The Thirty Years' War and German Memory in the Nineteenth Century

Kevin Cramer

The Thirty Years' War

and German Memory in the
Nineteenth Century

University of Nebraska Press • Lincoln & London

A version of chapter 2 previously
appeared as "The Cult of Gustavus
Adolphus: Protestant Identity
and German Nationalism" in
*Protestants, Catholics, and Jews in
Germany, 1800–1914*, ed. Helmut
Walser Smith (Oxford UK:
Berg, 2001).

♾

Library of Congress Cataloging-in-
Publication Data
Cramer, Kevin.
The Thirty Years' War and German
memory in the nineteenth century /
Kevin Cramer.
p. cm. — (Studies in war, society,
and the military)
Includes bibliographical references
and index.
ISBN-13: 978-0-8032-1562-7 (cloth :
alk. paper)
ISBN-10: 0-8032-1562-2 (cloth : alk.
paper)
1. Germany—History—19th century—Historiography. 2. Collective
memory—Germany 3. National
characteristics, German—Historiography. 4. Thirty Years' War,
1618–1648—Social aspects—Germany. I. Title.
DD203.C74 2007
943'.07—dc22
2006039637

Set in Sabon.

To my mother, Mary Helen Lewis Cramer, with love and gratitude

Contents

Acknowledgments

Since this is a book about war, memory, and place, I think I should begin by acknowledging the profound influence my childhood had on the conceptual origins of this study. Although I was born in Michigan, I grew up in Stone Mountain, Georgia, in the 1960s and 1970s when the town was being steadily absorbed into the vast sprawl of Atlanta, the self-declared capital of the "New South." The growth of Atlanta as a major American city meant, among other things, the gradual effacement of the more visible marks the Civil War had left on the north Georgia landscape. Yet traces remained. Backyards were marked by slowly eroding lines of fortifications. At many an intersection, cast-iron signs commemorated the battles, skirmishes, and cavalry raids of the Battle of Atlanta in 1864. Every spring on Confederate Memorial Day, across from the gas station where I worked as a teenager, the small cemetery blossomed with miniature Stars and Bars placed on veterans' graves. Blasted into the side of the most visible natural landmark in the area, the massive granite monolith that gave Stone Mountain its name, was a huge bas-relief sculpture of Robert E. Lee, Stonewall Jackson, and Jefferson Davis on horseback. A frequent destination of elementary school field trips was the Cyclorama in Grant Park Zoo that depicted the Battle of Atlanta. The memory of the Civil War was an inescapable presence. Even on the playground, lingering animosities of the war manifested themselves when my friends good-naturedly declared a sharp line of demarcation between those born in the South, "Rebels," and those unfortunates like myself, "Yankees," who, through no fault of their own, had come into the world north of the Mason-Dixon Line. Suffice it to say, as I began exploring how Germans had refought the Thirty Years' War in the nineteenth century, I immediately recognized the preoccupation with a past that would not pass. That moment of recognition was the beginning of this book.

Many people made this book possible. I owe my wife, Linda Santoro (fighter girl from the future), more gratitude than the English language can convey for her love and encouragement. Our friends in Massachusetts—Lucas, Joe and Trish, Nancy, Susan, Gerard, Dom, Rob and Jude—maintained our sanity with good music, strong drink, and much laughter. Leslie Poe talked baseball and Einstürzende Neubauten with me in the kitchen of our dorm that first alienating year of graduate school. Robert Fisher distracted me with feats of strength. David and Joelle Paulson, Frank Trentmann and Lizza Ruddick, and Andrew Port never once let me lose confidence in my ideas. It is no exaggeration to say that, without the spiritual and intellectual generosity of David Craig and Jocelyn Sisson, I could not have finished this book. I owe more to their insight, humor, and camaraderie than they know.

The intellectual debts I have incurred in the course of this project are substantial. Walter Struve and Emmanuel Chill at the City College of New York changed my life by encouraging me to be a historian. At Harvard University the wisdom of Franklin Ford, Charles Maier, James Hankins, Olwen Hufton, and Daniel Aaron guided me through the first stages of my apprenticeship. I hope this study approaches the very high standards they set as intellectual mentors. I owe the most, however, to my adviser, David Blackbourn. In the beginning his great gift was to comprehend the ramifications of this project better than I did myself. As the book finally took shape on paper, his erudition and conceptual discipline led me clear of many dead ends and set an example I have tried to emulate every day. Yet, as I finished the manuscript, I realized that his most valuable gift was his friendship.

Several true gentlemen and scholars were unstinting in their advice and encouragement during the revision of the manuscript. Geoff Eley, Mike Harris, Michael Geyer, Hartmut Lehmann, Roland Löffler, Charles McClelland, Keith Pickus, Till van Rhaden, James Sheehan, Helmut Smith, Geoffrey Wawro, Siegfried Weichlein, and Steven Welch all took valuable time at conferences and in correspondence to offer crucial insights that immeasurably sharpened the book's focus and strengthened its organization.

My initial research in Germany got its bearings from the suggestions and formidable collective wisdom of Dr. Karl Otmar Frhr. von

Aretin, Dr. Hans Fenske, Dr. Lothar Gall, Dr. Gottfried Korff, Dr. Jörn Rüsen, Dr. Claus Scharf, Dr. Helmut Seier, and Dr. Rudolf Vierhaus. Dr. Manfred Drexl and Renate Maneval at the Bavarian State Library, Peter Spanos at the Ludwig Maximilian University in Munich, and Ulrike Schöpperele at the university library in Freiburg opened every door and made me feel welcome.

The Minda de Gunzburg Center for European Studies at Harvard provided a perfect place to work and generously funded my research and writing with a Krupp Foundation Fellowship in European Studies and a Dissertation Writing Fellowship granted by the Program for the Study of Germany and Europe.

Finally, I want to thank my friends and colleagues (past and present) at Indiana University–Purdue University, Indianapolis, for their intellectual and moral support: Wietse de Boer, Annie Gilbert Coleman, Jon Coleman, Stephen Heathorn, Monroe Little, Nancy Robertson, Phil Scarpino, Bill Schneider, Michael Snodgrass, Marianne Wokeck, and Xin Zhang.

I owe a late colleague the final word. If I hadn't clearly heard him reacting to the idea with an appalled, "Oh, no, you can't do that. You have to dedicate it to your mom," this book would have been dedicated to the memory of Scott Seregny, friend, fellow Gram Parsons fan, and professor of Russian history. Scott, as usual, you were right. Keep looking over my shoulder.

The Thirty Years' War and German Memory in the Nineteenth Century

Introduction

The Thirty Years' War! What a fateful epoch for Germany, an epoch of the most fanatical and savage conflict, a bloody time of religious war, whose flame was lit in Bohemia in 1618 to rage through Germany with devastation and fire for a quarter of a century. Misery without parallel spread from the Baltic to the Danube. We see ancient and rich provinces afflicted by the fury of rebellion, the bonds of government torn asunder, only to be restored with blood and iron—a time filled with shame and horror!

This advertisement appeared on the end sheet of Luise Mühlbach's *Die Opfer des religiösen Fanatismus: Historicher Roman aus dem dreißigjährigen Krieg* (The Victims of Religious Fanaticism: A Historical Novel of the Thirty Years' War) (1871–72). The publisher, Sigmund Bensinger, was clearly not promising light reading for Mühlbach's devoted fans throughout German-speaking Central Europe. Bensinger knew what his audience wanted.[1] Mühlbach's novel was part of a tremendous flood of histories, plays, novels, poems, and "rediscovered" memoirs and documents dealing with the Thirty Years' War that appeared in Germany in the mid-nineteenth century. In an era that saw the birth of German nationalism and the unification of Germany as a powerful nation-state, the reading public's obsession with the most destructive and divisive war in German history is a remarkable example of the interplay between collective memory, history, and national identity. This interplay is the distinguishing characteristic of nationalist thinking as it evolved in the nineteenth century. But what is remarkable about the German case is that a story of defeat and humiliation should exert such influence on an emerging national consciousness.[2] This should draw the histori-

an's attention immediately, since national narratives are conventionally understood as stories of triumph. At first glance there seems to be
very little to celebrate in the events and outcome of the Thirty Years'
War. This catastrophe overshadowed every milestone of Germany's
progress toward nationhood and European and global power: 1813,
1866, 1871, 1917, and 1941. Yet the collective memory of this seventeenth-century war shaped every debate in the nineteenth century over
the ideal form of the German nation.

There are many reasons for the Germans' morbid fascination with
the Thirty Years' War. The popularity of Gustav Freytag's *Bilder aus
der deutschen vergangenheit* (Pictures from the German Past) and
Grimmelshausen's *Simplicissimus* (both appearing in countless versions and reprintings) was based in part on pride in how far Germany
had come in overcoming the material destruction and political weakness the war had left in its wake. Interest in the war was also stimulated by the midcentury apotheosis of Friedrich Schiller as the German
national poet. His interpretation of the Thirty Years' War as a struggle
for German liberty led to a new appreciation of the work as one of the
key texts influencing the creation of a national German history. Finally,
Prussian historians used Germany's degradation in the war as a way to
further mythologize the Hohenzollern triumph in 1871. Why did the
argument over the meaning of the war become so violent, prolonged,
and partisan? Why were the battles of the "Great War" of the seventeenth century fought again, in popular remembrance, history, and literature, in the nineteenth? After two hundred years, the unresolved issues
that had originally sparked the conflict lingered in collective memory
as obstacles to German unification. Germany's rediscovery of the war
in the nineteenth century was ultimately driven by a need to overcome
those obstacles through a new understanding of the war as the decisive
political event that shaped modern Germany.

As Germans looked cautiously forward to political unification in the
mid-nineteenth century, the popular memory of the Thirty Years' War,
the presence of a past that refused to pass, caused them to look over
their shoulders constantly. Germans relived the Thirty Years' War as
that "sad, joyless time," in Gustav Freytag's words, and the defining
episode of the German tragedy. To fully understand the broad accep-

tance of Prussian leadership of German unification, the issues at the center of the "greater Germany–little Germany" (*Großdeutschland/Kleindeutschland*) debate, and the cultural and political marginalization of Germany's Catholics, we must understand how and why the Thirty Years' War haunted German memory in the nineteenth century. To understand the clash between the Protestant and Catholic visions of a unified Germany, one must understand how Germans reconceptualized the experience of war for partisan purposes. Their rediscovery of the Thirty Years' War in the nineteenth century shaped a concept of German national development that, for all its secular nationalist trajectory, explicitly relied on confessional allegiance as the definitive criterion of what it meant to be German. The experience of total war itself was integrated within these narratives as a decisive factor in the formation of German national identity. One remarkable feature of these histories is a tendency to characterize war in religious terms, as the sacrifice demanded to fulfill the covenant between God and his chosen people. This covenant promised nationhood—not just in unification but in ascendancy to European and global power, a conviction that was fundamental to the harsh faith of German nationalism. Such faith would demand the martyrdom of Germans in the twentieth century and, ultimately, the sacrifice of millions who were not German. At the end of his novel *Doctor Faustus*, Thomas Mann looked back on nineteenth-century Germany's troubled rise to nationhood and the ruin of that nation under the leadership of Adolf Hitler, and wondered about the origins of what he called the "blood state."[3] By studying Germany's confrontation with the meaning of the Thirty Years' War in the nineteenth century, we can add to our understanding of how and why the foundations of the blood state were laid.

Extracting meaning from this seventeenth-century catastrophe was a violently polemical process that reveals much about how the give and take between history writing and collective memory shaped the discipline in Germany. In the *Historical Journal* in 1865, Bernhard Erdmannsdörffer, a prominent scholar of the constitutional history of the German states, observed how bitter and divisive the argument over the meaning of the Thirty Years' War had become:

> We stand in the midst of a struggle between new political and religious factions. Admittedly, they are not the same old debates from the past. However, in looking back on former times, we return to their common origins and old formulas of opposition and again fan the flames of ancient discords as if, in pronouncing on the right or wrong of past positions, we are passing judgment on the faults or merits of our own endeavors. These days scarcely a line can be written on this subject without the implicit or explicit aim of attack or defense. Our entire literature in this area has become polemical—less in regard to the confirmation or disputation of individual facts than in the general view of the motivations and values of the men and parties under discussion.[4]

Erdmannsdörffer's criticisms sum up the state of mind of German historians in the nineteenth century as they attempted to construct a coherent German history that had the gravitas of the histories of France and Britain. Given the historiographical conventions of the era, and given Germany's history of weakness and disunity (and thus a lack of a unifying secular identity), this meant reworking a story of religious and civil war into a founding act of revolutionary violence.

After the defeat of Napoleon in the Battle of the Nations at Leipzig in 1813, a novel feeling of national pride and solidarity swept through the German states. Germany's debilitating confessional and political fragmentation seemed banished forever by the unifying war of liberation against imperial France. Napoleon's dissolution of the moribund Holy Roman Empire and his creation of the Confederation of the Rhine also seemed, for many, to point the way toward a unified German nation. A new sense of national community, at least among an increasingly assertive *Bildungsbürgertum*, was born in this war. The sudden vision of political unity that followed in its wake naturally stimulated a desire for a national history. Where could Germans find the epochal conflict that had laid the foundation for the development of the modern state and disclosed the connecting historical thread to 1813? The glory of eternal France was manifest in the story of the rise of the expansionist Bourbon monarchy under Louis XIV, reborn in the millenarian hope of 1789 and in the Napoleonic imperial myth, which melded the two ideas of France. The Whig tradition in English history writing traced the triumph of parliamentary government from the disunity of the Wars of the Roses through the English Civil War and the Glorious Revolution of 1688. German historians certainly tried to interpret the Wars of Liberation against Napoleon as a crusade or revolutionary war that had led to the birth of a modern nationalist consciousness. The history of the Reformation offered a possible basis for a national narrative based on the idea of the Protestant struggle to liberate Germany from the tyranny of Rome. However, this nascent Protestant nationalism, essential to the conviction that it was Prussia's mission to fulfill the promise of German greatness, would not find its footing unless and until it could be grounded in some idea of a territorial state. It was not until the 1860s, when Prussian history writing connected the rise of the Hohenzollerns with German unification, that a viable (though not uncontested) German national history seemed possible. But in the period before 1871 this approach appealed mainly to those already convinced of the inevitability (and desirability) of Prussian leadership of unification. Its assumptions were less convincing to those who envisioned alternative unitary schemes that challenged Prussian and Austrian domination of the German Confederation.

What is noteworthy about this struggle to create a unifying history is that German historians used the story of the Thirty Years' War, the most divisive and humiliating episode in modern German history, as the matrix within which a compelling story of the German rise to unity, nationhood, and power could be presented. Reconstructing histories of the Thirty Years' War gave historians the opportunity to reflect on a German event in the relatively recent past that had become just distant enough to permit the drawing of conclusions about its significance. In its diplomatic, territorial, ideological, and political consequences for Germany, the war was seen to have prefigured the epochal transformations put in play by the French Revolution. In comparing the great seventeenth-century upheaval with that of the late eighteenth and early nineteenth centuries, German historians identified the Thirty Years' War as the most decisive and formative conflict in the long and halting progress toward German nationhood.

The divide between Catholic and Protestant made this past a bitterly contested ground. No aspect of the German religious schism offered a more compelling forum for debating the political, cultural, and psychological consequences of the Reformation than the history of the Thirty Years' War. The confessional division turned history writing about the war into a clash between two epics of victimization, one Protestant and one Catholic. Protestant historians insisted on the religious origins of the conflict as they reconceptualized the war as part of a longer struggle against foreign rule, beginning with the Reformation, for German liberty. By presenting Habsburg rule as a Jesuit tyranny directed from Rome and enforced by barbaric foreign mercenaries, they could point to the war as a justification for a Germany unified under Prussian (and Protestant) leadership, the kleindeutsch idea that excluded Austria and consigned Catholics to second-class status in the national community. Catholic historians defended the Habsburg Counter-Reformation as a struggle to preserve, modernize, and expand the imperial constitutional state as the historically legitimate defender of German culture and civilization. They believed that the war conclusively demonstrated the desirability of a Germany organized along confederal lines, a constitutional model partially realized in the German Confederation. This großdeutsch idea also implied a reincarnation of the Holy Roman Empire that included Austria. As German political and historical thought in the nineteenth century attempted to define a modern idea of the nation, this kleindeutsch/großdeutsch argument was at the core of every political and cultural discussion about Germany's destiny as a unified nation.

The historians' arguments over the lessons of the war reflected a more general uncertainty among educated Germans over what, exactly, "Germany" had been or was meant to be. Heine's observation that in Germany there was no present, only a past and a future, perfectly captured their anxiety over this question. At the heart of the debate over the meaning of the Thirty Years' War was a fractious exchange between Catholic and Protestant. Both sides attempted to explain the meaning of German suffering and the reasons for Germany's long exile from the promised land of nationhood. Of course, an important justification for the discipline of history in the nineteenth century was an abiding belief in the power of a national narrative to develop and strengthen allegiance to the nation-state. The difficulty in this particular case was reconciling Germany's laggard progress toward unification, generally understood as a consequence of the Thirty Years' War, with the triumphant narrative required to solidify that allegiance. It was obviously difficult for German historians to substantively challenge the conventional view that this catastrophic and divisive war, and the peace settlement that confirmed German division, were the first chapters of modern Germany's problematic story. Another problem was that this history of civil war and foreign intervention undermined any claim to great power status. The solution was to reimagine the confessional conflict that sparked the war in epic terms that resonated in the nineteenth-century historical imagination. The story of the Thirty Years' War was refashioned into an epochal confrontation between the forces of reaction and liberty, legitimacy and revolution. German historians raised the stakes of this confrontation into nothing less than the future constitutional and territorial shape of Germany. The human, material, and psychological losses of the war were surveyed in detail as explanations for Germany's continually interrupted progress toward becoming a nation. Nineteenth-century Germany's remembrance of the Thirty Years' War became a cathartic national confrontation with the constitutional, ideological, and spiritual assumptions that underlay modern German identity.[5] The development of history as a professionalized and scientific discipline in the nineteenth century justified this process. In their books Macaulay, Buckle, Michelet, and Thierry conspicuously celebrated the role of transcendent principles, manifested in various heroic and inspiring episodes, in creating the modern British and French nations. It is useful to bear in mind that historians were, as Eugen Weber writes, "the clerisy of the nineteenth century because it fell to them to rewrite foundational myths; and history was the theology of the nineteenth century because it provided societies cast loose from the moorings of custom and habit with new anchorage in a rediscovered—or reinvented—past."[6] For their part, German historians of the Thirty Years' War revealed the crucial connection between confessional allegiance and national identity and how it had contributed to Germany's present "unfinished" status.

Certainly, this was not the *only* way Germans read their history, but

but this religiously inflected interpretation of German national development, revealed in the commemoration and cultural remembrance of the Thirty Years' War, consistently employed biblical narrative tropes of "chosen-ness" in descriptions of sacrifice and the extirpative wrath of God. The fear of the nation's annihilation was always present. But out of the chaos of war a new order, a renewal, and rebirth would always be possible. If, as Heinrich von Srbik suggests, German idealist philosophy politicized history and historicized politics in the nineteenth century, perhaps these tendencies can be partially explained as attempts to impose meaning on the chaos of revolution and war. Srbik's intuition is reflected in the work of historians Georg Iggers and Bernd Faulenbach, who have examined the idealist roots of German political thought as a key influence on a militantly nationalist historiography.[7] Iggers's classic study, *The German Conception of History*, identified the strains of philosophical idealism found in the methodological assumptions of German *Historismus*. Embodied in the work of the so-called Prussian School, it articulated a notion of political order based on the waging of war to make and preserve the state.[8] Faulenbach's work on the ideological functions of history writing also attempts to explain how these premises drove a process of historical self-interpretation that easily and willingly lent itself to an authoritarian concept of the state.[9] Iggers and Faulenbach take a biographical approach to the study of German history writing that focuses on the links between idealist philosophy, philosophies of history, and various ideological commitments of historians to a vision of the nation. This interpretation was firmly established in Franz X. von Wegele's *Geschichte der deutschen Historiographie* (History of German Historiography) (1885), Eduard Feuter's *Geschichte der neueren Historiographie* (History of Modern Historiography) (1911), Georg von Below's *Die deutsche Geschichtschreibung von den Befreiungskriegen bis zu unsern Tagen* (German History Writing from the Wars of Liberation to the Present Day) (1916), and Moriz Ritter's *Die Entwicklung der Geschichtswissenschaft an den führenden Werken betrachtet* (The Development of the Science of History) (1919).[10] Given the prominent cultural and political role historians played in the Second Reich, this approach is logical and remains useful.[11] The consensus is that the tenets of philosophical idealism, manifested in philosophies of history, encouraged a dangerous eschatological attitude in German nationalism, which was especially noticeable in a general historical fascination with war. Otto Hintze ruefully acknowledged this in 1915 when he quoted an English writer to the effect that "Prussian history is endlessly boring because it speaks so much of war and so little of revolution."[12] The result has been an extensive literature on the historical thinking and influence of Kant, Herder, Hegel, and Schiller. These studies provide the background for other works that examine the intemperate collisions of historical scholarship, nationalism, and politics that continuously disturbed German academic life in the nineteenth century.[13] Disputes over methodologies, sources, and political agendas invariably degenerated into the open questioning of opponents' allegiance to the nation. This Teutonic turmoil was as much a part of the nineteenth-century writing dealing with the Thirty Years' War as it was of the twentieth-century arguments over certain continuities and discontinuities in German history, most notably in the Fischer controversy in the 1960s over twentieth-century German war aims and the historians' debate (*Historikerstreit*) of the 1980s over "normalizing" the Holocaust.[14]

By focusing on the philosophical and ideological energies driving the ascent of the Prussian School, historians have missed some opportunities to explore the deeper connections between history, politics, and national identity in nineteenth-century Germany. There have been few studies examining the pull of specific episodes in German history (other than those that glorify the rise of the Hohenzollerns, such as German unification) on historians' imaginations.[15] How do historians come to choose and shape the subjects and themes of their narratives? This is an important question. National histories are both a catalyst and a by-product of the rise of the nation-state, and they are made to compel allegiance and solidarity.[16] Historians of history writing are studying the historical debates over the meaning of the transformative episodes of violence in the life of a nation: war, revolution, and mass death. Their work has produced a significant body of scholarship on the most interpreted event of the modern era of history writing, the French Revolution, followed closely by studies of the historical interpretations of the seventeenth-century British civil war, the American Civil War, the Russian Revolution, and the Holocaust.[17] This innovative scholarship demonstrates that if we truly want to understand the place of history writing in the cultural and intellectual life of a nation, we must take a page from Voltaire and ask what tricks the living have played on the dead. We can recover an era's passionate belief in the meaning of the past by showing how historians' topical choices are closely linked to contemporary political and ideological concerns.[18] Frank Ankersmit points to these links when he emphasizes that historical narratives function by distinguishing "between what *did* happen and what *might* have happened but *did not.*" The "what-if questions" raised by this groping toward meaning must, it seems to me, reveal something of supreme importance.[19] Nineteenth-century histories of the Thirty Years' War were not only about the war; they were also arguments about the past, present, and future of the German nation. The presence of this seventeenth-century war in the nineteenth century was felt in the ever-present fear of war, revolution, occupation, and dissolution that turned every dispute over the proper interpretation of the war into a debate over the possibility of German nationhood. The authors of these histories were convinced that the story of the Thirty Years' War, in showing what might have happened but did not, captured the essence of Germany's struggle toward nationhood, a tragic and frustrating cycle of *becoming*, and also showed the way to breaking that cycle.

The significance of nineteenth-century German history writing about the Thirty Years' War lies in the clash between two competing historical vocabularies, one Protestant, one Catholic, which tried to impose coherence on, and extract meaning from, the defeats and discontinuities of Germany's struggle to unify.[20] The narratives constructed from these vocabularies, stories of sacrifice and redemption, promised fulfillment of the German aspiration to unity. These stories were painful to tell, but they allowed Germans to understand the Thirty Years' War as an epic struggle to make the nation. For the first time Germans could begin to see their country's past as something other than an obscure and mystifying chaos. The injunction to sacrifice, the fundamental idea behind the historical consciousness of the West (and modern nationalism), is the reason the past weighs so heavily on the present. Modern history writing, in the service of nationalism, adopted for secular ends the story of Abraham leading Isaac to the altar. This command to sacrifice is what made the German debates over the meaning of the Thirty Years' War so violent and uncompromising. It lay beneath all arguments over the political form of the nation. Disputing the veracity of the national narrative dishonored the sacrifices of the dead and invited the punishment of occupation, partition, and enslavement. Michel de Certeau sees in these debates "the presence of the dead who still haunt the present ... [that] phantasm of historiography, the object that it seeks, honors, buries." For Certeau, history writing evolved to provide the state with the moral authority to command obedience.[21] It animates institutions with ideas that are worth dying for, a function once the domain of religious, theological, and philosophical writings. Defining and articulating those ideas drove the professionalization of the discipline of history (and the rise in its intellectual status) in the nineteenth century. German disunity made this definition and articulation an overriding obligation for German historians and led to a bitter confrontation between two historical-moral genealogies and two ideas of the German nation-state.

This book explores the reasons for this clash as it arose out of the connections between the experience of war, historical and collective memory, religious division, and German national identity. It examines a century of history writing in the work of over two hundred historians contained in some four hundred texts, augmented by reviews, criticism, memoirs, letters, speeches, and political and religious writings. The most intense debate over the interpretation of the Thirty Years' War occurred during the period between the Wars of Liberation and the Wars of Unification, that is, between the 1820s, when the grip of Metternich's Restoration tightened on the German Confederation, and the 1860s, when Prussia emerged as the presumptive leader of German unification. The Confederation regimes gradually clamped down on open demonstrations of German nationalism, and vigorous political debate about the shape of a unified German nation was driven underground. As a result, public discourse on the unification question mainly came under the influence of Germany's historians. The narrative of the war presented historians with a very useful template for framing questions about the national destiny of Germany without conspicuously challenging the prerogatives of absolutism, particularism (*Kleinstaaterei*), and the legitimacy of the settlement of the Congress of Vienna. The uncertainty of that destiny, and the rising civic and intellectual prestige of historians, created a relatively open forum (in the context of the censorship enforced by the German Confederation) in which many competing solutions for the fulfillment of that destiny could be debated. However, although intellectual debates and cultural preoccupations can be broadly understood as influencing politics and policy over the long term, this process is not the focus of this book. If anything, shifts in policy, political alignments, and ideological orientation were reflected in the changing terms of the debate itself.

It is also important to emphasize that this debate, a conspicuous and long-running episode in the intellectual history of nineteenth-century Germany, was by no means confined to the academy. It was an argument that, because it spoke so strongly to competing notions of national identity, compelled and fascinated the broad stratum of educated Germans for almost a century. I therefore take an inclusive approach in this book to what constitutes history writing and include in that category not only scholarly monographs, general histories, and articles but also poetry, drama, and historical fiction. In the early nineteenth century the work of hundreds (if not thousands) of amateur historians in regional archives made significant contributions to a rapidly growing corpus of documentary material from the war. Writing for journals published by an expanding network of regional historical associations, these lay practitioners wrote many of the histories under discussion. On the other hand, many professional historians wrote novels, plays, and poems about the war. They also often included fictional material in anthologies dealing with the war and borrowed uncritically and verbatim from popular and fictional accounts of the war, such as those written by Schiller and Grimmelshausen, while emphasizing to readers the enduring historical value of such works. This disregard for genre boundaries had no discernible impact on the critical or popular reception of these histories until after midcentury, when it began to be called into question by new professional standards.

Most of these historians have been forgotten, some more deservedly than others. Luminaries such as Schiller, Ranke, Droysen, Sybel, and Treitschke all wrote about the war. Recent scholarship has called to our attention the work of some less familiar names: Vogt, Westenrieder, Förster, Klopp, and Biedermann. Most of these historians of the Thirty Years' War were reviewed, praised, and criticized in the context of their tumultuous century. For the most part they died in obscurity, leaving nothing to posterity but their books, perhaps a few lines in the *Universal German Biography* (if they were fortunate), and the fading echoes of their arguments. Were they mediocre writers? Were their interpretations of evidence prejudiced and incomplete? Were their historical judgments fallacious? In many cases, the answer is yes. There are few historians in any century whose work has been left unmarked by the brickbats of their peers and later, more self-consciously enlightened, generations. But the famous and obscure alike were united by a predilection that was Schiller's most enduring legacy to German history writing (if not literature): a fascination with war and revolution.

The positions these historians took on the war were fundamentally shaped by their confessional identities. Chiefly characterized by an uncompromising animosity, the divide between Protestant and Catholic was deep and enduring. This confessional enmity, so much stronger than had been the case in the eighteenth century, was the most important ideological factor that determined how these historians defined a unified German nation. The argument between Protestant and Catholic over interpreting the meaning of the Thirty Years' War came down to one historico-theological question: Whose sacrifice on behalf of the nation would be accepted? Protestant historians, preferring to write a national history that marginalized or excluded Catholics, insisted on the essentially religious nature of the Thirty Years' War. They cast the war as a struggle against the foreign tyranny of the Habsburg Counter-Reformation to preserve the foundation of "German liberty" established in 1517. Theirs was a vision of a war fought to establish the kingdom of the elect, a Protestant German Reich, an interpretation that was easily incorporated into a coherent nationalist narrative of Prussian triumph. Catholic historians viewed the German Confederation as the legitimate successor to the Holy Roman Empire as a guarantor of Catholic interests and the constitutional protections that preserved all the German states, large and small. In support of this idea they refuted their opponents' vision of the nation by condemning the Reformation as an essentially political revolution against the legitimate authority and constitution of the empire. With the dissolution of the German Confederation in 1866, Catholic historians, who had long fought to be heard from the periphery of the German historical consciousness, lost what was left of the institutional manifestation of the idea of Germany that they had tried to legitimate. Once the Second Reich was founded in 1871, a winner of the argument over the meaning of the Thirty Years' War could be declared. To both sides it seemed that, two hundred years later, for better or for worse, the great issue of the Thirty Years' War had finally been resolved by unification.

The themes of war, revolution, and liberation, Schiller's bequest to German history writing, formed the framework of the debate over the meaning of the Thirty Years' War, which historians used to pose three questions that were fundamental to the articulation of a German national history after 1815. Which constitutional and territorial vision of the nation had the greatest legitimacy? Which "world-historical figure" of the war could be most usefully mythologized as a nation builder? Which community's sacrifice in the war, Protestant Germany's or Catholic Germany's, established the most authentic criteria that defined what it meant to be German? Trying to answer these questions, German historians focused on five crucial (and overlapping) periods and events. They determined the organization of this book: the campaign of the Counter-Reformation from 1618 to 1629, the crusade and apotheosis of the Swedish king Gustavus Adolphus from 1630 to 1632, the dramatic rise and fall of Wallenstein from 1630 to 1634, the destruction of the Protestant city of Magdeburg in 1631, and the Swedish War from 1631 to 1638. In German collective remembrance this twenty-year period, from 1618 to 1638, encompassed the decisive turns and defining miseries of the war.

Chapter 1, "The Great War," focuses on the interpretations of the Counter-Reformation that Kaiser Ferdinand II pursued in the first decade of the war. This debate on the origins of the war was framed by a larger nineteenth-century argument, which dominated the opening sessions of the Frankfurt Parliament in 1848, over the ideal constitutional structure of the German nation. Invoking the fearful upheavals of the French Revolution, Catholic historians condemned the Bohemian Rebellion in 1618 as nothing less than a revolution against the constitution of the Holy Roman Empire, the shield of German culture and Christian civilization. They argued that the visionary Habsburg response to this revolution was in effect a counterrevolution, and the first war of German unification, that aimed to reform and expand the empire as a unified "greater Germany."

Chapter 2, "The War of Protestant Liberation," examines the response of Protestant historians to this großdeutsch interpretation of the war. Their advocacy of the kleindeutsch solution to German unification took the form of a Protestant nationalism that found expression in the transformation of the Swedish king Gustavus Adolphus into a German national hero. The popular memory of his epic march through Germany in 1631 and 1632 was refashioned into a history of a crusade to liberate the German Protestants from the foreign tyranny of the Habsburgs. Protestant historians claimed that Gustavus Adolphus planned to dismantle the old Holy Roman Empire and establish a Protestant German Reich in its place. This interpretation of the Swedish king's plans for Germany was used to justify and legitimate Prussia's leadership of German unification.

Chapter 3, "Wallenstein's Revolution," examines a debate that echoed the argument over Gustavus Adolphus's ambitions for Germany. The dominant theme was the recurring question of German nationalist thinking, "What might have been?" Germany's efforts at nation building in the nineteenth century were beset with doubts about the legitimacy of the history of its political development. German historians compared German history with the national histories of France and Britain and lamented the absence of a transforming revolutionary warlord on a par with Henry IV, Cromwell, or Napoleon. German historians took up the old debate of Wallenstein's "treason" and refashioned this enigmatic figure into a far-seeing statesman who saw in the chaos of war the world-historical moment to challenge the medieval order with the idea of national power. Presented as the model for Bismarck, Wallenstein's revolutionary vision for Germany was of a powerful and unified central European state liberated from the debilitating confessional conflict and territorial fragmentation of the old empire.

No episode of the great nineteenth-century debate over the meaning of the Thirty Years' War was more revealing of the war's central importance to conceptions of German identity than the clash over the question "Who destroyed Magdeburg?" Chapter 4, "The Martyrdom of Magdeburg," looks at the prolonged and bitter argument over this defining moment in the nineteenth-century memory of the war. The "Magdeburg question" was a serious moral, political, and nationalist issue in nineteenth-century Germany. The graphic portrayals of the city's destruction in 1631 firmly anchored the Protestant national narrative in the idea of the Germans as a chosen people. Nationalist aspirations were justified in a detailed catalogue of Protestant suffering and sacrifice at the hands of an alien and barbaric imperial soldiery. Protestant insistence on Catholic responsibility for the crime, in turn, nullified any Catholic claim to national kinship with the "true" (i.e., Protestant) Germans. As a consequence, Catholic historians made strenuous, and ultimately futile, attempts to refute what they called the "lie" of Magdeburg.

Chapter 5, "German Gothic," examines the narratives of the Swedish War, the period between 1631 and 1638 also remembered by Catholics as the "time of annihilation." These years lived in modern German memory as the traumatic heart of the war—a time of mass death that surpassed the ravages of the Great Plague. Nineteenth-century historians characterized Germany's suffering during the war, in the scale of its cruelty and the depth of the material and psychological wounds it had inflicted on the German nation, as a catastrophe unique in history. This suffering was the focus of an extensive literature of what I call "atrocity narratives" written by both Catholic and Protestant historians that can only be described as competing epics of victimization. Like the memories of Magdeburg, the lingering trauma of the Swedish War had a profound impact on the construction of German national identity because it inextricably bound that identity to sacrifice and suffering in war. Protestant atrocity narratives added luster to the Hohenzollern triumph in reviving German power and prosperity. Catholic histories of the Swedish War articulated a profound dread of physical annihilation and the threat to identity, place, and community implied by Protestant (and Prussian) ascendancy.

Studied as a single body of interpretation, the nineteenth-century histories of the Thirty Years' War stand revealed as a profoundly dark and gothic literature, filled with blood and emotion and driven by grievance and accusation, charge and countercharge. The graphic depiction of violence in these histories both fascinates and repels. It lurches in many directions, pulled simultaneously by distress, anger, pride, and shame. It was not characterized by qualifications, compromise, or restraint. Both Protestant and Catholic historians passionately believed that there was one true history of the war to be revealed; anyone challenging that truth was quickly accused of distorting the meaning of German history. The war's presence in the German national consciousness in the nineteenth century was an uneasy and disturbing spirit. It was a constant reminder of the consequences of disunity.

Germans felt their national destiny was tied to the catastrophe and aftermath of the Thirty Years' War. Retold as the defining event in German history, it became an epochal moment when grand designs collapsed in defeat. Ultimately the Thirty Years' War became the dark glass through which Germans viewed their future. What they saw gave them hope, but that hope could not completely banish a crippling dread of dissolution and annihilation. In his novel *The Meeting at Telgte*, Günter Grass acknowledges that dread (as he does in all of his books) when he uses the Thirty Years' War as the background for his fable about his country's eternal wandering in the wilderness of history: "The thing that hath been tomorrow is that which shall be yesterday. Our stories of today need not have taken place in the present. This one began more than three hundred years ago. So did many other stories. Every story set in Germany goes back that far."[22]

1. The Great War

Remaking the Holy Roman Empire

How did historians in nineteenth-century Germany come to grips with the complex sequence of events that ignited a fratricidal thirty-year conflict that was also remembered as the Great German War, the Great War, the Great Schism, and Germany's Darkest Hour? The debate over the origins of the war was a critical part of the decades-long project of historical and collective remembrance that reinterpreted the impact of the war on modern Germany's national aspirations. The clash between Catholic and Protestant historians also determined to a large extent their competing concepts of a unified Germany and their respective claims to an authentic German identity. It is appropriate, then, that this study of the popular and historical consciousness of the war in nineteenth-century Germany begin at the beginning.

Protestant historians essentially denied the German identity of Catholics, who were in constant fear of marginalization within the German national community, by condemning the imperial cause as part of a brutal Counter-Reformation campaign to bring Germany under the yoke of Rome. Catholic historians vigorously challenged this prejudice. They created an alternative narrative that reimagined the first decade of the war not as a religious war (the consensus Protestant characterization) but as a Habsburg-led counterrevolution and war of unification that aimed at remaking the Holy Roman Empire into a powerful Central European state. This interpretation has been cursorily examined by historians, usually in discussions of Catholic conservatism, and has been generally dismissed as nostalgia for medieval glories. The midcentury debate over how "national" and "German" the medieval empire really was and how the history of this period was manipulated by "greater Germany" (Großdeutschland) advocates has received the most attention.[1] Opinion is divided on the extent to which remembrance of the medieval binary of "emperor and empire" (*Kaiser und Reich*) continued to influence nineteenth-century Catholic ideas regarding a unified Germany. There is a tradition of viewing this imperial patriotism (*Reichspatriotismus*) as an attempt to preserve notions of a constitutional structure that balanced unity with the preservation of traditional German liberties within a limited, decentralized monarchy. This perspective asserts the positive political legacy of the empire as a "national-German" institution.[2] Dissenters point out that the post-1815 tensions between Austria and Prussia over influence within the German Confederation and the irreconcilable großdeutsch/kleindeutsch argument effectively destroyed whatever common idea of Germany that the empire had still represented.[3] Besides dismissing it as a romantic protest against Prussian triumphalism, there has been little interest in looking more closely at the pro-imperial stance as a historical justification for a united Germany that was not dominated by Prussia (or, in some cases, Austria). We find this justification in an iconoclastic corpus of history writing that focused on the origins of the Great War. Studying these narratives affords us a clearer understanding of the nineteenth-century Catholic conception of, and allegiance to, the German nation as a confederal entity than has otherwise emerged from studies of romantic Catholic medievalism.

Out of the interlocked series of regional conflicts bracketed by the Bohemian Revolt in 1618 and the imperial conquest of northern Germany under Tilly and Wallenstein in 1629, Catholic historians fashioned a narrative that cast the victory of Ferdinand II over the rebellious Protestant princes as the beginning of a Habsburg counterrevolution that seized the historical moment to remake the Holy Roman Empire. Unfortunately for the future of Germany, in their view, this chance went glimmering when foreign armies, on the invitation of the renegade Protestant princes, intervened in the German civil war. Catholic historians developed the thesis of counterrevolution to legitimate a Catholic vision of a united Germany that could challenge the self-proclaimed Protestant monopoly on German patriotism and national feeling. A significant component of the confrontation with Protestant remembrance and interpretation of the war was the Catholic insistence that the war had its origins in a political crisis. They claimed that the uprising of the Protestant nobility in Bohemia in 1618 was the beginning of a revolution against the legitimate authority of Kaiser and Reich.

Catholic histories of the Thirty Years' War assumed a certain positive continuity in German political institutions. The lessons they derived from studying the war did little to undermine that assumption. A vision of Germany as a confederal-imperial state—or rather the potential for Germany to unite itself on that basis—was promoted and defended in Catholic histories dealing with the initial phases of the war. This idea of the German nation challenged Protestant claims about the inevitability (and desirability) of Prussian leadership of a unified Germany. Interpreting the Thirty Years' War as a German civil war and the imperial cause as a modernizing counterrevolution was intended to back up this vision. Catholic historians described the start of the war as a plainly seditious act in which the Protestant rebels had concealed their revolutionary political goals beneath the cloak of religion. Protestant historians, asserting the fundamental connection between the Reformation and German liberty, continued to insist that religion was the main issue that led to the war. This stance buttressed Protestant and Prussian claims to leadership in Germany.[4] Conversely, a political interpretation of the origins of the war could be used to make a case for the legitimacy of the Catholic concept of the German nation and membership in the national community. At the heart of the emerging German national consciousness in the nineteenth century was the conviction, on both sides of the confessional divide, that the origins of the Thirty Years' War lay in the clash between two revolutionary visions of Germany. In short, what was at issue in the Great War was nothing less than the triumph of one of two competing designs for the German nation.

To fully understand this clash of visions, it is necessary to take another look at the famous debate between the Protestant historian Heinrich Sybel and the Catholic Julius Ficker that took place between 1859 and 1861, a debate over the meaning of the medieval empire to modern

German national identity. Sybel, arguing on behalf of the "little Germany" (Kleindeutschland) viewpoint, claimed that the medieval emperors' lust for non-German territories (especially in Italy) had seriously damaged German national interests in the long term because the cosmopolitan polity that emerged was ultimately doomed to failure as the basis of a modern nation-state. Sybel concluded that the Catholic idealization of the medieval empire as a way to articulate a solution for the German national question was anachronistic and wrong-headed.

Ficker defended that solution by arguing for the utility of the imperial constitution as a basically sound mechanism that balanced unity and cohesion with the benefits of decentralization.[5] Ficker's argument was part of the Catholic attack on the kleindeutsch notion of German history that had started to find its voice soon after 1815. Essentially, Catholic historians and intellectuals refused to accept the linking of German national identity with the spirit of the Reformation and Protestantism.[6] The Catholic advocacy for "greater Germany" envisioned a centralized imperial Germany under Habsburg rule, hegemony in Central Europe, and the neutralization of the territorial ambitions of France and the great power aspirations of Prussia. The clash between the Protestant and Catholic historians over what exactly had started the war, like the argument over the legacy of the medieval empire, was part of the broader nineteenth-century debate over the national borders and political form of any future German state.[7]

The subject of the Thirty Years' War, because of the many unresolved issues concerning German unity that it raised, had been a flashpoint within the großdeutsch/kleindeutsch argument going back to the early years of the nineteenth century. No period of the war better served Catholic and großdeutsch arguments than the events of the period between 1607 and 1629, which spanned the years between the formation of the Protestant Union and the Catholic League and the near-total victory of Catholic arms in Germany that was marked by the promulgation of the Edict of Restitution.[8] It was no wonder, as one contemporary commentator pointed out, that the brief establishment of a revitalized and unitary imperial authority over half of Germany in 1629 animated the imaginations of Catholics as they attacked the exclusionary kleindeutsch bias they saw in Protestant histories of the war.[9]

Two beliefs were the foundation of the Catholic consensus that the war had, in fact, begun as a political rebellion and subsequently spread over the empire as a revolutionary war. The first was that interpreting the start of the war as a rebellion against the imperial constitution justified a claim for the legitimacy of the institutions of the empire. The other was that the victories of 1629 were easily incorporated into an account of a Habsburg counterrevolution that attempted to unify and modernize the Holy Roman Empire. Catholic historians seized on that brief moment of triumph in 1629 as a model for the modern German state. The success of the imperial armies in 1629 became the backdrop for the nineteenth-century Catholic fantasy of the "Baltic project" of Wallenstein and Ferdinand II, which aimed at projecting German power into the North and Baltic seas in order to make Germany a northern European maritime and commercial power to rival Sweden, the Netherlands, Denmark, and Britain.

This argument over the place of a unified Germany within the European balance of power, the "German question" of the nineteenth century, was also a debate over the constitutional structure that best preserved German unity and sovereignty. The Napoleonic occupation and the potential for a new and unified nation revealed by the Wars of Liberation made arguments over the form of a German constitution the driving force in German political debate until the upheavals of 1848. Proposals for the future political structure of the German state relied implicitly on some type of reform of the old imperial constitution. Historians disagree over exactly how the concept of Reich was used in this period, but there is no doubt that the idea of Germany was closely tied to an idealization of the medieval unity of Kaiser and Reich.[10] The latter could stand in opposition to each other if, as Protestant historians proposed, the Habsburg-led empire was dissolved or, as Catholic historians believed, together they could represent a notion of a constitutional order that was uniquely suited to defending German interests. "Kaiser and Reich" could symbolize a lost independence and power, or they could be seen pragmatically as complementary mechanisms of a legitimate German polity. Despite the profound disagreements over the role that the medieval empire had played in the evolution (or eventual degradation) of the German nation, it seems clear that in the nineteenth century the idea of Germany had imperial connotations, whether expressed in the Catholic preference for a modernized confederation of sovereign states or in the Protestant advocacy of a more centralized polity under Prussian leadership.[11]

The großdeutsch model of the German nation celebrated the almost complete conquest of Germany by the imperial armies in the decade after the Bohemian defeat at White Mountain in 1620. Changing perspectives that mirrored the arguments over what political form the German nation should take marked the interpretations of this achievement. They shift from a positive advocacy of "what might be" prior to Bismarck's wars of unification between 1866 and 1870, to a defeated defense of "what could have been" after a Hohenzollern was made Kaiser of a unified Germany in 1871. As we shall see, in the great nineteenth-century debate over what constituted a viable historical understanding of the German nation and the basis of German national identity, the alternative vision of the national community offered by Catholic historians would ultimately lose out to the Protestant-Prussian idea.[12]

The Revolution of 1618

Catholic historians' understanding of the period from 1607 to 1629 was marked by three successive phases of interpretation. The first arose out of the pro and con arguments about constitutional rule (animated by pervasive fear of revolution) that dominated political debate in Germany in the three decades after the French Revolution. This phase emphasized the possibilities of modernizing and reforming the old imperial constitution (*Reichsverfassung*). Another distinguishing feature of this period was speculation about Bavarian leadership in a confederal Germany in which neither Prussia nor Austria could dominate or absorb the smaller states. The second phase encompassed the period of the alarmed Catholic reaction from the early 1850s through the early 1860s, when the ascendancy of Prussia to dominance and leadership in Germany appeared unstoppable. This phase was marked by an increasingly desperate defense of the status quo represented by the German Confederation, which was seen as the legitimate successor to the Holy Roman Empire dissolved by Napoleon in 1806. In the vanguard of this position was a concerted effort to rehabilitate the reputation, aims, and legacy of the rule of Ferdinand II.[13] The third phase confronted the founding of the Second Reich under Prussian leadership and its consolidation. Catholics pragmatically realized that the exclusion and marginalization of their participation in the historical definition of the German state was inevitable and unstoppable. Those Catholic historians who continued to defend the legitimacy of the old Reich began to reframe their argument with a modern nationalist vocabulary that challenged Prussian ascendancy on its own terms. In an attempt to reconcile Catholic claims to membership in the new nation with the reality of unification under Prussian leadership, they argued that the old empire was a German, not a Catholic, institution and that it had always defended German interests.

The memory of the French occupation of Germany between 1806 and 1813 had an enormous impact on the Catholic historians writing in this period. Their conservative reaction to the triumph of revolution and French arms found much that was instructive in the old empire's confrontation in 1618 with a radicalized German Protestantism that eventually allied itself with France. The historical parallels were consistently pointed out. It was this profound fear of revolution, combined with the ever-present threat of French expansion, which drove Catholic historians' reexamination of the themes and events of the Thirty Years' War.

Michael Ignaz Schmidt's twelve-volume *Neuere Geschichte der Deutschen* (Modern History of the Germans), which appeared between 1778 and 1789, was widely read throughout Germany by Catholics and Protestants alike. It was an essential and much cited reference work for Catholic historians in the nineteenth century, who took as inspiration Schmidt's attempt to write a history of the German nation from a Catholic perspective. Schmidt, a Jesuit-educated historian who taught imperial history at Würzburg and was later director of the State Archives in Vienna, was a champion of a robust imperial political authority founded on the constitutional structure of the empire.[14] Completing his work in the shadow of the French Revolution, Schmidt concluded that the rebellion of the Protestant Bohemian nobles in 1618 against the imperial regency in Prague was the beginning of a much more ambitious assault on the authority of the Kaiser, the constitution, and the legally constituted religious peace. He asserted that the Bohemian revolutionaries had conspired with a French-sponsored Protestant Union to launch a "great revolution" that would turn Europe upside down. In the volume (1789), Schmidt regretfully noted that only a few Protestant princes were enlightened enough to defend imperial law and authority, even if that meant acquiescing in the evolution of the empire as a "German monarchical state."[15] Under the words *"Zustand der deutschen Nation"* (state of the German nation), this commentary pointedly addressed the danger that France posed to German independence.

Andreas Sebastian Stumpf (1772–1820), also from Würzburg, adapted Schmidt's thesis to comment directly on the danger that the French Revolution posed for Germany. Fleeing revolutionary upheaval in Strasbourg in 1790, Stumpf was forced to return to the university in his hometown to complete his education.[16] While in Bavarian service as an archivist in Munich, he wrote his *Diplomatische Geschichte der teutschen Liga im siebzehnten Jahrhunderte* (Diplomatic History of the German League in the Seventeenth Century), which was published in 1800. He pointed out that the history of the Catholic League (which he insisted on calling the *German* League in his book), formed in 1609 to counter the Protestant Union, had received little attention from modern historians, and what had been written about it had at best dismissed its importance and at worst been sharply critical of its aims. Stumpf's rehabilitation of the League's role in the Thirty Years' War became an influential and standard reference for some sixty years. Basing his work on an examination of the diplomatic documentation, Stumpf was confident that his new interpretation would be welcomed by those German readers who were not "blinded by preconceptions." He cited as the chief inspiration for his work a "special desire" to take the modern reader back to a time, because of its "many similarities and parallels to the present," he believed might have interest for Germany's current statesmen because they revealed "the foundations and policies of a union that deserves emulation in our time in order to maintain the peace and the constitution in Germany."[17]

Stumpf's argument emphasized the role that Maximilian I (1573–1651), the ruler of Bavaria, had played in forming the League because, unlike Schmidt, Stumpf was less sanguine about the potential of reconceiving the empire along monarchical lines. Stumpf argued that the history of the Catholic League offered an instructive example of how the estates and territories of the empire could be bound more closely as a political union to create an effective instrument of defense that preserved and enhanced imperial authority while maintaining the independence and security of the empire's sovereign states.[18] In any case, Stumpf believed that the threat from revolutionary France should be in itself a strong stimulant to Austrian leadership of constitutional reform as a means to improve the military posture of the empire. Stumpf's preferences, however, inclined toward Bavarian leadership within the empire as the best way to forestall an absolutist expansion of Habsburg power as well as the lust of the other princes for imperial territories. Here one can see the bare outline of a reformed imperial polity that checked both Prussian and Austrian ambitions in central Europe.[19]

As Napoleon extended French hegemony throughout Europe, the dean of Bavarian historians, Lorenz von Westenrieder (1748–1829), undertook his history of the Thirty Years' War. Westenrieder unequivocally viewed the war as "the most important and instructive" period in German and European history.[20] His main argument was that the subversive plans of the Protestant Union and the Bohemian "rebels" were actually part of a grander scheme of Louis XIII and Cardinal Richelieu to overthrow the empire and conquer Germany.[21] According to Westenrieder, the French, determined to undermine the Habsburgs and partition Germany, tried to stop the Catholic League's attempt to uphold and expand the legal authority and prestige of the Kaiser and the binding power of the imperial constitution. Kaiser Ferdinand's alternatives, Westenrieder pointed out, were stark: Either he could do nothing while the Reich collapsed into lawless anarchy, or he could use force to uphold imperial authority and put down the "Bohemian rebellion."[22] He characterized the uprising as a mortal threat to the "ancient and lawful" German constitution and the authority of the Reichstag.[23] For Westenrieder it was obvious that the modern threat of revolution and subversion emanating from France was a continuation of age-old French attempts to undermine German unity, which he believed was best preserved within the structure of the imperial constitution.[24]

Napoleon's dissolution of the Holy Roman Empire in 1806 and his creation of the Confederation of the Rhine stimulated a major project by Bavarian historians to revise the image of Maximilian I by casting him in the role of a visionary German leader who emerged in a time of crisis to save Germany.[25] Karl Kristian von Mann, in a public lecture at the Academy of Sciences in Munich in 1806, went so far as to condemn Maximilian's failure to seize the imperial crown when he had the chance and consolidate his rule over all of southern Germany, thus preserving "the prestige and power of the German Reich."[26] Maximilian was an obvious candidate for idealization by conservative Catholic opinion, which endorsed his defense of the universal church while consolidating Bavarian leadership within an imperial German polity. Maximilian's policies were praised as a model for preserving the constitutional status quo (and Bavaria's status within it) and the links to Vienna while keeping French, Austrian, and Prussian ambitions in check. Maximilian's attempt to play these powers against each other (which was only partially successful) inspired admiration from those who found themselves in a similar perilous situation. As we shall see, however, the lessons that historians could derive from an examination of his diplomacy were potentially useful only as long as the successor to the empire established by the Congress of Vienna in 1815, the German Confederation, endured.

The first major reexamination of Maximilian and his policies was Peter Philipp Wolf's "pragmatic" history, which appeared in four volumes between 1807 and 1811. Undertaking to counter Protestant "distortions" of the Elector's policies and provide instruction for future policy decisions, Wolf (1761–1808) claimed that Maximilian and the Catholic League not only defended the old imperial structures but put them on the path to reform that benefited the entire body of the German state (*gesammten Deutschen Staatskörpers*).[27] Maximilian, according to Wolf, saw in the expanding constitutional crisis created by the Bohemian Rebellion a revolutionary opportunity to simultaneously pursue the goals of the Counter-Reformation while bringing Germany under a more centralized imperial authority.[28] His instrument was the army of the Catholic League.

Westenrieder, Mann, and Wolf laid the groundwork for the most influential nineteenth-century reexamination of the policies of Maximilian, which came from the pen of a Munich historian who spent his entire life in the service of the Bavarian government, Karl Maria von Aretin (1796–1868).[29] Aretin's 1839 History of Bavarian Foreign Policy since 1500 significantly revised the conventional judgment that Maximilian had sacrificed political advantage to a religious cause that ultimately benefited only Austria.[30] Aretin saw Maximilian's defense of Catholicism as a fateful moment when the establishment of a more unitary imperial authority in Germany had briefly seemed possible. In Aretin's analysis the achievements of the Catholic League in subduing the Protestant revolt between 1618 and 1629 served as a formidable historical "demonstration" of how a revived imperial power could check French expansionism and awaken in Germans a "moral impression" of imperial prestige and authority.[31]

Aretin's general history of Bavaria's Wittelsbach rulers, appearing in 1842, was an even more explicit defense of Maximilian's policy of linking the unity and strength of the German nation to the preservation of some form of the empire. Aretin generously characterized his work as a continuation of Westenrieder's research even as he acknowledged that "historians of the modern era," such as Karl Menzel, Heinrich Leo, and Leopold von Ranke, also recognized the leading political position Bavaria had gained in Germany as a result of Maximilian's farsighted defense of the imperial order.[32] Aretin carefully pointed out, however, that the stress he laid on Maximilian's loyalty to the Habsburgs should not be construed as condoning the damage that Wittelsbach dynastic ambitions had caused to Germany's long-term interests. Rather, he offered his history in the confident hope that enmity between Austria and Bavaria, which had such tragic consequences to the maintenance of the political and religious order in Europe, would never occur again. Here Aretin suggested that Maximilian's true successor was the "illustrious statesman" Metternich, whose conservative policies had preserved European civilization behind the protective wall of the Austrian imperial state.[33] But with the revolution of 1848 and Metternich's fall, Catholic advocacy of a revitalized empire gradually gave way to more reactionary arguments. This shift in perspective by Catholic historians largely manifested itself in a comprehensive reevaluation of the policies and goals of the regime of Kaiser Ferdinand II.

Catholic intellectual life in Germany had always been marked by conservative tendencies. The mainstream of Catholic political thought opposed radical republicanism, or "Jacobinism," at large, and kleindeutsch Protestant nationalism in particular, the latter seen as merely a cover for Prussia's destabilizing territorial ambitions. The leading journal of conservative opinion in Catholic Germany was the *Historisch-politische Blätter für das katholische Deutschland* (*HpB*). Founded by Joseph Görres and Karl Ernst Jarcke in 1838, it started out as a forum to air opposition to Prussian rule over Catholic populations in the Rhineland, which Prussia had acquired as part of the peace settlement of 1815. Its broader mandate, as conceived by Jarcke, was to advocate for Catholic interests through defense of the German Confederation. After 1852, under the leadership of Joseph Edmund Jörg, the *HpB* served as the main ideological voice for proponents of a "greater Germany" that would preserve Germany's power position in Central Europe, counter French and Prussian territorial ambitions, and stem the rising tide of liberalism. It aggressively and consistently condemned the Protestant dominance of political and cultural discourse in nineteenth-century Germany as preparing the ground for revolution and civil war.[34]

In its first year of publication, the *HpB* published a lengthy article by Jodok Stülz, whose purpose was to rescue the historical reputation of Ferdinand II from the "rubbish heap of lies and slanders" to which it had been consigned by subversive Protestant historians.[35] The main claim of this rehabilitation was that Ferdinand, in suppressing the Bohemian Rebellion, had acted in a timely and legal fashion to crush revolution in his crown lands before it could spread to the empire. According to Stülz, Bohemia's Protestant rebels had shown themselves to be members of a "party of revolution" that was the historical precursor and model for the great political revolution in France in 1789. Stülz pointed out that the leaders of the revolt in Prague had extolled the "sovereignty of the people" in language that showed all too clearly the origins of the "revolutionary practice of our days."[36] In this analysis Protestantism (and, by association, Prussia) was the driving force behind the dangerous ideas that again threatened to foment civil war in Germany. This article established the *HpB* as a consistent defender of the conservative antirevolutionary agenda of the Restoration regimes.

Nowhere was this reactionary ideology more comprehensively promoted than in the landmark revisionist history of Ferdinand II written by Friedrich Emanuel von Hurter (1787–1865), an original and lifelong contributor to the *HpB* and a passionate and consistent opponent of constitutional liberalism. During his tenure as an imperial historiographer in Vienna (a post secured for him by Jarcke, who was a friend of Metternich), Hurter wrote his massive eleven-volume *Geschichte Kaiser Ferdinands II. und seiner Eltern* (History of Emperor Ferdinand II and His Predecessors), which was published over the course of fourteen years. The first volume appeared in 1850; the last was published the year before Hurter's death. Volumes 8 through 11 were subtitled as a separate four-volume history of the reign of Ferdinand II. In his foreword, Hurter proposed to rescue the historical reputation of the emperor who had reestablished the authority of the imperial constitution and the prestige of the Habsburgs. Hurter accused modern historians of ignoring the fact that the Bohemian rebels, inflamed by "the divisive democratic elements in Calvinism," had not been primarily interested in an expansion of religious rights and freedoms, which Ferdinand had been willing to entertain within the extant constitutional order. Their real goal, he said, was the dissolution of the empire. How could Ferdinand, Hurter asked, have stood idly by while the Reich was torn apart and left open to, among other dangers, Turkish and Hungarian invasion?[37]

It is clear that Hurter had been deeply traumatized by the revolution of 1848, which had interrupted his research and forced him to flee Vienna. However, his conservatism had much deeper roots. As a theology student in Göttingen between 1804 and 1806, he had acquired an abiding distaste not only for "Protestant rationalism" but also for all things French. His first attempts at writing history brought him to the attention of Johannes von Müller, the Swiss jurist who believed that it was Germany's very political fragmentation that preserved the liberties of Germans.[38] A long intellectual friendship followed that profoundly influenced Hurter's conservative notion of a confederal Germany based on the old imperial constitution, though he deviated from Müller in his belief that such a state could be more unitary in structure.

Hurter believed that there were demonstrable historical links between the revolutionary Protestantism of the seventeenth century and the French Revolution.[39] His interpretation of the origins of the Thirty Years' War is a key example of the historical consciousness that was at the center of political Catholicism in the decades before 1871. Catholic intellectuals' attempts to shape and influence the constitutional debate in Germany were based on the belief that the lessons of the past must govern the policies of the present.[40] This notion of historical remembrance is, of course, the essence of conservatism, and it is fair to say that most Catholic history writing about the Thirty Years' War was not an outlet for liberal political theorizing. Ultimately, the conservative Catholic defense of the political and religious structures of the old empire (roundly condemned, in the epithet "ultramontanism," by Protestant, Prussian, and liberal critics as part and parcel of German Catholics' reactionary fealty to the pope) was no match for the accelerating dynamism of Protestant nationalism. If political Catholicism was going to remain a viable alternative in the debate over German nationhood, a conservative concept of the Reich had to be more than a blind defense of outmoded institutions. One way to do this was to reimagine the beginning of the Thirty Years' War as the start of a civil war between the "revolutionary-republican" Protestant-Calvinist rebels and the defenders of the legitimate constitutional order, the Habsburgs.

Hurter justified the Catholic model of a united Germany by reconceiving the history of Habsburg policy in the Thirty Years' War as a visionary attempt to seize the opportunity this civil war offered to reestablish the Holy Roman Empire on new and firmer foundations. This interpretation was initially formulated in the context of the conservative horror at the subversive forces unleashed by the French Revolution.

But Hurter's successors gradually came to be more alarmed by the ambitions of Prussia. In the events of 1848 and the reaction that followed, they saw a fearful prospect: the arbitrary and autocratic rule of the Hohenzollerns spread over all of Germany. The kleindeutsch idea, they argued, obscured Prussia's shameful history of selfishly and consistently selling out German interests in central Europe in alliance with France, Germany's archenemy. Prussia and Protestantism were identified as the true enemies of a strong, united Germany.

The most violent, consistent, and tendentious of these accusations came from what would seem to be an unlikely source: a young Protestant historian from Ostfriesland named Onno Klopp (1822–1903). His first article in the *HpB*, "Magdeburg, Tilly, and Gustavus Adolphus," appeared in 1860. It was a detailed and highly polemical refutation of the cherished Protestant legend of Johann Tserclaes, Count of Tilly, the bloodthirsty imperial general who commanded the Catholic League army between 1610 and 1632. The piece established Klopp as the legitimate heir to Hurter and the chief voice of the anti-Prussian and anti-nationalist school of Catholic history writing. In the long debate between Catholic and Protestant historians in the nineteenth century, Klopp was the sharpest critic of the assumption that Prussia was historically predestined to lead German unification.[41] It is easy to understand why Klopp spent his entire career outside the university. But, despite the ideological sympathies that made him persona non grata among Protestant scholars, he was effectively barred from securing a teaching position in Bavaria or Austria because he was a Protestant.[42] He would eventually convert to Catholicism and relocate to Austria. Before taking that step, he earned his living as a journalist, an editor of Leibniz's papers, a secondary school teacher, and a court historian in Hanover, eventually solidifying his reputation in the 1860s as one of the most widely read and controversial historians of his time.

Klopp's opposition to absolutism had initially made him an enthusiastic supporter of the democratic ideas that blossomed in Germany during the 1848 revolution. Yet, like many young liberals of his generation, the violence of revolution would push him in a more conservative direction. For disenchanted Catholic 48'ers such as himself, the constitutional structure of the German Confederation, the legitimate (in their eyes) successor to the old empire, offered a model of political stability. But the imperial ideal Klopp advocated in his iconoclastic histories of the Thirty Years' War was not only praised as a conservative bulwark against revolution. Klopp also defended the Holy Roman Empire as a fundamentally sound political system that protected its less powerful constituents from the tyranny of the princes. Behind the propaganda of religious war Klopp saw in the Protestant cause in the Thirty Years' War the destabilizing aims of several petty despots. He saw the same goals being pursued in the nineteenth century, as Prussia's statesmen (given a free pass by Protestant historians) cloaked their absolutist designs in the rhetoric of unification. In his lifelong study of the Thirty Years' War, Klopp methodically refuted the lies he believed were at the heart of Protestant history writing. He elaborated on the constitutional arguments of Westenrieder and Hurter by claiming that the "positive order" of the confederal empire was the essence of the German nation and that the Prussian slogan of "Unity leads to freedom!" (*Einheit führt zur Freiheit!*) did not necessarily mean positive things for Germany's future.[43] The assertion of the historic anti-French mission of the Prussian state was, in Klopp's opinion, mendacious and dangerous in the extreme.[44] Klopp, like Hurter, believed that the preservation of German liberty and the defense of German interests had always been guaranteed by the Catholic empire, not the dissolutive ideas propagated by the Reformation. He vigorously disputed the hegemony over the direction of German history and the collective remembrance of the Thirty Years' War that Protestant historians had bestowed on Prussia. Klopp was, as one might imagine, vigorously denounced by Protestant critics as a liar, a lunatic, a traitor, or a combination of all three.

Klopp's views gained their first broad notoriety with the publication of his three-volume History of Ostfriesland (1854–58), the third volume of which was a vociferous attack on Prussia and Friedrich II.[45] But a year before that third volume appeared, Klopp published, under the cover of anonymity, his *Studien über Katholizismus, Protestantismus, und Gewissensfreiheit in Deutschland* (Studies on Catholicism, Protestantism, and Freedom of Belief in Germany). This book challenged the monopoly on patriotism claimed by the Protestant kleindeutsch party. In it Klopp advanced two main arguments that formed the basis of his research for the next forty years. His first claim was that the Protestant interpretation of the war as a religious conflict was a cynical historical falsehood that was intended to obscure the past and present sins of the German princes. The second was that the so-called Bohemian Revolution, far from being a justified uprising in defense of religious prerogatives, was nothing more than a plot by the Czech-Slavic "feudal aristocracy" to reestablish their tyranny over the estates.[46] Klopp was thus able to make the claim that the political legacy of Catholicism, as embodied in the constitution of the old empire, was one of freedom, modernization, domestic stability, and constitutional rule. This counterattack against the guiding principle of Protestant history writing, namely, that 1517 represented the birth of German aspirations to independence and unity, took Hurter's conservative arguments and turned them upside down by making Ferdinand II the scourge of feudal tyranny.

Two other critical components of Klopp's defense of the empire was a recognizably pan-German argument that the empire was the bulwark of western civilization and, as a corollary, a view of the Thirty Years' War as an epochal clash between Slavic barbarism and Christian civilization (a view of the war that would become prominent after 1918): "We see that the cause of the Habsburgs, in their fight against the Bohemian elites, was the protection of the German language and German culture in the Reich against the Slav threat."[47] In short, Klopp saw in the Holy Roman Empire a combination of religious and secular power that made German civilization unique. Essentially, this interpretation allowed Klopp to claim that Catholicism, not Protestantism, had the more historically valid claim to being the foundation of true "Germanness" and that therefore the empire was the political institution that had the greatest impact on the formation of a modern German national identity. By waging war against the Protestant princes, Ferdinand clearly placed the interests of German power and culture uppermost in his policies. In Klopp's view, Protestant historians in the nineteenth century were no different than their pamphleteering predecessors in the seventeenth century in using religion to conceal "the dismemberment of the German

Reich and the German nation." According to Klopp, the Protestant histories of the origins of the war, when they wrote of a "national war" or a "people's war" against the Kaiser, were simply concealing, behind a crude and disingenuous appeal to the memory of the 1813 uprising against Napoleon, the Protestant princes' aims of dissolving the empire in pursuit of particularistic and dynastic advantage.[48]

Klopp's writings mirrored a prevailing mood of apprehension among Germany's Catholics about the fate of the German Confederation, particularly during the late 1850s and early 1860s, when Austria's waning ability to influence events in central Europe was becoming more and more apparent. French military support of Cavour's attempt to unify Italy in 1859 had begun the expulsion of Austria from the peninsula, while Prussia studiously avoided intervention on Austria's side, as Vienna argued the statutes of the Confederation obligated it to do. The formation of the Nationalverein that same year to promote Prussian leadership of German unification seemed to indicate that, after a decade of relative quiet, the "German question" was again becoming urgent and that Prussia (backed by the advocacy of Protestant historians) was seizing the high ground in the debate over unification. The old fear of Germany's Catholic community, dissolution and marginalization, which was in itself a legacy of the war, loomed once again.

Klopp's main claim, that the Thirty Years' War was political in its origins and that the religiously inspired "nationalist uprising" (as he accused Protestant historians of labeling it) of the Bohemians was a petty feudal revolt against a benevolent and legally constituted monarchy, was central to his indictment of the Protestants for deliberately instigating a civil war that threatened not only the legitimate constitutional order but the destruction of Germany itself. No other conclusion could be reached except that Catholicism was the historical champion of Germany's interests, which were best defended and preserved within the fortress of the empire. Klopp believed that the Protestant historians' defense of a religious interpretation of the origins of the Thirty Years' War echoed seventeenth-century propaganda because both obscured the anti-German ambitions of the Protestant princes. For Klopp these ambitions were writ large in the nineteenth century as

"Prussia."[49] In 1863, Klopp recalled his reaction to Heinrich Sybel's provocative address to the Bavarian Academy of Sciences in 1859, in which Sybel challenged the historiographical "cult of empire." It was at that moment, Klopp remembered, that he saw his life's work clearly: "I would put General Tilly, one of the personalities of the war who had been most shamefully treated by the kleindeutsch, tendentious and false 'Protestant interpretation' of the past, in the foreground of a history of the first half of the war."[50]

Klopp calculated the stakes of his fight with Protestant and Prussian history writing in simple terms: German national interests demanded the maintenance of some version of the imperial-confederal polity bound closely to Austria. Other Catholic scholars, however, confronting the reality of the rise of Prussia in the 1860s, began to distance themselves from this viewpoint, which would be subsumed under the liberal epithet of "ultramontanism." This shift began even before Bismarck launched his wars of unification in 1866 and 1870. Unlike Klopp, who had asserted a Catholic-German patriotism by maligning the motives behind the Protestant-Prussian variety, his younger successors emphasized how Catholic Germany had defended the status quo in the Thirty Years' War and thus preserved German constitutional integrity against the territorial ambitions of the Habsburgs. Catholic historians' defense of "German Catholicism" began in 1863 with a reassessment of the founding of the Catholic League by Carl Adolph Cornelius (1819–1903). Cornelius, a close friend of Sybel, taught history in Munich, where he was prominent in the circle of church historians such as Johann Adam Möhler and Ignaz Döllinger, who believed that the Catholic Church could evolve and modernize away from its rigid hierarchy without abandoning its fundamental spiritual mission.[51] Similarly, Cornelius's interpretation of the origins and aims of the Catholic League, which exerted much influence on the work of his students Moriz Ritter and Felix Stieve, marked the emergence of a much less conservative (in comparison to Westenrieder, Hurter, and Klopp) Catholic history writing that emphasized the "national" motivations behind the League's founding. Cornelius praised the federal, constitutional, and cooperative nature of the League, in essence its modernizing dynamic, as it was directed against Germany's foreign enemies and their domestic allies.[52] Ritter retained this perspective of the two antagonists in the first decade of the war in his history of the Protestant Union that appeared in 1867, which asserted that, for their part, the Protestant princes of the Union had only pursued reforms, no different than the aims of the League, that were directed toward containing Habsburg ambitions in the face of the Spanish and French threats.[53] The imperial solution advocated by the legitimist and ultramontane historiography of Westenrieder, Hurter, and Klopp was replaced by a new generation of Catholic historians less committed to defending the confederal status quo than they were to an analysis of the Thirty Years' War that defended Catholic membership in the German national community.[54]

The most prominent advocate of this new Catholic-German perspective was Felix Stieve (1845–98), a professor of history at the Technical Academy in Munich. Stieve, a Westphalian Catholic who was an enthusiastic supporter of unification under Prussia, gradually came to reject the interpretations of the legitimist school as represented by Hurter and Klopp.[55] Stieve's revisionism was founded on a "policy of restoration" (*Restaurationspolitik*), which was the term he used to describe the Catholic League's simultaneous commitment to the protection of Catholic interests and the preservation of the imperial constitution. In Stieve's view, these goals were not necessarily congruent with Habsburg dynastic interests. For Stieve, the Union/League division could plausibly be interpreted as representing two approaches to the same goal of remaking the Holy Roman Empire as a more unitary German state.

Like Klopp, Stieve realized that Catholic history writing could only make a claim to represent a "German" vision of a unified nation if it insisted on the political origins of the Thirty Years' War. Unlike Klopp, however, he did not do this by attacking Prussia. Instead, Stieve told a story that demonstrated the anti-Austrian and German motivations behind the formation of the Catholic League. In his formulation of the "restoration idea" (*Restaurationsidee*), Stieve attempted to integrate the history of the Catholic League within the context of a coherent German national narrative. This interpretation of the origins of the war was founded on four main claims: first, the League was the military instrument through which the laws and structure of the empire were maintained and enforced in order that the revitalization of the empire could be pursued; second, the empire and its institutions were not fundamentally anti-Protestant but representative of Germany as a whole; third, these institutions opposed absolutism and defended German liberty; and fourth, the attempt to remake these institutions during the crisis of civil war aimed at the preservation of a "powerful national sense."[56]

Stieve's history of the League offered a historical justification of the continuing relevance of the political legacy of the empire for nineteenth-century Germany. What he had achieved was a Catholic narrative of German national development that largely avoided falling into the trap of a dogmatic confessional animosity. Like Cornelius, Stieve believed that Maximilian's leadership of the Catholic League was dedicated to the maintenance of the integrity and structure of the empire and motivated by a genuine national dynamic that could serve as the basis for remaking the empire as a truly German institution. Stieve came to believe that the founding of the Second Reich in 1871 confirmed this interpretation, and he made an appeal for a nonconfessional national mode of history writing: "German history writing, Protestant as well as Catholic, observes the past through the political and religious viewpoints of the present, and finds in them weapons for current battles, and thus is accustomed to celebrating the religious fanatic or the representative of the most petty particularism as national heroes."[57]

The Habsburg War of Unification

The argument over the origins of the war became a forum in which Catholic historians, and those historians opposed to the possibility of Prussian hegemony, could reimagine the Holy Roman Empire as the most historically legitimate model for a viable German state. Nevertheless, arguments for the inherent strength of the old empire and attempts to rehabilitate the reputation of Ferdinand II as defender of the legitimate political order could be seen as lacking both visceral nationalist appeal and modern relevance. But the story of the first decade of the war, a series of imperial victories over the Protestant princes of the western empire and their ally Denmark that culminated in the Peace of Lübeck in 1629, could be used to present a more fully realized vision of "what could have been / what could yet be." Catholic historians took up the tale of the first third of the war and wrote a series of speculative "what if" histories that imagined a radically different kind of imperial German state emerging from the chaos of civil war.

These histories described a triumphant imperium that restored a hegemonic German power from the Baltic Sea to the Alps. Many were unquestionably influenced by the example and experience of Napoleon's bold redrawing of the map of Central Europe. Napoleon's reorganization of the German states, and his molding of France into a dominating imperial power, not only inspired a German nationalist reaction to French hegemony but also spurred a speculative reflection on the power of the medieval German emperors, which was also a response to defeat at the hands of Napoleonic France.[58] Großdeutsch and Catholic historians envisioned a resurrected German empire in three ways: first, as the defender of Christian civilization in Europe; second, as the preserver of German unity from the threat of French conquest and partition; and third, as the model for a modern German state that, as a maritime rival to Sweden, the Netherlands, Denmark, and Britain, defended German interests in the North and Baltic seas.

As we have seen, the conservative Catholic interpretation of Germany's role in Europe argued for recognizing the importance of the Holy Roman Empire as the main defender of European Christian civilization (that is to say, "Germany," a popular narcissism that persisted well into the twentieth century). This argument also broached the possibility that Catholic and Protestant might be reconciled and reunited in a modernized version of the medieval empire. But during the traumatic years of the Napoleonic occupation, and while the patriotic euphoria of 1813 lasted after the Congress of Vienna, these interpretations began to focus more on the "lost opportunity" in the Thirty Years' War to create a powerful unified empire in central Europe. Nostalgia for the empire of Charlemagne was superseded, if not entirely replaced, by a reexamination of the abortive unifying project of Ferdinand II. As Napoleonic France extended its power over the Rhine, Lorenz von Westenrieder dedicated his 1804 history of the Thirty Years' War to the task of providing his contemporaries with "instructive and warning examples for our reflection and counsel in similar cases."[59] For Westenrieder, Kaiser Ferdinand II's attempt to turn a counterrevolutionary war toward remaking the empire as a unified power under a single ruler "in the footsteps of Charlemagne and the Saxon Otto" was a singular example from the past that offered a way out of Germany's present humiliation.[60]

Karl Ludwig von Woltmann (1770–1817), a Protestant historian who held no particular brief for Prussian hegemony, had studied at Göttingen and taught at Jena with Schiller. He offered a more specific and sophisticated version, relatively unmarked by nostalgia or conservatism, of Westenrieder's unified imperial state. Woltmann wrote during a time that, like the thirty years between 1618 and 1648, was roiled by a violent flux of revolution, occupation, and liberation.[61] Foreign armies had again crossed the German frontiers intent on the dissolution of the empire. Woltmann reacted to this crisis by developing a radically new idea of the political structure of Germany, one that envisioned Austria at the head of a confessionally united German "European Republic," in which the unifying idea of Kaiser and Reich and the modern nationalist spirit of 1813 brought Germans together against the French, Russian, and Ottoman threats.[62] Woltmann's interpretation of the origins of the German political structure took very little from the traditional idea of empire held by Westenrieder, Hurter, and Klopp. Like the Mainz historian Nicolaus Vogt, who did the same in his analyses of the aims of Gustavus Adolphus, Woltmann was inspired by the achievements of Napoleon to rethink the unification of Germany in more modern terms.[63] Counterintuitively, he cited the empire of Charlemagne as the original model of a politically united Germany that triumphed over Teutonic "tribalism" and noted that whenever the Germans had tampered with the unity of Kaiser and Reich, as in the Thirty Years' War, "Germany drowned in the blood of its sons."[64]

Woltmann was intrigued by the unitary possibilities of the imperial structure, but was much less interested than conservative Catholic historians in debating the merits of the imperial constitution. He advocated a more modern notion of German sovereignty that was quasi-popular in nature. In a "supplement" he wrote for an 1816 edition of Friedrich

Schiller's history of the Thirty Years' War, Woltmann described an enlightened Habsburg policy pursued from the rule of Rudolph II to Ferdinand II, that is, from 1576 to 1637, that aimed at breaking the "intermediary" powers of the princes, the Protestant Church, and Rome, while uniting Germany within strong borders under one crown.[65] Reflecting on the model of Napoleon's Confederation of the Rhine and its successor, the German Confederation, Woltmann came to the conclusion that Ferdinand was less interested in reimposing Habsburg dynastic rule over all of Germany than he was in trying to unite Germany as a confederation of sovereign territorial rulers who, under the overall authority of the emperor, would control and direct Germany's "national power."[66] In the flush of the victory over Napoleon in 1813, Woltmann found in this great project of the Habsburg rulers in the Thirty Years' War a compelling model for a modern German state.

Karl Adolf Menzel (1784–1855), another Protestant historian who was less than enthusiastic about Prussian leadership in Germany, was also inspired in his analysis of the early years of the war by what he saw as a Habsburg attempt to unify Germany under a single ruler. However, he had a much clearer (and more ambitious) take on the possibilities that a history of the war's origins offered as a template for German unification in the nineteenth century. In his provocative and influential Modern History of the Germans (1826–48), Menzel defended Ferdinand's bloody suppression of the Bohemian revolt and approved of Ferdinand's determination to uphold the principle that the empire was "one state." He attributed to Ferdinand a decidedly modern determination to wield his prerogatives as emperor to crush the forces of dissolution and to revitalize imperial authority to the point that Germany could become "not only in name, but in fact, a Reich that was equal to the other nations in Europe." Menzel believed the reason that nineteenth-century Germany now found herself 200 years behind France and Britain in terms of political and economic progress was because Ferdinand had been thwarted at a fateful moment (the recurring lament we find in all of the nineteenth-century histories of the war) in his attempt to found an "effective and real state authority" that encompassed the national community.[67]

However, this interpretation was problematic for the majority of Catholic großdeutsch historians of the 1850s and 1860s. It did not serve very well to justify a confederal solution to German unification, and because it slighted constitutional questions they were trying to highlight, it tended to undermine the legitimacy of the Habsburg claim to having a voice in German affairs. Finally, Menzel's reluctance to criticize Protestantism's political agenda in support of Prussia also made it unsatisfactory. Nevertheless, the legitimist school of Catholic historiography would gradually adopt this grander scheme of a Habsburg project of unification as a way of buttressing the Catholic national idea.[68] Onno Klopp, as the leading voice of the legitimist school after Hurter, made a passionate argument for the unifying "moral power" of the imperial tradition. But simply asserting the moral and cultural virtues of the empire as a defender of German civilization was increasingly recognized as a somewhat desperate argument rooted in political weakness and intellectual marginalization. Klopp revealed as much in a typically sharp response to Sybel in 1862, in which he attacked any scholarship that "oriented itself to support the claims of the state."[69] But beyond blindly rejecting Prussian leadership of German unification, what could Catholic history writing offer to nineteenth-century Germans as a patriotically compelling, modern, and historically justified model of a unified and powerful Germany?

By attacking the "Slavic" identity of the Bohemian nobility, Klopp revived the notion of the Christian imperium as defender of western civilization (and hinted at what would become a central idea legitimating German war aims in the twentieth century). According to Klopp, the holder of the imperial office occupied a "moral position" unique among the rulers of Europe. In pursuing the unification of Germany in a counterrevolutionary war, Ferdinand was in fact creating the necessary foundation for the defense of Christian culture and civilization. Thus Klopp claimed, "In upholding his rights against the rebellious princes, [Ferdinand] defended the unity, the might, and the liberty of the German nation. While he turned foreign princes and kings from German soil, he defended not only his nation but also the potential for repulsing the common enemies of Christendom. As he protected his throne, his dynasty, and his authority, he saved Christian culture."[70] Klopp had recast the Thirty Years' War as an epochal clash between civilization and barbarism in which the survival of European culture itself hung in the balance.

Klopp accused Protestant historians in general (with the exception of renegades like Woltmann and Menzel) of willfully denigrating, if not actually ignoring, this historical and moral mission of the Holy Roman Empire. Klopp had come to the conclusion that the possibility of a strong and united Germany (created by the victories of 1629) so alarmed the other European powers, especially France, that the myth of a "Habsburg domination" of Europe, or the establishment of a "universal monarchy," had been created out of whole cloth by interests that feared a revival of German power.[71] Klopp blamed this "treasonous" falsehood for the fact that no genuine "German national" history writing existed. Under the influence of this foreign canard, the Protestant tradition of history writing had developed. As it gravitated toward Prussian power, it inevitably contributed, Klopp believed, to the political weakness and fragmentation of Germany by cynically discrediting the Catholic idea of the nation.[72] Klopp found the latter to be historically grounded in the vital role the empire had played in the medieval period as the "ruling nation of Europe," defending the continent from the depredations of the Slavs, Magyars, and Vikings. Ferdinand had nobly attempted to uphold and fulfill this holy mission. And it was this idea that Klopp cited as the justification for his claim that "a defensive and protective alliance between Austria and Prussia and all of the other German states against every enemy and every attack, that is what would profit the German Fatherland."[73]

In nineteenth-century Germany the sincerity and persuasiveness of nationalist and patriotic sentiments were largely determined by the level of hostility they directed toward France. The simple argument that justified the Catholic national idea asserted the consistent anti-French mission of the empire and the Habsburg counterrevolutionary policy during the Thirty Years' War. The imperial victories of 1629 were glorified as decisive and preemptive blows against the grand plan to dethrone the Habsburgs and dominate Europe, which Catholic historians believed was at the core of French foreign policy from Henry IV to Napoleon. This interpretation claimed that the empire had historically been the most effective bulwark against French ambitions in Germany. Protestant particularism, and the Protestant princes' open and self-serving alliances with the eternal enemy France, had undermined and betrayed this paramount mission.

Catholic history writing believed implicitly in the reality of Henry IV's ambition to create a "United Europe" once he had stabilized France after the Wars of Religion. This plan, it was claimed, had envisioned the establishment of a new political order and balance of power in Europe, a complete remaking of the continent's map at the expense of Germany. As the legitimist interpretations of Westenrieder and Hurter had justified the Counter-Reformation as essentially counterrevolutionary, this idea of a new European order pursued by Henry IV raised the memory of the Napoleonic occupation to buttress the legitimacy of the empire as the historical defender of German interests. Writing during the French occupation, Peter Philipp Wolf speculated on the plans of Henry IV, basing his account on recently discovered documents from Henry's court.[74] Wolf's analysis of this new material revealed that Henry IV wanted to establish a new balance of power in Europe comprising six hereditary monarchies: France, Spain, England, Denmark, Sweden, and Lombardy; five "elective monarchies": the "German Empire," Bohemia, Poland, Hungary, and the Papal States; and four "republics": Switzerland, Italy, Venice, and Belgium. Obviously this meant the partition of the Habsburg lands. Wolf also revealed that the new confederation was to have been governed by a "European Senate" located near the "center" of Europe, perhaps Cologne, Trier, Mainz, or Strasbourg.[75] Wolf was carefully neutral in his assessment of this plan, though it is hard to escape the impression that he believed it contained what would have been positive aspects for Bavaria, if not for Germany as a whole. His fellow Bavarian Aretin, writing on Henry IV twenty-five years later, was equally circumspect.[76] Such a reorganization of the map of Europe, had it been accomplished (Henry IV was assassinated in 1610—his murderer was convinced he wanted to destroy the Catholic Church), would have meant a considerable enlargement of Bavaria's power and territory. Mere consideration of a scheme to reestablish a genuinely elective empire reflected a concept of German unity and imperial reform that excluded Austria and potentially checked Prussian influence. By emphasizing the elective nature of the emperor's office, Wolf and Aretin exhibited a true Bavarian patriotism that would always reserve judgment regarding Habsburg intentions. What is more interesting is that they regarded a French king as a "bringer of peace" (*Friedensbringer*) emerging from the chaos of the religious wars: the successor to Caesar or Augustus or the precursor to Napoleon.[77]

Karl Adolf Menzel, as always, was more direct and polemical, explicitly labeling Protestantism the stalking horse for French plans for empire. The Protestant Union, in his view, was the subversive instrument through which Henry IV's "Christian-European Republic" would be established in Germany, thus extending French power over the Rhine. Menzel's German-national/pro-imperial perspective came from a deep skepticism regarding the motives behind proposals for any political reorganization of Europe. Whether it was the Treaty of Westphalia in 1648, the Confederation of the Rhine in 1806, or the German Confederation in 1815, the result was always the same: diminution of German unity and power. Unfortunately, Menzel concluded, German rulers more often than not had collaborated in these enterprises. Nevertheless, until 1806 the empire, as preserved by the Treaty of Westphalia, had been in his opinion the last, best defense against partition. Karl Müller, also an advocate of this German-national interpretation, supported Menzel's conclusions: "Had this [Henry IV's] plan succeeded, two hundred years ago Germany would have had the same relationship with France that it had two hundred years later through the Confederation of the Rhine."[78]

Since the 1820s, French ambitions, in the shape of Talleyrand's intrigues, Adolphe Thiers's militantly nationalist foreign policy, or Louis Napoleon's saber rattling, were perceived by Catholic historians as being primarily interested in destabilizing the European balance of power established by the Congress of Vienna in 1815 and thus again opening Europe to French hegemony. For many Germans, naked French expansionism, as once practiced by Louis XIV and Napoleon, had given way to the export of radical political ideas or diplomatic maneuvers to undermine the peace settlement of 1815. Aretin reflected these apprehensions in his interpretation of the "great plan" of Henry IV to "foment rebellion" among the Protestants of Austria, Bohemia, and Hungary.[79] Johann Sporschil (1800–1863), a popular and widely read Catholic historian who also worked as a journalist, upheld the empire as the best guarantor of German interests by labeling the Protestant Union a mere tool in Richelieu's hands. For Sporschil, Germany's security in Europe was best served by the existence of the empire. Of course, nationalism was a grave threat to this existence, so Sporschil summarily dismissed the liberal belief in the possibility of creating a more secular and political "German Catholicism."[80] In 1861 Johannes Janssen would decisively characterize the French nemesis from the legitimist perspective when he concluded that Richelieu was the "diabolic" successor to Henry IV and the "founder of a spiritually empty absolutism" that aimed at the destruction of the German empire and the stability of Europe.[81]

Ultimately, the articulation of a persuasive and compelling Catholic national idea depended on legitimating the empire by attributing to it a historical anti-French (and, by extrapolation, antirevolutionary) mission. Comparing the imperial triumph of 1629 to the Prussian-led victory over Napoleon in 1813 was one way to challenge the Protestant monopoly on German patriotism on its own ground. But how could Catholic historians challenge Prussian claims of superiority in the more pragmatic realm of European power politics, the basis of Prussia's claims to be the best defender of German interests? How could Catholic historians and their anti-Prussian sympathizers justify their alternative national idea within the nineteenth-century context of economic and political modernization? Could the empire ever have been seen as demonstrating the potential to make Germany a commercial and military power capable of challenging Sweden, the Netherlands, Denmark, and Britain?

They offered concrete evidence of this potential in speculations about what was variously termed the Wallenstein plan, the Baltic project, or the trade plan. These historians integrated their narratives of the victory of 1629 with claims about how Kaiser Ferdinand II and Wallenstein, the commander of the imperial forces not part of the Catholic League, intended not only to unite Germany but to make the new state a maritime power equal to be reckoned with. Their interpretations addressed nineteenth-century concerns about Germany's ability to compete on the global economic stage.[82] On the other side, Protestant narratives from the late eighteenth and early nineteenth centuries also stressed the ambitions of Ferdinand and Wallenstein to establish "one kingdom" on the French model in Germany at the expense of the imperial constitution and the religious peace. In these Protestant histories defeating Denmark, expropriating Mecklenburg, and subduing the strategic Baltic port of Stralsund were all steps taken to forestall Gustavus Adolphus's invasion of Germany to rescue Protestantism and to further the establishment of the dreaded "universal monarchy."[83] Although these interpretations emphasized Wallenstein's territorial ambitions over trade and maritime policy, this perspective would change in the 1820s and 1830s as the economic benefits of a Customs Union (*Zollverein*) between the German states became clear. Protestant as well as Catholic historians found the lessons of 1629 particularly compelling. When Denmark and the German Confederation came to blows over control of the northern states of Schleswig-Holstein in 1848 and 1864, both times the small Danish navy had blockaded German ports, which added urgency and national meaning to the debate over Wallenstein's maritime plans. The formation of a strong German navy, and the protection of German commerce in the North and Baltic seas in competition with Britain, the Netherlands, Denmark, and Sweden, became an important issue to those keen on seeing Germany become a major power.[84] However, the fact that Catholic historians made a good case for attributing this kind of national foresight to Ferdinand II and Wallenstein was a little hard to swallow for most Protestant historians, except for apostates like Karl Menzel.

The dream of restoring the economic power of the Hanseatic League, though it was usually linked to the unbounded ambitions of Wallenstein, nevertheless moved Protestant historians as they contemplated the extension of Habsburg power to the Baltic between 1627 and 1629.[85] The historical notes appended to the 1760 German edition of Walter Harte's biography of Gustavus Adolphus pointed out that, in 1570, the Speyer Reichstag appointed admirals to the Burgundian, Westphalian, and

Upper and Lower Saxon administrative districts (*Kreise*). Ferdinand obviously had precedent on his side in his attempt to wrest the Baltic and North Sea trade from Sweden and Denmark.[86] What Protestant historians also admired about Wallenstein was his realistic and uninhibited practice of power politics on a strategic scale. Karl Woltmann was convinced that the Wallenstein plan was part of the Duke of Friedland's secessionist scheme to turn Mecklenburg into a base of operations as a major north German principality that could control trade in the Baltic.[87] Johann Söltl believed, on the contrary, that Wallenstein was methodically carrying out the Kaiser's plan to take control of the Hanseatic ports, build a fleet, and make Germany a land and sea power.[88] In a phrase that would be repeated again and again, in one form or another, in all nineteenth-century histories of the Thirty Years' War, Karl Menzel mused that a "turning point in German history" had briefly beckoned in 1629.[89] Johann Sporschil concluded that if the Wallenstein plan had succeeded, it would have been "as much in Germany's interest as in the Kaiser's"[90] By the mid-nineteenth century, German historians were becoming increasingly concerned with economic and strategic considerations, concerns that only became more acute as Germany's economic modernization accelerated in the 1850s and 1860s. Gustav Droysen still invoked the specter, now somewhat long in the tooth, of the "universal monarchy" of Philip II when he asserted that in 1629 "imperial absolutism" was finally nearing its long-sought goal: the conquest of northern Europe. But he also acknowledged that in the Baltic project the empire had pursued a sound strategic idea, a "profoundly comprehensive plan." In an eerily prescient aside, Droysen added that all Wallenstein and the Kaiser lacked to carry it out were ships to cross the sea.[91]

Catholic historians, in their speculations about the Baltic project, saw the opportunity to seize the high ground in the unification debate and to reorient German remembrance of the Thirty Years' War toward Catholic accomplishments (rather than Catholic crimes) by integrating into their narrative the idea of German national progress. The obstacles to German unity and greatness, in this interpretation, were not the Protestant princes per se but the predatory powers that stood behind them and supported their rebellion: Sweden, Denmark, Britain, the

Netherlands, and France. The empire was praised for having fought for German national interests by trying to restore the maritime dominance of the Hanseatic League, build a navy, and reestablish the authority of the empire on the two German seas.[92] Friedrich von Hurter saw the Kaiser's "forward-looking idea" of a commercial union between Spain and the Hanseatic League as opening "glittering prospects" to Germany: "The great German people must control their sea, and take back what had been stolen from them by England."[93] This vision of the "imperial flag waving from the Alps to the Baltic" was before Onno Klopp's eyes as well as he linked the Catholic imperial idea to the aspirations of a modern state: "The kings and powers of Europe watched the swelling power of Ferdinand with shock and horror. The danger, that Germany was able to become a single unified Reich under one ruler and thus the first and decisive power, the arbiter in Europe, lay before their eyes." Ferdinand's grand scheme called for a rejuvenation of the Hansa and the lifting of the tolls in the Skagerrak and the Sound, "a shabby and vile tribute levied on the whole of Germany."[94] Addressing potential critics, Klopp maintained that this "trade plan," as he called it, was not a delusion but a clear-eyed strategic vision that had come close to fulfillment: "Ferdinand fully recognized the importance of trade for the wealth and culture of the nation."[95] One Protestant historian grudgingly conceded that the plan to gain control of the Baltic "was, from the German point of view, undoubtedly justified. . . . But the Kaiser did not receive a favorable response to this idea precisely because it had come from him, the Kaiser."[96] This was one issue in the long nineteenth-century debate over the meaning and legacy of the Thirty Years' War in which Protestant historians obviously felt they did not have a prima facie case against the Catholic interpretation. Still, in 1867 Konrad Reichard declared in his much-cited Maritime Policy of the Habsburgs that the Baltic project of the Habsburgs should be seen as nothing more than a plan through which Spain had sought the destruction of the Protestant sea powers in its attempt to impose the Catholic universal monarchy on Europe. It was a "Spanish plan" that simultaneously aimed at the destruction of the "Dutch Republicans" and the forging of the last link of the chain that shackled central Europe from Poland to Lombardy and from Alsace to the mouth of the Scheldt.[97]

By asserting the existence of this Baltic project, Catholic historians tried to update their defense of the old empire. The unification of Germany's economic strength into an instrument of continental and global power had become a recognizable and popular "national" goal by midcentury.[98] Catholic advocacy of the Baltic project promoted a national goal in a way that partially neutralized the confessional divide and lent legitimacy to the Catholic national idea. In emphasizing the historical anti-French mission of the old empire and in discerning a nascent German Weltpolitik driving Habsburg plans in the Thirty Years' War, these historians tried to tell a story that undermined Protestant-Prussian claims to German leadership in the nineteenth century. But the unification of Germany in 1871 settled the großdeutsch-kleindeutsch argument once and for all. Franz Keym, writing in 1873, bitterly acknowledged that Catholic historians and their supporters had never been successful in fundamentally altering the parameters of the debate in the historical consciousness of most Germans. He believed that the nineteenth-century interpretations of the Thirty Years' War's meaning were always perceived to have been divided into two camps, one "national," that is, Protestant, and the other "anti-national," that is, Catholic.[99]

Catholic historians tried to reimagine the history of the opening phases of the Thirty Years' War as the beginning of a Habsburg counterrevolution and war of unification that aimed at the restoration of German power in Central Europe. But the credibility of their story was handicapped in one significant way: It could not compete with the dynamism of the Protestant concept of the German nation, which not only claimed a monopoly on national feeling, as well as all modern and forward-looking ideas, but also was based on an interpretation of the Great War not as a civil war but as the War of Protestant Liberation. It is to that narrative I now turn.

2. The War of Protestant Liberation

The Angel of Deliverance
In 1844 Friedrich Moser, an amateur historian who lived in Zwickau, published a pamphlet describing the 1837 unveiling of the Gustavus Adolphus memorial in the Saxon village of Lützen, outside Leipzig. Moser recalled the anguished prayers of Germany's Protestants in 1629 as Wallenstein's imperial army, seemingly unstoppable, extended the reach of the Habsburg Counter-Reformation to the Baltic Sea: "Thousands and thousands of voices called and prayed to God: have you then, Lord our God, completely forsaken us? Oh, make an end to our misfortune and misery, dry our tears, still our sighs! Send us an angel of deliverance in our distress and affliction!" For Moser, the Lützen battlefield where the Swedish king fell defending Protestant liberty was "holy land," doubly consecrated because of its proximity to the site of the 1813 Battle of Nations (*Völkerschlacht*) outside Leipzig, where Germans had come together to defeat Napoleon and end the French occupation of Germany. Moser called on Germans not only to remember 1629, when Protestant Germany seemed to be defeated, but also to recall 1813, when it rose again. For Moser and most of Germany's Protestants in the first half of the nineteenth century, the Swedish king's intervention in the Thirty Years' War in 1631 and 1632 was the first great war of German liberation, inextricably linked in collective remembrance to the second war of liberation against Napoleon in the early nineteenth century. Both were remembered as moments when a vision of a unified Germany had beckoned briefly before it cruelly disappeared.[1]

The devotion of Germany's Protestants to the memory of Gustavus Adolphus was a remarkable cultural and religious phenomenon of the first half of the nineteenth century. But the transformation of a Swedish king into a German national hero was much more than just an expression of nineteenth-century Protestant piety. The cult of Gustavus Adolphus emerged out of the hopes and anxieties Germans had concerning the question of German unification. Historians, poets, playwrights, and novelists celebrated his crusade against imperial tyranny by reimagining his intervention in the Thirty Years' War as a war of Protestant (and German) liberation. This new interpretation, completely in tune with contemporary aspirations, claimed that Gustavus Adolphus had tried to establish a unified German state on the ruins of the Holy Roman Empire.[2] The preceding chapter described how Catholic historians had placed the "lost opportunity" of 1629, the establishment of a revitalized imperial authority over Germany, at the center of a story of the Habsburg counterrevolution and war of unification. In a narrative that refashioned the Swede Gustavus Adolphus into a unifying symbol and German national hero, Protestant writers legitimated a kleindeutsch, or "little Germany," solution to German unification oriented toward Prussia. Speculating on the details and ramifications of his unfulfilled vision of German unity, this story focused on the tragedy of Gustavus Adolphus's premature death in battle. Like Catholic historians, Protestants lamented a "lost opportunity": the establishment of a unified Protestant German Reich.[3]

The making of Gustavus Adolphus into a German hero in the first half of the nineteenth century was a defining moment in the evolution of Protestant nationalism and a key element in the historiographical legitimation of Prussian leadership and unification. It bound together notions of confessional allegiance, national identity, and emancipation from foreign (i.e., Catholic) rule. The Swedish king, the most popularly recognized symbol of German unity before 1871, was an ideal candidate for historical reinvention as a symbol of German national aspirations. The plot of this new hagiography was simple and extraordinarily compelling in its details: motivated by profound religious convictions, he had landed at Rügen on the Baltic coast in a dark hour to save Germany's oppressed Protestants from Catholic tyranny. He restored the "German liberties" of the Protestant princes that had been trampled under imperial occupation. He was a warrior and a king who had German blood, spoke the German language, and professed the true German faith. Reexamining the history of his campaign in Germany, many historians came to the conclusion that he had in fact attempted to carry out a radical plan for the constitutional reorganization of Germany. Finally, when his crusade seemed about to achieve its aim, the overthrow of the Catholic empire and the establishment of a new Protestant Reich, he was martyred, some said assassinated, on the field of Lützen while leading his soldiers against Wallenstein's imperial army. For Protestants in nineteenth-century Germany, Gustavus Adolphus's appeal as a symbol of the struggle for German independence exceeded even that of Luther.[4] In a relatively short time he was mythologized into an all-embracing symbol for the Protestant idea of the German nation, that is, a unified state created out of the old empire, under Protestant rule, and, with its center of gravity in the northern states, free of both Habsburg authority and influence. Gustavus Adolphus became the savior (*Retter*) in these narratives—a locution that powerfully suggests the idea of the Germans as a "chosen people." Through the collective remembrance of his martyrdom, this idea was closely connected to notions of national, social, and religious renewal and a regeneration of those German-Protestant virtues of independence and defiance that had resisted Roman and French ambitions for three hundred years. Gustavus Adolphus stood as the embodiment of those virtues and the true heir of Luther.[5] It must be emphasized, however, that the nineteenth-century glorification of the Swedish king was thoroughly modern in that it articulated a conception of a unified German nation built around the northern Protestant states of the old empire.

Modern nationalism has been exhaustively explained as a phenomenon that emerged out of democratic revolution, secularization, and economic and institutional modernization. Considerably less attention has been paid to the enduring influence of religiously inflected thinking on nationalist concepts.[6] The study of nineteenth-century German nationalism has, with a few exceptions, avoided in-depth analysis of the influence that the schism between Protestant and Catholic continued to exert on competing models of the nation.[7] Protestant histories of the Thirty Years' War placed Gustavus Adolphus at the center of a new and self-consciously "national" German history. Conceived as part of a unifying master narrative, these histories became the core of a modern nationalist ideology that united past glories with present needs through the use of popular and easily recognized biblical tropes of the covenant between God and the chosen people, sacrifice, and religious war.[8] Analyses of German nationalism have more or less successfully addressed a crucial issue originally raised by Friedrich Meinecke: The main obstacle to successful state building, which required the fashioning of a truly national consciousness, was the difficulty of integrating the German "political nation" with the "cultural nation." Focusing on the centralizing impetus of modernization and secularization in the nation-building process in the nineteenth century tends, however, to push the role of the cultural nation in this process into the background.[9] Our understanding of nationalism can be broadened by examining the intersection of religion and nationalism in the early stages of national identity formation, especially as it emerged out of regional and "transnational," or imperial, loyalties.[10]

The cult of Gustavus Adolphus arose out of a confluence of traditional religious and cultural allegiances to the Protestant-German "nation" with modern nationalist desires for political unity. The national narrative that emerged out of the cult was initially somewhat heterogeneous, referring as much to older notions of allegiance to the "confederal" systems established by the Treaty of Westphalia in 1648 and the Congress of Vienna in 1815 as it did to nineteenth-century political views regarding a centralized nation-state.[11] As Protestant nationalism, defined as a vision of Germany free of Catholic influence and imperial authority, evolved over fifty years, the manipulation of the symbolism of Gustavus Adolphus reflected successive ideas of the nation ranging from the democratic aspirations of the generation of 1813 through the constitutional demands of the liberals of 1848 to the militant and expansionist nationalism of the Second Reich. Through the symbolism of Gustavus Adolphus, historians created and legitimated the Protestant-Prussian variant of German unification by emphasizing the connection between confessional and national identity.

Because they believed it pointed toward the creation of a unified Protestant German Reich, Gustavus Adolphus's campaign in Germany between 1630 and 1632 was recalled by German Protestants as the defining event in modern German history. Protestant nationalism envisioned the German state as "the one true church"—a morally, culturally, and politically regenerated community built on the ruins of the Holy Roman Empire. In short, it was to be a modernized Protestant nation as a "republic of German virtue."[12] These virtues—willingness to sacrifice, devotion to liberty, and defiance of Rome—were seen as the essential qualities of "Germanness" and were linked in German historical consciousness and collective remembrance to the delivery from bondage that the Reformation symbolized. This "Deutero-Isaianic vein" in the Protestant history writing about the Thirty Years' War, to use Salo Baron's phrase, was basically a theology of liberation that identified the Germans as a "chosen people," anointed to rule, if only after trial and tribulation. Gustavus Adolphus became, like Luther, a central figure in this secularized Old Testament narrative adapted to the needs of nineteenth-century nation building.[13]

In his study of the connections between German nationalist thought and Protestantism, Horst Zillessen concludes that secularization and modernization transformed the religious and cultural foundations of German identity into a more compelling political "national spirit" (*Volksgeist*). Zillessen notes that, in fulfilling Ludwig von Gerlach's conviction that the Germans "must give [their] consciousness of God a political form," this spirit was "apolitical in its expression, but not unpolitical."[14] Recent studies have modified this notion of secularization by suggesting that what occurred was not so much a substitution of nationalism for religion as a "nationalization of religion." In this view, German nationalism arose in part as a consequence of putting Christianity in the service of political ends. The confessional conflict in Germany was not subordinated to or subsumed beneath the demands of modernization. Instead, the seventeenth-century war between Catholic and Protestant Germany, between the two attempts to remake the Holy Roman Empire that was the central conflict of the Thirty Years' War, was refought in a nineteenth-century context. To put it differently, the confessional divide was modernized as an ideological conflict over the structure and purpose of state and nation.[15] Helmut Walser Smith expands on Wolfgang Altgeld's idea of "confessional milieus" battling over the "conceived order of the state" to speculate that multiple and competing national ideas emerged out of the intersection of religion and political ideology.[16] This approach is important for an analysis of the symbolic function of Gustavus Adolphus. Protestant histories of the Thirty Years' War created a spiritual and functional narrative link between past and present as a means of establishing the "cultural criteria for national authenticity."[17] These criteria were founded on three basic assumptions and beliefs: Protestantism and the spirit of the Reformation embodied the core aspiration of freedom from Rome that defined the German national community; this community, through centuries of sacrifice and oppression, was bound together by the notion of "chosenness" and thus a covenant with God; and this covenant implied a sacred national "mission" that conceived the nation in moral as well as political terms. To this set of essential convictions should be added the belief that Protestant Germany was the defender of true Christian and European civilization.

Protestant nationalism in nineteenth-century Germany reflected both Friedrich Schlegel's understanding of the historian as a prophet turned toward the past and Novalis's definition of history as the gospel of the future. These histories of Gustavus Adolphus and the Thirty Years' War must be examined not only for what they reveal of an emerging German nationalism that tied authentic identity (or lack thereof) to confession but also, in its mixture of nostalgia and prophecy, as an expression of the romantic idea of the nation. The connection between the German idea of history and romanticism is important because the narratives written in the nineteenth century were, as Peter Herbst defines them, essentially "mythogenic." History, even as it was "professionalized" through application of scientific principles in the nineteenth century, was still valued for its allegorical function in locating useful patterns and symbols. Only through such an understanding of the past could the present be understood and the future divined. The romantic idea of the nation required the invention of a heroic individual whose story embodied the virtues and aspirations of the national community. Gustavus Adolphus's idealized portrait functioned as an integrative symbol around which this narrative could be constructed. In the Protestant historical imagination, he represented the true and original character of the modern German nation born during the long war of liberation that had begun in 1517. His death in battle, at the head of a crusading army, was reconceived as a martyr's sacrifice for a cause whose realization was postponed.[18] Romantic history writing, or a historical nostalgia that sifted the past for portents of the future, invested these narratives with a somewhat incoherent belief in history as "progressive regression," to use Dietrich von Engelhardt's phrase.[19] For both Protestant and Catholic historians, the narratives of the Thirty Years' War, at least as they were written in the first two decades after 1815, were part of a larger romantic historical project of recovering a mythic past for present needs.[20] As was shown in chapter 1, Catholic history writing idealized the old empire as the legitimate foundation of a unified German state, while Protestant historians, in a more visceral appeal to the romantic imagination, speculated on Gustavus Adolphus's tragically unfulfilled vision of a united nation. Both visions, in short, were paradoxical exercises in forward-looking nostalgia.

The Protestant vision of the unfulfilled nation was at the heart of the "Gustavus Adolphus question" that animated debate between German historians for much of the nineteenth century. Protestant and Catholic historians violently clashed over the answer to two fundamental questions: Why did Gustavus Adolphus intervene in the German civil war? And what were his ultimate goals? The answers, at least from the mid-nineteenth century on, were more or less shaped by changing ideas about exactly how a unified German state could be established. As far as the German historical discipline was concerned, adumbrating the various trajectories toward this goal had been the overriding task of political history.[21] This analytical perspective also dominated reviews of the historical literature on Gustavus Adolphus in the twentieth century as it variously embraced Schiller's "liberation thesis," Gustav Droysen's justification of a pragmatic Bismarckian power politics immediately prior to 1871, and Heinrich von Treitschke's later reemphasis on the religious motives behind the formation of a Corpus Evangelicorum as a model for the North German Confederation.[22]

The idealization of Gustavus Adolphus in German history writing began in the optimistically patriotic years between the victory over Napoleon in 1813 and 1814 and the nationalist Hambach Festival of 1832. These two decades witnessed a largely liberal celebration of the unifying idea of the Protestant Reich represented by Gustavus Adolphus as "liberator," which found its clearest expression in the commemorative ceremonies at Breitenfeld in 1831 and Lützen in 1832 and the subsequent foundation of the Gustavus Adolphus Association in 1832. The unifying (and largely ecumenical) German nationalism that had emerged from the victories of 1813 gradually evaporated as undiminished confessional animosities (among other ideas) strained the weak bonds of the German Confederation. The rise of Prussian economic and political power in the Confederation between the expansion of the Customs Union in 1834 and the war with Denmark over Schleswig-Holstein in 1864 worked to cast historical perceptions of Gustavus Adolphus into new forms. The imagining of the Protestant Reich through the idealization of the Swedish king increasingly acquired marked chauvinistic overtones, especially as political and social contestation over Germany's constitutional and economic future stirred again in the years before 1848. Protestant historians' increasingly explicit advocacy of a Prussian-led unification of Germany, filtered through analyses of the Realpolitik of Gustavus Adolphus, provoked a vigorous Catholic response that invoked the memory of Napoleon to offer a counterhistory of the Swedish king as just another bloodthirsty conqueror. By 1871 Protestant historians of the Thirty Years' War had in large part succeeded in recasting Gustavus Adolphus as a warlord in the Hohenzollern mold. Their interpretations of his motivations and goals legitimated a distinctly Prussian idea of a monarchical and authoritarian nation-state. Gustavus Adolphus, initially lionized as a romantic symbol of an unfulfilled Protestant Reich, was transformed into the pragmatic forefather of Prussian (and Bismarckian) power politics.

Two Wars for Unity and Freedom

Observing the nationalist climate in Restoration Germany, Johannes Willms perceptively points out that "the national idealism of these years wanted a 'German Reich'; however, this Reich was not of this world."[23]

To understand the emergence of Gustavus Adolphus as a nationalist symbol in Protestant history writing, we must take another look at the transformation of German national feeling during the period of French hegemony and occupation between 1806 and 1813, or roughly the period between Jena and Auerstädt and the Battle of Nations at Leipzig. The key elements of this developing national consciousness were the idea of a national "rebirth" in the popular crusade against Napoleon and the identification of this renewal with the emancipatory dynamic of the Reformation. In the construction of the Protestant national narrative, the Swedish king became the genius loci that integrated the "real" experience of the War of Liberation against Napoleonic France with its "ideal" and unrealized (yet necessary and inevitable) result: a unified Protestant German Reich. Essentially Gustavus Adolphus was remade into the leader of the first war of German liberation. In the first decades of the Restoration, the celebration of the Swedish king diligently traced the various continuities that linked his unfulfilled vision of a united Germany with the aspirations of 1813. Fusing the national-religious idea in the historical figure of Gustavus Adolphus was a not surprising result of the profoundly eschatological nature of German nationalist feeling as it emerged from the Napoleonic captivity. His beatification promised and legitimated not only a new Germany but also a new European moral and political order centered on a unified Germany. The Protestant narratives of the Thirty Years' War in the nineteenth century confirmed the belief in the German "mission" founded in the Reformation and continued in the war against Napoleon. As justifications of a united Germany, they offered the compelling picture of a Protestant monarch leading a popular "holy war" out of northern Germany against a decadent and foreign Catholic tyranny.[24] The legend of Gustavus Adolphus became an essential part of the historical project to link the destiny of the Hohenzollerns with that of Germany.

Initially reflecting the political thought of the late Enlightenment, this discussion of the German "mission" in Europe emphasized a view of the balance of power in which Germany was the keystone of a stable European system. Much effort went into schemes outlining a constellation of sovereign states that functioned as a "European Republic," which was to be based on rational political hierarchies organized on the basis of the Roman civil code, operated by an enlightened absolutism, and motivated by a belief in progress. In the late eighteenth century, the proposals for reforming the European state system away from its inclination for war assumed that in the establishment of a new moral and political order in Europe, a radically reorganized German empire would be the decisive achievement that would guarantee the success of this grand enterprise.[25]

Nicolaus Vogt (1756–1836), a Mainz historian and an important figure of the late Enlightenment in Germany, placed Gustavus Adolphus at the center of his speculations on the possibilities of creating such a new order in Europe. Vogt believed that the European war unleashed by the French Revolution would become the catalyst for the transformation of the European state system. One thing Vogt brought away from his education at Göttingen was a deep and abiding admiration of the office of the Teutonic kings as the classical basis of German constitutional theory. Though nominally a Catholic, his writings were closer in spirit to the Protestant idealization of the Germanic virtues of liberty and independence than the legitimist arguments of Catholic historians like Lorenz von Westenrieder, Friedrich von Hurter, and Onno Klopp. Vogt was also inspired by what Heinz Gollwitzer calls the "European patriotism" that initially greeted the advancing armies of republican and imperial France. The revolutionary and Napoleonic reforms, Vogt was convinced, pragmatically synthesized republican and monarchical ideas with a vision of a modernized and stable balance of power in Europe, one based on a reorganized and united Germany. In his later works, Vogt placed Gustavus Adolphus within an elite genealogy of visionary European rulers that included Charlemagne, Henry IV, Charles V, Friedrich II, and Napoleon.[26] In Vogt's view Napoleon's bold remaking of the map of Germany and the European state system made him the obvious successor to Gustavus Adolphus. Both waged war to overturn an obsolete empire and reestablish the unitary monarchical idea in Germany.[27]

Even before the French Revolution, Vogt had outlined his idea of this "Germano-centric" new order in Europe in an influential theoretical work, *Ueber die Europäische Republik* (On the European Republic) (1787). He envisioned Germany, organized as a constitutional union of sovereign rulers, again becoming the "unification point" of the European nations and the nexus of a more stable state system. This is the grand design that Vogt believed was also the main goal of Gustavus Adolphus's intervention in the Thirty Years' War.[28] In 1790 Vogt wrote, as a "supplement" to On the European Republic, a drama in verse honoring the Swedish king. It consisted of a fictional dialogue between Gustavus Adolphus and his chief minister and adviser, Oxenstierna, and featured walk-on roles for the approving spirits of Charlemagne and Otto the Great. This experiment in counterfactual speculation was derived from the memoirs of the Swedish royal historian Bogislav Philipp von Chemnitz (1605–78).[29] Vogt had Oxenstierna advising his king to seize the opportunity to carry out the great plan of Henry IV for the political and territorial reorganization of Europe. In Vogt's imagination, Gustavus Adolphus chose an even more ambitious course. He would throw down the Habsburg-ruled Holy Roman Empire and make himself the new "Roman king" of a Germanic nation that excluded Austria.[30] Vogt's initially positive evaluation of the aims of Napoleon was reflected in his interpretation of the Swedish king's revolutionary plans, which also indicated the nationalist inclinations of this enlightened intellectual. He could fantasize about the possibilities opened up by the consolidation of the Confederation of the Rhine even as he lamented the disunity of the German rulers that allowed the extension of French hegemony over central Europe.[31] Although Vogt, like many other German reformers, eventually became disenchanted with Napoleon, he did not abandon his conviction that the Corsican had demonstrated the political and strategic viability of an imperial overlord reigning over a politically and territorially reorganized continent. However, his idea of a new German imperial state was conceived in opposition to a French-led reorganization of Europe, and he saw some value in calls for a modernized Holy Roman Empire.[32] Nevertheless, the dim outlines of a proposal for a type of "North German Confederation" can be discerned in Vogt's analysis of the plans of Gustavus Adolphus.

Vogt also speculated on what would have happened if, as had long been rumored, a marriage alliance between the Vasa and Hohenzollern dynasties had been concluded. He believed that even the discussion of this union revealed much about Gustavus Adolphus's plans to unify the northern German Protestant states, a scheme that, according to Vogt, included combining Holstein and Pomerania into a new electoral territory (although this also implied the territorial mutilation of Brandenburg).[33] The significance of Vogt's speculations is that he was the first to systematically link the history of Napoleon's redrawing of the German map with an interpretation of Gustavus Adolphus that emphasized how a united Germany could anchor a new distribution of power in Europe. Vogt's interpretation of the motives and aims of the Swedish king represented an intermediate definition of Germany's place in the European state system (and a united Germany), that is, it was located somewhere between the eighteenth-century constitutional conceptions of Pütter, Gatterer, and Spittler, with their defense of the utility of the empire in protecting the sovereignty of its smaller members, and the nineteenth-century idea of the nation-state. Combining admiration of Hohenzollern bureaucratic absolutism, the liberally inclined constitutional theories of the Göttingen School, and a faith in the progressive dynamic of Protestantism, Vogt's analysis of the aims of the Swedish king was a crucial stage in the evolution of the Protestant national narrative within the history writing about the Thirty Years' War.[34]

Nationalist Protestant historians, inspired by the lessons of Prussia's defeat in 1806 as well as the victory of 1813, followed Vogt's lead in finding in the story of Gustavus Adolphus historical guideposts to German unification. Their speculations about a "Swedish-Prussian monarchy" allied with a protectorate of the other Protestant German states as the cornerstone of an alliance of Europe's Protestant powers proposed another possible intermediary stage in the progress toward a unified Germany.[35] In 1831, the pro-Prussian historian Friedrich von Raumer (1781–1875) claimed that the German princes had seriously considered just such an alliance as early as 1614.[36] The territorial consolidation achieved by the Confederation of the Rhine, Prussia's defensive modernization after 1806, and the unifying national feeling generated by the Wars of Liberation were crucial influences on the creation of a modern German national consciousness during the early nineteenth century. Vogt's vision of Gustavus Adolphus and Napoleon demolishing an obsolescent Holy Roman Empire to create a new and unified Germany (and a new state order in Europe) expressed the optimism of the German national movement during the years between the celebrations of the victory over Napoleon in 1814 and the dismissal of the "Göttingen Seven" after those intellectuals protested the abrogation of the Hanoverian constitution in 1833. The exhilarating feeling of unity created by the victory over the French would eventually dissipate in uneasiness over the answer to a question that patriots were reluctant to ask: Whose victory was it, "Germany's" or Prussia's? The two different answers to this question illustrated the split between liberal constitutionalism and absolutist conservatism. But for a few years in the 1830s, the emergence of the cult of Gustavus Adolphus offered the heroic myth of the Swedish king as a narrative of unification, reconciliation, and mediation between those two camps. The first period of the popular and historical mythologizing of Gustavus Adolphus between 1831 and 1833 took place when invoking the spirit of 1813 still had the power to unite most Germans in nationalist hopes and enthusiasm.[37] Gustavus Adolphus symbolized the cultural and political expressions of the German "mission" as it was articulated at the time. He represented the possibilities of binding the Protestant "nation" to a unified and modern state. The systematic legitimation of this idea in a Protestant national narrative began with his anointment as a German hero during the bicentennial commemorations in 1831 and 1832 of his victory over Tilly and the Catholic League armies at Breitenfeld and his death in battle against Wallenstein at Lützen.

At one level, these commemorative ceremonies were expressions of the nationalist calls for unity and freedom after 1813. They also reveal the powerful influence of religion and confessional identity on the new German patriotism as it was exhibited at the nationalist festival in Heidelberg in 1814, the Reformation Jubilee and the demonstration of the student associations at the Wartburg in 1817, and the Hambach Festival of 1832.[38] The nineteenth-century enthusiasm for Gustavus Adolphus was a part of this series of secular convocations that celebrated the rebirth of German liberty and national feeling in the struggle against Napoleon.[39] Both phenomena emerged from the powerful flux of nationalist and liberal anticipation and disappointment that marked the early 1830s, beginning with the July Revolution in France and the uprising in Poland in 1830 and culminating in the increasingly repressive and censorious police regimes put in place by the Confederation ministries to squelch popular demands for constitutional reform.[40] The celebration of the heroic myth of Gustavus Adolphus avoided a direct confrontation with the authorities and the penalties that would have been incurred by more explicit demonstrations of nationalist (read revolutionary) activism.[41] The period 1830–35 also witnessed (as elsewhere in Europe) the advent of a nationalist Young Germany movement calling for German unification and its almost simultaneous prohibition, the passing of Goethe (and his elevation into the German pantheon), the creation of a form of economic unity with the establishment of the Customs Union, and the publication of the first edition of Karl von Rotteck and Karl Welcker's Encyclopedia of Political Economy (*Staats-Lexikon*), German liberalism's handbook of constitutional theory. However, the 1830s also witnessed the common national feeling of the Wars of Liberation fragmenting into a muted yet passionate argument about the territorial shape and political structure of a unified German state.

The commemorations of Gustavus Adolphus's rise and fall at Breitenfeld and Lützen derived much of their emotional impact and symbolic power from those sites' proximity to the hallowed ground of the 1813 Battle of Nations near Leipzig. The rituals that marked the events were saturated with a consciousness of recent history that brought together the themes of liberation and unity within the longer continuum of Protestant Germany's struggle for liberty whose milestones were 1517, 1632, and 1813.[42] As public acts of collective remembrance, these commemorations anchored that narrative in popular memory and, in Patrick Hutton's phrase, "immobilized it in time." Hutton's schematic of commemoration helps explain the invention of the cult of Gustavus Adolphus. As an act of political advocacy, these ceremonies also established sacred sites that would serve as places of pilgrimage for the chosen people.[43] Gustavus Adolphus's death on the battlefield or his martyrdom was reconceived as a sacrifice for German liberty and unity. Lützen was the holy ground of that sacrifice, and the chosen community for whom the sacrifice was made was the Protestant German "nation."[44] Protestant Germany's remembrance of the Swedish king, as patriotic communion with the dead of two wars of liberation, invoked the causes of liberty, independence, and unity that bound 1632 and 1813 in the consciousness of Protestant nationalism. Friedrich Ludwig von Rango, a Silesian grenadier officer who had won the Iron Cross in 1813, memorialized Gustavus Adolphus's death in the "holy fight for freedom" in his 1815 poem "Mein deutsches Vaterland," which celebrated the victory over Napoleon and the older enemy of Catholic France by calling on the spirit of the Teutonic warrior-king Hermann, who, when he defeated the imperial legions in the Teutobergerwald in 9 AD, had also "shattered the chains of Rome."[45] Ten years later Rango wrote a hagiography of Gustavus Adolphus dedicated to the Prussian king Friedrich Wilhelm III and the soldiers who had fought at Leipzig in 1813. Rango prefaced this work with another poem that brought Vasa and Hohenzollern, 1632 and 1813, together. This dedication envisioned "God and king leading the victorious soldiers to bring Europe's freedom out of the ruins," as Rango recalled his inspiration:

> Suddenly, I came upon that monument
> Which so modestly from the lap of time
> Lovingly offers itself to the wanderer;
> I stood before Lützen's holy Sweden Stone.[46]

Fifteen years later Otto Jacobi, a popular dramatist well regarded by contemporaries, if not posterity, made Rango's mystical connection between 1632 and 1813 more explicit:

> As in our own day,
> We see here how they fought for justice and freedom.
> The same fields soaked with blood,
> Are the same fields that brought us glory,
> And struck away our chains.[47]

Bounded by Lützen, Breitenfeld, and Leipzig (Wittenberg, the birth-

place of the Reformation, was thirty miles to the north), this tiny tri-
angle of German soil in western Saxony, because of its close connection
to the history of Protestantism and the German Wars of Liberation,
had become the center of gravity of German nationalism in the early
nineteenth century.[48]

The Protestant-nationalist cult dedicated to the memory of the Swedish
king asserted itself in earnest with the commemoration of the two
hundredth anniversary of Gustavus Adolphus's victory over Tilly at
Breitenfeld in 1631. A detailed account left by an anonymous participant in the ceremony that took place on September 7, 1831, stressed
the spiritual connection to the Battle of Nations, when another war
for German liberty had raged. On a sunny and warm afternoon, the
population of Breitenfeld and the neighboring villages were summoned
by church bells to the field owned by the Leipzig merchant Ferdinand
Grüner. Local clergy and officials and the Leipzig choir and university
choral group gathered around a shrouded memorial. Children stood
behind them, holding aloft wreaths and flags bearing the arms of Saxony
and Sweden. With hymns and prayers giving thanks for the deliverance
of the German Protestant Church and the freedom of belief, the monument, a massive cube of Mannsdorfer granite set on a hill surrounded by
eight spruce trees, was unveiled as Pastor Ketzler of Gross-Wiederitzsch
prayed, "The Lord is nigh and never parted from his people." Dr. Gottlob
Grossmann, a church official from Leipzig, stepped to the rostrum to
dedicate the memorial in the name of the Swedish and Saxon people
and in the name of the "renewed and redeemed" German nation. He
reminded his audience that without Gustavus Adolphus's great victory
at Breitenfeld, which had preserved the religious liberty of Germany
and indeed of the world, Germany's Protestants would today be living
under the cruel tyranny and lack of civil freedoms that oppressed the
peoples of Catholic Europe. For Grossmann, the Gustavus Adolphus
memorial not only marked a great turning point in German history but
also served as the border stone in the German lands that marked the
frontier between delusion and belief, freedom and slavery.[49] The ceremony concluded as three flags, each bearing the Swedish and Saxon
arms on one side and a representation of the monument on the other,

were planted around the memorial. Each face of the massive rectangular stone was inscribed with these words:

RELIGIOUS FREEDOM FOR THE WORLD
SAVED AT BREITENFELD
BY GUSTAVUS ADOLPHUS, CHRISTIAN AND HERO
ON 7 SEPTEMBER 1631[50]

This religious and patriotic ceremony still drew significant inspiration from the liberating and unifying spirit of the Wars of Liberation. But the restrained nationalist tone was diffused, if not deliberately muted, within the emancipatory rhetoric of the Protestant pulpit and tempered by the political quietism enforced in Confederation Germany. However, even those moved by more frankly radical sentiments could also be inspired by the symbolism of Breitenfeld:

> The world lay torn by religious war,
> The dark religion of night
> Advanced in musket smoke and cannon's roar
> Shielded by a Kaiser's might,
> Yet already racked by faint death throes
> It saw the new day's triumphant light,
> It saw a sun rise out of the North,
> As never rose from the East.[51]

The author of these lines, Ernst Ortlepp, was a translator of Shakespeare and Byron and one of the more notorious political poets in Saxony (and future teacher of Friedrich Nietzsche). Contemporaries compared his work to that of Georg Herwegh, Georg Büchner, Ferdinand Freiligrath, and Karl Gutzkow. Ortlepp's involvement with radical democratic movements led to his expulsion from Leipzig in 1836, where he had belonged to a circle of young revolutionaries such as Richard Wagner and Heinrich Laube who, inspired by the 1830 revolutions in France and Poland, took up their pens as champions of the republican ideals of "liberty, equality, and fraternity."[52] Ortlepp's reverence for the memory of Gustavus Adolphus indicates that there was more to the symbolism of Breitenfeld than the celebration of nationalist aspirations for a unified Protestant

German nation. His victories over the Catholic armies also represented the possibility of German national resurrection founded on the liberation of the human spirit from medieval and absolutist dogmas. Even an aristocratic member of the Prussian general staff could somewhat awkwardly embrace the spirit of the new age, sententiously proclaiming in 1832 that "in our time we judge war from the standpoint of how it serves the great interests of the people and indeed of all humanity. One such war was the Thirty Years' War."[53]

As J. C. Pfister put it in his 1833 *Geschichte der Teutschen* (History of the Germans), "[Gustavus Adolphus] died on the same fields from which the first call for religious freedom came."[54] The nineteenth-century remaking of the Swedish king into a German national hero, as well as the compelling (for educated Germans) German history that emerged from this mythogenesis, was largely made possible by the connections that could be made between his march through Germany between 1630 and 1632 and the revolutionary struggle for German independence that had begun in 1517. Among other persuasive details, it was established that Gustavus Adolphus had landed in Germany on the hundredth anniversary of the Augsburg Confession to restore the rights and liberties of Protestant Germany that had been earlier confirmed on that very date. His greatest triumph and his martyrdom for Protestant Germany's liberation had occurred within a few miles of each other in close proximity to that other holy ground of German independence and unity, the site of the Battle of Nations. Wittenberg, where Luther had made his first stand against Rome, was not far off. These nationalist propinquities had great popular appeal for Germany's Protestants. After all, their liberator might just as easily have landed on another date, declared his intentions to secure the strategic interests of his kingdom, and been defeated at Breitenfeld at the hands of the renowned Tilly, who had never lost a battle. Or he might have fallen in his momentous confrontation with Wallenstein at the Old Fortress outside of Nuremberg, after having partitioned the Holy Roman Empire amongst his allies. This was the counterhistory, the alternative that would have refuted Protestant Germany's sense of chosenness. The Wars of Liberation against Napoleon made the symbolism of the Swedish king even more striking because they fit together in a seamless narrative that demonstrated the essential bond between the aspirations of German nationalism and the desire for liberty that had driven the Protestant Reformation. The story of Gustavus Adolphus was transformed by historians and acts of popular and collective remembrance into the unifying myth at the center of the Protestant national narrative. As we shall see, the main complaint of Catholic Germany was that this story seemed literally too good to be true.

The apotheosis of the Swedish king culminated with the 1832 commemoration of his martyrdom at Lützen, the campaign to build a suitable memorial on the site, and the subsequent foundation in Leipzig of the Gustavus Adolphus Association (*Gustav Adolf-Verein*) in 1832.[55] Commemorative literature began to appear in the early 1830s that celebrated his march into central Germany during the winter of 1631–32 (after Breitenfeld) as a crusade that came within a hairsbreadth of overthrowing the Holy Roman Empire. According to these accounts, pealing bells and adulatory throngs greeted the "Nordic Lion" as his army passed through Naumburg, Erfurt, Frankfurt am Main, and Nuremberg. One chronicler claimed that in Erfurt the Elector of Saxony had risen before an assembly that included Elector Georg Wilhelm of Brandenburg to give the toast, "The crown of a king belongs to the worthiest—hail Germany's king, Gustavus Adolphus!" whereupon, according to the narrator, the princely guests outdid themselves in demanding that Gustavus Adolphus accept the imperial crown (as Vogt had speculated) or, failing that, the crown of a united Swedish-German kingdom.[56] For many who recounted variations of this history, the symbolism of Gustavus Adolphus's brief residence in Frankfurt am Main, the site of the imperial coronations, was particularly compelling.[57] Reinforcing the appeal of these accounts, a popular German saying had it that whoever occupied Frankfurt for a year would become Kaiser. Long before the anniversary year of 1832, some asserted that Gustavus Adolphus himself was aware of this particular legend and that he felt "so at home in Frankfurt that he sent for his queen." There were Catholic as well as Protestant versions of this story, with a predictable difference in interpretation.[58] Friedrich Förster, a student of Hegel and a prominent Berlin historian noted for his work on the development of the Prussian state and his revisionist interpretation of Wallenstein, took the opportunity of the 1832 anniversary to compose in verse what he called a "historical drama" about the life of Gustavus Adolphus.[59] Förster, who had won the Iron Cross at the battle of Belle Alliance during the final campaign against Napoleon, described the king's progress across central Germany after Breitenfeld as a de facto coronation procession. After the defeat of Tilly at Breitenfeld, Förster imagined the people of Saxony discussing the possibility that Gustav Adolf might take up the imperial crown:

> When he realizes,
> That we guard the imperial regalia,
> The crown jewels, and the crown of Charlemagne,
> In our fortress, the appetite might
> Grow in him to bite the golden apple
> Of the Holy Roman Empire.

Förster then shifted the scene to Nuremberg and the chamber in the city's fortress where the imperial regalia was kept. Gustavus Adolphus and his queen approached the crown of Charlemagne:

> This is the crown that adorned Charlemagne's
> Glorious head; true, it is
> A colossal thing, weighty in gold,
> And weightier still in cares.

At this point Förster imagined Gustavus Adolphus taking up the imperial scepter as his queen Eleanora exclaimed, "Your arm is strong enough to rule!"[60]

The legend of Gustavus Adolphus gripped the German imagination from the moment of his death. For two hundred years, tradition claimed that the Sweden Stone (Schwedenstein), a large granite boulder that stood northeast of the village of Lützen by the side of the road to Leipzig, marked the spot where Gustavus Adolphus fell. Local lore said that it had been set up by the king's valet, Jakob Erikson, with the help of peasants from the nearby village of Meuchen. Other accounts claimed that it originally was a milestone that dated from the mid-sixteenth century.[61] The roughly pyramidal boulder, about four feet tall, was inscribed on one of its faces "G A 1632." The rock marked a sacred spot, and over the years its setting became more formally monumental. In 1803 a ring of eight poplar trees had been planted around the stone. In the annus mirabilis of 1813, a Prussian general had a stone cairn in the shape of a cross built around the Sweden Stone (only two of the poplars had survived the ravages of the Napoleonic wars).[62] This was more or less how the site looked in 1832, with the only new addition being a wooden sign facing the road to Leipzig that read, "Gustav Adolph, King of Sweden, here fell in battle for religious freedom on 6 November 1632."[63] According to J. C. Pfister, the first chronicler of the history of the site, patriotic Germans began calling for a more formal monument in 1798 when Freiherr von Zink in the *Philosophical Monthly* and Herr von Eberstein in Leopold von Göckingk's liberal *Journal of and for Germany* pointed out the inadequacy of the solitary stone as an appropriate monument to the Swedish king.[64] In 1830 Capt. F. C. F. Philippi, a civil servant who lived in Lützen, proposed that a more substantial and fitting memorial be built to honor the savior of German religion and liberty. Lützen's mayor and other notables endorsed this plan, and in August 1830 a public campaign was announced to raise funds for a general improvement of the site and the erection of a more imposing marker.[65] Little was accomplished over the next two years, but the project gained momentum as the bicentennial of Gustavus Adolphus's death approached in the autumn of 1832, when a formal ceremony of remembrance was planned.

The commemorative ceremonies that took place in Lützen in 1832 were documented in a collection of poems, recollections, and historical notes published in 1833 by C. H. F. Hartmann, a Leipzig book dealer who was one of the organizers. In the preface to his description of the commemorative ceremony, Hartmann took the opportunity to express his pessimism about the current state of public support for German unification and complained that, in his opinion, the German people were far from attaining the unity that best served their true national interest. Hartmann was nevertheless hopeful that the public and collective remembrance of the Swedish king's sacrifice would demonstrate that the sparks of national feeling and confessional unity had not been completely extinguished in Germany.[66]

The memorial services began November 5 in the small church in the nearby village of Meuchen and at other sites in the neighborhood where the local folklore recalled that Gustavus Adolphus had stopped, however briefly. For many years the church in Meuchen had been a destination of Protestant pilgrimages because it was there that the king's body had been brought after the battle and prepared for the journey back to Sweden.[67] After a visit to the Sweden Stone, the participants gathered for a service in this church, which had been decorated with blue and yellow banners. Dr. Gottlob Grossmann, who had presided over the ceremonies at Breitenfeld and was on his way to Lützen, was a surprise guest. Philippi's memoir praised Grossmann's speech as "powerful and heartfelt" and expressed the belief that such commemorations showed the possibilities of a wider raising of national consciousness in Germany.[68]

At ten the next morning Lützen's church bells began to ring, and the celebrants assembled in the marketplace, including Grossmann, Haasenritter (a church official from Merseberg), the French ambassador to the Saxon court in Dresden, and several local clergymen. Schoolchildren wearing the Swedish blue and yellow and students from the Weissenfels Seminary escorted the procession to the battlefield. Hymns sung by the Leipzig choir created the appropriate mood of solemnity, while mounted Prussian and Saxon gendarmes and the Lützen militia supplied the requisite martial touches. A crowd of poorer citizens from Lützen and Leipzig brought up the rear. Arriving at the holy ground, the notables took their places on a wooden grandstand. A prayer, accompanied by a rendition of Handel's *Messiah* by the seminarians, opened the ceremony. Haasenritter delivered the formal dedication, asking the assembly to remember the sacrifice of Gustavus Adolphus, who had given his life to reestablish the lawful constitution of Germany and to deliver her princes and people from slavery. As he concluded, young women laid wreaths and garlands at the base of the Sweden Stone, while intoning these words:

This act of remembrance, which serves as only a pale reflection
Of the deep emotion in our breasts and our gratitude to the
   noblest of beings
Who came to our salvation on this battlefield,
Is offered here to you, Gustavus, Hero of the Faith.

They placed a blue silk cushion embossed with the three crowns of Sweden on the stone. Another prayer ended the ceremony, and the participants made their way back to the market square, where they joined the choir in a motet before dispersing to home and tavern.[69]

At the concluding banquet that evening in Lützen's Huntsmen's Lodge, Dr. Grossmann was joined by Provost Holleuser of Merseberg, Chief Administrator von Rochow, and the archdeacon of the Thomaskirche in Leipzig, Dr. Goldhorn. Their conversation turned to the plan for a more formal monument to the Swedish king. They agreed that a new public subscription would be necessary to collect the required funds. In good German fashion, a committee was formed that included Philippi, who started things off with a generous contribution of 400 talers. The local appeal for contributions appeared the next day in the *Saxon Journal*. Somewhat unimaginatively, the committee already had an idea about what the monument should look like: a colossal granite cube whose cost was estimated at three thousand talers.[70] The campaign was launched in Germany at large with the announcement on December 7, 1832, in the *Leipzig Daily* of an English-style "penny subscription." This plan was the brainchild of C. A. Schild, an enterprising Leipzig merchant motivated as much, it would seem, by commercial considerations as by patriotic sentiments. In the announcement Schild deplored Germany's political fragmentation and declared that he still believed that the idea of national unity was manifest in the historical solidarity of Protestant Germany. Schild was convinced that building a memorial to Gustavus Adolphus offered a unique opportunity to at least unite Protestant Germany in remembrance: "Obviously, our poor Fatherland is torn into many small states, but it lives still in a unity of conviction, despite the different colors that fly on the border posts that keep our brothers from freely pursuing their business. . . . Let us erect a memorial that will also be a monument to the German national character."[71] The appeal for contributions quickly took off. The Kingdom of Saxony donated 1,000 talers. Friedrich Wilhelm III, the king who had led Prussia in the war against Napoleon and the Hohenzollern Crown Prince, also took a keen interest in the plans for a monument to Gustavus Adolphus. Diligently pursuing every possibility, Hartmann sent copies of a poem from his anthology to the grand duke in Weimar. It included these lines: "A foreigner passed by who had heard of the battle, / Asking, 'Where is the monument that honors your hero?' / A plowman came toward him and pointed beneath the poplar trees, calling out: 'There is the Sweden Stone!'"[72]

To Hartmann's chagrin, the packet was returned without a contribution. But the secretary of the Saxon legation in Weimar, von Carlowitz, forwarded a copy to Friedrich Wilhelm for consideration in his office as guardian of the Protestant Church in Germany. The parsimonious Prussian king donated 100 talers.[73] But to be fair, Friedrich Wilhelm's interest did not end with this donation. He made up for his stinginess by asking his court architect, Karl Friedrich Schinkel, to come up with some ideas for the memorial. Schinkel originally proposed a neoclassical open stone and masonry temple to be erected over the Sweden Stone. A less expensive variation of this idea, a ten-meter high cast-iron baldachin, or canopy, was finally executed.[74] On November 6, 1837, Bishop Johann Draseke dedicated this new monument in the presence of 25,000 festive spectators. With dramatic flair, he called upon the memorial to uncover itself and speak to the gathered pilgrims and to posterity of Gustavus Adolphus's heroic deeds.[75] This ceremony, which had the blessing of the Prussian monarchy, was more conspicuously martial than the one in 1832. The Thuringian Hussar Regiment and uniformed university students escorted the procession to the monument. Four cannons were fired to announce the unveiling. More significantly, in an unmistakable gesture toward another war of liberation, the new caretaker of the grounds was a disabled veteran of the Battle of Nations.[76]

The campaign to raise funds for the monument also inspired the creation of a foundation dedicated to the spiritual and financial support of oppressed and impoverished German Protestants under Catholic rule in Europe. In contemporary usage these unfortunates were called the "Protestant diaspora." This foundation, which held its first annual meeting on November 6, 1833, was christened the Gustavus Adolphus Association.[77] The idea of the Protestant diaspora, and its manifestation in the historiographical and public remembrance of Gustavus Adolphus, was at the heart of Protestant nationalism in the first half of the nineteenth century.[78] German identity, independence, and unity were sought in a once and future realm of the historical imagination. Grossmann's use of the "border marker" metaphor in his Breitenfeld speech, and the act of monumental remembrance itself, are revealing. The commemorations were rituals of demarcation, the setting of boundary stones, which located and defined the "sacred" soil of the community.[79] This community was, in Gerhard Kaiser's phrase, the "unrealized nation" of the Protestant German Reich. These commemorative rites also drew on the mystical vocabulary of Pietism described by George Mosse that spoke of the Fatherland as a "magic" and "hidden" space.[80] The belief in the existence of this diaspora poignantly expressed German anxieties about the elusive nature of their Fatherland, a grasp at a national solidarity created by victimization, and the hope of a return to the Promised Land, in this case a strong and unified Germany. Ultimately, the Protestant remembrance of Gustavus Adolphus was a defiant act of self-definition that challenged the idea that weakness and fragmentation were Germany's destiny. But the idea of the Protestant diaspora also revealed the essential pathos and frustration at the core of the German sense of "chosenness." The monuments at Breitenfeld and Lützen made the unrealized idea of Germany somewhat more tangible and expressed hope that the unfinished nation could indeed be made reality. The symbolism of Gustavus Adolphus incorporated the solemn German faith in monarchy, liberty, independence, and unity, and his story anchored those ideas in a hopeful historical narrative.[81]

A New Protestant Reich

The optimism of 1813 and the early 1830s regarding Germany's progress toward political modernization, if not actual unification, gradually dissipated in the reaction to the nationalist Hambach festival in 1832 and the abortive republican revolt in Frankfurt in 1833, both of which resulted in the extension of repressive laws that had been in place since the Karlsbad Decrees of 1819. The new nationalist patriotism of the early Restoration period embodied in the commemorations at Lützen gradually faded as the 1830s ran their course.[82] The construction of a viable idea of the German nation and the ideological objectives and style of German history writing shifted direction toward pragmatic analysis and political realism. A new school of political historians, represented by Leopold von Ranke and Johann Gustav Droysen, shaped the historiographical "Prussian" project by emphasizing the political utility of historical investigation. The issue of German unification was addressed within a more realistic analytical approach that implicitly and explicitly endorsed Prussian leadership. This turn toward what Heinz Gollwitzer has termed "pragmatic political nationalism" abandoned the democratic and participatory constitutional thinking of liberalism since 1813 for a more realistic embrace of state power.[83] This transformation was confirmed in the reaction to the revolution of 1848 as many advocates of a unified Germany jettisoned parliamentary resolutions in favor of Prussian arms as the best means of achieving their goal. But realism about what was necessary to achieve German unification did not mean that Protestant nationalism lost its appeal. If anything, it became more accentuated and exclusionary, as demonstrated by the enthusiasm that greeted the Schiller centenary in 1859.[84]

This shift toward pragmatism was reflected in the historical writing dealing with Gustavus Adolphus. His roles as rescuer, liberator, and defender of Protestant liberties were moved into the background while his strategic and geopolitical aims received more attention. During the 1840s a more clear-eyed examination of his policies searched for a road map to a unified north German state. The idealistic patriotism of 1813 had made its last appearances at the commemoration at Lützen and the dedication of the new memorial in 1837. In the decade that followed, Protestant history writing about the Thirty Years' War turned from the nationalist symbolism of Gustavus Adolphus toward a closer examination of his intentions and policies. Historians, both Catholic and Protestant, wanted to know what he would have done as ruler of Germany. In concentrating on how Gustavus Adolphus might have established a radically different kind of state on the ruins of the Holy Roman Empire, this phase of interpretation was influenced by new currents within a maturing German nationalism. A more pragmatic and less religiously polarized (though not by much) history writing would gradually supercede the interpretations that had been driven by Protestant nationalism in the first three decades of the nineteenth century. The history of Gustavus Adolphus was reshaped into a narrative that illustrated and legitimated the modern project of state building.

With this new approach, historians speculated about the plans of the Swedish king to rechannel the energies of the war of Protestant liberation into a war to dissolve the Holy Roman Empire and create a new state on its foundations. In this interpretation, Gustavus Adolphus was celebrated less as a savior of religious and political liberties than as a revolutionary warlord and statesman of far-reaching vision. The unified Protestant Reich that historians claimed he had tried to establish was presented as the historical template for the unified nation that became the goal of the more pragmatic German nationalism that emerged after 1848. This interpretation of Gustavus Adolphus examined a new model of German unity in the form of a confederation of Protestant states in the north and southwest closely allied with Sweden. According to this school of thought, as "a new, fresh Protestant ruler," the Swedish king would have ruled this confederation from Mainz or Frankfurt, while possibly retaining some formal connection to a reorganized Holy Roman Empire. These histories argued that the old fear of the Habsburg "universal monarchy" was anachronistic and that the real threat to German liberty was the political infirmity created by the multiple sovereignties contained within the German Confederation, a state of affairs that only benefited France, Germany's ancient and eternal enemy.[85]

In order to make this argument, these historians set up their thesis with this question: How would Gustavus Adolphus have changed the political structure of Germany? In a slightly different form, this question had originally been posed (and answered negatively) by Friedrich Schiller, who asked, "Was Gustavus Adolphus's death a misfortune for Germany?"[86] In 1839 Karl Adolf Menzel challenged the historical judgment of the German national poet in a deliberately provocative analysis of the career of Gustavus Adolphus that set the terms of the debate for the next thirty years. But Menzel's rabid anti-Prussian animus ultimately meant that his conclusions would be unacceptable to most Protestant historians. His interpretation of Gustavus Adolphus's career was in part inspired by his admiration of Britain's constitutional monarchy. He rejected Schiller's appraisal of the king as a tyrannical "absolutist" who had little regard for traditional German liberties. According to Menzel, Gustavus Adolphus saw clearly the fatal infirmities of the Holy Roman Empire and the revolutionary possibilities offered by the German civil war, as revealed by the king's much-debated decision to strike into central and southern Germany after his victory over the Catholic League army at Breitenfeld, instead of striking directly at Vienna and Prague. In Menzel's view, by occupying the imperial cities in the heart of Germany, especially Frankfurt and Nuremberg, Gustavus Adolphus shrewdly seized places "which bound the political imagination of the nation" and were essential elements in the plan "to declare himself the supreme ruler of the German Reich."[87] After all, Menzel pointedly observed, the bond between the Habsburg emperor and the Germans had never been that strong, and "other nations have successfully chosen foreign kings."[88] Menzel was confident that, had Gustavus Adolphus lived to complete his plan, Germany would have been well served in the centuries to come because "Prussia would never have risen to its position in Germany as a significant European power had Gustavus Adolphus consolidated the Swedish protectorate over Protestant Germany and produced a male heir." Warming to his anti-Prussian theme, Menzel declared himself in agreement with those "imperially inclined historians" (i.e., Catholics) who maintained that Gustavus Adolphus would have restricted princely autonomy much more than Ferdinand had ever contemplated. However, Menzel was quick to point out that the Swedish king would have taken such action only in the course of a revolutionary transformation of the imperial constitution.[89]

Friedrich Wilhelm Barthold (1799–1858) in his controversial *Geschichte des großen deutschen Krieges* (History of the Great German War) (1842–43) elaborated on Menzel's revisionist interpretation of the Protestant liberator. A student of Friedrich von Raumer, Barthold had been profoundly influenced by his liberal professor's support for constitutional rule and political modernization in Germany.[90] Barthold's study focused on the second half of the Thirty Years' War, a period he believed historians had neglected. His main purpose, he asserted, was to remind all Germans that France, their old enemy, had cynically used Gustavus Adolphus as the instrument to divide and conquer Germany. In other words, he came not to praise the "great Gustavus Adolphus, who, fortunately, died early," but to bury him. Barthold mocked those "credulous souls, inflamed by the traditions of their school years," who had so piously gathered around the Sweden Stone at Lützen. Nor was he greatly concerned about what would turn out to be the considerable wrath of other Protestant historians, those "unconscious servants of the French" who, in their attacks on the empire, displayed the gratitude of ignorance as they thanked Germany's true enemy for what they believed to be their "rescue from absolutism." Barthold concluded the foreword to his work by stating that as a "Protestant and a Prussian" he categorically refused to ally himself with the nationalist zealots and their misguided "dogma" proclaiming the "the nation's glory, unity, and prosperity." He only hoped that another Ferdinand II would arise to turn back the French.[91] Barthold's hatred of France (a vital component of modern German nationalism) transformed the hero of Protestant nationalism, and the champion of German independence and unity, into the uncomprehending dupe of Louis XIII's chief minister, Richelieu, who plotted the conquest and partition of Germany. Barthold's conclusions, combined with, as his critics put it, his "anachronistic" and "Ghibelline" (i.e., pro-imperial) characterization of Ferdinand II as the true representative of German national interests, were roundly condemned by his fellow Protestant historians.[92] Barthold's transgression was that he had exposed the manipulation of the historical symbolism of Gustavus Adolphus by what he characterized as an unsophisticated and naive Protestant history writing that played right into the hands of Germany's autocratic princes (represented by Prussia) and external enemies (represented by France). Barthold concluded that the "national feeling" that the schoolmasters found embodied in Gustavus Adolphus was in reality the ambition of a conqueror that sought to overturn the Holy Roman Empire so it could be partitioned among its "greedy neighbors."[93] Presumably recalling to his readers Prussia's confrontation with Adolphe Thiers's bellicose foreign policy in the war scare of 1840, in the preface to the second volume of his history Barthold warned: "The events reported here are old, but the lessons that they teach, are they superfluous for our day?"[94]

Menzel and Barthold provoked outrage because they were Protestant historians who used the history of Gustavus Adolphus to challenge the legitimacy of the Prussian ascendancy in nineteenth-century Germany. For his part, Menzel was convinced that an unreflective enthusiasm for Prussian leadership of German unification only prolonged the hold of autocratic absolutism on the German states, while Barthold accused Gustavus Adolphus of complicity in French plans to divide and destroy Germany. What was particularly galling about Barthold, as far as his critics were concerned, was that his condemnation of the Swedish king's motives deliberately appealed to German memories of the French occupation. One of these critics, Gottlieb Mohnike, believed that speculation about Gustavus Adolphus's intentions was basically "unhistorical" and that it besmirched the glory of a great man; however, if the "what if" game had to be played, Mohnike deferred to Barthold Georg Niebuhr's judgment: "Had Gustavus Adolphus won the imperial crown, he would have been considered a German by the entire nation."[95]

When he pointed out the historical precedent for a foreigner being offered a native throne, Menzel put his finger on one of the key themes that was developing in the Protestant history writing about Gustavus Adolphus in the decade before 1848. While the king's narrative was offered as the historical justification of Prussian power politics, it could also serve to legitimate the liberal idea of a popular limited monarchy based on a substantial alteration of the imperial constitution. For most nineteenth-century Germans, conservative or liberal, the moral power and authority of monarchy was the cornerstone of any desirable political system.[96] German liberalism's belief in the flexibility of the German constitutional tradition tended to mute reservations about the admittedly awkward fact that Protestant Germany's hero was a Swedish king. It was commonly argued that Sweden had ruled territories that were part of the Holy Roman Empire and that the royal house of Vasa was linked through marriage to several German princely dynasties. The folk-lore concerning the popular acclaim that greeted his march into central Germany after Breitenfeld was interpreted in order to give credence to the king's supposed aspirations to become the ruler of Germany. Johann Sporschil asked in 1843, "Is it any wonder that the idea took root in his thinking to bind the German Reich to his person and to become its Kaiser and ruler?" This popularity, Sporschil claimed (using the anti-French litmus test), struck fear into the heart of Richelieu, who began to plot against him.[97] And even if he had attempted to usurp the imperial throne, a German biographer asked, "A free and independent Germany, would that have been such a misfortune?"[98] Ultimately, it was the traditional appeal of his status as liberator and defender of the faith that made it very difficult to discredit Gustavus Adolphus as a symbol of German nationalism and champion of a strong and unified Germany.

This symbolism was most powerful and evocative when it was used by historians, such as Wilhelm Bötticher and Ludwig Flathe, to articulate an idea of the German "mission" in Europe that was rooted in its essentially Protestant identity. Couched in the vocabulary of religious war, the messianic overtones of this idea dominated every aspect of the nineteenth-century histories of the Thirty Years' War. Bötticher invoked the "evangelical and godly unity" of the German Volk, for whom Gustavus Adolphus had sacrificed his life, in the long war against the "Roman and Slavic peoples." Bötticher believed that the Swedish king had attempted to establish a "monarchical, Protestant Germany" as a bulwark against the tyranny and decadence of the Catholic empire. After his death, the Great Elector and the House of Hohenzollern took up this holy mission. Bötticher asked his readers to consider whether a German union with Sweden would have been more shameful than the dependency of Hanover on England, or Holstein on Denmark, or Luxembourg on the Netherlands. Bötticher was convinced that a great Protestant power in Europe had to arise: "History will show the fulfillment of the prophetic designs and visions of the great Swedish king."[99] Ludwig Flathe, a professor of history at the University of Leipzig, shared this conviction. He pointed out that Protestantism was "the essential religion of the German tribe" and that the German princes' alliance with Gustavus Adolphus was actually a reunion with a "diaspora" tribe of a single great "family of peoples" (*Völker-Familie*). For Flathe, it logically followed from this interpretation that "Roman Catholics," in their allegiance to Rome and their loyalty to the old empire, were fundamentally "un-German" (he asserted that a people's "Germanness" was directly proportional to their distance from the Catholic world).[100] Flathe concluded that Gustavus Adolphus had demonstrated that the only way to turn back the French threat was to transform Germany into a unified Protestant Reich founded on the German-national patriotism. Anyone who challenged this view by reviving the old demons of religious division were, in Flathe's eyes, guilty of high treason in letting the foreigner again gain a foothold in Germany.[101]

Who, exactly, were these betrayers of the German Volk in this long war of Protestant and German liberation which had begun in 1517? Catholic historians had long contested the dominance of the Protestant version of German history. As was shown in chapter 1, Michael Ignaz Schmidt and Lorenz von Westenrieder used a legitimist defense of the empire to create an inclusive "national-Catholic history" that distanced itself from the juridical tradition of "imperial history" associated with the work of Johann Jakob Moser.[102] Their conservative rejection of the "emancipation" offered by the French Revolution and the Napoleonic reforms also allowed them to reject the myth of Gustavus Adolphus as a "liberator" and portray him instead as a conqueror who aimed at nothing less than the revolutionary overthrow of the Holy Roman Empire. In short, as Westenrieder tartly observed, "liberating" the Protestant princes should not be seen as the same thing as liberating the German people. He further pointed out that this so-called liberation often took the form of abrogating existing constitutional liberties that would have led in effect to a Swedish despotism over Germany and the states of the north becoming vassals to the Swedish crown.[103] In obvious frustration, Westenrieder complained that, despite all the evidence proving that Gustavus Adolphus's goal was to create a new kingdom of conquered vassal states, Germans were still inundated with "a whole flood of panegyrics, poems, songs, tales, and eulogies in which everything that the king once thought, said, did, or could and should have thought, said, or done, has been repeated a thousand times."[104]

The anti-Prussian historians Menzel and Barthold, with their groß-deutsch sympathies, had exposed a wider audience to the long-standing argument of Catholic historians that blamed selfish Protestant princes for Germany's political weakness. They were also afraid that the historical symbolism of Gustavus Adolphus was being manipulated to justify Prussian hegemony, which was not quite the same project as creating an independent and unified Reich. The most influential synthesis of these arguments was written by the son of a Protestant clergyman who had converted to Catholicism in 1853, the Swabian historian and archivist August Friedrich Gfrörer (1803–61). His *Gustav Adolph, König von Schweden und seine Zeit* (Gustavus Adolphus, the King of Sweden, and His Time) went through four editions and sold a more than respectable 15,000 copies between 1835 and 1864. Until Gustav Droysen's biography appeared in 1869, Gfrörer's work was the most widely read and cited book (and the most controversial from the Protestant point of view) on the Swedish king in Germany. Like his friend Heinrich Leo, Gfrörer was a staunch liberal (though not radical) opponent of Prussia who believed that historical scholarship had a "present usefulness" in forcefully addressing contemporary social and political issues.[105]

Although the 1835 and 1837 editions sold well, the considerably revised third edition that appeared in 1852 did even better.[106] Although he acknowledged his debt to the studies of Westenrieder and Aretin, Gfrörer offered new arguments based on Karl Müller's work on the origins of the Bohemian revolt.[107] Gfrörer defended the policies of Ferdinand and Wallenstein by contrasting Wallenstein's revolutionary efforts to unify the Reich on a "national" basis with the Swedish king's naked lust for glory, territory, and power. Gfrörer accused Gustavus Adolphus of plotting to invade Germany as early as 1629, despite the opposition of the Swedish estates. In Gfrörer's view he was motivated, like Alexander the Great, "by the lust for military glory and the spirit of conquest which drove the Swedes across the Baltic, disguised by the glitter of religious ideas."[108] Like Menzel, Gfrörer believed that Gustavus Adolphus's decision to strike into central Germany after Breitenfeld, instead of marching on Vienna, revealed his true ambitions: "As soon as Protestants and Catholics united against him and public opinion turned, the mask of the 'champion of the faith' fell away and out stretched the hated hand of the conqueror."[109] Gfrörer went on, "No one called him to Germany; he broke into our Reich like a thief. . . . Our nation was not so stupid, as some theologians would have it, to put a royal adventurer at its head." Gfrörer had no doubt that, had Gustavus Adolphus lived, he would have established what amounted to a military dictatorship in Germany. To refute the Protestant narrative of the liberator, Gfrörer appealed to German memories of the French occupation under Napoleon. His conclusion echoed Barthold's as it discerned an unreconstructed Prussian absolutism lurking within the current historical misinterpretation of Gustavus Adolphus. Gfrörer hoped that "if the German nation is again to be united, it will only be as a constitutional monarchy on the English model."[110]

The conservative legitimist historians that followed Gfrörer, particularly Onno Klopp and Friedrich von Hurter, rejected the liberal core of Gfrörer's attack on the cult of Gustavus Adolphus. Klopp, who edited the fourth revised edition of Gfrörer's work, criticized him for his neglect of important political issues.[111] In challenging the patriotic monopoly of the Prussian narrative, Klopp and Hurter were concerned with disputing the historical justification for establishing a unified Protestant Reich. Of course, in the late 1850s and early 1860s, the Protestant threat, in the shape of Bismarck's maneuverings to undermine the German Confederation to Prussia's advantage, was much more menacing and clearly defined for them than it had been for Gfrörer. The central thesis of Klopp and Hurter was that Gustavus Adolphus had intended to destroy the rejuvenated empire of Ferdinand (and, indeed, that he had been primarily motivated to intervene in the German civil war by the threat this new empire posed) and set up on the ruins a state with a completely new constitutional structure based solely on the Protestant estates and ruled by a Protestant emperor.[112] Like their Protestant counterparts, they had looked into the past, but the future they saw there was much less appealing.[113]

The *Historisch-politische Blätter für das katholische Deutschland* (*HpB*) was in the vanguard of the Catholic response to the increasingly nationalist and exclusionary tone of the Protestant historiography celebrating Gustavus Adolphus in the 1840s.[114] Like Menzel, Barthold, and Gfrörer, this journal's editors were concerned about the tendency of what they called "poetic history" to "glorify injustice" in celebrating a foreign dictator's bloody intervention in a German civil war: "Here lay an example to warn us that we should never again let a foreigner, whether he comes from the north like Gustavus Adolphus or the west like Louis XIV, intervene in our internal affairs, because the price we pay in honor, in wealth, and in blood is too dear, much too dear."[115] The journal's editors lamented that only the Germans, among all the peoples of Europe, were so apparently deficient in an instinct for self-preservation and a sense of their own worth that they built monuments on those fields where brother had murdered brother in civil war. Could a nation sink lower, the *HpB* asked, than when it celebrated the memory of a foreign conqueror, in league with France, who had laid waste to the land and murdered its inhabitants?[116] It was in the pages of the *HpB* during the 1840s that Albert Heising, a Catholic amateur historian with a highly developed gift for polemic, gained almost as much notoriety as Gfrörer because of his attack on the "romantic idea" of Gustavus Adolphus as the liberator of Protestant Germany. Heising paired his reappraisal of the Swedish king with an arguably even more controversial defense of Tilly (which Klopp would continue) that ignited a long-running historians' debate over who was responsible for the destruction of Magdeburg.[117] These articles were later combined in a book, which appeared in a second and revised edition in 1854.[118] Heising ridiculed the picture of a crusading Gustavus Adolphus as a romantic anachronism that had been created by the Protestant "theologians." That this view was widely accepted was, in Heising's view, clear and convincing "evidence that the Germans valued their confession more than their nation." Like Frederick the Great and Napoleon, Gustavus Adolphus had been an "interloper and conqueror" more interested in ruling Germany than in liberating it.[119] Heising maintained that if the Swedish king were judged on the basis of his actions alone and without the distorting prejudices that had accumulated over two centuries, only one conclusion could be reached: Gustavus Adolphus had intended to create a quasi-independent Protestant confederation indistinguishable in its basic structure and purpose from Napoleon's Confederation of the Rhine. Pursuing this comparison further, Heising pointed out that Gustavus Adolphus, like Napoleon, had robbed the Germans of their wealth, exiled their princes, and expropriated their lands. Yet, he concluded incredulously, for two hundred years German historians had "treasonously" celebrated this robber.[120] Attempting to sever the mystical bond between two wars of liberation, 1632 and 1813, Heising wielded the sharpest blade in the Catholic arsenal: equating Gustavus Adolphus's "liberation" with the tyranny of Napoleon. It was a compelling argument; certainly no Catholic historian had previously made it so coherently and eloquently. Johannes Janssen proclaimed the latest Catholic revisionist interpretation of Gustavus Adolphus as a triumph for the "German-national" historical viewpoint over the partisan and Protestant "rational-scientific" perspective.[121] All of the assumptions of the Protestant interpretation were turned on their heads in Janssen's indictment: "The German princes thus assumed the same relationship to Sweden as they did in our century to Napoleon. . . . Any German that celebrates Gustavus Adolphus must also celebrate Napoleon, and the celebration of Napoleon is as base a sin against the German national feeling and the honor of the nation as any that pay homage to the Swedish conqueror."[122]

Heising's provocative reinterpretation of the career of Gustavus Adolphus, as a critique of German weakness and exploitation by France, ironically began to be echoed by Protestant historians in the same period. In the 1850s, the history of Gustavus Adolphus was increasingly used to legitimate the idea of a unified German nation constructed around a Prussian-dominated northern Germany. Gustavus Adolphus evolved as the symbol of the possibilities (and necessity) of a Prussian-directed Realpolitik. Several factors pushed Protestant historians to revise their picture of the Swedish king as the savior of German Protestantism to conform to a more modern nationalist vision of German hegemony in central Europe. The settlement of 1815, and Austria's role as principal guarantor of the system created by the Congress of Vienna, was seen, by 1848 at the latest, to be approaching obsolescence. The reappearance of the old French danger in the shape of Louis Napoleon's Second

Empire and the shift of Austrian interests away from Germany and toward the Balkans was the new reality brought home by Austria's loss of control of northern Italy during the peninsula's wars of unification between 1859 and 1861, in which Prussia had declined to intervene. The Schiller Centenary of 1859 and the death of Friedrich Wilhelm IV in 1861 seemed to many to mark the beginning of an optimistic "New Era" in which the nationalist dreams of 1848 (and 1813) might be peacefully fulfilled. Further, the Prussian "constitutional crisis" of the mid-1860s was eventually resolved by Bismarck as he bartered liberal acquiescence to the monarchical principle (the core of Protestant constitutional thinking) in return for German unification.[123] Finally, the Schleswig-Holstein conflict in 1864 and Prussia's defeat of Austria at Königgratz in 1866 decisively put to rest any doubts about the unifying power of Prussian arms. Moving with the currents of these events, Protestant and Prussian-oriented history writing recast the symbolism of Gustavus Adolphus in order to express a more modern and militant idea of national identity and German sovereignty within the Protestant national narrative.[124]

"Sovereignty is a conception of power (*Machtbegriff*) and when it is wielded as a conception of law (*Rechtsbegriff*) it will always produce untenable results."[125] August Ludwig von Rochau, writing in 1853, thus justified the utility and necessity of Realpolitik, a term he introduced into the German political lexicon. Rochau crystallized the change in thinking about the best means to create a united German state. The new interpretations of Gustavus Adolphus reflected this change. It is interesting to note, however, the extent to which Protestant nationalism endured as a component of a Realpolitik solution to the German question. The nationalist fervor of the fifteen years before unification, as it became ever more confident in its assertion of what was "German," retained its fundamental attachment to Protestant identity. In the history writing of this period, Gustavus Adolphus was still a useful nationalist symbol of the war for German independence that had begun with the Reformation in 1517 and was continued in the two wars of liberation in 1632 and 1813 and the wars of unification of Bismarck.[126] We can see the continued relevance of this symbolism in the popular folklorist Friedrich

Karl Wild's assertion that "if the Protestant religion wanted to secure equal rights and freedoms with the Catholics, then it was necessary to establish a powerful, German-Protestant Reich with a Protestant ruler. Because Gustavus Adolphus seriously tried to secure the liberty of his fellow Protestants and the power of the Protestant Church in Germany, he had to contemplate the foundation of such a Reich."[127]

The utility of the symbolism of Gustavus Adolphus in constructing the Protestant national narrative was closely connected to basic nineteenth-century assumptions about the nature of the German "mission" in Europe and the German "national consciousness." Chief among them was the idea that Germany was naturally bound to England and Scandinavia as part of a northern Protestant alliance engaged in a prolonged war to the death against the encircling Catholic threats of French expansionism, "southern European despotism" (perpetuated by Jesuit machinations), and Slavic barbarism (barely concealed beneath the veneer of Eastern Orthodox Christianity). The rabid nationalist Wolfgang Menzel (1798–1873) had long made this connection clear (as had Flathe), which sheds light on the perceived affinity between the "Lion of the Midnight Sun" and German nationalism. Amid the upheavals of 1848 Menzel promoted the resurrection of the Swedish-German alliance of the Thirty Years' War to forestall the predatory designs of France and Russia. Menzel believed that Germany and Sweden were "natural allies" and, moreover, that this alliance was the only means through which Sweden could "regain its former glories" and Germany could rule again wherever German was spoken. Obviously, an essential precondition for the success of this plan was a strong and united Germany.[128] Menzel deplored the support of reactionary Prussian policy for Russian repression of nationalist uprisings in Poland and the Baltic states in 1830 and 1848, stating unequivocally in 1854: "From a confessional standpoint we do not expect the *Kreuzzeitung* to display Catholic sympathies; however, the same standpoint admits of no other policy than the support of an alliance with England and Scandinavia, the cradle nations (*Stammländer*) of Protestantism. In embracing the 'Russian party,' the *Kreuzzeitung* is supporting a power which aims at nothing less than the suppression of the Protestant Church to the advantage of the Orthodox confession."[129]

In the discourse of German nationalism in the nineteenth century, the apotheosis of Gustavus Adolphus at midcentury marked the boundary between two ages. As demonstrated in the ceremonies at Breitenfeld and Lützen, evolving nationalist thinking contrasted the Reformation's promise of German emancipation with the papal and Jesuit tyranny of Rome and, eventually, Vienna. As a symbol, Gustavus Adolphus would always represent confessional solidarity and Protestant cultural values, but his story became increasingly useful as a means of demonstrating the possibilities of German power in Europe. By reimagining his march into Germany as a key episode in the longer war of German liberation and independence begun in 1517, Protestant history writing confronted and refuted the psychologically crippling history of German weakness and laid the foundation for a triumphant and unifying national narrative. In 1856 one commentator pointed out that when Catholics dismissed his symbolism for Germany's Protestants as inherently divisive, they missed a crucial point: In honoring him, in erecting a "boundary stone between two epochs," Germans were finally acknowledging the revitalization of an old power and a "unitary national consciousness" that proclaimed the arrival of a "German party." In short, his unrealized aims were finding fulfillment in the ambitions of Prussia's Hohenzollerns.[130]

Protestant history writing in the 1860s increasingly viewed Gustavus Adolphus's ambitions through the lens of Realpolitik as the potential of Prussian power was brought into sharp focus. The first two editions of the *Staats-Lexikon* (1835 and 1845) had no entries under "Gustav II. Adolf." The third edition (1862) had a six-page analysis of the king's career by the Saxon liberal politician and historian Karl Biedermann. Biedermann, who supported the Prussian-led unification of Germany as the surest means of establishing a modern state, interpreted Gustavus Adolphus's intervention in Germany as being driven largely by strategic and trade considerations.[131] That Biedermann concentrated on these issues is not surprising, given the heated nationalist arguments at the time about the importance of Germany reasserting control of

Schleswig-Holstein and the Baltic littoral and the obsolescence of the German Confederation. As the Confederation tottered on the brink of dissolution with Bismarck threatening unilateral Prussian withdrawal in 1866, the prophetic example of Gustavus Adolphus was proclaimed: "What could have been better for the German Reich than the replacement of the Roman Catholic imperium, with all of its southern European deadweight, with a German kingdom that embraced the new age and the noblest aspirations of humanity? If the dissolution of the German Reich was to be avoided, the only possible solution was the ascension of a German federative monarchy to the place of the Roman Catholic imperium's caesaristic majesty. . . . [In this regard] if Gustav Adolf had a failing, it was that he was more German than the German princes."[132] Heinrich Thiersch asserted in 1869 that Gustavus Adolphus was the "German Cromwell" who had been thwarted in his plans to "establish a new order in the Reich under a Protestant ruler."[133]

Gustav Droysen (1838–1908), the son of Johann Gustav Droysen, the founder of the "Prussian School" in German history writing, produced what became the standard modern interpretation of Gustavus Adolphus in his two-volume biography, which appeared in 1869–70. It was his only major work. Deviating little from his father's ideas about the essence and aims of state power, Droysen portrayed Gustavus Adolphus as a consummate practitioner of Realpolitik who understood that the state was a political instrument that pursued rationally defined strategic goals to further the national interest.[134] As Droysen saw it, the goal of the Swedish king's intervention in the German civil war had been the establishment of a unitary state that would stabilize and maintain the balance of power in Europe. Droysen's Protestant nationalism is revealed in the introduction to his biography, which appropriates the images and language of religious war: "As the Apostle Paul was pictured, with the open Bible in his left hand and a naked sword in the right, so stands the Northerner in the gaze of an admiring posterity."[135] Droysen believed that the Swedish king's war of liberation had fallen short of its goal because he had allowed himself to be diverted by the "unholy light" of the imperial crown. His mistaken attempt to remake the empire prevented him from creating a strong, united Protestant

Germany that would stand against and eclipse the old imperial power and thus establish a new balance of power in Germany that secured both Sweden's and Europe's peace and security.[136] Droysen's interpretation of Gustavus Adolphus as Realpolitiker could easily be mistaken for a description of the policies of Bismarck.[137] In the annus mirabilis of 1870, a poem appeared dedicated to the "savior with the German heart":

> Once before Germany had had unity
> And law and enlightenment ruled the land.
> And she would have been spared much disgrace
> If Germans had offered an emperor's crown
> To the great Gustavus Adolphus,
> If that had happened, Friedrich Wilhelm,
> Elected as son-in-law,
> Anointed at his tomb,
> Would have passed on as his legacy
> Germany's imperial scepter.[138]

With the proclamation of a unified Germany in the form of the Second Reich in the Hall of Mirrors in Versailles in January 1871, Protestant history writing lost much of the impetus to interpret the career of Gustavus Adolphus as the legitimation of Prussia's unification of Germany. The Swedish king's place at the center of a narrative of a possible, yet unrealized, nation had diminished somewhat with the establishment of the real thing. While Catholic history writing was, if anything, even more frustrated and bitter that the history of a "murderous conqueror" and "carrier of the Protestant imperial idea" was being used to justify the Hohenzollern imperial monarchy, the winning side was rethinking its glorification of a foreign king.[139] Droysen still basically adhered to his original views, but, using newly discovered diplomatic records, he revised the conventional wisdom regarding Elector Georg Wilhelm's pusillanimous dealings with the Swedish king. By 1878, Droysen portrays Gustavus Adolphus as ruthlessly dismissive of the Prussian ruler's attempts to remain neutral, recover Pomerania, and serve as a mediator between Sweden and the empire.[140] The Saxon historian Julius Otto

Opel (1829–95), in a pamphlet published by the Protestant Union in 1894, similarly took the opportunity to portray Johann Georg of Saxony as a peace-loving statesman who cooperated with Gustavus Adolphus only in pursuit of the latter's main goal of establishing a new religious peace. At most, Opel speculated, the Swedish king might have been duly elected to the throne by the Protestant princes to preserve and protect the existing constitutional order.[141] It is clear that, as Bismarckian Germany consolidated itself and as its citizens gained confidence in the solidity of its historical narrative (which assumed the inevitable rise of Prussia under the Hohenzollerns), German nationalism was able to wean itself somewhat from its reliance on the symbolism of a foreign hero by embracing a story with the rise of the Hohenzollerns at its center. Gustavus Adolphus lost none of his nationalist allure in being returned to the religious and cultural pantheon, but his symbolism as a political model and polemical rallying point was no longer so urgently required. In Heinrich von Treitschke's judgment, "Brandenburg obtained at Westphalia the complete victory of Gustavus Adolphus's ideas—Brandenburg effected an honorable religious peace which guaranteed the unconditional equality of the confessions. . . . The model of his uncle taught Friedrich Wilhelm to master the power of his estates and to maintain a strong military and monarchical authority."[142]

The war of Protestant liberation that Gustavus Adolphus had waged was gradually absorbed into the more compelling and triumphant history of the wars of unification led by Bismarck, which were themselves turned into the culmination of the longer war for German independence that had begun with Luther's challenge to Rome in 1517, failed in 1632 with Gustavus Adolphus's death at Lützen, and fallen short after the victory over Napoleon with the restoration of the absolutist status quo by the Congress of Vienna in 1815. Ultimately, it was this bigger story, dramatically lit by the sunrise of 1871, which accounted for nineteenth-century Germany's equally intense fascination with the Swedish king's nemesis, Wallenstein. As German collective remembrance reshaped the legends of these two leaders into forms reflecting nineteenth-century concerns, this process revealed a basic belief at the heart of the German national consciousness: the need of a strong military and monarchical authority to ensure the survival of the nation. The story of Wallenstein, the subject of the next chapter, exposed the intractable nature of this aspect of the "German problem" in central Europe, its fundamental connection to expansionist war, and ultimately the limitations of Protestant nationalism as the foundation of modern German national identity.

3. Wallenstein's Revolution

The Wallenstein Question

"In life," wrote Friedrich Schiller in 1793, "it was his misfortune to make himself the enemy of the victorious party; in death it was his misfortune to be survived by his enemies, who then wrote his history."[1] Schiller's observation captures the essence of the "Wallenstein question," which occupied such a central place in the German historical consciousness of the Thirty Years' War. Schiller's take on Albrecht von Wallenstein, Duke of Friedland, exerted an enormous influence on the nineteenth-century historical reinterpretation of the war and the popular memory of the conflict. It became a cornerstone of Germany's political folklore and the debate over the war's legacy. Schiller's mounting stature as the poet of the German national revival was undoubtedly a major reason for the steadily rising flood of Wallenstein literature in the nineteenth century.[2] But compared with the history writing about the origins of the Thirty Years' War and Gustavus Adolphus's intervention, the burgeoning histories dealing with Wallenstein appealed much less consistently (and emotionally) to the animosity between Catholic and Protestant. In successive stages of interpretation driven increasingly by maturing "German-national" preoccupations, Wallenstein came to symbolize the power of Realpolitik to make the German nation-state. As a story of a revolutionary leader emerging from civil war (his similarity to Cromwell was often pointed out), the career of Wallenstein provided a pragmatic contrast to the religious martyrdom of Gustavus Adolphus even as both men were indissolubly linked in German memory as the great antagonists of the Thirty Years' War. The nineteenth-century histories of Wallenstein also represented an important stage in the evolution of German history writing because they were driven by the recognition that the discipline of history had an intellectual and cultural obligation, necessitated by the rise of nation-state, to construct a unifying and coherent narrative that contextualized and justified political action.[3] We shall see how his legacy as a visionary and revolutionary German statesman who had tried to unify Germany was firmly established long before Prussian history writing mythologized the achievements of the Hohenzollerns and Bismarck after 1871.

In the nineteenth century, as in the seventeenth, this story resisted a conclusive interpretation. An enigma that captured the German historical and nationalist imagination, Wallenstein's true motivations and goals, summed up in the vexing "guilt question" (*Schuldfrage*) first posed by Schiller, still remain something of a mystery for modern historians, despite the extensive documentary discoveries of their nineteenth-century predecessors. Golo Mann, whose massive biography of Wallenstein is supported by seventeen pages of bibliography and eighty pages of notes, confronted this enigma by falling back on the belletristic tradition of the early nineteenth century. Mann's stated ambition was to write the "definitive" Wallenstein biography, but he had to acknowledge the ultimate mystery of the Duke of Friedland: "This is a true story, not an invented one . . . the issue is an individuality at once very strong and exuberant, eventually erupting into forfeiture of his own identity. I have given no summing up, no final verdict. Reality knows none."[4] Mann's admission gestured toward the abyss that lay between twentieth-century doubts and nineteenth-century certainties. Leopold von Ranke abhorred the ambiguities he felt to be inherent in biography, yet he wrote a "history" of Wallenstein that was, significantly, his only work that focused on an individual.[5] The Wallenstein question, as it came to be called, attracted historians seeking a forum in which to debate various approaches to the practical realization of German unification.[6] But a definitive answer to the question remained elusive, and a number of interpretations competed for primacy. As a result, the problem of Wallenstein served as a formative case study in the writing of political history in Germany, and the proposed solutions to this problem came to have considerable impact on the historical articulation of a vision of the modern German state.

Schiller's portrayal of Wallenstein, largely a product of the turmoil of the French Revolution, set the terms of the historical argument over his nineteenth-century legacy because it influenced German historians, in their response to the modernizing energies unleashed by their old enemy, to write a "national" German history that could make its own claim to a transformative revolutionary tradition and buttress aspirations to German unity.[7] In putting Wallenstein at the center of this tradition, historians emphasized the part he played in the turbulent era of the seventeenth century, a momentous period of war and revolution that had seen both France and Britain make significant strides, as secular and centralized nation-states, toward "great power" status. Wallenstein's plans were interpreted and presented as a model for a similar German transformation in the nineteenth century. A crucial context of this reinterpretation is that the historical consciousness of nineteenth-century Europe was profoundly shaped by the threat (and promise) of revolution.[8] The political folklore that had long surrounded Wallenstein was refashioned to explain his career in a narrative that emphasized his abortive attempt to radically transform the Holy Roman Empire into a great central European power that could defy France, Scandinavia, and the Turkish threat. In the nineteenth century, the legend of the terrible Duke of Friedland, who ravaged Germany as he "stamped armies out of the ground," was historicized and given contemporary significance and meaning.

This historiographical transformation bore some similarity to the post-1815 reconsideration of Napoleon, to whom he was often compared.[9] However, the revisionist phenomenon to which Wallenstein's reinterpretation bears the most striking resemblance, in terms of both the historical parallels drawn and the ideological and political causes advanced, can be found in the nineteenth-century British historians' debate over Oliver Cromwell. British historians were pushed by contemporary concerns to reevaluate the legacy of this central figure of the English civil war, which, in terms of chronology and some of the ideas in conflict, was roughly contemporaneous with the Thirty Years' War. As in the popular German recollection of Wallenstein, the very ambiguity woven into the memory of Cromwell (modernizing revolutionary or regicide? visionary statesman or dictator?) permitted historical reassessments that co-opted his achievements in the service of various and even opposed ideologies: conservatism, republicanism, imperialism.[10] The important role of this "polemical process," as Olive Anderson calls it, in shaping the political use of history in nineteenth-century Britain is equally apparent in the parallel German phenomenon that centered around Wallenstein. In both cases historians and collective remembrance created political myths that incorporated and fixed the elusive anxieties of modern statehood. They confronted similar concerns: national identity, "great power status," imperial expansion, revolution and radicalism, reform versus reaction, constitutional modernization, and fears of civil war and dictatorship.[11] As it turned out, the two bodies of reinterpretation reached dramatically different conclusions. British historians analyzed their nation's emergence from civil war to legitimate the victory of parliamentarianism at a crucial moment in the creation of the British nation. Similarly, though in a different ideological direction, the lesson that German historians drew from the Thirty Years' War and Wallenstein's central role in the conflict was that German unification could only be achieved on the basis of a bold repudiation of old ways of thinking.

In writing a modern and unifying German national history, German historians attempted to anchor that narrative in key "revolutionary" and transformative historical moments in the recent past, moments that heralded the break with obsolete political institutions. One particularly decisive moment in the German civil war, the "Wallenstein catastrophe" (as many German historians came to call his assassination in 1634), was retold, in much the same way that the story of Gustavus Adolphus had been retold, as yet another turning point in the history of the war of German liberation when a new and unified state was snatched from the Germans' grasp. The year 1634, illuminated by the bright hope of possibility, was inserted into the history of the unrealized nation along the equally dazzling prospects that had seemed manifest in 1517, 1629, 1632, 1813, 1848, and 1871 (and eventually 1918). The debate over the Wallenstein question, the argument over the significance of the ambitions left unrealized with the warlord's assassination in 1634, began with Schiller's iconic portrait of Wallenstein in his history of the Thirty Years' War, which Christoph Wieland observed "had so many readers that, of all the books in the German language, it alone allowed people to make an intellectual claim to some level of culture."[12] Schiller's elevation to the status of German "national poet" came during the repressive era of the post-1815 Restoration, when centenary celebrations of his birth in 1859 praised his work as the purest embodiment of the German spirit and national rebirth.[13] The gradual revision of the Wallenstein tradition created by Schiller represented the latter stages of the transition from romantic (that is, more spiritual than political) concepts of the heroic historical protagonist toward the modern "world-historical" figure as revolutionary warlord. That component of Schiller's historical vision that influenced German history writing most critically was his inclination to view history as a series of confrontations between the rearguard of obsolete ideas and the forces of human liberation. This vision compelled German historians because it could be interpreted to justify revolutionary action to challenge the status quo.[14] Schiller's theory of history also bequeathed to his successors a fascination with revolution and war by raising the profile of the "political man" who fought to establish a new order on the ruins of the old. Still, Schiller's Wallenstein retained much of the romantic and tragic appeal, omnipresent in the political folklore of Germany (from Heinrich IV to Götz von Berlichingen), of a Shakespearean protagonist in battle with what John Farrell calls a "schismatic political universe."[15] But nineteenth-century interpretations of Wallenstein also took from the Schiller tradition a more self-consciously modern iconography of the revolutionary in order to justify the imperatives of modern state building. This vision was naturally rejected by Catholic history writing, which tenaciously insisted, as part of their defense of a confederal vision of Germany, on his betrayal of the Holy Roman Empire, the only historically legitimate German polity. Protestant historians, on the other hand, seeking to legitimate the establishment of a centralized and powerful German state, revised the traditional picture of the hated defender of the reactionary imperial Counter-Reformation to portray Wallenstein as a visionary statesman on a par with Cromwell, Napoleon, and Bismarck.

Nineteenth-century critics reevaluated Schiller's dramatic Wallenstein trilogy (1798–99) as canonical texts that grappled with the apprehensions about the role that a politically ambiguous German philosophical idealism had played in the development of the German national consciousness.[16] In the late 1830s, Hermann Hinrichs praised Schiller as the "authentic voice of Germany," calling the Wallenstein trilogy a "great patriotic poem" that, in its "bitter melancholy," was representative of the German "national feeling." That melancholy, in this reading, had its origins in Wallenstein's failure to remake the Holy Roman Empire into a powerful German state. Hinrichs interpreted Schiller's drama as an allegory describing the modern breakup of "old Europe" set against the background of the French Revolution. Wallenstein, the Napoleonic warlord at the center of this drama, represented the modernizing force striking at the foundations of the obsolete medieval polity of the Holy Roman Empire.[17] The highest of patriotic motives were ascribed to Schiller's Wallenstein, the revolutionary who, like Gustavus Adolphus, had tragically fallen while attempting to establish a united Germany dominant within a new European order. In 1858 Karl Tomaschek rationalized Schiller's probable alteration of historical reality (in modern parlance, his counterfactual history) as an attempt to show the "possible Wallenstein" as he was confronted with three "world-historical choices": the seizure of territorial power for himself, the reestablishment of imperial power on a just peace, or the founding of a "genuinely new Reich."[18] This view was summed up by Johann Hess during the 1859 Schiller centennial: "Therefore we can speak of it not only as literature but as a national work like no other, which, as a profound study of the human character, is a masterful expression of an especially compelling catastrophe in the history of our Fatherland."[19]

For many German historians in the nineteenth century, finding an answer to the Wallenstein question was urgent because it promised to recover the lost historical map that pointed toward German unification. Portraying Wallenstein as a revolutionary German statesman brought down by a "Jesuit" conspiracy allowed Protestant historians to emphasize the resistance of reactionary Catholic obscurantism to the establishment of a powerful German state in central Europe. This interpretation of Wallenstein blamed the Habsburgs for perpetuating German weakness. It argued that Wallenstein had tried to turn the course of the German civil war away from the cause of religion and toward political revolution. Because the Habsburgs had assassinated him, they were accused of condemning Germany to two hundred years of political impotence, disunion, and foreign interference. This conclusion believed implicitly that Germany had, before that tragic moment, the opportunity under Wallenstein's leadership to become a European power of consequence in the second half of the seventeenth century, just like France, Britain, and Sweden. Not surprisingly, Catholic historians would challenge this hypothesis, which in their view was nothing but another justification for Prussian ambitions in the nineteenth century. They insisted on the justice of the conventional indictment of Wallenstein as an ambitious *condottiere* who turned against his monarch for personal gain. This interpretation, familiar from the legitimist arguments of the Westenrieder-Hurter-Klopp school regarding the war's origins, emphasized the legitimacy of the Holy Roman Empire as the basis of the German state. It portrayed Wallenstein as just another, albeit more dramatic, example of the territorial prince who, in cynical alliance with Germany's enemies, pursued his own interests at the expense of the integrity of the Reich.

When Karl Gustav Helbig christened this debate "the trial of Wallenstein" in 1853, he was commenting on how sharply polarized the ideological commitments to two different conceptions of a unified Germany had become in an era of intense historical awareness. This debate also shows a quality unique to German history writing: the belief in what I call the appellate function of historical inquiry. The trial of Wallenstein demonstrated how political history in Germany evolved as a compendium of briefs argued before the bar of collective memory. We can also see in this perspective a keenly felt lack, on the part of educated and forward-looking Germans, of a genuinely unifying "national" narrative on a par with Britain and France. This perceived handicap drove the development of a political history in which solutions to the "German problem" were extracted from the past and offered as blueprints for successful state building. Successive reinventions of Wallenstein within a unifying national narrative separated obsolete historical models from modern ones at successive revolutionary moments in the evolution toward German nationhood in the nineteenth century: the dissolution of the Holy Roman Empire by Napoleon, the national uprising of 1813, the revolution of 1848, the ascendancy of Prussia within the German Confederation, and Bismarck's wars of unification between 1866 and 1871. This nineteenth-century continuum of struggle became, in turn, part of the longer narrative of the German war of liberation, whose revolutionary moments were 1517, 1629, 1632, and 1813. The various nineteenth-century interpretations of Wallenstein's revolution reflected a succession of fixations on possible solutions to the German problem: a Napoleonic redrawing of the Central European map to consolidate the remains of the Holy Roman Empire, a modernizing bureaucratic absolutism that began nation building with economic unification and constitutional reforms, and the use of the hammer of Prussian power politics to break the old order and forge the new. Wallenstein's trial by the historians demonstrated how political history in nineteenth-century Germany, unlike in Britain and France, became the most important forum for presenting systemized theories of state building.[20]

Like so many other aspects of modern political and national consciousness in Germany, the recasting of the historical Wallenstein in a revolutionary mold owed much to the impact of the French Revolution on loyalties to traditional institutional, political, and territorial structures. Wallenstein was embraced by the new nationalist faith in post-revolutionary and post-Napoleonic Germany as the German model for the revolutionary "new political man." Although they attributed its original concept to the sagacity of Ferdinand II, Catholic historians were able to praise Wallenstein's "Baltic project" of 1629–30, discussed in chapter 1, as the model for a modernized unitary imperial state. But the period of Wallenstein's career that spanned the time between his dismissal from command at Regensburg in 1630 and his assassination in Eger in 1634 was subjected to a dramatic shift in interpretation. The events of this period, revisited in the nineteenth-century "trial of Wallenstein," began with a reevaluation of the political folklore of Wallenstein as rebel and traitor. This was the story told most famously by Schiller, who set the fall of the Duke of Friedland against the lurid backdrop of the French Revolution. Following Schiller's lead, Protestant historians were no longer so inclined to accept without reservation the traditional image of the ambitious, bloodthirsty, and superstitious *condottiere*. When German historians argued about accepting Wallenstein into the pantheon of German heroes, they were mainly arguing about the answer to one question: "What was Wallenstein rebelling against?" From the Protestant side the short answer was ultramontane Catholic reaction, their updated indictment of the opponent of German greatness known as the Habsburg-led Counter-Reformation. Wallenstein was idealized by historians who advocated the creation of a powerful and modernized German state that excluded Austrian leadership and participation. The generalissimo's motivations and plans during the fateful years between 1630 and 1634 were presented as a possible road map to that goal.[21] In a series of reinterpretations, Wallenstein's assassination in his Eger castle by agents of the emperor in 1634 became yet another setback in Germany's halting progress toward unification. These new narratives told the tale of Wallenstein's scheme to remake Germany into a European power before he was brought down by a conspiracy of Jesuits, Bavarians, and Spanish agents who surrounded Kaiser Ferdinand II in the Hofburg.

The French Revolution created a new understanding of political action, state building, and historical agency for historians in the nineteenth century, which manifested itself in the decades-long debate about the aims of Wallenstein's revolution. Further, the audacity of the French revolutionaries changed perspectives of the role of the "great man" in history, which Schiller had explored in his fascination with the revolutionary hero.[22] But this emphasis on the heroic figure in history came to be modified by the course of the Revolution and Schiller's own changing perspective of that event. The Schillerian portrait of the enlightened warrior (embodied in his portrait of William of Orange leading the Dutch war of independence against Spanish rule) fighting the dark forces of reaction, the latter represented by the Church and the institutional remnants of medieval feudalism, subtly changed after the execution of Louis XVI in 1792 and during the subsequent period of Jacobin and Girondin dictatorship preceding the advent of Napoleon in 1799. Wallenstein was remade into the champion of a new rationalized and secularized political and strategic order in central Europe and a proto-nationalist symbol of Germany's reawakening in the first decade of the nineteenth century.[23] Wallenstein no longer solely symbolized the "revolutionary" in the romantic sense of a man standing against the currents of his time; he now represented a modernizing and emancipatory force.

German historians did not start to systematically reexamine the Wallenstein question until some time after Schiller's death. For much of the eighteenth century, histories of Wallenstein, like works on Gustavus Adolphus, had been based on contemporaneous and propagandistic accounts from French, Swedish, and Protestant sources, as well as Austrian "official" accounts written after the fact to justify his assassination. Reaching more conclusive and relevant (given nineteenth-century preoccupations) judgments about his "treason" was seriously hampered because his remaining personal papers, a surprisingly substantial collection scattered in different archives in Holland, Stockholm, Mecklenburg, Berlin, Dresden, Prague, and Vienna, had not been thoroughly examined.[24] One reason the popular tradition of his betrayal of the Kaiser persisted was because of the inaccessibility, or ignorance, of documentation that could challenge that view (or the presumption that most of it had been destroyed during the war). Schiller's *History of the Thirty Years' War* (1791–93) relied primarily on the seventeenth-century literature, as well as the important late-eighteenth-century syntheses by Johann Herchenhahn, Michael Schmidt, and Johann Galletti. As a consequence, Schiller's Wallenstein began life as the hybrid offspring of the conventional legitimist portrait of the plotter against the imperial throne and the more sympathetic "German-national" Protestant view, as expressed by one of Wallenstein's eighteenth-century biographers, of a revolutionary in the mold of Cromwell: "today a patriot, tomorrow a traitor," whose ultimate aim had been "to invade the imperial dynastic lands and not to lay down arms until the Kaiser himself had been vanquished and, wherever possible, the entire House of Habsburg had been extirpated at its roots."[25]

Given the accelerating violence of the revolutionary energies released in France in the early 1790s, and all that it portended for the survival of the traditional political and social order in Europe, it is not surprising that conservative Catholic historians tenaciously defended the dogma of Wallenstein's treasonous rebellion against Kaiser Ferdinand II. Johann Christian Herchenhahn (1754–95) wrote the first and, for some time, the authoritative modern biography of Wallenstein. Herchenhahn was a German-educated jurist and diplomat in Austrian service and an advocate for the enlightened absolutism behind Joseph II's modernizing reforms.[26] His portrait of Wallenstein typified the Catholic legitimist argument. Herchenhahn's indictment of the Duke of Friedland asserted that the evidence left no doubt that Wallenstein, in his "treasonous" negotiations with the enemy, "regarded with scorn the imperial constitution [*Reichsverfassung*] of the German Fatherland," and aimed at nothing less than the complete overthrow of the Kaiser.[27] Michael Schmidt, the imperial historian in Würzburg, shared Herchenhahn's view. In his widely cited history of Germany that appeared in 1791, Schmidt compared Wallenstein's plans for the partition of the Holy Roman Empire with those of that eternal Catholic bête noire, the French monarch Henry IV (1589–1610).[28] Nevertheless, Schmidt conceded that, even as he had "plotted" against the Kaiser, Wallenstein recognized the Swedish threat to German sovereignty and fought to drive the Swedes out of Germany. Despite this acknowledgment of Wallenstein's strategic acumen, Schmidt pointed out that the fundamental question historians had to decide was who wanted peace more, Wallenstein or Ferdinand II? Who was ultimately the bringer of peace, and who was the destroyer?[29] He had identified the central issue driving the debate over the "true" historical picture of Wallenstein and how it fit into a national German history. If he was motivated by personal ambition alone, Catholic historians could accuse him of wrecking the possibility of an imperial unitary state, the reformed Holy Roman Empire, that had briefly beckoned as a consequence of the imperial victories of 1629 and 1630. On the other hand, if Wallenstein had opposed the Kaiser out of the conviction that Habsburg war aims militated against a general peace, Protestant historians could plausibly argue that he had sought a settlement as the first step toward a unified Germany. Protestant revision of the political folklore of Wallenstein's treason transformed him from the bloodthirsty enforcer of the Counter-Reformation into a revolutionary statesman who had tried to end centuries of German weakness and vulnerability. The Protestant Johann Georg Galletti (1750–1828), court historian at Gotha and an important source for Schiller, wrote in 1791 that, though Wallenstein was a "tyrant," his opposition to Ferdinand II had aimed at ending Spanish and Habsburg control of central Europe and countering French expansion. A peace settlement, according to Galletti, was an absolutely essential precondition for the success of this plan. Ferdinand's reactionary ambition to re-Catholicize Germany gave Wallenstein no choice but to ally himself with France and the Protestant powers.[30]

Schiller's version of this Protestant nationalist interpretation had a major influence on all subsequent histories of Wallenstein, for or against. Schiller speculated that the raising of a Spanish army in northern Italy in 1634, intended for direct intervention in the Rhineland and Dutch provinces, freed Ferdinand II from his dependence on Wallenstein, whose position had already been eroded by the Bavarian and Spanish factions in the court: "But as no one since the days of Samuel the Prophet has come to a good end who opposed the Church, so even Wallenstein must be numbered among its victims. Through the intrigues of monks he lost his marshal's baton at Regensburg and at the Eger his life. But, perhaps more important than either, he lost his honor and reputation before posterity."[31] Unlikely as it seems, Wallenstein, the terrible sword of the Counter-Reformation in the traditional history of the Thirty Years' War, was being reinvented not only as a revolutionary martyr brought down by the forces of reaction and tyranny but also as a Protestant hero and a German patriot battling foreign invaders.

This interpretation of Wallenstein gained currency and at the same time acquired a distinctly nationalist veneer as the armies of revolutionary France crossed the Rhine in 1792 to bring down the old order. By 1796, the iconic image of the soldier-statesman in European history, embodied in such rulers as Cromwell, William of Orange, Charles XII, Peter the Great, and Frederick the Great, was modernized with the advent of Napoleon, a radically different type of ruler: the revolutionary figure rising out of obscurity. A radical alteration of the territorial and political order of Europe seemed possible. The Napoleonic reorganization of Europe between 1796 and 1807, in first superimposing a republican topography on the map of the old regime, and then creating a completely new constellation of subordinate states within the orbit of the French empire, was initially an inspiration to those Germans who dreamed of a radical political solution that ended their nation's fragmentation and weakness. For some German thinkers of the late Enlightenment, such as Andreas Georg Friedrich Rebmann and Nicolaus Vogt, the history of Wallenstein was particularly compelling because it revealed the possibilities of revolutionary action in changing the map of Europe. From a late-nineteenth-century perspective, the plans of Wallenstein could be interpreted to legitimate a program of political and territorial modernization that had four main goals: the unification and constitutional modernization of Germany; the integration of this new state within a reshaped European balance of power; the institutionalization of modern ideas of social and political organization; and the establishment of a "Third Germany" as a counterweight against Prussian and Austrian power.

Rebmann (1768–1824) was a Jena-educated jurist turned "German Jacobin" who devoted most of his career to writing slashing political satire in support of the revolutionary idea of constitutional monarchy.[32] In 1794, shortly before his exile from Germany because of his support for revolutionaries in Mainz, he wrote what he called a "half history–half novel" that interpreted the fall of Wallenstein as the "miscarried revolution of the seventeenth century."[33] Depicted against the background of seventeenth-century revolution, Rebmann's Wallenstein was a political visionary who had seized the opportunity offered by civil war to try and establish a "new Germany." According to Rebmann, this new state, modern, secular ("free from the power of the priests"), and built on a constitutional foundation that balanced confessional rights, religious freedom, and the rights of the estates, could have made Germany "an example to the world's princes."[34] Rebmann fleshed out his counterfactual history by inventing bold revolutionary speeches for his hero: "You know my designs, you are privy to my boldest thoughts, so you know that I want to seize this power only so that I might free humanity from its chains and, in these lands that I hope to win, to offer those blessings hitherto unknown among men." History, Rebmann was convinced, offered only one such chance to a "great man."[35] Though "Rebmanniana" became a contemporary epithet describing German republicanism, Rebmann had clearly tried to reconcile his interpretation of Wallenstein the revolutionary with a vision of a modern German constitutional state. As an advocate for Benjamin Constant's political theories (they had become acquainted in Paris), Rebmann insisted that the ideals of the revolution be preserved even as he condemned the excesses of the Terror, asking, in one of his most famous tracts, "Just because an arsonist had to light a candle, does one then forbid all light?"[36] Rebmann was sure that the moment for revolutionary change had come at last for Germany, arguing: "Our system of rule and our legal and religious institutions have for some time stood in conspicuous discontinuity with our political situation, our Enlightenment convictions, and our public opinion."[37] Rebmann's "bourgeois republicanism," or "republicanism from below," strove to justify revolution by depicting Wallenstein as the martyred "good prince": the personification of the rational, yet seemingly frustrated, ambitions of the political Enlightenment.[38]

Revolutionary France, as it extended its control over western Europe, soon revealed itself in many German eyes as essentially the ancient French enemy masquerading as the liberator of mankind. As a consequence, Wallenstein became a much more compelling figure for German historians as a statesman whose historical reputation could be rehabilitated as a symbol of resistance to the French. In a memoir of the Seven Years' War published in 1797, a Prussian general recalled standing as a young officer before Wallenstein's tomb in Gitschin and wondering, "Was he a traitor, or was he innocent?" Repudiating the "always falsified" history of Wallenstein perpetuated by historians like Herchenhahn, this old soldier's "true life story" would show that the Duke of Friedland had the authority to make peace in order to isolate the empire's foreign invaders from their German allies. It was clear, the general concluded, that an anti-German conspiracy of "clerics, Spaniards, and Bavarians" had wrecked this plan by willfully misrepresenting Wallenstein's plans to the

Kaiser.[39] Schiller's dramatic trilogy about Wallenstein was also a product of the revolutionary war of the late eighteenth century. His earlier history of the Thirty Years' War had portrayed Wallenstein as a romantic hero brought down by the forces of reaction and tyranny. Appearing in 1798 and 1799, the three plays had a more distinctly nationalist tone, recasting Wallenstein as a German hero torn between loyalty to the empire (as a German, not a Catholic, institution) and the patriotic conviction that the empire needed to be drastically remade if German power was to be resurrected. Like the old Prussian general, Schiller still gave credence to the traditional canard accusing the Jesuits of subverting Wallenstein's plans, but his updated picture of the Duke of Friedland was much more political in its exposition than the one presented in his earlier history of the Thirty Years' War. Two late-eighteenth-century concerns appear to have guided Schiller's plotting of Wallenstein's rise and fall. The first was contained in Wallenstein's presentiment that the dissolution of the Holy Roman Empire was imminent: "Here there is no Kaiser. The Prince is Kaiser!" Schiller's Wallenstein sensed the coming of "a new order of things" that would topple the ancient power:

> And what brought you to this moment? In all
> Honesty, do you know yourself? You dare to
> Overthrow the power that, secure on its throne,
> Occupied for centuries, and resting on time-honored custom,
> Is bound to the pious and trusting
> People with a thousand tenacious roots.[40]

Schiller's protagonist also articulated the idea that if Germany could free itself from the religious division and foreign influence that left her vulnerable to invasion, the "greater good" of Europe would be served as well:

> It shall not be said of me that I parceled out
> Germany and betrayed it to the foreigner
> So that I might pocket my share.
> Rather, the Empire will honor me as its protector
> And, having proven myself as a prince of the Empire,

It will be my right to sit among the Empire's princes.
No foreign power shall grasp the Empire
In its tentacles, least of all
These Goths, these beggars
Who gaze so enviously and greedily
At the riches of our German nation. . . .

Because it is *I* who seeks peace, so must I fall.
Austria does not care if this unending war
Exhausts the armies and desolates the world,
Austria only wants to expand forever, winning more land.

Only I care for the whole. Understand, I have
A heart and I am moved to pity by the miseries of the German people. . . .

Take heed! For fifteen years the torch of war has burned
And still there is no end. Swedes against Germans! Papists against
Lutherans! No one will yield to the other! Every hand is turned against
the other! Everything is disputed! And nowhere is there a judge! Where
will it end? Who
Can unravel the knot which grows endlessly
More tangled? It must be cut.
I feel that I am the man destiny has chosen.
With your help I hope to carry it out.[41]

Schiller's Wallenstein was realized not only as a German tragic hero but
also as a political visionary. Wallenstein the revolutionary, the architect
of a new Germany within a new Europe, would become an even more
compelling figure for Germans with the rise of Napoleon. Early-nineteenth-century Protestant historians emphasized Wallenstein's "German-
national" credentials as an opponent of both France and the Catholic
Habsburgs. Catholic historians did not entirely reject this view. Karl
Woltmann (1770–1817), a liberal Catholic historian sympathetic to
many of the modernizing aims of the French revolutionaries, basically
agreed with the "Enlightenment pragmatism" that informed Schiller's
and Rebmann's portrayals of Wallenstein. Woltmann, however, still
looked to Austrian leadership of a German "European Republic" in

the face of the French threat. Woltmann's analysis, which condemned Wallenstein's later "betrayal" of the Kaiser, focused on the first half of Wallenstein's career. It is not surprising that Woltmann's großdeutsch predilections gravitated toward the Wallenstein who was the instrument of Ferdinand II's project to unite Germany within a new centralized Holy Roman Empire.[42] His notion of the empire as a unique combination of German, multinational, and European interests that was worth modernizing made him much more sympathetic to Wallenstein the revolutionary than later generations of more conservative Catholic historians.[43]

Nicolaus Vogt, the theorist of a federative "European republic" of modernized nation-states, referred to the work of Schiller and Rebmann in a comprehensive reinterpretation of Wallenstein he presented in a series of works written between 1787 and 1808. As we saw in chapter 2, Vogt was influenced by the flux of the revolutionary and Napoleonic experience to shape an interpretation of Gustavus Adolphus as the creator of a unified north German state.[44] Vogt was able to reconcile the aims of both the Swedish king and the Duke of Friedland, conventionally presented as the two great antagonists of the war, within a broader historical justification of a united Germany in a reorganized Europe. He explicitly compared Wallenstein to Napoleon in a laudatory explication of the Duke of Friedland's revolutionary attempt to create a German-dominated Central European polity that united "under one flag" the German-speaking lands, the Netherlands, northern Italy, and Bohemia. Vogt dramatically described Wallenstein's hesitation at the brink of rebellion: "[He could remain a true servant of the Habsburgs or] raise himself and the German nation over the two sundered factions in the Fatherland." This was a critical moment, requiring new leadership and a new approach. After all, speculated Vogt, "what would have been the effect of the undertakings of this new Caesar on the German nation and its constitution?" Had not many so-called criminals, in the judgment of conventional history, had the best interests of the state at heart? Vogt concluded: "[Wallenstein] wanted to give the Germans a more unitary constitution, her people pride and unity, and the Reich its lost power and influence."[45] Napoleon's comprehensive demolition of the old state structure of Europe (in which Vogt foresaw the potential unification of Germany), and his larger imperial project in general, provided Vogt with a compelling backdrop for his portrait of Wallenstein as a revolutionary warlord who had also tried to create a unified German state and in the process remake the European state system.[46] Seeing the latter as the inevitable consequence of German unification was central to the nineteenth century's reimagination of Gustavus Adolphus, and it was an equally crucial component of the historical rehabilitation of Wallenstein.

A Traitor's Trial

The blossoming of German nationalist thinking after the defeat of Napoleon in 1813 significantly altered the portrait of Wallenstein as revolutionary created by Schiller, Rebmann, and Vogt. Wallenstein would be increasingly portrayed as a patriotic defender of German interests against foreign powers intent on Germany's destruction. Defeat and occupation at the hands of the French and the awakening of a nationalist consciousness in the Wars of Liberation eventually undermined interpretations of Wallenstein based on the radical aspirations of late Enlightenment thinking. However, as a result of the defensive modernization that Prussia and the other German states embarked upon after Napoleon's crushing victories in 1806, the debate over the unresolved question of German unification gradually came to focus on the relative desirability and practical form of either Prussian or Austrian leadership toward that goal. Prussia's claim to German leadership was based in part on its claim that it had taken the lead in liberating Germany from French rule, a feat largely attributed to the reorganization of the Prussian state and army by Stein, Hardenberg, and Scharnhorst between 1807 and 1810. But increasing pressure from an emergent liberal civil society for comprehensive political reform was met with an emphasis on the consolidation of a modernized absolutism in the form of a more streamlined and efficient administrative state. The modernization of the German political structure in the direction of genuine constitutional rule, with all of its implications for unification, ultimately faltered because it subordinated "constitution" (*Verfassung*) to "administration" (*Verwaltung*) as the bureaucracy consolidated its primacy in public affairs.[47]

The events of the French Revolution had driven a major rethinking of Wallenstein as a revolutionary with a radical plan to build a new Germany on the ruins of the old order. To use Thomas Nipperdey's phrase, the more prosaic accomplishments of the Prussian reformers' pursuit of "liberty through administration" were the background of the Duke of Friedland's next incarnation as a paragon of rational governance.[48] Economic modernization, as embodied in the Customs Union established under Prussian leadership in 1834, emerged in this period as the least controversial component of German unification (or the only one that was officially sanctioned by the Confederation regimes). This victory of bureaucratic absolutism built on the cameralist philosophy of the Prussian Enlightenment.[49] It promoted the ideas of the rationally governed, well-ordered state as it made issues of competence, efficiency, and organization the primary focus of open political discourse in the years before 1848.[50] As new archival sources were discovered in the first half of the nineteenth century, this new paradigm came to dominate Wallenstein historiography. The first phase in the creation of a modern interpretation of Wallenstein that legitimated Prussian leadership in Germany was part of what might be called the "political Hegelianism" of the early Restoration period. Friedrich Förster (1791–1868), an influential member of the original generation of the Berlin Hegelians, offered the first historical interpretation of Wallenstein as a modern ruler. To put it another way, Förster's Wallenstein appeared clothed in distinctly nineteenth-century garb. In the view of John Toews, Förster and his contemporaries Heinrich Leo, Eduard Gans, Johannes Schulze, and Leopold Henning embraced Hegel's state-oriented philosophy of history out of a profound disillusionment with the apparent failure of the "romantic nationalism" of the War of Liberation to create a unified German nation. For Förster and other patriotic young veterans of the war against Napoleon, the reality of the restored absolutist status quo created by the Congress of Vienna in 1815 dictated an accommodation with conservative politics as a rational organizational activity (rather than revolution) that culminated in the establishment of the modern state, in this case Prussia.[51] Förster presented Wallenstein as the first "world-historical" figure in modern German history who pursued the politics of state building in the Hegelian sense. In Förster's hands Wallenstein, as both catalyst and victim of an epochal collision between traditional forces and rationalist dynamics, became the "new political man" who represented the essential truth of his age. Yet, as Hegel had noted in frustration, "no Ideal result," that is, the emergence of the modern state, came out of the Thirty Years' War.[52] German historians writing about Wallenstein during the Restoration, like their French counterparts looking back at the consequences of 1789, wanted to reestablish a sense of historical continuity and rational progress that justified the institutions and political choices of postrevolutionary and postwar society. French historiography, as represented by Michelet and Thierry in Linda Orr's analysis, sought to integrate 1789 within a coherent national narrative. Orr's conclusion suggests that French historians succeeded in doing this because they had confidence in the basic historical foundations of the French state. For contemporary German historians, the state was still evanescent. The search for legitimating precedents, strategies, and political vocabularies was made contentious by awareness of their own continually interrupted progress toward nationhood: a continuum of German history repeatedly broken by war and failed attempts at nation building. The German historical debate during this period was about the establishment of the state itself and, as a necessary corollary, the establishment of its unifying narrative.[53]

The revolutionary upheavals set in motion in 1789—or more precisely, defeat in 1806—seemed to wipe the slate of German history clean. The revolutionary interruption of a century and a half of political somnolence by French armies revived a sense of the possibilities of German nationhood, even as it made clear to another generation of young patriots that the main obstacle to this aspiration must always be France (and, to lesser extent, Austria). Förster recalled his optimism at the age of seventeen when Austria and Prussia seemed ready to throw off the French yoke. He had longed to enter the ranks of the liberators of the Fatherland, as "the hatred of the French and the yearning for revenge became ever more deeply rooted in my patriotic heart." Förster got his revenge—and an Iron Cross in 1815 in the Battle of La Belle Alliance as an officer in the famous Lützow Freikorps.[54] Förster and others of his generation condemned the Congress of Vienna's restoration of the status quo ante bellum, believing that it had deliberately imposed a form of historical amnesia on Europe, especially Germany. The antidote to this affliction, a new unifying history, Förster was convinced, lay in the archives waiting to be discovered. Patriotic reawakening had to be accompanied by a historical reawakening that made German history a source of national pride and solidarity, as was the case in Britain and France. Förster looked to Wallenstein as the world-historical figure who, like Cromwell and Napoleon, could lend power and glory to the German national narrative. The very popularity of Schiller's portrait of the great man had, Förster pointed out, in its flights of fiction encouraged German forgetfulness and disinclination to confront and master political realities, so that the true Wallenstein lay buried in the archives, a victim of sectarian condemnation and falsification: "Through Schiller's history of the Thirty Years' War, and still more through his great drama, would public opinion be confirmed forever in its judgment of Wallenstein as a traitor."[55] Förster believed that the rehabilitation of Wallenstein as a German national hero had to begin by challenging Schiller's verdict of treason. Announcing his intention to focus on the period 1630–34, the years that he believed had been the subject of the greatest "falsifications," Förster characterized the tenor of his research as more "critical" than "historical." If the unjust verdict on "a remarkable man" was finally to be reversed, Förster believed he had no choice but to shed new light on old arguments. He concluded, on the basis of his research, that French intrigues had been behind Wallenstein's dismissal from command in 1630 and that his later peace negotiations with Saxony and Brandenburg Prussia, the foundation of the case condemning him as a traitor, had been conducted with the Kaiser's full approval with the sole aim of isolating and expelling the Swedish invader. In the chaos of war Wallenstein had seized the opportunity to make himself head of a new "German party." This revolutionary and patriotic act made him, inevitably, the target of the Jesuit conspiracy that dominated the Habsburg court.[56] As Förster elaborated this thesis further, it became the basis for an argument among German historians about Wallenstein's motives that lasted over forty years.

After 1815, politics in the German Confederation were characterized by the consolidation of bureaucratic authoritarianism and a muted discourse in civil society that focused on relatively limited constitutional reform. These two currents of thinking about the organization of the state complemented and opposed each other in an uneasy (and unequal) dialogue that broke down in 1830 and 1848, resumed with little practical consequence after 1871, and collapsed completely in 1918. Before German unification in 1871, the revisionist histories of Wallenstein tried to reconcile these two trajectories of modernization in the figure of the Duke of Friedland. Johann Sporschil (1800–1863), a pro-Austrian liberal "German Catholic," did not deny the fact of Wallenstein's "treason." This acknowledgment did not, however, prevent him from endorsing Wallenstein's revolutionary scheme to establish a new Germany free of Austrian and foreign influence. According to Sporschil, in defying France and trying to unify Germany, Wallenstein was "no protector of old structures." Sporschil believed that the princes' (and Habsburg) resistance to Wallenstein's plan paved the way for foreign intervention and partition and ultimately left Germany open to the depredations of Louis XIV and Napoleon.[57] German historians in the 1820s and 1830s, trying to construct a coherent national history, haltingly made their way from defending bureaucratic authoritarianism (essentially a modernized status quo) toward advocacy of unification and constitutional reform. Joseph von Hormayr (1781–1848) captured this uncertain mood as it was embodied in the enigma of Wallenstein: "The present century is characterized by a predilection for patriotic history, which has quickly established itself since the turn of the century among all classes of people. . . . The difficulties of our times have led to reflection on the past, where one searches for the hope and consolation which the present seems to deny."[58] In Hormayr's judgment, there were few figures from the German past superior to Wallenstein as an anchor for a unifying national German history. Hormayr, like Sporschil, interpreted Wallenstein's peace negotiations with Brandenburg and Saxony as an effort to establish himself, as an independent prince, at the head of a "third party" in Germany free of Prussian and Austrian influence.[59] Hormayr was vehemently anti-Habsburg and thus more inclined to blame the failure of Wallenstein's plan on Ferdinand's obstinacy than on the princes. His Digest of Patriotic History (published between 1811 and 1849) was Hormayr's vehicle for publicizing a "patriotic history" that combined, in Heinrich von Srbik's view, imperial patriotism and "German unification theory" (he had left Austria in 1828 and ended his career in Bavarian service).[60] Hormayr was one of the first to point out that the reassessment of Wallenstein as a German patriot had to take into account his attempt to unify the German nation on the basis of a new constitutional structure.[61]

Two years after Hormayr, another Austrian-born historian, Julius Schottky (1794–1849), also criticized conventional German histories for ignoring Wallenstein's constitutional innovations during his brief ducal reign in Mecklenburg (1627–28) and his abiding concern for the education and wealth of his subjects, the productivity of his lands, and building and arts. Schottky was of the opinion that, although it spoke more of duties than rights, Wallenstein's Charter of 1628, as a precursor to the enlightened absolutism of Frederick the Great, was a radical innovation in the history of German political thought.[62] It was Förster, however, who most fully developed the interpretation of Wallenstein as a revolutionary ruler who had pursued the modernization of the state. He dismissed what he felt to be the "one-sided" focus on Wallenstein's military exploits that ignored his political acumen, most notably manifested in his creation of a new "constitutional relationship" that not only confirmed the rights and obligations of the knights and the aristocracy but also gave representation to the urban communes as a "Third Estate." Clearly, Förster concluded, Wallenstein was a ruler far ahead of his time.[63]

Förster's 1834 plea for a new interpretation of Wallenstein as a modernizer stimulated a thorough reassessment of the generalissimo's motivations and plans. Not surprisingly, in 1837 Karl Adolf Menzel was one of the first to question what he interpreted as Förster's conservative attempt to legitimate Prussian dominance in Germany by scaling down the revolutionary scope of Wallenstein's ambitions.[64] Like Hormayr,

Menzel acknowledged that Wallenstein's negotiations with Sweden and France, and the fact that his officers swore personal fealty to him in January 1634, were self-evidently treasonous. But Menzel also believed that Wallenstein took those steps to consolidate his power, preserve his freedom of action, and position himself against the "clerical court party." In short, according to Menzel, Wallenstein was trying to force the Kaiser to make peace as the precondition for the constitutional reorganization of the Holy Roman Empire.[65] Menzel's fellow iconoclast Friedrich Wilhelm Barthold, who had poured scorn on the Protestant-Prussian appropriation of Gustavus Adolphus as a German national hero and whose anti-French animus was, if anything, more virulent than Menzel's, dismissed Wallenstein in 1842 as a dupe manipulated by Richelieu—a standard accusation of the anti-Prussian faction in German history writing.[66] In 1844 Förster finally responded to these criticisms in a lengthy recapitulation of his arguments that included 120 pages of documentation. He continued to maintain that imperial apologists after 1634 had a vested interest in the fabrication of evidence pointing to Wallenstein's "treason." As for the issue of Wallenstein's negotiations with France, Förster theorized that he had been motivated by the desire to secure a general peace and, in any case, the French had known all along that he was acting in the interests, if not with the explicit approval, of Vienna. In clearing Wallenstein's name before what he called the "tribunal of history," Förster's brief on behalf of the general concluded: "Should such a time of danger for Germany come again, we hope and wish that the Fatherland will never again find it necessary to turn its eyes to foreign soil, but find its heroes and salvation at home!"[67] Catholic historians, who had praised Wallenstein as the instrument of Ferdinand II's 1629 "Baltic project," were led by Karl Maria Freiherr von Aretin and Albert Heising in cautious approval of Förster's view as an indication of a "German-national sensibility" toward Wallenstein as the instrument of imperial unitary designs. However, they still insisted that Wallenstein had ultimately sabotaged the Habsburg war of unification by plotting rebellion against the Kaiser.[68] If Förster's defense of Wallenstein was judged overly tendentious (and limited in vision), and if his advocacy of Wallenstein as a model enlightened ruler was rendered suspect in light of his pro-Prussian views, his broader conclusions about Wallenstein's motivations retained their influence as political debate in Germany showed signs of life in the 1840s. The Breslau historian Richard Roepell (1808–93), a member of the "Young Hegelian" circle and a National Liberal politician, was able to turn the accusations against Wallenstein into an argument for his innocence. In Roepell's opinion, the goal of peace in Germany, so bitterly opposed by the "Spanish party" because they saw in it a serious diminution of Habsburg authority, justified any means, including negotiation with France.[69] Another commentator on the "scholars' battle" over Wallenstein in the mid-1840s emphasized that his "guilt" could only be adduced from his goals. "What, ultimately, had these been? To drive the Swedes out of Germany and secure a general peace. His 'treason' lay in his defiance of the Kaiser in pursuit of that goal."[70]

As the two decades after 1830 saw a gradual return to a more lively discussion of the possibilities of political reform in Germany, the abortive revolution of 1848, a "failure" in the sense that the Frankfurt Parliament had failed in its hope of unifying Germany, changed the parameters of the debate. Constitutional arguments still dominated, but the search for a solution to the "German question" shifted toward pragmatic considerations of what combination of powers within the Confederation could reenergize the process of consolidation begun by Napoleon. One major reason for this reassessment is that the events of 1848 had shaken the fragile status quo of "dualism," that is, the roughly equal status of Prussian and Austrian influence within the German Confederation.[71] Two other factors influenced the midcentury trajectory toward a "German-national" history writing that rejected the cautious reforms advocated by Förster's generation. First, Protestant nationalism had not disappeared. It still had the power, as the clash between the Prussian government and the archbishop of Cologne in 1837 demonstrated, to mobilize Germans in defense of their confessional prerogatives. It remained an important element buttressing Prussian claims to cultural and political leadership in Germany. Second, there was the revival of a powerful anti-French animus in response to the nationalist foreign policy of Adolphe Thiers in 1840, which highlighted Prussia's credentials as the power best fitted to guarantee German security. These circumstances were the background for a revision of the Förster thesis in the 1850s. The nature of Wallenstein's revolution and the issue of his "treason," especially the purposes behind his negotiations with Saxony, Brandenburg, Sweden, France, and the Bohemian rebels in exile, were reexamined in light of newly unearthed archival evidence. With the erosion of the vestigial loyalties to what remained of the old imperial constitution, as embodied in the German Confederation, arguments that insisted on Wallenstein's treason to the empire lost much of their power to persuade. The Napoleonic revolutionary and the Prussian modernizer of the Restoration was gradually recast at midcentury as the symbol of an assertive nationalist power politics in central Europe.

The Saxon historian Karl Gustav Helbig (1808–75) was a political moderate who represented a new generation of historians who tried to reconcile preservation of key elements of the conservative worldview with the liberals' new pragmatism. His pathbreaking 1850 monograph portrayed Wallenstein as the consummate political realist who had pursued any means to end French and Swedish intervention in Germany and establish a general peace.[72] In making the first extensive use of the royal Saxon archives in Dresden, Helbig rejected the "partisan" quarrels of Förster, Mailath, and Aretin as being erroneously fixated on a juridical "either/or" judgment of Wallenstein, even as he acknowledged the essentially "traitorous" nature of the Duke of Friedland. This was the midcentury "historicist moment" revealed in its break with eighteenth-century philosophical idealism: practical political goals must be judged, not moral questions of criminal intent or character. Helbig claimed that the negotiations between Wallenstein and Hans Georg von Arnim, the Saxon general and emissary representing the Protestant princes, had been undertaken with imperial approval and were intended to detach Brandenburg and Saxony from their alliance with Sweden. Helbig believed that, if successful, this initiative would have created the conditions for the establishment of an "advantageous peace" that would have served as the foundation of a new constitutional arrangement between the empire and the princes, one that would have been a significant advance toward realizing the hope of a more unified imperial state. Helbig hoped that his presentation of this "exonerating material" from the archives might inspire a historical reassessment of Wallenstein. In particular he wanted his fellow historians to reconsider how the "evolution of the tragedy" played out as Wallenstein and a few patriotic German princes had tried to eject the foreigners out of Germany, preserve the Holy Roman Empire, and create a new constitutional foundation of a unified state.[73] Helbig was the first to emphasize the improvisational nature of Wallenstein's plans as he pursued a policy determined primarily by German, rather than Habsburg, interests. This portrait of the general resembled the Napoleonic warlord of Rebmann and Vogt, but Wallenstein's revolution was now represented as more recognizably German than European.

It is clear that the historical puzzle of Wallenstein showed, as its many pieces were shuffled and rearranged, the still fragmented approaches to a solution to the German question at midcentury. Two futile gestures toward unity, 1813 and 1848, loomed in the background of recent German history. These misfired attempts at nationhood were interpreted as two more episodes in a longer continuum of failure that included 1629, 1632, and, as we shall see, 1634. German historians were still divided over whether Wallenstein should be judged as the instrument of imperial centralization, an essentially pro-Habsburg perspective that was congenial to Catholics, or viewed from the monarchical perspective as a salutary example of power politics in the Prussian mold. For both schools of thought, the invocation of Wallenstein's "German" vision was closely tied to the assumption that any configuration of the German nation would be based on hegemony in Central Europe, the oft-asserted historical necessity of dominating the continent's "central position." Bearing this aspect of the debate in mind, it is important to remember that contested interpretations of Wallenstein's legacy were also part of the development of Bohemian nationalism in the mid-nineteenth century. Examining the Bohemian context of the Wallenstein question allows a clearer understanding, from a perspective outside of Germany proper, of the strong pull his story had on German nationalists. Beda Dudik (1815–90), one of the leading lights (along with Franz Palacky, Jan Kollar, and Christian d'Elvert) of modern Bohemian history writing, had been put in charge of retrieving the Moravian archives that had been carried off to Stockholm by Swedish troops during the Thirty Years' War. In 1852 Dudik announced "an essential modification" to Förster's conclusions. He believed that new evidence from the recovered archives showed that Wallenstein's negotiations with the French were part of his plan to gain support for his seizure of the Bohemian crown.[74] This romantic nostalgia for an independent or autonomous kingdom had become central to Bohemian "nationalist" thinking during the 1830s and 1840s. However, at the time of Dudik's writing, this dream of self-determination had apparently been indefinitely postponed by the imperial declaration of 1851, which confirmed Bohemia (and Moravia and Silesia) as part of the Habsburg crown lands. This disappointment marked the beginning of the split in Bohemian national thinking between "ethnic federalism" and the militantly separatist nationalism of the Young Czech movement.[75] The "German tradition" of Bohemian history writing, represented by Dudik and d'Elvert, had developed from the perspective of a regional patriotism that emphasized the privileges and liberties afforded by the Habsburg possession of the Bohemian crown.[76] But they nevertheless rejected the popular attachment to Schiller's Germanized Wallenstein. Instead he was "Waldstein," a Bohemian patriot and hero who had fought to preserve the empire but had still acted in the interests of Bohemia's autonomy and traditional rights.[77] The Czech debate over the "guilt" of Wallenstein in the late nineteenth century, and in the interwar and postwar decades of the twentieth, mirrored its nineteenth-century German counterpart in that it pitted those who insisted on his betrayal of the old order against those who saw him as a revolutionary state builder.[78]

Helbig commented on this midcentury confrontation between tradition and revolution, or between a passive allegiance to the status quo and a dynamic faith in the future, in his observation that, despite the ongoing project of revising and modernizing Schiller's interpretation of Wallenstein (initiated by Förster, Menzel, Aretin, and Mailath), the "judgment of the public" obviously preferred Schiller's poetic idealization to the historical Wallenstein. In Helbig's view this bias was primarily determined by a romantic attachment to the story of the tragic hero brought down by the forces of reaction: "They embraced Wallenstein enthusiastically, undisturbed by his terrible atrocities in northern Germany, while Tilly, a man whose character was considerably more honorable and praiseworthy, and whose soldiers did nothing worse than Wallenstein's, has been branded a cruel Attila."[79] Helbig's reflexive anti-Habsburg animus (after all, Tilly had commanded the Catholic League forces, not the imperial army) remained strong in Protestant nationalism, and it greatly facilitated Wallenstein's metamorphosis from Counter-Reformation scourge to German revolutionary. On the other side of the confessional divide, the debunker of the Gustavus Adolphus myth, Friedrich August Gfrörer, managed to idealize the Swedish king's great antagonist in the "national war" while promoting the "greater Germany" vision: "With Wallenstein's elevation came a conspicuous turn to the Ghibelline [imperial] plan. . . . As Wallenstein raised his banner, the national spirit awoke in our soldiers—German Protestants and Catholics joined hands in order to return to the emperor his rightful authority and to reestablish the old religion on which the German Empire had been originally built and on which alone, even if Providence should decide differently, it can be built in the future."[80] When Helbig reviewed the burgeoning literature on Wallenstein in 1853, he recognized what he called, in the first use of the phrase, a modern "trial of Wallenstein" by historians who no longer relied so heavily on Schiller. He sharply criticized Gfrörer's pro-imperial interpretation of the Duke of Friedland's plans for German unity as anachronistic fantasy: "This work is a tasteless apologia for Wallenstein. . . . Gfrörer's overwrought Ghibelline patriotism transformed his dreams of German glory into Wallenstein's."[81] But in dismissing Gfrörer, Helbig had identified the "trial of Wallenstein" as a decisive moment in the process of creating a unifying and national German history.

The Unifier

In the four decades following Helbig's groundbreaking reappraisal, historians produced a massive amount of scholarship focusing on Förster's framing of the Wallenstein question. Prussia's ascendancy as the dominant economic (as well as political) power within the German Confederation in the late 1850s (or the waning of Austria's capacity to maintain its influence) made it apparent to most observers that the settlement of 1815 was on shaky ground. Austria's loss of Lombardy in 1860, the collapse of the comity of the Holy Alliance as Russia and Austria confronted each other in the Balkans, the rise of the militantly pro-Prussian Nationalverein in the German Confederation, and the continuing irritant to German sensibilities caused by Danish control of Schleswig-Holstein—all appeared to contemporaries as signs of the coming collapse of the system created in 1815 by the Congress of Vienna. This sense of impending dissolution, focused as it was on the senescence of the German Confederation, was the background for an explosion of historical interest in Wallenstein. The perceived weakening of Austrian power, or Vienna's apparent ambivalence about the long-term desirability of trying to maintain its influence in German affairs, appeared to signal a turning point in the process of German unification. Like the period from 1632 to 1634, the escalating confrontation between Austria and Prussia between 1859 and 1866 culminated in a weakening of Austrian power that promised, finally, a resolution to the German question. During the climacteric in the first war of German liberation, Gustavus Adolphus and Wallenstein had threatened the universal monarchy with a revolutionary new order, only to fall short of their goals. However, nineteenth-century enthusiasm for what might be called the "Gustavian" model for German unification, that is, some sort of rearrangement of the sovereignties of the various German states based on confessional solidarity, began to wane, largely because of a growing doubt about the limitations of Protestant nationalism as the exclusive and sufficient basis for the new state. The debate over the "Wallensteinian" model, on the other hand, only increased in intensity because of the revolutionary dynamism perceived in the Duke of Friedland's anti-Austrian brand of Realpolitik.

Austria's waning influence and power within the German Confederation lent urgency to a last-ditch effort by the two main voices of the Catholic legitimist school of history writing, Friedrich Hurter and Onno Klopp, to discredit Wallenstein's motives and intentions. Their defense of the constitutional status quo, as embodied in the German Confederation, reiterated the traditional assertion of Wallenstein's treasonous plot against the legitimate constitutional order of the empire. But by focusing on Wallenstein's alleged dictatorial ambitions, they appealed to contemporary anti-Prussian apprehensions. They emphasized how Wallenstein's subversion of the imperial constitution had thwarted Ferdinand's plans to modernize and unify the Holy Roman Empire. In this view Wallenstein's alleged plans to create a unitary and hereditary monarchy in Germany masked crude ambitions to set up a despotic military dictatorship. Hurter, a consistent and reactionary advocate of what Heinrich Srbik called a "medieval aristocratic-monarchical feudalism," insisted that the issue of treason remain central to new research on Wallenstein. Hurter dismissed praise for Wallenstein's "constitutional innovations" as dangerously anachronistic and unacceptably biased by German-nationalist inclinations, asking, "Should the perspectives of the present thus be allowed to become embedded in the past?"[82] For his part, Klopp warned of the tendency for despotic rulers to emerge in times of civil war: "[Wallenstein] may not have spoken exactly the words which have often been put in his mouth: ' . . . the Reich no longer needs Electors and Princes, they must be put out to pasture; as in France and Spain, in Germany there must also be only one ruler. . . .' Wallenstein may not have expressed this idea so explicitly, but the concept arose naturally enough out of the circumstances."[83] In his massive two-volume defense of Tilly, published in 1861 (while debate in the Prussian assembly over expansion of the army raged), Klopp claimed that, with French help, Wallenstein had plotted from as early as 1630 to become the "unlimited military dictator" of Germany, which Klopp compared to the "military despotism" of Cromwell. According to Klopp, this "total transformation" of Germany into a hereditary monarchy with Wallenstein as king would have been based on a comprehensive process of secularization, a claim Klopp supported by asserting that Wallenstein had always secretly opposed the Edict of Restitution (enacted in 1629 to restore church lands seized since 1552).[84] Klopp was tarring Wallenstein, just as he had tarred Gustavus Adolphus, with the brush of the "revolutionary" political aims of Protestant nationalism. Hurter seconded this opinion in 1862 in a monograph that focused on the last four years of Wallenstein's life. Wallenstein's contacts with the French-backed Bohemian rebels in

exile were, in Hurter's view, irrefutable evidence of the general's treasonous plans to seize the Bohemian crown as the necessary first step
toward overthrowing the legal constitutional order and becoming the
"dictator of Germany." Adducing Wallenstein's guilt from a "mountain
of evidence," Hurter dismissed what he called the "German" theory of
the existence of a Jesuit-directed Spanish conspiracy against Wallenstein
as a mere "fairy tale."[85] For Klopp and Hurter, Wallenstein's revolution
was nothing more than a self-serving *putsch* against the emperor no less
subversive of the legitimate constitutional order than the initial spark
of the war, the Protestant rebellion of 1618. It seemed to them that the
threat now loomed again in the policies of the new minister president
serving the Hohenzollern king, Otto von Bismarck.

For a historian whose philosophy seemed to have led to the German
infatuation with the "world-historical individual" as a catalyst and
manifestation of historical progress, it is revealing that Leopold von
Ranke (1795–1886) wrote, out of all his voluminous output, only one
major work from the biographical perspective, his influential History of
Wallenstein (1869). Ranke had apparently contemplated such a study
quite early in his career. In a letter written in 1830 to Friedrich von Gentz,
he made the observation that he was sure it would be quite easy to refute
what he termed Friedrich Förster's outdated "Wallensteiniade."[86] When
Ranke finally published his refutation almost forty years later, it did
indeed represent, in its emphasis on the response of human agency to a
unique set of circumstances, the significant historicist shift away from
Förster's Hegelian "enlightened absolutist" portrayal of Wallenstein.
Ranke's biography confirmed the "German-national" interpretation
that Heising had advanced in 1846 in his work on Gustavus Adolphus
and that Helbig had systematically pursued in the early 1850s. Ranke's
study appeared in the same year that Gustav Droysen published the
first volume of his equally influential biography of Gustavus Adolphus.
Essentially, both Ranke and Droysen sought to justify a Realpolitik
solution to the problem of German unification. Both historians, as
far as possible, avoided the divisive religious arguments that had long
dominated the history writing about the Thirty Years' War in favor
of a pragmatic argument for seeing Germany as the nexus of a new

European order.[87] Ranke's portrayal of Wallenstein, a product of his conservative inclinations, shaped the debate over the Wallenstein question for the next quarter century. He ultimately advocated a more cautious approach to European balance-of-power politics than was completely congenial to the ardent Bismarck enthusiasts among his peers and students.[88] Peter Gay has perceptively noted Ranke's admiration for the grand plans of Henry IV to reorganize the European state system, so it is not surprising that his search for a historical illustration of the dialectic that drove the rise of the state settled on Wallenstein as a paradigmatic historical figure in conflict with his times, or the "pathological man," in Karl Metz's phrase, who embodied the force of change toward "coherence" in history.[89]

Ranke regarded Wallenstein as a statesman of ambitious and innovative designs. He pointed out, however, that the ambitious "monarchical aims" of the first command (1625–30) had evolved into the more limited and pragmatic "peace policy" (*Friedenspolitik*) of the second (1632–34).[90] Nevertheless, it is clear that Ranke identified an epochal "conflict of ideas" in Wallenstein's clash with Gustavus Adolphus. The same battle, the struggle between the Habsburg-backed constitutional order and the "national" idea that fought for the "secularization" and unification of political authority, was being fought again as Ranke wrote.[91] Beginning with the recovery of Schleswig from Denmark and ending with Austria's defeat at Königgratz, the years between 1864 and 1866 saw the dissolution of Austrian power, along with the German Confederation itself, in a remarkable succession of withdrawals and defeats engineered by Bismarck. This sequence of events is the essential context for Ranke's conclusion that Wallenstein's attempts to negotiate peace between 1632 and 1634 had "great national meaning" because they were fundamental to a policy that challenged the divisive Counter-Reformation politics of the "zealous Catholic party" and the "religious opposition" to peace in Germany of the Jesuit cabal advising Ferdinand II. Although they ultimately failed, Wallenstein's attempts to expel France, Sweden, and Spain from German affairs, and his pursuit of a "reunification of the confessions," were, according to Ranke, entirely consistent with "Protestant and [German] national interests ever since the Schmalkaldic War [1546–1547]." Ranke concluded that Wallenstein's "overriding priority was still the possible settlement of the religious and territorial disunion of the German Reich and the assertion of its national character, its integrity, and the entire binding force of the imperial constitution."[92] Ranke's analysis of Wallenstein's diplomacy was driven by a conservative appreciation for the constitutional legacy of the old empire and a preference for a German-national Realpolitik that pursued German unity and hegemony in central Europe. However, the Rankean imprimatur that was applied to most of the Wallenstein historiography of the Bismarckian era usually invoked only the second half of that perspective.[93] By focusing on Wallenstein's abortive attempt to impose some sort of unitary structure on the "religious and territorial disunion" of the German states, Ranke offered a paradigm of political and territorial centralization that appeared to be triumphantly confirmed in the founding of the German Empire in 1871. The resistance to this interpretation came from those historians whose confessional loyalties, particularist allegiances, or liberal convictions were best protected within the traditional imperial-confederal structure. They accused Wallenstein of conspiring to undermine this idea, the guarantor of ancient German liberties, which was systematically demolished by Bismarck in the nineteenth century. Post-unification Catholic history writing about Wallenstein, bitterly acknowledging the achievement of 1866–71, ruefully concurred in Ranke's judgment of Wallenstein's "world-historical" centralizing ambitions: "The methodical centralization of Germany, built on an unlimited military despotism, and an absolute imperial rule, whose fiat would become the law for the whole of Germany, this was the overweening idea that arose out of the limitless pride of the Duke of Friedland."[94]

The debate was not over, however. It had a significant coda outside of Germany that must be examined. The final phase of the debate over the Wallenstein question occurred during the 1870s and 1880s. These arguments pitted those "pro-imperial" Bohemian historians who continued to insist on the traditional judgment of Wallenstein's guilt against the "pro-German" depictions of Wallenstein as an authentic and distinctly modern German hero.[95] This last debate took place against the background of federalist reform in the Austro-Hungarian empire and the consolidation of Bismarck's Second Reich. As Vienna's attention was turned to the promotion in the Balkans of Austria's true interests as the "Danubian monarchy," the long-awaited German hegemony in central Europe appeared to be dawning. The story of Wallenstein remained central to legitimating this hegemony, even if the story was told by historians outside the borders of the new nation. The German-Bohemian Wallenstein debate, within the broader nineteenth-century reconsideration of the Duke of Friedland's legacy, is revealing because of the central question under dispute: How German was Wallenstein? The last two decades of the nineteenth century witnessed a heated confrontation in German-speaking academia in Central Europe between the "German Slavophile" Anton Gindely (1829–92), who insisted on Wallenstein's guilt, and the pro-German Bohemian Hermann Hallwich (1838–1913), who defended the Helbig-Ranke thesis that asserted the realistic and necessary pro-German goals of Wallenstein's "peace policy." Gindely, like Hallwich, had studied with the Bavarian historian and "greater Germany" advocate Konstantin von Höfler and had gone on to teach history at Charles University in Prague, where he was a founding member of the German-Bohemian Party. Between 1869 and 1880, he published one of the most widely read histories of the Thirty Years' War, not only in the German-speaking world but in its English translation as well. Gindely's interpretation of Wallenstein (or "Waldstein," as he pedantically insisted) arose out of imperial and south German Catholic (his mother was German) loyalties that saw the new German nationalism (and the new German nation-state) as a mortal threat to the sovereignty of the Habsburg empire.[96] Gindely's first work dealing with Wallenstein, published in 1875, was basically an elaboration of the Hurter-Klopp argument that warned of the dangers of a Prussian-dominated unified Germany. Gindely believed that Wallenstein had attempted, both in Mecklenburg and in Bohemia, to create a "state within a state" (which also, significantly, coveted Silesia) allied with the empire's enemies as a base from which he could eventually challenge the Kaiser. For Gindely these stood revealed as dangerous "German" goals, which posed as serious a threat to Austria's position in Central Europe in the 1870s as they had been in the 1630s.

Like Gindely, Hermann Hallwich had been a student of Höfler, but he was also a protégé of Helbig and considered himself a follower of Ranke. As a liberal member of the Bohemian provincial diet and the Imperial Council (*Reichsrat*), Hallwich spent his career, both as a state economic and trade adviser (which accounted for his Försterian view of Wallenstein as, among other things, an innovator in the field of political economy) and a historian, mediating German and Czech economic relations in the Austrian empire. He supported a federalist compromise to solve the nationalities problem, as part of the modernization of Austria, Bohemia, and Moravia (in 1890 he served on the German-Czech commission that oversaw federalist reform). As a historian his most significant achievement was the collation and publication of an extensive collection of previously unknown documents and letters from the scattered Wallenstein papers. These source materials became the basis for a new wave of research on Wallenstein during the last two decades of the nineteenth century.[97] Hallwich first challenged Gindely in 1876, when he made his first appearance in the trial of Wallenstein as a self-described "witness for the defense" (*Entlastungszeuge*), at least as far as the question of Wallenstein's negotiations with Saxony were concerned. Hewing closely to Ranke's interpretation, and marshalling new evidence from the Saxon archives, Hallwich concluded that Wallenstein, spurred by his "striking recognition" of the danger that the "Spanish party" posed to the empire and after having received "distinct signals" that a negotiated general peace might be possible, aggressively pursued contacts with the Protestant princes with full imperial approval.[98] Another Bohemian historian, Vinzenz Prökl, concurred with what he called Hallwich's "German" interpretation (that is, that the enemies of Wallenstein were the enemies of Germany). For Prökl it was clear that Wallenstein's negotiations aimed at the pacification and unification of the empire through the expulsion of the Catholic and foreign invaders. Only when those goals were accomplished, according to Prökl, could Wallenstein begin to carry out his revolutionary "national idea" of remaking the Holy Roman Empire.[99]

The founding of the Second Reich in 1871 profoundly influenced the transformation of the Duke of Friedland into the historical champion of the German national idea and protector, as one enthusiast put it, of "all the good spirits of Germany" (that is, German-speaking Central Europe).[100] In a volume of the Modern People's Library that appeared in 1876, Martin Philippson, a professor in Bonn, informed his readers exactly what had been lost because Wallenstein's revolutionary project to establish "monarchical unity" in Germany had failed:

> Reconciliation of the confessional division, unification of the whole Reich under imperial authority, chasing the foreigners from German soil: these are projects which deserve more of our recognition, as they stand in glaring opposition to the later achievements of Habsburg policy symbolized by the Peace of Westphalia. In defiance of the Kaiser, Wallenstein wanted to make Germany great, free, and united. After defeating Wallenstein the Kaiser took the road which led to fragmentation, partition, powerlessness, and the loss of fair German provinces to France, Denmark, and Sweden. This unholy state of affairs endured until another, younger state, Prussia, took the leadership of Germany away from Austria when, six years after the death of Wallenstein, the actual creator of the Prussian state, Friedrich Wilhelm, ascended the throne in Berlin.[101]

In the early years of the Second Reich, historians deliberately used the history of the Duke of Friedland to justify and legitimate the Prussian-led unification of Germany. In a review of the Wallenstein literature of the 1860s and 1870s, Ottokar Lorenz (1832–1904), an Austrian-born Jena historian who as an anticlerical émigré had become a leading exponent of the necessity of Prussian power politics to unify Germany, dismissed the preoccupation of historians with the question of Wallenstein's guilt or innocence, asking instead, "Can historical scholarship encompass the subjective question of guilt, according to moral or legal viewpoints, within the field of its judgment?"[102] Following Wilhelm Dilthey, Lorenz took the position that historical evidence was the basis of a rational "construction" of a narrative that made the past comprehensible from the perspective of present needs and anxieties.[103] Lorenz therefore believed that the question of Wallenstein's criminality was a completely "unsatisfactory" field of investigation for the historian. Instead, he argued, the sole focus of any study of Wallenstein should be on the practical consequences of his fall from power, since it derailed progress toward a lasting religious peace and the "certain unification" and "radical territorial reorganization" of the Reich in which all foreign influence would have been eliminated.[104]

In 1879 Hermann Hallwich published Wallenstein's End: Unpublished Correspondence and Documents, the first volume of his collection of new documentary material from the Wallenstein papers. In the foreword he maintained that the 150-year-old historians' "trial of Wallenstein" had produced nothing more than a series of apologias, dubious official "proofs" of his guilt, and all manner of pro-Bavarian, pro-Swedish, and anti-French tracts. In sum, he noted, all the parties concerned had been duly interrogated *except* Wallenstein, who until now had been denied the chance to testify in his own defense: "After all his gainsayers have spoken, he has a right to be heard."[105] Hallwich concluded that the Spaniards, the Jesuits, Bavaria's Maximilian, and the other princes of the Catholic League were completely justified in their apprehensions that Wallenstein, through his "peace policy," was actually mounting a revolution to establish a unitary, monarchical authority in Germany. Surveying the results of the "complete victory" of the Spanish faction in Vienna that led to Wallenstein's removal from command and eventual assassination, Hallwich asked: "And yet, what course would world history have taken if Wallenstein had been successful in carrying out his plans! What respected and honored place might Germany have claimed in the pages of this chronicle if she had been politically united for two hundred and fifty years! The heart of a true German cannot contemplate this without feelings of the deepest sorrow."[106]

A final confrontation took place in the 1880s between the defenders of a legitimist interpretation of the Thirty Years' War, who stood behind Gindely, and the "Wallenstein Men," the authors of a unifying national narrative and backers of Hallwich who saw in the events of the war a historical demonstration of the possibilities of a united and hegemonic Germany in central Europe. This final argument about Wallenstein's revolution clashed over whether or not it was possible (or desirable) to reconcile the modern idea of the nation-state with the traditional notion of the imperial polity. Hostility toward France also became more marked, and there was a shift in emphasis toward the centralized and authoritarian nature of Wallenstein's military organization and rule. As the Second Reich consolidated and Germany grew as a first-rank power in the two decades after unification, the proposed solutions to the Wallenstein question increasingly pointed toward a European state system centered on Germany and established and maintained through military power. Wallenstein's "national idea," it was argued, clearly envisioned Germany as an imperial state.

In 1881 Edmund Schebek (1819–95), a Moravian jurist and imperial civil servant, published what he called a "brief for the defense" (*Vertheidigungschrift*) under the provocative title The Solution to the Wallenstein Question. Citing new evidence, Schebek challenged what he believed to be 150 years of "falsified history" about Wallenstein by claiming that the glory of the Kaiser and the independence of the Reich had been Wallenstein's main priorities. Schebek praised the Duke of Friedland as "the single decisive champion of the imperial idea."[107] His most imaginative contribution to the rehabilitation of Wallenstein's reputation was the suggestion, based on his reading of new sources, that the slander campaign of the "Catholic party" undermining Wallenstein's peace initiatives had in fact been based on forged evidence provided by a member of the original 1618 cabal of Bohemian rebels, the lord high chancellor of Bohemia, Wilhelm von Slawata, a cousin of Wallenstein.[108] Schebek concluded that, by trying to negotiate a peace that undermined imperial war aims, Wallenstein was guilty at most of an error in judgment but certainly not treason. If Wallenstein was "guilty," he went on, then his only crime was that he had tried to unify the German Reich on a "new basis." Wallenstein's visionary plan, according to Schebek, charted the course for Bismarck's founding of a new German empire in the nineteenth century. Indeed, Schebek pointed out, when one considered the array of forces that conspired to bring Wallenstein down, his "failure" made Bismarck's success in 1871 all the more remarkable.[109] In a second monograph published in 1882, Schebek reasserted the by now familiar German view of the proper role of the historian as it applied in this case. He must act as a "legal advocate" in defending the "most slandered man in German history."[110] Schebek dismissed the claims of connections between Wallenstein and the rebel Bohemian émigrés as a canard originating in a French disinformation campaign that leaked fabricated details of Wallenstein's negotiations to undermine the general's influence in Vienna. Schebek hoped that his new findings had "shed some mitigating light on the monstrous injustice that befell this great and worthy man in his life, in history, and in literature."[111]

In a piece written in 1883 to mark the three hundredth anniversary of the "great man's" birth, Hermann Hallwich professed his admiration for the "Sisyphean labor" of those historians who, like Schebek, strove to find the single conclusive document that proved Wallenstein guilty or innocent. But the fact remained, Hallwich reminded his readers, that "thousands and thousands" of pieces of documentation had been examined without the least evidence of Wallenstein's guilt coming to light. Hallwich could not help wondering at the motives of those who continued to deny the Duke of Friedland's innocence.[112] Hallwich was confident that his own work on this "world-historical question" had definitively closed the debate even as, inevitably, this "last word" encountered resistance: "Whenever the name of Wallenstein is mentioned, political, dynastic, anti-dynastic, national, and confessional interests attempt to validate themselves with either condemnation or acquittal."[113] Hallwich's conclusion that anti-Wallenstein historians were essentially anti-German is repeated in another commemorative pamphlet published in 1884 to mark the 250th anniversary of Wallenstein's death. Recapitulating Schebek's and Hallwich's arguments, the author, Richard Wapler, offered his work as a German nationalist's rebuttal against the "Jesuitical baseness" of a "servile Austrian historiography" and as a memorial to "our greatest national hero, a Germanic patriot to the bone, and a lamentable victim of perfidious politics and an unjust and arbitrary tribunal."[114]

Hallwich's satisfaction that he had delivered the last word in the debate about Wallenstein's revolution was premature, however. Between 1869 and 1880 the first three volumes of Anton Gindely's massive history of the Thirty Years' War, which dealt with the events of the Bohemian Rebellion in 1618 up through the transfer of the Palatine Electorate to

Bavaria in 1623, came out in Prague.[115] But Gindely had also completed a popular history of the entire war published in Germany between 1882 and 1884. Written for a general audience, this book, based on extensive archival research, sold an impressive twenty thousand copies and became the most widely read nineteenth-century history of the Thirty Years' War since the appearance of Schiller's history. It was the standard reference until after the turn of the century, when it was superseded by Moriz Ritter's German History in the Age of the Counter-Reformation and the Thirty Years' War (1889–1908).[116] In his preface to the German edition of 1884, Gindely immediately attacked Hallwich by claiming that Hallwich's own evidence condemned Wallenstein as a traitor.[117] The book's conclusions were marked by a general anti-German tenor that distinguished Gindely's work from the more specifically anti-Prussian animus of Westenrieder, Hurter, and Klopp. For Gindely, Wallenstein's vision of a new German imperium had become an accomplished fact in 1871 with the creation of a unified Germany that threatened the independence of Central Europeans. In insisting on Wallenstein's treason, Gindely was resisting an interpretation that he saw as a politicization of history that undermined the fragile consensus binding the dual monarchy together. Between 1879 and 1884, the German (that is, Austrian and German-Bohemian) members of the Imperial Council had rejected several demands that some measure of official parity be granted to the Czech language in public life and education. When the burned Czech National Theater was rededicated in 1883, it turned into a celebration of Czech nationalism, and the Czech "federalist" party went on to win a majority in the provincial elections of 1883. Gindely was a powerful, if somewhat isolated, voice of warning in this tense period when Germanophile Austrian historians such as Hallwich and Lorenz, through their interpretations of Wallenstein's career, were openly shifting their ideological loyalties toward the new German state. Wallenstein stood convicted of treason, in Gindely's counterargument, on four counts: his contacts with Gustavus Adolphus, his negotiations with France, his attempt to conclude a premature and "unfavorable" peace with Brandenburg and Saxony, and the simple fact that the secrecy in which these contacts were shrouded was sufficient in itself to demonstrate Wallenstein's intent to betray the empire. Gindely paid little attention to what he called the "recent lively discussion" about Wallenstein's assassination, noting only that it was probably necessary in order for the Kaiser to regain control of his army.[118] Nevertheless, outside of Bohemia most German historians were inclined, on the evidence, to support the treason argument (which was essentially the view of Ranke), albeit with cautious language that referred to "compromising correspondence" and the "indiscretion" of the Bohemian-French connection. These points aside, the fact remained, according to the Dresden historian Arnold Gaedeke, that Wallenstein had realistically recognized the necessity of peace as well as the mortal danger to Germany of an escalating French involvement in the war. Wallenstein's moves to check French ambitions and avoid a prolongation of the war had been vigorously opposed by the Catholic party, who understandably feared a diminution of Habsburg authority, and by the Swedes, who wanted to annex German territory.[119]

Although Gindely mocked Schebek's theory that Wallenstein had been set up, he betrayed some uncertainty whether the evidence regarding Wallenstein's activities in the period 1633–34, which his defenders hailed as the culmination of his revolutionary "peace policy," incontrovertibly condemned him as a traitor by basically ignoring it. His next sally in the debate about Wallenstein's revolution simply elaborated the conventional judgments of the Duke of Friedland's traitorous nature. Gindely insisted that, taken as a whole, the new archival discoveries affirmatively answered the question of Wallenstein's guilt. Citing Dudik's research, Gindely demanded that Wallenstein's accusers focus on two main questions: first, did Wallenstein deliberately undermine the aims of the Catholic League, and second, did he seek the imperial crown for himself? As discussed in chapter 2, the second question was also posed by Gustavus Adolphus's defenders and detractors. Throughout the nineteenth century the German "national question" often boiled down to an argument about how *German* the Holy Roman Empire was. Should it be resurrected or replaced? The debate over the origins of the Thirty Years' War, the aims of Gustavus Adolphus, and Wallenstein's revolution all revolved, in one form or another, around this question. Gindely believed that a definitive answer would come from further investigation of an earlier period in Wallenstein's career, the "First Command" of 1625–30, which was celebrated by Catholic and großdeutsch historians as a moment when a rejuvenated and centralized Holy Roman Empire seemed close to realization. Gindely was convinced that "in the five years of his first command Waldstein completed his education as a traitor."[120] Gindely cited as proof the fact that Wallenstein's contemporaries, particularly Maximilian of Bavaria, were aware from the start of his "imperial plans" and desire for the Habsburg crown, ambitions that were revealed in his well-known opposition to the Catholic League and the Edict of Restitution. Gindely believed that through this opposition Wallenstein hoped to curry favor with the Protestant princes. Wallenstein's claims that he only wanted to do for Germany what Richelieu had done for France accounted, in Gindely's opinion, for the misplaced "sympathy" of many modern German historians for Wallenstein's alleged goals of modernizing imperial power through unifying the German state. If Wallenstein's aim had been to make the Kaiser a king, Gindely went on in a bluntly ironic vein, then the means Wallenstein had pursued to this end—crushing the princes, ruining their lands, and trampling the liberties of the estates—might be justified in the eyes of history. But the documents proved that claims of Wallenstein's world-historical status were mendacious and politically motivated. Instead, he stood revealed to posterity as a "violent man" who had schemed only to aggrandize himself.[121]

Hallwich's first response to Gindely, as a self-proclaimed "expert on the Wallenstein question," appeared in the journal of the Association for the History of the Germans in Bohemia. Hallwich poured scorn on Gindely's debunking of Wallenstein's "honorable peace policy" as dubious "nonsense" and "soap bubbles" based on "untenable" scholarly premises: "There is not a page in his book in which there are not a number of serious mistakes."[122] Hallwich not only deplored Gindely's "caricature of history" for its complete lack of "objectivity" but, in one very telling attack that equated historical acumen with national culture, also complained that, as a Czech, Gindely was writing in a language that was not his own: "He has no more sense for historical truth than he does for the spirit of the German language." Hallwich remained unconvinced that Wallenstein's dismissal at Regensburg in 1630 was anything other than the work of the enemies of Germany's greatness and imperial unity.[123] In 1887 Hallwich devoted an entire book, *Wallenstein und Waldstein: Ein offener Brief an Dr. Gindely* (Wallenstein and Waldstein: An Open Letter to Dr. Gindely), to a point-by-point rebuttal of Gindely's main arguments. This attack, published in Germany, was liberally laced with derisive commentary on Gindely's style and savage apostrophes impugning Gindely's scholarly integrity. Hallwich began by noting that Gindely was only the latest of a long line of Czech Bohemian historians, such as Jan Kollar (1793–1852) and Palacky, who had always condemned any interpretation of Wallenstein that was "too German" in its conclusions. Therefore, in considering Gindely's "partisan and dilettantish "claim of rendering a "final judgment" (*Endurtheil*) on the Wallenstein question, the reader was put in the position of deciding between Ranke's German "Wallenstein" ("the first historically true portrait of one of [Germany's] more significant and important generals and statesmen") and Gindely's Bohemian traitor "Waldstein."[124] Obviously, Hallwich had no doubt about which interpretation a German patriot would believe. As for Gindely's claims that Wallenstein had plotted to seize the imperial crown, an accusation backed up by "only a small sampling of thoroughly dubious (*verdächtiger*) sources," Hallwich could only ask: "Could deluded and malicious defamation go any further?"[125] Hallwich seized upon this particular claim with the same alacrity as had Catholic historians when they denounced Protestant historians who attributed the same ambition to Gustavus Adolphus. In the case of the Swedish king, it had been a matter of casting doubt on the legitimacy of claims that Gustavus Adolphus had aimed at creating a unified Protestant–North German state. Hallwich believed that Wallenstein had a vision for Germany far more revolutionary in its aims than merely taking control of an obsolescent medieval empire. Hallwich described Gindely's Wallenstein as a portrait stitched together "out of old scraps and rags cut from the same cloth of *soi-disant* political Catholicism and the legitimist ultramontane and reactionary party in Germany and Austria which tries to rescue the honor of their beloved Tilly by defaming the policies of Wallenstein. . . . Any court would undoubtedly pronounce you guilty of slandering the illustrious dead. In my view, however, yours is a genuinely pathetic scholarly enterprise that transgresses the laws and obligations which are and must be sacred in civil society [*bürgerliche Gesellschaft*]. . . . Our differences lay not in expression but in method."[126] Hallwich obviously shared the common intellectual prejudice of his time, namely, that German science must always triumph over Catholic obscurantism. Stung, Gindely replied to those he called the "Wallenstein Admirers" by announcing that he would not defend his position by resorting to the "polemics" of Hallwich but would "calmly" refute him with the facts. Aside from accusing Hallwich of indulging in "fantasy" and "standing the truth on its head," Gindely was otherwise restrained in rejecting Hallwich's "insinuation" that he had failed to examine, or had deliberately ignored, the evidence in Wallenstein's correspondence. In his opinion Arnold Gaedeke and Emil Hildebrand had already examined that particular body of evidence to conclusively prove that Wallenstein had actively conspired with the Bohemian exiles to enter into an alliance with Sweden. Gindely's sharpest retort, however, was saved for his categorical repudiation of Hallwich's accusation that he harbored reactionary and ultramontane sympathies. This was, Gindely implied, an unworthy appeal by Hallwich to his readers' baser (read German) nationalist instincts.[127]

But by the end of the 1880s, with the waning of the divisive passions of the Kulturkampf and the consolidation of the Second Reich as a major European power, the old legitimist arguments, the pro-imperial school of history writing dating back to Westenrieder, Hurter, and Klopp that insisted on Wallenstein's guilt as a traitor, had lost most of their power to provoke. The history of Wallenstein had been successfully refashioned to justify a revolutionary and nationalist power politics that aimed at constructing a new European balance of power centered on a united Germany. The Rankean interpretation of Wallenstein, with its emphasis on the historical processes through which great powers emerge, won out in a decidedly "Germanicized" version propagated by historians like Helbig, Lorenz, and Hallwich. In 1888 the conservative nationalist historian Max Lenz (1850–1932), the torchbearer of the Ranke Renaissance of the 1880s, scourge of großdeutsch and ultramontane history writing, and plotter of the "Luther to Bismarck" genealogy to legitimate the Wilhelmine imperial state, summed up the significance of Wallenstein's place in the German national narrative. In prose marked by what Heinrich von Srbik later labeled a peculiar combination of German unitary thinking, Rankean "universalism," and großdeutsch imperial fantasies, Lenz concluded, "If [Wallenstein] had gained control of the German armies, he would not have remained merely a rebel against the Kaiser, but a representative of the highest and most longed-for good: peace and the national welfare, freedom of religion and the interests of the estates—the head of a European federation against Habsburg domination. The time would have come to dispense with all pretense and make a beginning."[128] That beginning, as it turned out, would have to be postponed until 1871.

The nineteenth-century "trial of Wallenstein," that is, the debate about the aims and consequences of his failed "revolution," was driven primarily by the search for historical models and precedents that could legitimate the unification of Germany (and German hegemony in Europe) under the aegis of Prussia. Casting back to the revolutionary warlord represented by Henry IV, Cromwell, and Napoleon, this ideological buttressing of a Bismarckian power politics used the history of Wallenstein as a model and lesson that exemplified the virtues necessary for modern state-building: a disdain for an obsolete imperial-constitutional German political tradition; a strategic vision that pursued German dominance in central Europe; and a commitment to the radical territorial reorganization, through war if necessary, of the German states.

"What, in short, is his historical significance for the nourishing of that boundless trust in the national power state (*Machtstaat*) which, in the last analysis, has become a pagan faith in a new and temporal redeemer-god, and which in our century has driven millions of men to throw themselves as sacrifices into the jaws of Leviathan?"[129] Gerhard Ritter wrote these words in a Gestapo cell in Berlin during the winter of the collapse of 1944–45 as he contemplated the catastrophic consequences of the elevation of power politics as the guiding principle of the modern German foreign policy. Ritter was referring to the influence of nineteenth-century interpretations of Machiavelli on nationalist concepts of the state, but he easily could have been talking about the historiographical remaking of Wallenstein into an archetypal German statesman.[130] Discussion of how the concept of "Machiavellianism" has influenced modern German political history may seem, perhaps, a somewhat archaic approach to analyzing the abstract notion of "power" as articulated in German political thinking and history writing. But given the prolonged argument about whether Wallenstein's ends justified the means, and the affirmative answer given after the foundation of the Second Reich, it provides an important key to understanding the profound tensions inherent in the Wallenstein historiography of the nineteenth century, which made explicit and frequent reference to Machiavelli.[131] Friedrich Meinecke, writing, like Ritter, in the aftermath of an apocalyptically destructive war, also saw in the "catastrophe" of Wallenstein a Promethean moment in the German historical consciousness, the bringing of fire, so to speak, to an inanimate sense of the possibilities of nationhood: "The assassination of Wallenstein was for the Germanic world what the massacre of St. Bartholomew had been for the Latin world—the most glaring and blazing of the flashes of lightning which had burst out of the clouds of raison d'état."[132] The histories of Gustavus Adolphus and Wallenstein were arguments about the hope and possibility of German unification that had beckoned through the chaos of civil war. They sought to uncover a German historical continuum, a revolutionary gravitas and vision that revealed the meaning of Germany's long obstructed road to nationhood. But this anxious search for meaning also revealed pessimism about the catastrophic impact of the Thirty Years' War on the German national consciousness. As Germans recalled the story of the war's destruction, a dread of war and dissolution was apparent. The poles of the modern German sense of nationhood, the celebration of sacrifice and the fear of annihilation, are examined in the next two chapters.

4. The Martyrdom of Magdeburg

The German Jerusalem

The nineteenth-century reinterpretations of the origins of the Thirty Years' War and the motivations and aims of Gustavus Adolphus and Wallenstein were stories of triumphs and of grand designs that had failed. In the retelling of the story, and the debates that ensued, these histories looked to the past to find prophecies of a united and powerful Germany. There was, however, a darker side to nineteenth-century Germany's rediscovery of the war. If many of the new studies of the war were driven by a search for possible models for German unification, then the war's destruction, the epic scale of the material and human losses it caused, was reconceived in other narratives as the great test and sacrifice that refined and strengthened the national character and commitment to unity. In the histories of the siege of Magdeburg and the "time of annihilation" (*die Vertilgungszeit*), or the "Swedish War," historians elevated the notion of sacrifice into the founding principle of modern German nationalism.

Magdeburg was besieged, sacked, and burned in May 1631 by Catholic League forces commanded by Johann Tserclaes, Count of Tilly, immortalized as the "papist bloodhound" in Protestant folklore.[1] Even by seventeenth-century standards of conduct, the slaughter was shocking, so it is not surprising that in Protestant histories the destruction of Magdeburg became the defining horror of the Thirty Years' War.[2] In 1853 Otto Schmidt declared that "German freedom arose from Magdeburg's ashes."[3] In the hands of Protestant historians, the story of the city's martyrdom anchored the German national narrative in the context of the chosen people theme, which required exegesis in a plot of divine judgment, sacrifice and eventual redemption. Magdeburg became the "German Jerusalem" in what might be called an "Isaianic" or prophetic mode of historical interpretation that found in the catastrophe of the city's destruction the sacrifice that ensured the long-awaited foundation of a unified German state. Here the "Zion tradition" of the Old Testament narratives of the sufferings of Jerusalem, which foretold the foundation of the nation of Israel, was very prominent.[4] "What Jerusalem was for the old religion, what Rome was for the European church, Magdeburg will be for the German Reformation."[5] Magdeburg's suffering and steadfastness were also made part of a longer history of heroic cities from the biblical and classical canons. The horrors that Magdeburg's citizens endured, particularly the rape and torture of its women, were graphically emphasized to illustrate the greater victimization of Protestant Germany by Catholic tyranny in the war. For Protestant historians, the brutal sack of the city was the greatest single crime of the Thirty Years' War, and its history was recovered and retold to symbolize the profound evil and immorality of the Catholic-imperial cause, raising the "Magdeburg question" to the level of a serious moral, political, and nationalist issue in the nineteenth century. The fierce debate, which lasted more than fifty years, over who was responsible for the slaughter vividly illustrates how collective remembrance of the war was intertwined with anxieties about German national identity and the survival of the nation itself.

In the German historical imagination, the suffering of Magdeburg, as the paradigmatic episode of a horrific civil war, served as an enduring warning of the price paid for German disunity. Over the years the city's story was embellished and elaborated as one of the gospels of Protestant nationalism. A history of the siege written in 1719 related eyewitness accounts of how, just before the city's fall, an "unnatural and great storm wind" sprang up, dogs howled, and the cornices of the buildings on the city's Old Market streamed blood.[6] This oracular and apocalyptic language was common in eighteenth- and nineteenth-century histories of the fall of Magdeburg. More significantly, the city's destruction was frequently compared to that of Jerusalem by Rome in the first century AD. Protestant historians relied heavily on the conventions of biblical narrative to tell this story, particularly those found in the prophetic books of the Old Testament such as Deuteronomy and Isaiah. They traced the fulfillment of the national covenant in a narrative marked by a prolonged cycle of tests that alternated divine punishment for transgression and reward for obedience. Erich Auerbach's classic description of biblical narrative as an "ethically oriented historiography" designed to predict and confirm the unfolding of a divine plan remains probably the best hermeneutic perspective that reveals how German history writing, especially that written by Protestants, found its voice in the nineteenth century.[7]

The destruction of Magdeburg was interpreted from the perspective of this prophetic narrative tradition, which foretold Jerusalem's rebirth in triumph as the capital of the Davidic kingdom and spiritual antipode of pagan tyranny. But the fulfillment of this covenant was always postponed to an indefinite future, even as Jerusalem remained the final destination of a nation in exile that had endured massacre and enslavement as the price of nationhood and a sign of the covenant.[8] What is striking is how Protestant history writing interpreted the fall of Magdeburg as a prophetic event that, even as a defeat, pointed toward triumph in the eventual establishment of a united and triumphant Reich. René Girard's explanation of the plotting of the Old Testament as a cycle of "sacrificial crises" (and its formative influence on Christianity), in which violence and disorder demand sacrificial death to restore order and harmony, illuminates this recurring theme in German histories of the Thirty Years' War.[9] It is clear that the narrative trope of sacrifice was rooted in the models of classical myth and the Bible. This liberating notion of a "triumph in death," which would become essential to Christian martyrdom and modern romanticism, was especially marked in (though by no means exclusive to) German history writing. William Blake memorably appealed to this idea in his 1820 invocation of mystical Anglo-Saxon nationalism, *Jerusalem: The Emanation of the Giant Albion*:

> Such visions have appeared to me
> As I my ordered race have won
> Jerusalem is named liberty
> Among the sons of Albion.[10]

Magdeburg was also explicitly linked to those cities of antiquity, such as Troy, Saguntum, Numancia, and Masada, whose resistance to the imperial power of Greece and Rome later came to symbolize and legitimate the unitary aspirations of Britain, Spain, and Israel.[11] Underscored was the self-sacrifice of the community, preferring death to surrender (especially capitulation to an imperial despotism). One story from antiquity that seemed to have particularly influenced nineteenth-century Magdeburg narratives was that of the siege of Numancia in Iberia in 134 BC. Polybius, Lucilius, and Appian all wrote accounts of the six-year resistance of this mountain city.[12] Miguel de Cervantes's *La Numancia* (1585) was probably the most widely read retelling of this epic. Cervantes made the city symbolic of "lonely and unlucky Spain," whose heroic resistance to Rome foretold the future glory of the united and powerful kingdom under Philip II.[13] Cervantes's play was very popular in Germany between 1800 and 1815, when Napoleonic France dominated Europe. This fact helps explain the striking similarities between the play and nineteenth-century German accounts of the fall of Magdeburg, especially the descriptions of the Numancian women who chose to commit suicide rather than be raped by the Roman soldiers. Many patriotic Germans celebrated the "Gothic-Germanic" spirit of the Spanish war of independence against Napoleon as they endured French invasion and occupation. Fichte and the Schlegels mined the play for patriotic inspiration and praised it for its uplifting picture of tiny Numancia defying the mighty Roman Empire. No fewer than five versions of Cervantes's drama were published in Germany between 1806 and 1813, including an 1810 translation by Friedrich de La Motte-Fouque, a remarkable demonstration of how early German nationalism idealized Spain as the nation of patriotic insurgency.[14] In the nineteenth-century retelling of the destruction of Magdeburg, the heroism of the city was idealized in a similar nationalist context until it became the standard plot for almost every account of a German town that was besieged during the Thirty Years' War.

Magdeburg was used to symbolize the victimization of Protestant Germany at the hands of Catholic tyranny, which was captured in the immortal and evocative image of the violated maiden. Graphic descriptions of the rape and abuse of the town's female population were repeated in a rote and numbing litany of degradation.[15] But this victimization, reimagined as the sign of divine discipline and dispensation, also promised resurrection and renewal. A well-known eighteenth-century collection of pamphlets about the siege has a frontispiece engraving depicting a longhaired woman lying in an open coffin that rests on a bier framed by the rising sun. On her breast she holds a wreath from which springs a tree whose branches are formed by swords, muskets, cannons, and halberds. At the peak of the tree flies a flag. Underneath this picture is the caption "The maiden is not dead, she only sleeps."[16] Narratives of defeat commonly transpose the female body and the national body in order to emphasize national humiliation while inspiring revenge. Rape is the most potent and visceral image by which humiliation and conquest can be symbolized, and the Magdeburg histories exploit this imagery to the full. Within narratives of war, rape can symbolize three basic types of communal or national victimization: defeat, occupation, and racial defilement. Ultimately, the violation of women becomes a metaphor for male anguish at defeat.[17] In more general terms, the "taking" of a city in war is often described as rape, a violent act of possession symbolized in the abuse and torture of its female population. Further, women have long represented the innocent polity and the embodiment of national virtue, ideas we find, for example, in the story of the rape of Lucretia as told by Ovid, Livy, Dio Cassius, and Shakespeare. As a narrative device, rape is made the distinguishing act of the tyrant, and vengeance for the violation (usually through war and retributive atrocity) becomes the founding act of violence that establishes a new nation that is conceived as more virtuous than the tyranny that is being overthrown.[18] Beginning in the nineteenth century, modern rape narratives in histories of war have added a third component to this symbol of national violation: the dread of racial pollution by the invader. Mercenary (and Catholic) Croats, Walloons, Poles, Italians, and Hungarians figured prominently as predators on the women of Magdeburg. In contrast, the German commanders in Tilly's army were almost always depicted as trying to stop the rampage of the "barbarians." It was common for nineteenth-century epic-national literature to identify the rapist as a foreigner bent on sexual violation and impregnation. In its "Christian innocence," the female body came to represent the healthy body politic threatened by political, ideological, racial, and moral contamination. It is worth pointing out that, given the frequent references to the "rape of the maiden" in the Magdeburg histories, in Christian hagiography female martyrs were usually virgins, the virgin body being viewed as the perfect image of wholeness and integrity.[19] By the mid-nineteenth century, however, the legend of the destruction of Magdeburg began to be challenged by Catholic historians who believed that Catholic Germany had been collectively condemned as responsible for the crime and thus marked as enemies within the national community. "Who destroyed Magdeburg?" thus became a very important question in the shaping of German national identity. Catholic historians attempted to exonerate the imperial general Tilly and place the blame on Gustavus Adolphus, the city's Swedish commander, Dietrich von Falkenberg, and most provocatively (from the Protestant point of view) on Magdeburg's citizens themselves. Protestant historians, for the most part, reacted by defending the exclusionary orthodoxy of Catholic responsibility. No other episode of the war provoked such vehement and bitter argument. Why?

Clues can be found in a more recent German debate about another great crime of war. Observing the German historians' debate in the 1980s over the extent to which the murder of the European Jews by Nazi Germany could (or should) be seen as part of the longer continuum of German history, Immanuel Geiss came to the conclusion that the battle over a monopoly of historical interpretation inevitably becomes entangled with profound moral and ideological issues. The reason for this, he suggested, is that the nature of any historical debate about a "great crime" becomes dominated by "dualistic-fundamentalist thinking" that only recognizes good or evil, innocence or guilt.[20] Catholic historians, trying to refute Protestant insistence on Catholic responsibility for Magdeburg, wanted to free German Catholics of a stigma— continually renewed in the collective remembrance of the Thirty Years' War—which marked them as unworthy of German identity.[21] They did this by constructing what Amos Funkenstein has termed a "counter-history," which attacks the adversary's "foundational myth" by distorting (or calling into question) his positive self-image and identity.[22] As analyses of the historiography of the Holocaust have shown, debates over "meaning" are always attended by fears that even scrupulously objective accounts could undermine what was held to be the essential "truth," or moral lesson, of the foundational history.[23] The entire process of assigning responsibility drives the moral passion of any historians' debate. This was as true of the controversy created in 1846 by Albert Heising's *Magdeburg nicht durch Tilly zerstört* (Magdeburg Was Not Destroyed by Tilly) as it was for the furor that followed the publication in 1986 of Ernst Nolte's article "The Past That Will Not Pass," in which he suggested that the burden of guilt for the crimes of the Third Reich was inhibiting Germany's return to a "normal" history. One hundred and forty years apart, these two controversies reveal the existence of what Charles Maier has called the "plurality of truths" within the divided German historical consciousness. Both debates, as battles over the representation of a defining historical episode, arose from profound disagreement over the historical legitimation of national identity.[24]

For Protestants the destruction of Magdeburg, the "German Jerusalem," represented the ultimate sacrifice in defense of the true faith that promised nationhood, redemption in the Promised Land. It was the compelling power of this belief that made Magdeburg such a provocative issue as the Protestant and Catholic narratives of the Thirty Years' War clashed in the nineteenth century. But one must still ask, what circumstances allowed the confessional polemics of the seventeenth century to be resurrected in the nineteenth? Modern research methods and standards of evidence enabled a reappraisal of the contemporary accounts of the siege, and new archival work in the second half of the century uncovered previously unknown "eyewitness" reports (whose authenticity was always ferociously debated). The nineteenth-century advent of "scientific" evidence-based history gave Catholic historians the opportunity to legitimately question the Protestant version of the destruction of Magdeburg (or so they thought). From their point of view, an increasingly militant and exclusionary Protestant nationalism made it imperative that Catholic historians find a way to subvert the legend of Magdeburg, which, more than any other story of the Thirty Years'

War, perpetuated the "German/Un-German" dichotomy at the heart of the Protestant-Catholic divide. The debate over Magdeburg emerged out of the violent collision of two collective remembrances of the war, or what Henry Rousso calls "vectors of memory," during a moment in the nineteenth century when Germans were becoming keenly aware of how history established (and marginalized) national loyalties, identities, and patriotic values.[25]

During the first half of the nineteenth century, the historiography of the destruction of Magdeburg focused on the city as a symbol of Protestant German liberty and the martyrdom the city suffered as a consequence of its resistance to "Roman" tyranny. As shown in chapter 2, this theme, which was celebrated in the commemorations of the siege in 1831, was also prominent in the later commemorations of Breitenfeld and Gustavus Adolphus's death at Lützen. It also reflected the suppression in the 1830s of a more open and explicit discussion about the constitutional modernization of Germany. Magdeburg was transformed into the "heroic city" of Protestant nationalism, and its suffering was offered up as a demonstration of Germany's sacrifice for independence from the tyranny of a Catholic empire. The first phase of the debate over who destroyed Magdeburg, spanning the 1840s and 1850s, was ignited by the work of the Catholic revisionists Albert Heising and Onno Klopp, who attempted to undermine the foundation of the Protestant tradition by restoring Tilly's reputation. Refuting the tradition of the Catholic arsonist and murderer (*Mordbrenner*), Catholic historians attempted to place the blame for the city's destruction on the cold-blooded calculations of the Swedish invader, Gustavus Adolphus. By challenging the popular legend of Tilly's "guilt" (and indicting Gustavus Adolphus), they tried to discredit the idea of the city's martyrdom that did so much to buttress Protestant nationalism. The second phase, which manifested itself as a largely internecine Protestant quarrel, began in 1863 with Gustav Droysen's reexamination of the documents of the case. Droysen's judgment was that the answer to the central question of who destroyed Magdeburg must remain inconclusive. This determination, however, was resisted by many who refused to abandon the nationalist symbolism of Magdeburg's sacrifice. Another thirty years of passionate argument ensued among the Protestant "Magdeburg historians" Karl Wittich, Max Dittmar, and Robert Volkholz when Wittich, who speculated that the city had been deliberately set on fire by its own citizens to deny it to the enemy, attempted to recast the tradition as a simple and classical "nationalist" epic.

The Rape of the Maiden

The tale of the destruction of Magdeburg, and the singular horror of its trial by fire, was firmly established in German historical tradition by the end of the eighteenth century. Accounts of the siege dwelt unrestrainedly on the unparalleled sadism of the city's martyrdom with graphic (and nauseating) descriptions of the tortures inflicted on the citizens by the rampaging Croats and Walloons of the Catholic League commanders Tilly and Pappenheim. Until well into the nineteenth century, the orthodoxy concerning the sack of Magdeburg traced its genealogy back to a work of French anti-imperial propaganda that was first published in Geneva in 1633: The Swedish Soldier by Friedrich Spanheim (1600–1649). It was properly regarded as part of the pamphlet campaign to mobilize Protestant opinion after the fall of Magdeburg, and the ubiquity of Spanheim's book as a source for nineteenth-century historians was a major irritant that provoked Catholic counterhistories in the 1830s. In his widely cited history of the war that appeared in 1791, Johann Georg Galletti took his account of the siege from the standard life of Gustavus Adolphus by the English clergyman Walter Harte (1709–74), who had relied on Spanheim and the contemporaneous Swedish histories of Chemnitz and Pufendorf.[26] Galletti, a Protestant, prefaced his tale with the observation that "the fate of Magdeburg belonged to the most terrible and tragic scenes of the Thirty Years' War" before plunging into the standard description of the Croats decapitating thirty-five women in the Katherinenkirche, murdering pregnant women, hacking children in two, and impaling women on pikes after raping them. To avoid this fate, Galletti noted (invoking the Numancia legend) that many women threw themselves into the Elbe and drowned. "For three days the ruins echoed with the cries of the children looking for their parents and parents searching for their children. Some sat wailing in the blood of their dead parents. Suckling infants lay on the breasts of their dead mothers. . . . In modern times no other city has suffered a fate like Magdeburg's."[27] Galletti's description, as well as Schiller's, bears a striking resemblance to Henry V's speech outside the walls of Harfleur threatening the town with "heady murder, spoil, and villainy" if it did not surrender. There can be little doubt that Harte would be familiar with Shakespeare's famous paean to the cruelty of war in act 3 of *King Henry V*.[28]

But for nineteenth-century German readers it was Friedrich Schiller's history of the Thirty Years' War that created the popular legend of the destruction of Magdeburg. Schiller relied heavily on Harte and Galletti for his description of the sack of Magdeburg. His vivid descriptions of imperial brutality (establishing the canonical figure of thirty thousand dead) were responsible for perpetuating the memory of the destruction in the nineteenth-century German historical imagination. Schiller, writing for a women's periodical (Historical Almanac for Ladies for 1791–1793, where his history of the war originally appeared), lingered over the sexual depredations of the "barbarous" Croats and Walloons: "The butchery began and the craft of the historian and the art of the poet can find no language to describe it. Neither the innocence of childhood nor the infirmity of age, neither youth, sex, rank, nor beauty could deflect the fury of the conquerors. Women were brutalized in the arms of their husbands and daughters at the feet of their fathers. The weaker sex was exposed to the double sacrifice of their virtue and their lives to the rapacity of the victors."[29] Schiller employed the history of the Thirty Years' War in general and that of Magdeburg in particular to illustrate an episode in the German war of independence against the tyranny of Rome. His narrative of the war quickly became a key part of the basic patriotic lore of Protestant Germany. He had many imitators, such as Friedrich Ludwig Schmidt, who hoped his 1799 play about Magdeburg, inspired by Schiller's history, would "set aflame the love of Fatherland."[30] In challenging Schiller's version of Magdeburg, Catholic historians contended not only with the popularity of Schiller's histories among the educated classes. They also confronted the folklore of the cruelty of Tilly's soldiers in the Thirty Years' War at Magdeburg and during the campaigns of the Catholic League in the Lower Palatinate and Lower Silesia between 1619 and 1624, which had deep roots in the collective memory of nineteenth-century Germany. Every spring, during Whitsuntide, the town of Rothenburg ob der Tauber celebrated (as it does to this day) its deliverance from the wrath of Tilly, the grim conqueror of Magdeburg, that "small, lean, gaunt man with the pale sunken cheeks." In the 1880s the commemoration included a parade in historical costume, representing the combatants, and a reenactment of the Meistertrank, the ritual libation with which Tilly agreed to spare the town.[31] This kind of collective remembrance only reinforced the impact of Schiller: "those scenes of horror which, through Schiller's masterful descriptions, even today live vividly in the memory of the German people."[32]

Lorenz von Westenrieder, the first Catholic historian to challenge Protestant orthodoxy regarding Gustavus Adolphus, also wrote a counterhistory of the siege of Magdeburg that attacked the other gospel of Protestant nationalism. Proposing that the responsibility for the catastrophe belonged to the Swedish king, Westenrieder reasoned that, for strategic considerations alone, it was to Tilly's advantage to take the town intact: "No one had more reason than Tilly to regret the loss of the city."[33] It is important to remember that for Bavarian patriots Tilly was a hero (he is one of the commanders immortalized in the Feldherrnhalle in Munich). Westenrieder insisted that, in contrast to Wallenstein (of whom he had a very low opinion), Tilly was a devout Catholic and a "fair, restrained, and just man." Westenrieder believed that the fire that destroyed the city was started by accident: "Such a deed lay neither in Tilly's character nor in the facts. . . . The misfortune of Magdeburg was actually arranged by the King of Sweden who, as he established himself in Mecklenburg and Brandenburg, endeavored to keep Tilly at a distance and secure his position in Lower Saxony."[34] Westenrieder's first priority was to defend the honor of a hero from Bavarian history at a time when the kingdom's independence was threatened by Napoleonic France's domination of western Europe.[35] His second concern was to rally support for Austrian leadership in the struggle against Napoleon by recalling the example of the Catholic League.

Westenrieder's counterhistory was a solitary voice that was all but drowned out by the German nationalism emerging in this period. The histories of the destruction of Magdeburg that followed Schiller in the first half of the nineteenth century reflected the new national feeling. Their self-conscious patriotism mourned the broken covenant of 1813 that had briefly promised German liberty and unity. Sharing the romantic pathos found in the "liberation verse" (*Befreiungs-Lyrik*) of Schenkendorf, Körner, and Arndt and in the patriotic poetry of their successors, Ewald von Kleist, Uhland, and La Motte-Fouque, they celebrated the liberal idea of the unified nation-state as well as more conservative notions of political and moral renewal through war.[36] Their idealization of patriotic sacrifice, drawing on the older tradition of seventeenth-century war poetry (*Kriegsdichtung*), made explicit the connection between Gustavus Adolphus's War of Protestant Liberation between 1630 and 1632 and the Wars of Liberation against Napoleon between 1813 and 1814. Within this tradition, a young clergyman and poet from Halberstadt, Johann Karl August Rese (1783–1847), wrote one of the most powerful depictions of the destruction of Magdeburg to come out of the Napoleonic occupation. Rese was a minor poet of the "Halberstadt School" who spent his career in the ministry after leaving university at Halle. It was in Halle that Rese probably came under the influence of Johann Wilhelm Gleim, a widely read war poet whose main theme was the rise of Prussia under Frederick the Great.[37] As representatives of the genre, Gleim's famous "Grenadier Songs" were explicitly prophetic, apocalyptic, and idealistic as they adopted Schiller's emancipatory "death to tyrants" message. The vocabularies of martyrdom, sacrifice, and the Passion of Christ were all employed in the various portrayals of Magdeburg's suffering, making them important examples of what Gerhard Kaiser has called the "patriotic cult of blood and gore" that characterized German nationalist literature in the early nineteenth century.[38]

Rese began "The Destruction of Magdeburg by Tilly" with a standard classical reference that compared Magdeburg's fate with that of Troy and Tyre, the latter's fall having figured prominently in Isaianic prophetic allegories of destruction and rebirth.[39] He declared the patriotic story of Magdeburg the exception to the rule of anonymity that shrouded the stories of most towns that suffered in the Thirty Years' War: "The fate of this republican city as it fought for religion and freedom is of immortal value." For Rese, the French occupation of the German states drove home the main lesson of Magdeburg for nineteenth-century Germans who wanted to live in a unified nation-state: the city had fallen because it had neglected its defenses and had been fatally weakened by class divisions, treachery, and selfish individualism. Nevertheless, Rese believed that the city's resistance had demonstrated the "spirit of republican pride" and should be regarded by all patriotic Germans as "the model of noble and heroic struggle for religion and freedom."[40] Rese's graphic description of the rape and torture of Magdeburg's female population exceeded Schiller in luridness, with the addition of a detail that can be found consistently in all subsequent narratives of the sufferings of Germany's towns during the Thirty Years' War:

> The women of the town were the object of a twin fury: they were shamed on the streets before the eyes of their husbands and fathers. Then they were cruelly murdered, or tortured, bound and sold to be subjected to the lusts of the shameless barbarians. Ten- and twelve-year-old girls were raped. A woman of noble birth, after being raped by eight Croats, was impaled on a spike and displayed like a tavern sign from the window of a house. Another officer had three young girls, sisters of noble blood, sacrificed to his lusts. After he was finished, they were sent to the imperial camp to satisfy the hordes of Croats.

Many, Rese noted (adhering closely to the Numancia legend and Galletti), threw themselves off roofs, into the flames, or into the Elbe to avoid being raped. After this exhaustive (and almost pornographic) exposition, the modest clergyman pleaded, "I must abstain from mentioning any more of these monstrous outrages."[41] On the anniversary of the siege on Sunday, May 10, 1812, readers of the *Herald* in Nuremberg were treated to a similarly graphic description by the military historian Gottfried Becker (1778–1854): "The citizens were outnumbered twenty to one. . . . The streets were full of bodies. . . . Children suckled blood from their dead mothers' breasts. . . . The Croats gathered fifty women in a church. They kneeled and begged for their lives with upraised hands. They were answered with the swords that split their heads."[42] To classical symbols of tyranny and resistance and the biblical themes of sacrifice and martyrdom, Rese and Becker added a more modern dread of sexual defilement at the hands of the barbaric foreign invader.

In the histories of the Thirty Years' War written between 1830 and 1848, and especially in the commemorative literature about the siege that appeared in 1831, the destruction of Magdeburg symbolized Protestant Germany's sacrifice for the cause of unity and independence. These histories, as did other accounts of "heroic cities" in the war, saw the city's resistance as a defiant last stand against a foreign despotism. If Gustavus Adolphus was the great hero of the Protestant War of Liberation, then Magdeburg was its consecrated battleground. Using the classical narrative of the siege of Numancia as a model, Protestant historians celebrated Magdeburg's resistance (and the Protestant cause in the Thirty Years' War in general) as a legitimate uprising against a tyrannical empire.[43] After 1815 suppressed revolutionary (and nationalist) ideas undoubtedly influenced the transformation of Magdeburg into a symbol of the republican ideals of popular sovereignty and liberty, equality, and fraternity.[44] Following Rese, some accounts of the siege from the 1840s described a class conflict between rich and poor within the city in which the wealthier citizens avoided their military obligations and the poor were forced into the most dangerous duty, a situation that reportedly caused great resentment and disaffection among the townspeople.[45] Otto Schmidt's conviction that "German freedom rose out of Magdeburg's ashes" was as closely connected to the tradition of the inviolable civil freedoms that were the city's medieval legacy as it was to the notion that Magdeburg fell, as Wilhelm Bötticher wrote in 1845, "as a great sacrifice for the cause of the Reformation and for all Protestants, and indeed for the civil and religious freedom of Germany!"[46]

Juxtaposing defeat and triumph and resistance and humiliation, the nineteenth-century epics of Magdeburg's martyrdom confirmed the dualism of suffering and rebirth, the belief in regeneration through violence, within modern German nationalist thinking and history writing. These perspectives contributed significantly to the way the history of the siege was depicted in the first half of the nineteenth century. "I am the way into the doleful city, / I am the way into eternal grief, / I am the way to a forsaken race."[47] These are the first lines of the warning the pilgrim Dante saw inscribed above the gates of Hell. Jacob Burckhardt chose the verse as the epigraph for his History of Greek Civilization, Ulrich Raulff believes, out of the conviction that the Greeks had suffered more than any other nation and thus bequeathed to western history writing (and the German variant in particular) a fascination with horror and cruelty.[48] This observation helps explain the appeal of the symbolism of Magdeburg to the German historical consciousness. Like Jerusalem in the Book of Lamentations—"Enemies have stretched their hands over all her precious things; she has even seen the nations invade her sanctuary, those whom you forbade to enter your congregation"— Magdeburg's fall foretold the enslavement of a people and the dissolution of a nation.[49] At their most fundamental level, the Magdeburg histories were an attempt to extract meaning from suffering and defeat in prophecies of German unification. They were written in the style of a Passion play that became the center of the entire Protestant narrative of the Thirty Years' War (and that Catholic historians were so anxious to refute). It was the story at the heart of the German national consciousness, the sacrifice demanded to fulfill the national covenant. Equally important to this narrative was the idea that the city's destruction was a sacrifice of the elect that branded Catholics as unworthy of membership in the German nation. In accordance with the prophecies of the Jerusalem tradition, the rod of God's anger could only be directed at His chosen people, who were anointed to rule only after being tested by Providence.

Who Destroyed Magdeburg?

As in the propagation of the cult of Gustavus Adolphus, Magdeburg's symbolic sacrifice was embellished by historians to legitimate the chosen people theme in an emergent Protestant nationalism. Building the foundation of a Protestant national narrative and securing the ascendancy of the Prussian–North German idea of a unified Germany required an emphasis on confessional identity as the essential criterion of national allegiance. As shown in chapter 1, Protestant historians' insistence that the Thirty Years' War was fundamentally a religious war arose from the conviction that German unification was originally covenanted in the revolt against Rome in 1517. Rejecting the legitimacy of the Catholic idea of the German nation (the unitary imperial vision of 1629–30) also buttressed the advocacy of Prussian-led German unification and the continuation of Protestant political-cultural hegemony. Magdeburg history (as a fundamentally Protestant project) burdened Catholic Germans with the collective responsibility for a terrible crime that would forever mark them as unworthy of full membership in the German national community. Ultimately, this was the central issue of the historians' debate over Magdeburg. Unlike the debate over the apotheosis of Gustavus Adolphus and his vision of a unified Germany, which gradually lost momentum after 1871, the dispute over the Magdeburg question was characterized by a steady level of mutual vilification until the end of the century. Why? Ultimately, the definition of German national identity was at stake in the Magdeburg debate.

Catholic historians attempted to remove the mark of Cain from their community by restoring the reputation of Tilly, the leader of the army that had besieged Magdeburg. This project of historical rehabilitation proposed alternative theories that explained Magdeburg's destruction, beginning with the work of Karl Menzel, Johann Mailath, and Albert Heising between 1839 and 1846 and culminating in the controversy generated by the publication of Onno Klopp's magnum opus on Tilly in 1861. These revisionist histories called into question the historical basis of the legend of Magdeburg, specifically the story of the city's sacrifice for German freedom. Led by this quartet, Catholic historians pursued four main lines of attack against Protestant orthodoxy. The first was to exonerate Tilly (and his *German* Catholic soldiers) by blaming Pappenheim and his Croat soldiers for starting the fires that destroyed the city. The second was to accuse the city's Swedish commander, Dietrich von Falkenberg, of deliberately planning Magdeburg's destruction to deny the city to the victors (this claim had the additional advantage of impugning the motives of Gustavus Adolphus). The third was to maintain that internal division and loyalty to the empire allowed the imperial forces to breach the defenses. The fourth stratagem, and the most provocative, was to accuse the citizens themselves of setting the fires and planting the explosives that destroyed the city. In short, foreigners or Protestant zealots within the city destroyed Magdeburg, not the German soldiers of the Catholic League. The modern debate over who was responsible for the atrocity of Magdeburg was, in a sense, a continuation of the pamphlet campaigns of the seventeenth century that used Magdeburg for propaganda in the German civil war.[50] In the nineteenth century these pamphlets were reconsidered as eyewitness reports. As a result, they became the source of heated debates over their veracity and authenticity. Almost to a man, Protestant historians dismissed imperial accounts of the siege as self-evidently exculpatory and therefore completely untrustworthy. For their part, Catholic historians accused their Protestant opposition of rejecting any evidence that did not basically confirm Schiller's version of the massacre. This modern "pamphlet war" revealed a peculiar characteristic of nineteenth-century history writing in Germany: the belief that history itself was a sort of cosmic tribunal and that historians must approach their task as jurists arguing on behalf of plaintiffs and defendants. As one late-nineteenth-century observer of the debate recalled, the goal "was not so much to ascertain the true causes of the destruction as it was to free their religious compatriots, who had witnessed the catastrophe, from any judgment of guilt, while at the same time bringing an indictment against those of the opposing faith."[51] These indictments were based on a fairly limited number of documents purportedly written by witnesses to the events of the siege and its immediate aftermath. Their authenticity was usually challenged on three main points: whether the author was truly an eyewitness; whether the account in question was actually composed with events fresh in the mind of the observer; and whether and to what extent these accounts were based on dubious thirdhand descriptions of the siege. Document by document, the witnesses took the stand and were thoroughly examined and cross-examined. Two narratives were put before the tribunal of history with the expectation that one would be condemned as "false" and the other vindicated as "true" and, further, that this judgment would confirm the foundations on which German national identity rested.

Very little new documentation was uncovered during the first decade of the debate. New discoveries in the archives usually took the form of alternative manuscript versions gathered by Calvisius in a volume published in Magdeburg in 1727. This collection of Protestant testimonies was the main resource of Catholic historians attempting to discredit the Protestant horror story of Tilly the Mordbrenner. The reports in Calvisius were presented as eyewitness accounts of the final phase of the siege in which a massive fire, allegedly started by Pappenheim's Croats when they broke into the city's northern quarter, engulfed the entire city. Also included were Tilly's report to Maximilian in Munich and a few accounts that alluded to the possibility that Magdeburg's defenders had set the fires. But it is important to remember that the guilt or innocence of Tilly was not an important issue in the early eighteenth century. Calvisius was chiefly concerned with putting together an anthology that would serve as a patriotic memorial to the sufferings of his hometown. Two other sources figured prominently in the debate: the 1631 diary of Zacharias Bandhauer and the *Florus Germanicus* (1643) by Eberhard Wassenberg, which described how the defenders had planted explosives and started fires on Falkenberg's orders. Catholic historians also frequently cited Johann Mailath's research in the military archives in Vienna because Mailath claimed to have discovered new evidence of the factionalism that divided the city's leadership during the siege. Protestant defenders of the honor of Magdeburg, on the other hand, were for a long time dependent on the secondary Swedish and French accounts of Spanheim, Pufendorf, and Chemnitz. They also cited contemporary accounts collected in the *Theatrum Europaeum* (1662–1778), based almost entirely on Swedish and French sources. Franz Khevenhüller's (1588–1650) *Annales Ferdinandei*, a Catholic source and imperial apologia that distanced the Habsburgs from Tilly and the Catholic League, was, as might be imagined, a frequently cited source for Protestant historians.[52]

Karl Menzel, provocative as always, was one of the first to recognize what he called the "moral importance" of the Magdeburg question. A definitive answer, he believed, would have serious implications for Protestant Germany's moral claims to leadership in the struggle for German independence and unity. In his 1839 history of the Thirty Years' War, Menzel questioned the conventional condemnation of Tilly, noted the factionalism within the city's council, and suggested that Gustavus Adolphus may have callously left Magdeburg to its fate as an object lesson to intimidate Brandenburg and Saxony into openly supporting Sweden.[53] Menzel's argument, essentially a restatement of Westenrieder's doubts, inspired a vigorous Catholic attack on the legend of Magdeburg's martyrdom. An article in the *HpB* in 1839 (probably written by Albert Heising) eagerly embraced Menzel's speculation that "instead of an army, only a Swedish officer was sent" to recapitulate the reports in Calvisius that mines had been laid on Falkenberg's orders and that he had also set the fires to deny the city to the enemy.[54] Falkenberg's personal history and motivations were a compelling mystery at the center of the Magdeburg debate. There was some confusion about his true identity. One historian speculated that Falkenberg had reason to believe that a "Judas" had sold exact intelligence regarding Magdeburg's defenses to Tilly. Another claimed that once Falkenberg heard about this betrayal, he immediately ordered that fires be set to deny the city to the enemy, only to be murdered by traitors shortly thereafter.[55] Some conspiracy theorists claimed that he was a Catholic secret agent whose brother, also in the pay of the Habsburgs, was the assassin responsible for Gustavus Adolphus's murder at Lützen.[56] Among Protestants Falkenberg's shadowy history did raise the unsettling possibility that Swedish strategic considerations, not religious solidarity, had been the real reason for Magdeburg's sacrifice. That the city's citizens might have been responsible for the crime was only slightly less mortifying than the suggestion that a foreigner (or worse, a German in foreign service) might have orchestrated the whole thing. The Hungarian chronicler of the Habsburg imperial state, Johann Mailath (1786–1855), was the first historian to analyze new archival sources in addressing the possibility that Swedish intrigues might have been behind Magdeburg's destruction. Trying to prove that Tilly had attempted in good faith to negotiate the city's surrender, Mailath offered new evidence in 1842 from the imperial military archives on the factionalism within the city. He claimed that the majority of the populace was indeed loyal to, or had no particular quarrel with, the empire and had been pushed into a hopeless resistance by the sermons of a fanatical and politicized Protestant clergy. According to Mailath's scenario, the mysterious Falkenberg was the "discreet adventurer" and agent provocateur behind the divisions within the city's leadership.[57]

In 1846 the amateur historian Albert Heising synthesized previous Catholic critiques of partisan Protestant history writing in his incendiary book *Magdeburg nicht durch Tilly zerstört* (Magdeburg Was Not Destroyed by Tilly). A sustained attack on the Schiller tradition and the myth of Protestant unity and Catholic tyranny, Heising's broadside was a challenge by a committed German Catholic to the Protestant monopoly on German patriotism. His counterhistory struck a nerve among Germany's Protestant intelligentsia and marked the real beginning of the debate on the Magdeburg question. Heising, conscious of the threat that a militant Protestant nationalism posed to the continued existence of the German Confederation (and Catholic status within it), focused on the issue of factionalism within Magdeburg that Menzel and Mailath had originally raised. He claimed that fanatical and irresponsible members of the city council, abetted by the sermons of a "revolutionary" clergy (here recapitulating the legitimist arguments of Hurter and Klopp), persuaded Magdeburg's citizens to ally themselves with Sweden by appealing to religious hatred. According to Heising, a group of zealots, representing a majority on the Magdeburg city council since 1629, incited a reluctant city to rebellion against its constitution and emperor.[58] Instead of the traditional image of the united, heroic city, Heising's counterhistory of the opening maneuvers and the siege presented a damning picture of Magdeburg as an unwilling victim of religious fanaticism, revolutionary propaganda, and cold-blooded strategic calculation: "Despite the stories repeated a thousand times, from book to book and from mouth to mouth, up to this point Magdeburg had suffered like a thousand other towns. . . . The city had been led into error by fanatical preachers, inflamed by militant parties, divided by factions, betrayed by its own citizens, and forsaken by a king who had promised to help."[59]

Frustrated with a partisan historical tradition that, "for two hundred years, had branded Tilly an Alaric, an Attila, and a Genghis Khan," Heising complained that the true story of an event in which the Protestant side had such a clear interest in manipulating for propaganda purposes would be hard to establish: "As long as Schiller's history of the war remains the standard text for Germans, the history of Germany will always dishonor itself."[60] Nevertheless, his interpretation of contemporary eyewitness accounts concluded that Magdeburg's own citizens had intentionally destroyed their city under the leadership of Falkenberg. Moreover, Heising's counterhistory provoked Protestants by suggesting that there was "political advantage in martyrdom" because the city could demand restitution at the peace table in the form of the restoration of its traditional imperial liberties.[61] The first direct Protestant response to Heising predictably disputed his "Jesuit lies" and vigorously denied his claims of factionalism or indeed any interpretation that blamed Gustavus Adolphus, Falkenberg, or Magdeburg's citizens for the disaster. One of his critics, Wilhelm Hoffmann, was the head librarian at Magdeburg's city library. Hoffmann, in a determined bid to regain the moral high ground in this debate, resorted to the most graphic accounts yet of the Catholic atrocities as he described scenes of drunken necrophilia featuring the "cannibalistic Croats." Heising was unimpressed with this hair-raising tale, although he did profess sympathy for Hoffmann's attempt to "rescue the laurels of martyrdom that the city had worn for two hundred years; but a Magdeburger's personal feelings lead to bad history, as everyone knows."[62] The Catholic response in the *HpB* to Heising's thesis was enthusiastic and full of praise for Heising as the successor to Menzel and Gfrörer as the champion of truth against Protestant lies based on Schiller: "It had been some twenty years since German history writing, in dealing with German history since the Reformation, started to reject the lie-filled tradition of the seventeenth and eighteen centuries and started to rely on genuine sources." The review concluded that "a nation whose ruling classes receive such an education is scarcely fit to play a role in the world."[63]

Onno Klopp took up the torch as truth-teller from Heising. Klopp's life work, the rehabilitation of Tilly, shared Heising's concern that the Schiller tradition, deeply rooted in Protestant history writing and forever linking Tilly and Magdeburg, remained the most formidable obstacle to reclaiming a place for the Catholic narrative in a national German history: "There has been no other German work of history that has been so widely read than this [Schiller's] picture of the Thirty Years' War, in which truth and fiction are inextricably entwined in a motley web [*bunten Gewebe*]. . . . Above all, it is the ingrained tradition about the nature and manner of the destruction [of Magdeburg] that is the culmination of the delusion that the Thirty Years' War was a religious war. We must first rid ourselves of this delusion if confessional peace is to be restored among Germans."[64] Klopp obviously believed that a revisionist history of Magdeburg was urgently required and not only to rescue the honor of Tilly or to demonstrate the legitimist argument concerning the war's origins. A persuasive counterhistory of the destruction of Magdeburg would also cast doubt on Gustavus Adolphus's motives and thereby undermine the foundations of a story central to the claims of Protestant nationalism. Klopp further elaborated on Heising's account of factionalism within the city. By linking Magdeburg's internal feuds to the issues he believed central to the war's origins in Bohemia, Klopp offered another example of the betrayal of the people's interests by an absolutist nobility. His story of a city betrayed by a foreign king's machinations and divided between imperial loyalists and a treasonous "Swedish faction" overturned the Protestant-nationalist symbolism of Magdeburg history.

Klopp's claim that the Habsburg-led Holy Roman Empire and its legitimate (if denatured) successor, the German Confederation, constituted Germany's best defense against the establishment of Prussian absolutist despotism got a sympathetic hearing from the radical nationalist historian Heinrich Bensen (1798–1863). Bensen asserted that the meaning of Magdeburg for the nineteenth century was that it symbolized all of the divisions within Germany that still persisted after two centuries: Protestant versus Catholic, progress versus superstition, corporative rights versus absolutism, and territorial sovereignty versus imperial authority. Bensen condemned what he called "Magdeburg history" as an "illusion that is ritually worn as a fetish of worship and abomination" that perpetuated these divisions and prevented the creation of a truly "national" history.[65]

Klopp found this illusion useful because it gave traction to his argument that the Holy Roman Empire, not the princes or the nobility, had Germany's best interests at heart. During the winter of 1860–61, the *HpB* congratulated itself as it offered its readers the views of a "Protestant historian" on the so-called Magdeburg question. In this two-part article, Klopp outlined the themes he would eventually take up at much greater length in his massive work on Tilly. Using the Bandhauer diary and the reports in Calvisius, Klopp introduced his argument by portraying the division within Magdeburg's council as running not, as traditional historiography had it, between Lutheran and Catholic but between a "democratic" party of imperial loyalists (*Kaisertreue*) and an "aristocratic" faction that conspired with foreign powers in defiance of the "national feeling" of the inhabitants: "It was Germany itself, the empire, the nation, whose fate was decided within the walls of Magdeburg."[66] Klopp believed that the "monstrous strategy" of Gustavus Adolphus began with the arrival of the "mercenary" Falkenberg and that the Swedish king's plan had two overriding aims: first, Saxony and Brandenburg had to be intimidated into maintaining their support for the Protestant cause, and second, the fires of religious war had to be stoked to mobilize German public opinion behind Swedish intervention. For Gustavus Adolphus, Klopp asserted, the destruction of Magdeburg served both purposes perfectly. However, it was not enough that the city simply be taken or allowed to surrender; it had to be taken, according to Klopp, "with blood and horror." In short, the city was valuable to Gustavus Adolphus only if it were utterly destroyed. Klopp outlined the details of this conspiracy as follows: first, Falkenberg was ordered to ensure that the city's defenses were deliberately neglected, which meant, among other things, holding back a sufficient supply of powder for demolitions; second, bombs made from this "missing" powder were to be planted at strategic locations throughout the city, while the munitions in the arsenal on the Old Market in the city center were to be prepared for demolition when the city's fall was imminent; third, "fanatical" preachers, continually advocating rebellion against the emperor, were to dissuade the citizens from any thought of negotiation; and fourth, once Magdeburg had been reduced to ashes, the

"Swedish-theological" propaganda machine would spring into action, singling out Tilly as the author of the catastrophe.[67] Klopp's counterhistory claimed that Magdeburg had been chosen by Gustavus Adolphus and Protestant zealots as the German city to be sacrificed in order to fan the flames of a religious war: "Thus can be seen how the architect of the misery and lamentations of Germany so carefully planned his every step in advance."[68]

Klopp's two-volume *Tilly im dreißigjährigen Kriege* (Tilly in the Thirty Years' War) (1861), a revisionist history of the Counter-Reformation and the origins of the Thirty Years' War, centered on the destruction of Magdeburg. It added layer upon layer of justification of the Catholic confederal-imperial vision to the narrative of the city's immolation that he had developed in earlier articles. By 1891 his Tilly book had expanded into a massive four-volume second edition titled *Der dreißigjährigen Krieg biz zum Tode Gustav Adolf* (The Thirty Years' War up to the Death of Gustavus Adolphus in 1632) (1891). Klopp's basic argument never changed: Tilly was innocent and the martyrdom of Magdeburg was a Protestant lie perpetuated over two centuries in order to deny Germany's Catholics their rightful place in the national community. The true guilty party was Gustavus Adolphus, who, knowing that Magdeburgers and Germans yearned for peace and reconciliation, cynically resolved that, as Klopp reconstructed his thinking, "the fanaticism that was not there must be created and incited," in order that the city could be offered "as a sacrifice for the religious war. . . . [and] should become the torch which would ignite and proclaim the religious war, which hitherto had not moved the German people." Klopp's speculations confirmed his notoriety in Protestant eyes because it directly blamed "the savior of Protestantism" for the destruction of Magdeburg. Jacob Venedey, a liberal participant in the revolution of 1848 who had no great affection for Prussia, accused Klopp of trying to "make water flow uphill" in a desperate attempt to deny the essential fact that Rome, through the Habsburg Counter-Reformation, had tried to destroy Germany (a project Venedey believed continued to be pursued in the nineteenth century). Julius Opel was more restrained: "When the author whitewashes the situation at the beginning of the great struggle with a few threadbare political slogans, it becomes apparent that he is offering the book as a political pamphlet for our time."[69]

The Catholic counterhistories of Magdeburg ignited a debate that, given further stimulus by the Kulturkampf, raged well into the 1890s. By challenging the Schiller tradition of Magdeburg's sacrifice, the revisionists not only exonerated Tilly but also undermined the legend of Gustavus Adolphus and the entire narrative of the War of Protestant Liberation. If the destruction of Magdeburg could be proven a Protestant deed, then Protestant Germany's claims to be a chosen people (and the "true" Germans) became untenable. Therefore, it was fitting that the Protestant counterattack against the new histories of Magdeburg was initiated by Gustav Droysen, the biographer of Gustavus Adolphus and a member of the second generation of the statist "Prussian School" of political history.[70] After Droysen completed his doctoral studies in Göttingen with Georg Waitz, one of his first publications was a detailed critique of the revisionists' interpretations of the source material available on Magdeburg that appeared in the journal *Research on German History* in 1863. Droysen dismissed what he considered the partisan aims of Klopp and his predecessors by asserting an obligation to refocus the argument about sources on an analysis of their reliability as eyewitness accounts.[71] Droysen met the arguments of the Catholic historians with that by now familiar Protestant contempt for the "backwardness" and "fanaticism" of Catholic historians, while strongly implying that empirical rigor was a Protestant virtue and that dilettantism was a Catholic vice. Given this widespread intellectual prejudice, it is easy to see how Catholic revisionism became a form of cultural resistance that challenged the Prussian triumphalism of the 1860s and 1870s.[72] During the Kulturkampf in particular, this Protestant view of Catholic intellectual backwardness was couched in accusations of "ultramontane fanaticism" that questioned Catholic political loyalties. If the commitment of Catholic historians to the modern German national idea was in doubt, it followed that their willingness to recognize the imperatives and scholarly conventions of a nationally oriented and scientific historiography was open to question. As the nineteenth century came to a close, Protestant critiques of Catholic and other anti-Prussian counterhistories of the destruction of Magdeburg increasingly concentrated on what was considered methodological error. The "self-sufficient empiricism" of the Prussian School, to use Georg von Below's phrase, that emerged out of Protestant history writing after 1871 saw the documented historical event, objectively considered, as revealing the necessary and rational evolution of the German nation-state under Prussian leadership.[73] Any narrative that worked against the demonstration of this imperative was condemned by its own conclusions as false, subversive, and antithetical to a nationalist history of Germany. From this perspective Gustav Droysen briskly rejected as "untrustworthy," "aphoristic," "derivative," "trivial," and "subjective" the main documents that Heising and Klopp had cited from Calvisius to make the Catholic case. Droysen's main objection was that none of the accounts in Calvisius could be authoritatively demonstrated to have come from an eyewitness present at all of the key events of the siege of Magdeburg. Droysen concluded that the essential fact in the case, that Tilly's lieutenant Pappenheim had set some fires to break resistance at Magdeburg's northern gate, remained unaltered. In his opinion there was no compelling evidence that Falkenberg or the citizens had deliberately started the fires that led to the larger conflagration.[74] Rankean empirical rigor thus won out over the Catholic attempt to absolve Tilly of responsibility. Not everyone was satisfied with Droysen's refutation of the Catholic arguments. The medieval historian Rudolf Usinger (1835–74) deplored Droysen's unwillingness to engage in a polemical condemnation of the revisionist Catholic political agenda. Usinger, a founding member of the Nationalverein and the Protestant Union who would inherit Heinrich von Treitschke's chair in history at Kiel, inveighed against the "vulgar views" of the "zealous Catholic party" disseminated in the "party organ" of the *HpB*. Usinger took Droysen to task for avoiding, "perhaps more than could be wished," a more sharply expressed critique of certain "other works."[75]

However, the Magdeburg question was far from settled. A new and radical interpretation by a young historian from Jena, Karl Wittich (1840–1916), called Droysen's conclusions into question. Wittich's "Critical Commentary on the Destruction of Magdeburg" appeared in the *Journal of Prussian History* in 1869. This article offered the first fruits of Wittich's research in foreign archives, particularly in Stockholm and The Hague, gathered when he was amassing material for what he called a "German-national" interpretation of the career of Wallenstein.[76] It was a provocative challenge by a young scholar to an established historian of impeccable lineage. Wittich found Droysen's intervention in the Magdeburg debate useful but ultimately unsatisfying and unconvincing on the main question: Who destroyed Magdeburg? Wittich believed that his own findings offered compelling new evidence that Magdeburg was destroyed by its own citizens. Dismissing the Catholic and imperial accounts in Calvisius as essentially worthless because of their obvious biases, Wittich emphasized that the new evidence he had discovered was primarily of Protestant provenance. Probably conscious that his iconoclasm was a perilous career move for a young and aspiring historian who had not yet submitted his dissertation, Wittich prefaced his article with a disclaimer that his conclusions were of a preliminary nature.[77] He began by disputing Droysen's evaluation of the reliability of Bandhauer's account of the siege, that source "so beloved by Klopp and the other ultramontanes." Examining the manuscript, Wittich concluded that, even allowing for an ingrained pro-imperial bias and the likelihood that Bandhauer did not witness all the events he described, his account nevertheless confirmed that the fires set by Pappenheim's troops at Magdeburg's north gate were limited in scope and did not spread very far. In Wittich's view, the crucial question of how the city had been so quickly engulfed in flames remained open.[78]

Wittich's dissertation, "The Destruction of Magdeburg in the Year 1631," was passed by the faculty of philosophy at the University of Jena in 1870, the year of Bismarck's final war of unification against France. Wittich opened with the observation that the question about the destruction of Magdeburg remained "a point of controversy in every sense of the word." Demonstrating keen insight into what the debate was really about, he believed that the divisive issue of "guilt and innocence" that drove the debate obsessed historians because of its political implications for writing a German national history: "This is especially true in our time, when political-national factions increasingly look back with intense interest on the contentious past from the perspective of the contentious present. This past is interpreted with extreme and severe political judgments and all too frequently in a partisan spirit, which more or less arises from the modern tendency to politically exploit the past, despite completely altered present circumstances, from a one-sided standpoint."[79] Wittich had little use for the polemical accounts of the siege, which had been passed down since Calvisius and had become enshrined in German remembrance of the Thirty Years' War through Schiller: "The proper answer to the question does not lie in the accusations of the opposing sides. . . . Each side not only protested the innocence of its own party, but emphasized the sheer improbability and unbelievability of their guilt."[80] He was convinced that only new sources, used to cross-examine contemporary pamphlet accounts, could provide unbiased witness. Wittich believed he had discovered this witness in a previously unknown manuscript of Otto von Guericke's (1602–86) Chronicle of Magdeburg (1647), which he had found in the Royal Library in Berlin. This "Berlin specimen," Wittich claimed, contained material that had been excised from the original published version and the edition prepared from the Magdeburg manuscript by Friedrich Hoffmann in 1860.[81] For Wittich, a close reading of the stricken passages yielded two conclusions and one provocative question. Guericke's unexpurgated memoir of the siege appeared to confirm not only the revisionist descriptions of the intense factionalism that divided the city council before and during the siege but also the reports that a majority of the fires had broken out only some time after Magdeburg had been overrun by imperial forces. Extrapolating from these two revelations, Wittich asked: "Must one not conclude that the city had to have been set alight in many different areas by its own inhabitants?"[82] Gustav Droysen was reported to have been nonplussed by Wittich's "completely unexpected" dismissal of his conclusions.[83]

With this question Wittich laid the groundwork for a secularized version of Magdeburg history that was distinctly more nationalist than Protestant. His massive Magdeburg, Gustavus Adolphus, and Tilly (1874) subordinated the traditional confessional symbolism of Magdeburg to a more modern nationalist narrative of self-sacrifice or, to put it differently, an updated conception of "secular martyrdom" that romantically conflated the awakening German national consciousness with a last-ditch act of resistance. Citing diplomatic documents and secret correspondence he had discovered in the archives of The Hague, Stockholm, Dresden, Munich, Vienna, and Berlin, Wittich challenged conventional Protestant readings of the sources in Calvisius. Certain that the soldiers would not have intentionally destroyed the source of their plunder, Wittich asked, "Of all the manifold possibilities open to consideration, why not the possibility that Falkenberg or the citizens themselves deliberately destroyed the city? . . . If we examine the various sources closely, we find enough evidence to justify the view that the fires were set on a large scale in accordance with a unitary and systematic plan, rather than resulting from an impulsive act or simple accident."[84]

In the adversarial, or appellate, tradition of modern German history writing, the heart of Wittich's narrative was a ninety-page brief entitled "Factual Findings," which was subdivided into "Authors and Executors of the Deed," "Motives," and "Consequences." With no self-consciousness, Wittich admitted that his argument was based on intuition about a poem written by a Magdeburg refugee, the "Saguntina prosopopoeia weilandt die löblichen Anse nun Anzweh-Stadt Magdeburg," (Imitation of Saguntum: Magdeburg, the once beloved city of waters, now city of tears) that he found in the Dutch archive. "Certainly, it is only a poem" Wittich acknowledges, "and it does not claim to recount the actual course of events. It is offered, however, as an eloquent expression of the convictions of the city of Magdeburg, in whose name it speaks. . . . It celebrates the heroic constancy of this city, it celebrates its self-sacrifice, its suicide! . . . [Its language] is of transparent clarity. The allusions to Lucretia and Saguntum are unmistakable":

> The maiden and citadel, the indomitable city
> With a Roman deed sacrificed
> Its virgins to God.
>
> Just as seven times through fire
> Silver and every pure metal

> Must be thoroughly assayed:
>
> So too the Lutheran Lucretia,
> Unbowed German Constantia,
> Lives in eternal glory.[85]

Essentially, Wittich constructed his entire counterhistory of the destruction of Magdeburg around this remarkable invocation of the ideal of "triumph in death." By rejecting the traditional dichotomies of "guilt" and "innocence" created by the Protestant-Catholic conflict as divisive and parochial, Wittich moved the destruction of Magdeburg to the center of a unifying nationalist history that melded the tradition of the classical epic with notions of Christian martyrdom. He found in the more zealous factions within the city evidence of a "courage of despair" that preached self-destruction before surrender according to the example of Lucretia, Saguntum, and Numancia. The "authors" of this sacrifice were the Protestant clergy and the pro-Swedish faction, and the "executor" of the deed was Falkenberg. Wittich compared what he called this "Roman deed" to his century's most famous example of last-ditch resistance against the invader: the burning of Moscow in 1812 to deny it to the French invader. He pointed out that even Ranke had commented on the "astonishing" similarity in comparably desperate circumstances between the actions of Falkenberg and Rostopschin, the commander in Moscow. Wittich concluded by summoning the nationalist spirit of 1813 (and its connection to Gustavus Adolphus's sacrifice at Lützen): "As the burning of Magdeburg has been compared to that of Moscow, so, in fact, can one compare the significance of one catastrophe with another. E. M. Arndt wrote that the sun of Austerlitz set in the smoke and flames of Moscow. In the same way the fame [Tilly's] of Prague, Höchst, and Lutter died on the pyre of Magdeburg and a new sun twice arose from the smoke at Leipzig."[86]

Wittich was conscious of the possibility that his conclusions could be cited in support of Catholic assertions that Falkenberg had deliberately plotted the destruction of Magdeburg on the orders of Gustavus Adolphus.[87] Given the volatile atmosphere created by the Kulturkampf, he was cautious enough to distance himself from what he called the "extravagant accusations" of the Catholic camp. He rejected the "fantasy picture of Onno Klopp and his consorts" implicating the Swedish king in Magdeburg's fall, a view for which his critics initially gave him high marks for promoting a scientific and "nonconfessional" interpretation of the Magdeburg issue.[88] For a while, this stance allowed Wittich to separate himself from Catholic revisionists like Franz Keym, who in 1873 still characterized the history of Magdeburg's destruction as the "Swedish lie."[89] Eventually, however, Wittich's new account of the siege, based as it was on transforming Dietrich von Falkenberg, a "German Leonidas," into a national hero, began to encounter resistance. The debate over Magdeburg would last another twenty years because German nationalism, still somewhat insecurely rooted in the new state created in 1871, was clearly not yet ready to abandon one of its most cherished founding legends. Wittich's attempt to modernize this legend for a unified Germany was rejected by his Protestant peers, who tenaciously defended the old orthodoxy. That the battle over the meaning of Magdeburg continued as long as it did revealed the enduring parochial limitations of Protestant history writing and the power of a narrative of sacrifice that excluded Catholics. Max Dittmar (1858–98), a student of Droysen at Halle and Hoffmann's successor at the city library in Magdeburg, kept the debate alive in his 1884 dissertation by flatly declaring Wittich wrong both in his accusations against Falkenberg and the citizenry and in his questioning of Droysen. In a series of sharp exchanges with Dittmar over the next decade, Wittich refused to back down from his insistence that Falkenberg, resisting counsels of surrender, had resolved to destroy Magdeburg in a way that would dramatically discredit the imperial cause and inspire Germany's Protestants.

Dittmar admitted that the questions regarding the origins of the fires that had engulfed the city were difficult to answer. He nevertheless rejected the possibility that the Catholic forces could be absolved of responsibility for the crime. It was clear, Dittmar asserted, that the destruction of Magdeburg was the result of a "radical Catholic plan" to make it a "pure Catholic city . . . a Catholic 'Marienburg.'"[90] Dittmar believed that this plan accounted for the ambiguities and obfuscation in the imperial reports, while the accounts of the refugees and prisoners of war were unreliable because of their despair in exile and fear of retribution, respectively. He concluded that the reports in Calvisius that blamed Pappenheim's troops for starting the fires were probably correct, given the patterns of destruction. Dittmar, like Usinger, blamed Droysen's original reluctance to engage decisively in partisan battle for giving license to the revisionists. Further, Dittmar also agreed with Usinger that the best response was a vigorous reassertion of the Schiller tradition of Tilly the Mordbrenner, intent on exterminating the "nest of heretics."[91]

Wittich did not immediately respond to Dittmar's recapitulation of the traditional Protestant reading of Magdeburg. Since 1874 he had been hard at work in the archives investigating Falkenberg's activities just before Magdeburg's fall. In 1887 Wittich excitedly announced his discovery in the archives in Stockholm, among the papers of the Swedish "secret agent" Reichard Damerow, the "Corporal's Report," written by a soldier who said he carried out Falkenberg's direct order to blow up the arsenal located in the city's Old Market.[92] A few years later, in the pages of the *Historical Journal*, Wittich finally answered Dittmar directly by acknowledging the real and symbolic importance of occupying the city for the goals of the Counter-Reformation. But that being the case, Wittich argued that the total destruction of Magdeburg obviously served no useful purpose for the Catholic-imperial cause.[93] In 1892 Wittich published the first of three monographs intended to establish a new and definitive version of Magdeburg history. Highlighting the difficulty of Falkenberg's mission in the city—"where he had thought to find heroes, he found only shopkeepers"—Wittich opened his story with a narrative of the Swedish commander's struggle to rally Magdeburg around a greater cause than the divisive confessional fanaticism of the city's elders.[94] Wittich cited imperial military reports found in the Dresden archives to show how the defenders had set explosives to demolish the city's outer ring of fortifications the moment they were breached. Resorting again to the Spartan imagery he had used earlier, Wittich painted a picture of Falkenberg as a "second Leonidas" finally deciding that his last, best option was to sacrifice the city and its inhabitants rather than surrender such a valuable prize to the imperial forces. Wittich quoted a letter he had found in the Falkenberg family archives in Hanover in which Falkenberg confided to his brother, "If I can no longer hold the city, I will torch it!" He then turned to "eyewitness" accounts for the details of Falkenberg's final moments: "When he saw that everything was lost, [Falkenberg], right before he died, gave the order to detonate the arsenal." In this new German hero, Wittich believed "distinct contradictions were united . . . [those of] a Protestant Christian with a Roman of antiquity. His deeds proved that the 'Lutheran Lucretia' was not a contradiction."[95] Wittich's Falkenberg was a new national German hero who combined the classical ideal of Spartan sacrifice for the nation with the tradition of Protestant martyrdom for German liberty.

Even before Wittich had begun his Falkenberg hagiography, Felix Stieve expressed regret that Wittich's explanation of Magdeburg's destruction would not be accepted because it contradicted so much that was held sacred by Protestant nationalism, in particular the notion of Catholic responsibility.[96] Stieve's prediction was borne out. However, it is important to recognize that Protestant nationalism did not completely reject Wittich's argument about the Magdeburgers' self-immolation because it rejected the idea of sacrifice. Rather, it refused to contemplate a German identity not founded in victimization or sacrifice, a stance clearly shown in the work of Robert Volkholz, a native Magdeburger who taught at the high school in Halberstadt. His contribution to the great debate, *Die Zerstörung Magdeburgs [1631] im Lichte der neusten Forschung* (The Destruction of Magdeburg in Light of the Latest Research), came out in 1892 and was dedicated to Dittmar. Volkholz wanted to "steer the Magdeburg question back on course" with a defense of the Protestant orthodoxy concerning Magdeburg. Volkholz aimed to confirm that the imperial soldiery, under direct orders from Tilly and Pappenheim, had in fact set fires throughout the city to break the last-ditch resistance of the city's defenders: "This order found in his [Tilly's] soldiers only obedient servants and executioners. When the victory was decided, and as he finally thought about extinguishing the fires, the destruction was more than half complete." Volkholz denied that Falkenberg had even been alive when the Old Market arsenal was blown up and, citing a new account he had found in the pamphlet collection in the British Museum, dismissed the "extorted" testimony of prisoners who claimed that the fires had been started by zealots on the city council.[97]

Wittich took his time preparing a response to Dittmar and Volkholz. In Pappenheim and Falkenberg, published in 1894, he accused his opponents of surrendering to the same ideological fanaticism that distorted the judgment of Catholic historians: "The extremist partisans of these orthodoxies are, in respect to their views and theses, the antithesis of the ultramontanes, but in the way they approach controversy, their tactics are exactly the same."[98] Wittich accused Dittmar of "looking through the lens of local patriotism," Volkholz of rehashing "the pamphlet by [Johann] Kutscheit [*Herr Albert Heising für Tilly und gegen Gustav Adolf* (Albert Heising for Tilly and against Gustavus Adolphus), a critique of Heising published in 1847] of years ago and even surpassing it," and both historians of merely repeating the "folktale" of Tilly's guilt.[99] He remained convinced that Magdeburg deliberately destroyed itself following the example of Saguntum and that Falkenberg "sacrificed the city and himself to his king and the great Protestant principle." "Does it not appear," he asked, "given the evidence, as an unjustified skepticism to oppose so absolutely the simple possibility that it might have happened this way?"[100] For Wittich, the local patriotism and parochial confessional allegiances that persisted in Germany twenty years after unification were as much of an impediment to the creation of a national German history as was the obsolete legitimist perspective of Heising and Klopp.

In his "Open Answer to Professor Wittich," written in 1894, Dittmar declared himself deeply wounded by Wittich's accusations of partisanship and surprised by the spitefulness and "overbearing conceit" (*Eigendünkel*) of the attacks from a colleague he had regarded as a friend. Denying a credulous acceptance of a folktale as gospel truth, Dittmar protested that he had no reason to be embarrassed by the charge of being a "Magdeburg patriot" and that, if anything, his pride in his native city would only be increased if he could be convinced that Wittich's unlikely account of heroic self-sacrifice were true.[101] Dittmar reiterated that he had found no reliable evidence that Tilly had directly ordered the destruction of the city, nothing in the secret correspondence between Gustavus Adolphus and Falkenberg that indicated a scheme by the defenders to destroy the town, and no reason to believe that a small group of conspirators could even carry out such a plan: "My conviction is that what was first intended by the imperial leadership as a necessary tactical measure was turned into an act of pure destruction by the undisciplined, murderous, and plunder-crazed soldiery."[102] As regards Wittich's dubious infatuation with the poem "The Saguntina," Dittmar declared himself skeptical about a methodology that, in challenging the empirical standards of Droysen, could so highly esteem a piece of poetry: "Acknowledging that any historical tradition usually contains a small kernel of truth, I am in general still not convinced that the investigation of historical events should lay any special weight on these traditions."[103]

Much like Wittich, Robert Volkholz was convinced that any conclusive answer to the Magdeburg question could only be found in the answer to the Falkenberg question. In 1895 he published a monograph that offered a radically new interpretation of the famous "Ackermann report" contained in Calvisius, which had long been considered the most reliable account of Pappenheim's tactical decision to set a few fires to aid his breakthrough on the northern wall. Volkholz claimed that the manuscript Calvisius used, and the Berlin and Magdeburg specimens, examined by Wittich and Dittmar, respectively, were incomplete. Apparently Ackermann had written an addendum to his original memoir, which Volkholz uncovered in the church archives in Croppenstedt. Volkholz claimed a "world-historical significance" for this "Croppenstedt manuscript," written between 1636 and 1647, because he believed it demonstrated that Falkenberg had died in the vicinity of the St. Jacob Church, which was a few streets away from the northern gate, soon after Pappenheim's Croats had broken through, that is, no later than 8:30 a.m. "Herr Wittich, the biographer of Falkenberg, does not agree. He, who for a quarter of a century has made it his life's calling to inform the world that Falkenberg and the Magdeburgers intentionally and premeditatedly burned the city, emphasizes, contrary to the main witness Ackermann, the fact that the Swedish marshal, not by chance and not at an earlier hour, gave up his life around 8:45, when he saw that all was lost . . . 'like Leonidas at the head of his troops, fearlessly sacrificing himself and his soldiers.'" Volkholz rejected what he called Wittich's idealization of "the courage of despair" and instead pictured Falkenberg rushing to stem the influx of Pappenheim's Croats and falling still in the firm hope of success, "a victorious commander!"[104]

"It is very painful for me," Wittich replied, "to once again interrupt other work to return to a debate on the much discussed Magdeburg question, but it appears unavoidable, as a reckless and bitter opponent has made it, in this case, impossible to remain silent."[105] In fact, for more than a decade, solving the mystery of Magdeburg had practically been Wittich's sole vocation as an historian, and he certainly left no challenge to his thesis unanswered. And surely he must have been prepared for controversy, given that his counterhistory debunked the tradition of Magdeburg's martyrdom at the hands of a Catholic army, a story that was so central to the "chosen people" narrative of Protestant nationalism. Wittich had deliberately tried to secularize (without entirely abandoning religious themes) the story of sacrifice because he obviously believed the attachment to the old tradition weakened, rather than strengthened, German national unity and pride. This conviction accounted for the marked contempt he reserved for the "local patriotism" of his critics: "Or did Volkholz seriously believe that each and every informant from Magdeburg, especially those according to which the great conflagration was an act of despair perpetrated by its own inhabitants, could be dismissed merely on the strength of his objections? As a native Magdeburger, as a genuine local patriot, he has not been willing to tolerate the least hint of a suspicion in this direction."[106]

What is significant about Wittich's version of Magdeburg's destruction is that it emphasized the Götterdämmerung aspects of an almost pagan self-immolation, or nationalist act of self-determination, over the traditional biblical themes of sacrifice and martyrdom. He wanted to break the power of "Magdeburg history" (and all that it symbolized as a prop for a German identity founded in victimization) to divide Germany along religious lines. But Wittich's retelling of the story of Magdeburg was such a radical rejection of a key justification of the unified German state, the martyrdom and sacrifice of Germany's Protestants to demonstrate their faith in the covenant of 1517, that it could never be widely accepted. Ultimately, as the sharp judgments of Droysen's students Rammelt and Teitge show, Wittich's counterhistory of Falkenberg as secular pagan-romantic hero was dismissed as "breaking a lance for the imperial cause" and undermining the exclusionary Protestant national idea.[107] One prominent Catholic intellectual who came to Wittich's defense was the journalist and publisher (and future editor of the influential Catholic journal *Germania*) Eduard Marcour (1848–1924). His conclusions about the Magdeburg question sum up Catholic bitterness over Protestant Germany's refusal to relinquish the status of victim. "There is scarcely another example in history," Marcour writes almost incredulously, "in which the sinister power of the lie has so drastically demonstrated itself as in the question of guilt or innocence in the destruction of Magdeburg. . . . To try and shake this belief is considered a betrayal of the Protestant faith and an unpatriotic act."[108] Ultimately, Catholic revision of Magdeburg history must be seen as an act of cultural resistance, an assertion of identity, and an attempt to rescue a marginalized national idea.

Beneath all of the claims to a more perfect and legitimate vision of the German nation, behind all of the attempts to conjure a coherent national history out of the chaos of the Thirty Years' War, we can see two competing epics of victimization emerging. The scale and nature of each group's suffering, Protestant and Catholic, were offered as the defining experience that established authentic national identity. In the histories of what was known as the Swedish War, the subject of the final chapter, we will see how in Protestant narratives the destruction of the war was refashioned into the mark of divine grace and favor, whereas in Catholic collective remembrance the war evoked a dread of marginalization, expropriation, and exclusion.

5. German Gothic

Atrocity Narratives
Historians have long debated the actual extent of the material damage the Thirty Years' War inflicted on German economic development
and the veracity of contemporary accounts that described Germany
after the war as a wasteland of empty villages, overgrown fields, and
impoverished towns.[1] Robert Ergang, in a famous revisionist monograph published in 1956, attributed "the myth of the all-destructive fury
of the Thirty Years' War" to what he characterized as the "romantic"
inclinations of the historians of the early nineteenth century, particularly Schiller, who were "novelty seekers . . . interested in the fanciful,
the romantic, the sanguinary." Ergang explained their rediscovery of
Grimmelshausen, the seventeenth-century chronicler of the war, and
the frequent verbatim incorporation of details from his *Adventures of
Simplicissimus* into their histories, as a legacy of romanticism's affinity
for an earlier period's "Baroque delight" in exaggeration and cruelty; a
cultural predilection that persisted into the nineteenth century as what
I believe could be more accurately labeled "German Gothic."[2] Despite
the acknowledged unreliability and fragmentary nature of statistics
distilled from contemporary accounts and records, the consensus of
modern scholarship is that (the political, cultural, and psychological
damage aside) the material losses of Germany during the war were significant. A 60–70 percent loss in population (through mortality and
migration) has been noted in the most devastated areas, the Rhine
Palatinate, Bavaria, and Mecklenburg, while losses of between 15 and
30 percent of the entire prewar population of approximately 20 million have been estimated. At either end of this scale, it is clear that the

impact of the war on Germany was catastrophic. Equally obvious is the fact that, subject to regional variations, recovery would be slow and economic growth would be stagnant for a long period. The intuitions behind the admittedly inflated claims of the nineteenth-century historians were largely correct.[3]

The *Adventures of Simplicissimus*, written in 1668 and 1669 by the Catholic convert Hans Jacob Christoffel von Grimmelshausen (1625–76), provided nineteenth-century historians with an inexhaustible source for the narratives of atrocity, torture, and devastation that dominated collective German remembrance of the Thirty Years' War. Parts of Grimmelshausen's tale, especially those recounting the torture and rape of peasants by the Swedish soldiers and the retribution meted out by the peasants, were often reproduced word for word and, in the case of Protestant authors, the Catholic identity of the victims was switched to Protestant. Within the first sixty pages of the book, Grimmelshausen describes two scenes of mass rape, the administration of the infamous "Swedish Punch" (liquid offal and manure forced down the victim's throat), the roasting alive of a peasant in an oven, the binding and crushing of skulls with knotted ropes, the crushing of thumbs in the flintlocks of pistols, and the cutting off of ears and noses.[4] Just as the story of Magdeburg became the model for narratives of the heroic city, so the story of Simplicissimus, Grimmelshausen's protagonist, became the model for the narratives of German suffering. After Christoph Wagenseil's "modernized" edition appeared in the late eighteenth century, Grimmelshausen's novel steadily gained popularity in Germany. Barbara Salditt believes that the nineteenth-century enthusiasm for the tale stemmed from three main factors: the compelling theme of an authentic German literary hero and survivor emerging from the destruction of the war; the search to rediscover the lost treasures of an authentically German "people's art" (*Volkskunst*); and the nineteenth-century taste for the "realism" of historical novels and regional folktales (*Heimatserzählungen*). Between the mid-1830s and the 1870s, the book's reputation within an emerging national German literature was established and exploited as several scholarly, bowdlerized, and juvenile versions came off the presses.[5]

Another important element needs to be added to this explanation for nineteenth-century Germany's attraction to the explicitness of the atrocity narratives of the Thirty Years' War: profound anxiety about the transformative and potentially annihilative effects of war and revolution. Peter Paret has noted this same aesthetic and psychological inclination and the romantic obsession with ruin, decay, and regeneration in post–Napoleonic German historical art, particularly as it focused on detailed and realistic representations of the "central element of violence" in an age of revolution, as seen in Rethel's woodcut series *Another Dance of Death* (1848) and Menzel's *March Casualties Lying in State* (1848).[6] The German reaction to the bloody excesses of the French Revolution, and the experience of the epic slaughters of the major battles Napoleon fought on German soil, which far exceeded the human cost of the limited continental wars of the eighteenth century, gave new life and significance to the collective memory of the Thirty Years' War. Like the wars with revolutionary and Napoleonic France, the Thirty Years' War had also been, for those who lived through it and those who recalled it in collective memory, an epochal "clash of cosmologies," to use Michael Shapiro's term, that had threatened the physical annihilation of Germany.[7]

In German memory, folklore, and history, the period between 1630 and 1638, the "Swedish War," were years of mass death and destruction that defined the Thirty Years' War. For Catholic Germany the memory of this particularly horrific phase of the conflict was summed up in a more descriptive term: "the time of annihilation" (*die Vertilgungszeit*). Catholic and Protestant Germany's suffering in the war was remembered as unique in the scale of its cruelty and destructiveness and as having inflicted such damage on their country that the wounds were scarcely healed two hundred years later. As we will see it applied in the popular and historiographical recollection of this particular aspect of the war, the essential theme of "Magdeburg history" was the assertion of a community of suffering in which victimization was transcended through narratives of sacrifice. As a way to interpret modern German history in the creation of a unifying national history, this hermeneutic perspective guided the evolution of Protestant nationalism as an expression of *German* nationalism. The Thirty Years' War was reconceived as the fundamental experience that anointed the chosen people, as the first line of Johannes Brahms's 1868 "German Requiem" proclaims, "Blessed are those who mourn." But this patriotic hope of redemption in the Promised Land was always tempered by an anxiety that Germany would always be, somehow, a nation incomplete and unfinished. There always existed the possibility, revealed in the manifold sufferings of the Thirty Years' War, that the sacrifices offered to fulfill the national covenant would not be accepted. Most Protestant historians were convinced that unification in 1871, the miraculous year, marked the end of Germany's wanderings in the desert and that the Promised Land was finally within their grasp. In this moment of triumph Catholics were, in effect, pushed to the outer frontiers of the new kingdom, if not expelled completely. Protestant nationalism used histories of the Thirty Years' War not only to unite Germans in a community of suffering but also to blame Catholics for inflicting that trial by fire and weakening and dividing Germany for two hundred years. Challenging this indictment, and the cultural and political marginalization that it legitimated, Catholic historians tried to demonstrate that their "nation" had sacrificed for an idea of Germany. The "atrocity narratives" through which Protestant and Catholic Germany confronted the legacy of the war consistently employed three rubrics of suffering: heroic sacrifice, the destruction of order and morals, and the wanton tortures inflicted by foreign invaders on German victims. These rubrics do not by any means exhaust the extensive catalog of horrors detailed in the histories, but they do indicate basic tropology. Protestant historians used them to glorify the renascence of Germany under the leadership of the Hohenzollerns. Catholic historians used them to express a profound dread of Protestant-Prussian rule. These narratives transformed death and destruction into a mark of grace even as they revealed modern Germany's fear of invasion, revolution, and partition.

German collective remembrance of the Thirty Years' War in the nineteenth century recalled a time of chaos when the natural order of society and authority was inverted and Germany was plunged into an orgy of destruction unparalleled in modern history. While the histories of the origins of the war and the campaigns of Gustavus Adolphus and Wallenstein optimistically reexamined this traumatic past for clues indicating possible courses toward German unification, the atrocity narratives analyzed in this chapter are remarkable for their explicit cataloguing of every humiliation, every violation, every instance of weakness and powerlessness on Germany's part. Julius von Voß (1768–1832), a prolific writer of patriotic kitsch and light literature (*Eintagsliteratur*) in the early nineteenth century, employed the themes of Magdeburg history in lurid descriptions of the sack of the fictional town of Wendburg by the "wild Croats," down to the requisite detail of the town's women throwing themselves into the river to avoid being raped.[8] Friedrich Karl Wild (1807–71), the popular folklorist and author of several "moral tales" set during the Thirty Years' War, referred to the Jerusalem tradition of Old Testament narrative to describe the siege of Nördlingen in 1634 in his novel *Erhard Daubitz* (1866): "The second day of the siege was a Sunday, the second Sunday after the Festival of the Holy Trinity, which since olden times was marked by a sermon on the destruction of Jerusalem; indeed, I suppose the story of this tragic event was delivered in many churches. . . . What happened in Nördlingen that day was what once had befallen Jerusalem."[9] Otto Schmidt, a Protestant historian, lamented: "This was a time that men, created in the image of God, became accomplices of the Devil. . . . Everything good died under their hand; they brought death and fire and bestiality; lamentation and misery followed in their footsteps." The Catholic Franz Keym echoed Schmidt: "All bonds of order were destroyed, and all morals, and anarchy ruled; all of this was prolonged so that Sweden could conquer and enrich itself and France raise itself to be the first power in Europe!"[10] Working through the trauma caused by German religious division and political fragmentation, these narratives dwelled on the violation of Germany by foreign mercenary armies of Italians, Walloons, Spaniards, Hungarians, Croats, and Cossacks. But it was the recollection of Swedish depredations that lingered longest in German collective remembrance, as we see in Wild's evocation of the scars the Swedish War left on the land and memory: Perhaps no war is so well known and so often retold by the people than this one: "'The Swede is coming to take everything away!' All across Germany fathers have bounced their youngsters on their knees to these words; and when a peasant is asked about the ruins of the castle standing on the height, he says, 'That happened in the Swedish war—the Swede did that!'"[11]

Why this morbid and obsessive focus on a war that most Germans agreed had, in its consequences, been an epochal catastrophe for Germany? How, in effect, had "Magdeburg history" become *German* history? Some explanation of how history writing enables collective remembrance is required if we are going to answer that question. At their core, German histories of the war were "memory work," a therapeutic process of preserving and transmitting collective remembrance in order that the past might serve the present. Functioning in this way, history writing becomes a commemorative (and mnemonic) act. As such, it shares with monument building the pedagogic goal, in Maurice Halbwachs's phrase, of "immobilizing time" in a social process that re-creates the past for certain defined purposes (in this case, to warn of the perils of disunity). Historical consciousness operates as a crucial component of social memory, as Peter Burke points out when, modifying Halbwachs, he asserts that history writing turns collective remembrance into useful social memory by creating a "repertoire of stereotypes." Obviously, such mediated memory can have an infinite variety of purposes, but its creation reveals the most important function of history as rationalized social memory: the establishment in the popular mind of an easily accessible set of formally conceptualized images.[12] David Lowenthal believes that over time these narratives acquire a conviction and concreteness that penetrates the "curtain of doubt" that always shrouds the meaning of past events.[13] This process is clearly manifested in the German obsession with the mass death, destruction, and misery of the Thirty Years' War. What kind of "meaning," or meaningful interpretation, could be derived from this catastrophe? The descriptions of the ruined castle on the hill and the scars still visible on the land, the persistence of peasant memory in folklore, the regional nursery rhymes—all demonstrate the "movement into time," or the simultaneous awareness of past and present, that Edward Casey associates with the compelling force of what he calls "place memory."[14] German collective remembrance of the trauma of the war frequently called attention to the traces and relics the war had left on the landscape. However, what was "seen" in this landscape of memory was not necessarily "true" but an abstraction that served the purposes of healing and consolation: the time of annihilation had passed, but the German people remained, and there was an important story to be found in their survival. Victimization, the omnipresent theme in German history writing about the Thirty Years' War, transformed collective remembrance into narratives that confronted and, in the Protestant case, mastered German anxieties about the survival of their nation. The war was fixed in their memory as a common German experience that required constant reexamination, even if that meant revisiting its horror, to further the process of making German history a comprehensible and compelling whole. "One loves," Ernest Renan wrote in 1882, "in proportion to the sacrifices which one has approved and for which one has suffered."[15] What is remarkable about this literature of destruction is that it does not pause silently before and pass over the worst of the war, but plunges deeply into it. As it turns out, many Germans on both sides of the confessional line (but for very different reasons) in the nineteenth century were willing to forget (or forgive) very little about the war.

Transcendence of suffering as well as consolation (and explanation) for Germany's laggard progress toward nationhood were the psychological aims of much of the German history writing about the Thirty Years' War in the nineteenth century. Nowhere do we see these aims revealed more clearly than in the histories of the Swedish War. What does this focus on destruction tell us? Recent work on the remembrance and representation of the Holocaust is suggestive on this question, especially as it has stimulated a wide-ranging interdisciplinary discussion of the use of "trauma" as an analytical category. Specifically, how can remembrance of victimization be reconciled with the optimistic trajectory that master national narratives are required to support? In an attempt to answer this question, which has important implications for the understanding of the ideological and psychological functions of history writing, the concept of trauma as an individual reaction to catastrophic events in the past has been applied to the analysis of the vocabularies and strategies of historical narrative. Cathy Carruth has proposed that the assumption of a "referential literality" at work in the recording of historical experience must be modified by an awareness of how the fictive mixes with the functional in narratives that are working through trauma. Eric Santner defines this "narrative fetishism" as the simultaneous creation of distance from the event while controlling and numbing the remembered pain.[16] Trauma as an analytical category is problematic, however, if for no other reason than it is all too easy to see history as a narrative of "universalized" trauma. We must distinguish between the causes of the event, the experience of contemporaries, and collective remembrance. It is only in the latter that we find the "working through" of the trauma. Since this process combines the fictive with the factual, the truth claims are going to vary. Furthermore, without clearly identified victims and perpetrators, there is no trauma, or "tragedy," in the narrative sense. It is vital to remember that atrocity narratives divide the world into victims and perpetrators, a world in which the status of victim confers moral and political authority to control interpretation and meaning. We must also be aware that claims to victim status *always* imply a comparison to another group's suffering. Keeping these generalizations in mind, it must nevertheless be recognized that the concept of trauma has become a useful tool for studying how "communities of memory" are created or, to put it another way, how communities of suffering create identity. Iwona Irwin-Zarecka has examined the social and moral imperatives that turn witness into memory (testimony) in a process of collective remembrance that makes the past serve the present and future.[17] Thus we can see how the continuous renewal and survival of the community depends on establishing a history, or what Laurence Kirmayer calls a "consensual reality," that imposes closure on the wounds of the past and clearly marks the road into the future.[18] In short, the fear of destruction and annihilation of the community is transcended through history—Novalis's "backwards looking prophecy." These narratives of trauma do not rely on logic for their persuasiveness; their only purpose is to impose meaning, create coherence, and provide hope. Any given set of these narratives creates its own aesthetic conventions, or a set of vocabularies, symbols, and reference points, in an array of what Michael Lambek has called "cultural technologies" that order the past around specific moral, ethical, social, and political perspectives.[19] The descriptions of the trauma of the Thirty Years' War became "codified" to a considerable extent (as do the representations of the Holocaust); that is, the particular event in the past (*Erlebnis*) was transformed into an experience (*Erfahrung*) holding lessons for the present and future.[20] In the German mind, in the nineteenth-century histories of the Thirty Years' War, suffering became sacrifice because only the latter, through the covenant with God, promised survival and entrance into the Promised Land.

Ensuring the survival of the group (through preservation of identity) remains one of the most important functions of history writing as it has evolved in the modern period. I believe this cultural and social function has deep roots in the traditions of Judeo-Christian religious narrative and is nowhere demonstrated more strongly than in the German case, as exemplified in the histories of the Thirty Years' War. Western historical consciousness modernized itself during the Enlightenment as a conception of a "progressive" and "meaningful" narrative that is, in effect, a series of revelations of God's will manifested in the human experience. In Protestant Germany's remembrance, the catastrophe of the Thirty Years' War was reimagined as a series of sacrifices imposed and endured that would ultimately be redeemed in a unified nation. On the other side of the confessional divide, in Catholic Germany, the collective remembrance is of sacrifices rejected (the defeat of their idea of the nation; a noble but lost cause) and their subsequent marginalization in the new nation. Jacob Neusner believes that the Old Testament's narrative combination of remembrance (or witness) and prophecy became a crucial influence on the development of history writing in the West because it essentially bound a moral narrative to the needs of politics, or what he calls a "theological teleology."[21] Yosef Yerushalmi points out that the biblical injunction to "remember," the core of the Judaic intellectual tradition of testimony and memory work that imposes context and coherence on a history of suffering, slavery, and exile, was gradually appropriated by the Christian historical consciousness.[22] As an influence on history writing, this Judeo-Christian narrative tradition can be seen to have its origins in the rabbinical "amplification" of texts in Midrash, essentially the historiographical process of commentary and interpretation of the written witness of the community. Midrash, as an intellectual and cultural practice, preserves and reinforces the continuity of the community's narrative that ensures group survival.[23] In the Jewish narrative, slavery and exile created what Yerushalmi calls a "desperate pathos" and Daniel Boyarin calls an "ideology of death" within historical allegories that offered consolation for Jewish suffering and dispossession.[24] Memory work in German history writing, as it reflected on the sufferings endured during the Thirty Years' War, similarly aimed at the construction of a narrative that found meaning within the context of nineteenth-century anxieties about the path to national unification or, in the Catholic case, exclusion from that new nation.

These anxieties, originating in the collective remembrance of the Thirty Years' War, manifested themselves in fears of German backwardness, weakness, political disunion, and cultural and racial degeneration. Modern Germany was seen by many nineteenth-century historians as having been profoundly handicapped in the competition with other nations by the material and psychological damage inflicted by the war. On the other hand, they engaged in an obsessive cataloging of the injuries done to Germany in order to highlight their nation's fortitude, recovery, unity, and ascendancy (in Protestant claims) after midcentury. General histories written after the founding of the Second Reich in 1871 commonly juxtaposed graphic images of Germany's desolation in the war with references to the heights that Germany had scaled under the leadership of the Hohenzollerns. William Pierson writes of Germany's degradation in the seventeenth century: "In many areas famine drove the inhabitants to cannibalism. In Silesia, bands of peasants went hunting after men. One of their leaders, known as Melchior the Marksman, killed five hundred men with his own hands and ate them with his comrades. As in Silesia, so it went in most of the other German lands. . . . Thus Germany, once so powerful and flourishing, became transformed into a corpse-strewn waste of rubble heaps and murderers' dens. . . . By 1637, ten million had died." Pierson followed this description, which concluded a chapter on the destruction of Magdeburg, with a chapter extolling the achievements of Prussia's Friedrich Wilhelm, the "Great Elector."[25] We also find in both Catholic and Protestant histories a pervasive fear of revolution and social upheaval and, as in Grimmelshausen's depiction, a "world turned upside down." Germany's experience in the Thirty Years' War was the reason that a pervasive fear of physical annihilation as a nation and the extinction of German culture became a distinctive characteristic of the German national consciousness. The atrocity narratives discussed in this chapter had an important cultural function in the creation of a viable national identity. They consoled and bore witness against a repetition of this epochal catastrophe. "Never again," Karl Schmidt warned on the bicentennial of the Peace of Westphalia, "should such a shattering war be allowed to march over our German Fatherland, undermining all the foundations of civil, domestic, and moral life. Freedom of belief and conscience, the treasures bought at the price of so much noble blood, should remain eternally precious!"[26] Wilhelm Scherer, in his popular history of German literature, noted that the war "was a fatality not only to drama but to all the other branches of literature and to all intellectual progress generally in Germany. The fact that the literary life of Germany did not quite succumb under it is a proof of the vigor which it had already acquired."[27]

Narratives of war and civil conflict in the nineteenth century, driven by a visceral consciousness of the dire consequences of being on the losing side, portrayed a world divided into victims and perpetrators where the status of victim conferred moral and political authority and perpetrators were dehumanized as torturers and cannibals. Alain Corbin has described the serial upheavals of war and revolution in the nineteenth century as a "theater of massacre and torture," whose legacy in the modern historical consciousness was an obsession with the compilation of "martyrologies" and ritualistically repeated "images of savagery" prevalent in popular culture. Graphic descriptions of cannibalism, for example, were common in most of the German histories under discussion. Corbin and Frank Lestringant have observed that the cannibalistic massacre was one of the most profound images of persecution that represented a "disruption of the order of the universe," or "times out of joint," that dated from the religious schism of the sixteenth and seventeenth centuries. As in Germany, cannibalism was a central theme in the French discourse of Protestant martyrdom during the Wars of Religion.[28] The histories of the cruelties of the Thirty Years' War, as competing epics of victimization, were just such martyrologies, and they had a profound impact on the formation of modern German national identity. Ulf Hedetoft and Michael Geyer have both commented on the crippling ambivalence regarding a viable national identity caused by the tension in the German national consciousness between memories of grand aspirations fueled by militarism and the trauma and guilt created by the experience of mass death and genocide.[29] Protestant German history writing responded to this tension in the nineteenth century by creating a narrative of suffering that worked through the violence and disorder that marked German history with the story of the fulfillment of the nation's covenant with God.[30]

Protestant Survival

Writing in the early 1790s, Friedrich Schiller had come to the conclusion that history,

> so often confined to the dreary business of taking to pieces the uniform facade of human passion, is occasionally rewarded with manifestations that fall like a bolt of lightning on the smoothly ticking clockwork of human enterprise. . . . This power . . . without consultation, with no concern for the paltry creations of man, boldly and freely pursues its own goals. . . . But even as men are overwhelmed by the force of such an unexpected occurrence, they are moved to feel its genius and spiritual power and its transcendent source. . . . Such was the impact of the sudden departure of Gustavus Adolphus from the stage: the machine of politics was checked, and all judicious calculations were confused.[31]

Here Schiller clearly stated the conception of history behind his work on the Thirty Years' War and gave voice to the apprehension of his age, namely, that with the revolution of 1789 the continuum of history had been interrupted and the past would have to be reconstructed, and understood, according to new principles. F. R. Ankersmit has characterized the years after the French Revolution as that moment when the

Enlightenment's faith in a progressive sociohistorical reality, grounded in an understanding of natural law, was shaken, giving way to a more sober awareness of the individual caught in the mill of history.[32] In the German mind the French Revolution, far from demonstrating Condorcet's belief in the progressive perfection of man and his institutions, signaled a return to the chaos of the seventeenth century. The progressive hope of a cosmopolitan humanism offered no security in the new revolutionary era. But out of the flux of revolution, an emerging faith in the nation did offer sanctuary from annihilation. At the turn of the century we see Schiller uneasily suspended intellectually between a stricken humanism and a new and violent paradigm of historical change, which is undoubtedly why he found it difficult to completely abandon his commitment to a metahistorical narrative, even as this narrative increasingly relied on what Ulrich Muhlack calls "exemplary themes" to sustain the illusion of human progress.[33] Schiller's narrative technique, which heavily influenced Protestant German history writing, was liberally punctuated with apotheoses and symbolic resurrections that marked the invention, in Karl Pestalozzi's term, of a "historical theodicy."[34] This idea of history, a battle with evil and tyranny depicted in the histories of the Dutch Revolt and the Thirty Years' War, remained grounded in an enlightened humanism to the extent that it still celebrated the victory of the free individual in his necessarily bloody confrontation with unenlightened tyranny.[35] But the "chosen people" theme, or the conviction of Germany's unique historical struggle with the forces of superstition and oppression, appeared throughout Schiller's history of the war. It had apparently been on his mind for some time. "I have just been reading [histories] of the Thirty Years' War," he wrote to Theodor Körner in 1786, "and my head is still full of it. How curious it is, that this period of greatest national misery should also be one of the brightest pages of human greatness!"[36] We can see this in his description of the sack of Magdeburg, which appropriated (and reemphasized) the more sensational tropes of Protestant martyrdom:

> [Gustavus Adolphus] still had to battle an implacable foe within the breast of every Bavarian: religious fanaticism. In this land soldiers who did not believe in the pope were a new and unheard-of phenomenon; the blind

zeal of the priests had portrayed [the Swedes] as monsters, the children of hell, and their leader as the anti-Christ. . . . Woe to the lone Swedish soldier who fell into the hands of these savages! Every torture that a fiendish imagination could devise was practiced on these unlucky stragglers. The sight of their mutilated bodies inflamed the Swedish army to a terrible retribution.[37]

Schiller's embellishment of his chronicle of the struggle and sacrifice for freedom with such appeals to German anxieties about war and revolution was enthusiastically emulated in Protestant history writing.

Schiller's belief that historians had an obligation to reveal "essential truths," even at the expense of strict adherence to the facts, was a key element of nineteenth-century German historical practice, even after the advent of the Rankean insistence on scientific objectivity.[38] Ankersmit points to Novalis's dictum that "the historian organizes historical essences. The data of the past are the mass that is given a form by the historian, by empathy (*Belebung*)," as a clue that helps explain how history writing in the nineteenth century evolved as "proposals" for different ways of constructing the meaning of the past.[39] The histories of Protestant victimization and heroism in the Thirty Years' War manipulated a traumatic past in order to celebrate the German resurrection in the nineteenth century and, eventually, the fulfillment of the national covenant through unification in 1871. Even though Thomas Carlyle wrote that "it is mournful to see so many noble, tender, and high-aspiring souls standing sorrowful on the scene of past convulsions and controversies," the "Thirty Years' War" became a narrative metonym for Protestant and German resilience that also contained the promise of redemption and triumph.[40] In his foreword to Schiller's history, Christoph Wieland claimed that "such historical pictures from our past are one of the most effective means with which the German nation is brought together and this common spirit energized and maintained."[41] We should never lose sight of the fact that Schiller was taken very seriously as a historian in nineteenth-century Germany. Karl Hoffmeister approved of what he called Schiller's "pragmatic" attitude toward the exact rendering of historical details, as long as it stimulated "new debate and discussion" of those events which he identified as having "an essential, undeniable, and easily traceable influence on the current shape of the world and the condition of the present generation."[42] In his study of the evolution of historicism in Germany, Peter Reill largely concurs with Hoffmeister's view when he concludes that Schiller's artistic creation of "historical pictures" revealed a concern with a didactic "pragmatic history" rather than a strictly "scientific history."[43] By the time the centennial of his birth approached in 1859, the campaign to anoint Schiller as the spiritual father of a nationalist Protestant historiography was in full swing. "At a time when chaos was desolating Europe," his biographer Emil Palleske wrote in 1858, "such as prevailed in Germany during the Thirty Years' War, he summoned the youth of Germany, through his powerful imagery, to the battlefield, rousing them from the ignoble tranquility and inaction in which they had basked since the Seven Years' War."[44] Julian Schmidt, coeditor with Gustav Freytag of the influential national liberal journal *Border Courier*, praised the effect of Schiller's history of the Thirty Years' War on the German historical consciousness, somewhat smugly observing that, since its publication, "only a Protestant perception of German history is possible."[45] This view of Schiller, which promoted the idea that his historical works somehow disclosed the "essential" truth of the German historical experience, alarmed Catholic critics, who forcefully resisted the implication that what was "essential" in German history was also essentially Protestant. Johannes Janssen vigorously condemned Schiller's histories for perpetuating an interpretation of the Thirty Years' War that, while congenial to traditional prejudices, had been rendered obsolete by modern scholarship: "The views which Schiller laid down in his two great works on the Revolt of the Netherlands and the Thirty Years' War exercise an enduring influence, not only on the young, as no other work can claim, but, despite the advances of modern historiography, on the educated public, who have drawn most of their knowledge of the period from it."[46]

Schiller's influence as a historical popularizer is perhaps most visible in the work of Gustav Freytag (1816–95), whose best-selling series Pictures from the German Past carried on the Schillerian tradition of "pragmatic history." Inspired by an immersion in German military history, Freytag set out to chronicle what he called the "two thousand year old development of the national soul."[47] A confirmed "little Germany" advocate since the failure of the Frankfurt Parliament to establish a unified Germany in 1848, Freytag had become convinced that "the conservative forces appeared to have vanished, national self-esteem was weak, the liberal demands were contradictory," but that, for Germans like himself, "the period since 1861 was a time of renewed hopes," the beginning of a decade "in which the nation made the greatest progress," in a very short span of time, toward "the height of political power and the formation of a Reich which altered the power relationships between all the great powers and which presented Germany with a masterful portion of the world's inheritance."[48] Freytag believed that the steady rise of Brandenburg-Prussia under the Great Elector after the Thirty Years' War was the single most convincing demonstration of the vitality and vision of the Hohenzollern monarchy. Protestant suffering and heroism in the war, as he told the story, was a way to confer additional glory on Prussia's leadership of a unified Germany. It is clear that Freytag's success as a writer was based on a shrewd evaluation of what his audience wanted to hear. By linking their economic and social achievements to an emerging sense of identification with the nation-state, he appealed above all to the virtuous, self-regarding sense of industriousness and moral rectitude of the German middle classes. However, unlike the English gentleman or the French bourgeois, the German Bürger was unable to ground this identity in a firmly established national history or idea of the nation, relying instead on an assertion of German identity rooted in the history of the Protestant fight for German liberty that had begun with the Reformation. Pictures from the German Past did much to change this mind-set, as Freytag offered a national history that told of German cultural progress against great odds.[49] By celebrating the vitality of German Protestant civilization and restoring faith in the progressive dynamic of history, Freytag put the bourgeoisie at the center of this triumphant story.[50] Protestantism, having begun the war of German liberation in 1517, was the spiritual motor driving German historical progress and the struggle toward nationhood, a fact that Freytag felt was convincingly demonstrated by Germany's recovery from the economic, social, and cultural ruin of the Thirty Years' War. Freytag's history was very much representative of what Nancy Kaiser has labeled the school of "pragmatic realism" that emerged in German history writing at midcentury. It embraced the Schillerian idea of a historical truth which showed that Freytag, as Julian Schmidt put it, "had a sense for reality, for the true content of the thing."[51] Ultimately, Freytag's goal was the creation of a persuasive "positive reality" that rejected the implicit social criticism in French naturalism.[52] Very simply (and very successfully, from a remunerative point of view), Freytag was inspired to turn the story of catastrophe into a history of a triumph.

Those sections of Pictures from the German Past dealing with the Thirty Years' War first appeared in installments in 1858 in the *Border Courier*, which Ottokar Lorenz praised in its day as "one of the most prestigious journals of a national orientation," before being published as a multivolume work in 1859 and 1860.[53] In his introduction Freytag disclaimed any intention of dwelling on the cruelties of a remote past, instead choosing to depict Germany in 1618 as a bucolic and flourishing paradise of rich peasants, benign rulers, and efficient magistrates. This disclaimer notwithstanding, Freytag's first "sketch of daily life" during the war was a description of the enslavement and prostitution of the peasants' wives and daughters by the rampaging imperial armies.[54] He wrote of a Germany morally and spiritually prostrate after the death of Gustavus Adolphus, a land ravaged by plague and haunted by stillbirths, strange portents in the heavens, ghosts, spirits, holy visions, and terrible angelic visitations and prophecies. The morals of the family and community had degenerated and the people had sunk in an "apathetic brutality" as the peasants learned to imitate the virtuosity of the soldiers in torture and pillage: "There were few forest knolls, where once the peaceful woodcutter and stonebreaker had sung his careless song, in whose shadows such cruelties had not been committed." Here Freytag paused to anticipate the reader's question: how did the German people survive these calamities and rise again to reclaim wealth and power? He offered three reasons: the peasant's love for his soil, the courage of his rulers, and the piety of his spiritual caretakers, the village clergy.[55] His introduction to the history of what he called "the Great War" in volume 4 of Pictures from the German Past described it as a "terrible natural disaster": "The Thirty Years' War destroyed the strength of the German people and split the nation into its individual parts. It is a sad, joyless time which will be depicted here according to contemporary reports."[56] After condemning the corruption of the German language by the "camp dialect" (*Feldsprache*) of the foreign armies, and providing graphic descriptions of torture and rape drawn straight from Grimmelshausen, Freytag concluded his account of the destruction of Germany's economic, intellectual, and moral life by noting that even at that darkest hour, when Gustavus Adolphus lay dying, "his natural successor was already twelve years old. This heir was Friedrich Wilhelm, the Great Elector of Brandenburg."[57] Against conventional wisdom, which saw the Peace of Westphalia as the beginning of two centuries of German weakness, Freytag preferred a somewhat more optimistic view of 1648 as the beginning of a long test of Germany's strength that culminated in the political and spiritual revival of the uprising against Napoleon in 1813. His advocacy of Prussian leadership of German unification is clear: "Because of this war Germany would be thrown back two hundred years behind her more fortunate neighbors, the Dutch and the English. . . . Germany was free indeed. Ruined and powerless, for the next one hundred years her western border was a playground and prize for France."[58] There was another, less obvious (but no less important) subtext: without the war, no Prussia; without Prussia, no Germany. When Freytag finished the fifth volume of Pictures in 1866, he wrote, "This year Germans have regained what to many had become as unfamiliar as the settlement of central Europe by the Germanic tribes or the Crusades—their state. It has become a joy to be German, and it will soon be reckoned a great honor among the nations of the earth."[59]

More than any other historian after Schiller, Freytag confirmed in collective remembrance the belief that the depth and scale of German degradation during the "Swedish War" was unique in the history of nations.[60] Freytag's message, his "essential truth," however, was ultimately optimistic. By rendering German suffering as horrific and crushing, he celebrated modern Germany's resurrection. The obverse of Freytag's optimism was a morbid fascination with the horrors of the war and a compulsion to keep the old wounds open, as if to emphasize to the world that Germany, despite her resilience, had been permanently lamed by the destruction of the Thirty Years' War. In 1853 Carl Georg Lentz wrote, "The worst and, in its consequences, the most terrible effect of the war was the complete destruction of all the laws of humanity and society. ... The bonds of family life were torn asunder, and the places of learning had, in many areas, completely disappeared."[61] The cultural historian Karl Biedermann, looking back from the perspective of 1862 in a book titled Germany's Darkest Hour, saw the war as having destroyed the natural yearning for self-determination among Germans, leaving them powerless to resist the opportunistic and cynical absolutism of the princes: "The unparalleled ruin of the entire German national body," Biedermann observed, "which the Thirty Years' War left behind as its terrible legacy, and which manifested itself as much in a weakening of the national spirit as in the destruction of the national wealth, made it highly unlikely that the German people, by their own power and of their own accord, would soon raise themselves from the depths to which they had fallen."[62] Freytag's history seems detached and judicious in comparison to the zealous cataloging of Catholic crimes found in most of the other Protestant accounts. The central conventions of "Magdeburg history," Protestant martyrdom and Catholic evil, remained operative. The pro-Prussian historian and publisher Friedrich von Raumer (1781–1875), in his widely read history of Germany, set this darker tone for most later Protestant histories with his account of a brutal civil war whose inhumanity was Catholic in origin. Like Schiller, Raumer adopted wholesale the accounts of the seventeenth-century polemical literature, such as the *Theatrum Europaeum*, the *Florus Germanicus*, and Khevenhüller's *Annales Ferdinandei*.[63] Raumer described the sack of Pasewalk in Pomerania by the imperial colonel Götz on September 7, 1630, with the same outrage and prurient attention to detail that had characterized the histories of Magdeburg: "Women who had just given birth were not protected, but chased out of their beds and dishonored. This also befell women with child, old women, and small girls. The prettiest were bound to wagons, or tied by the hands to saddle horns, and dragged into the camp, where they were prostituted and then sold like cattle for a few miserable pieces of silver."[64] Raumer described the later stages of the war in the same sensational language, repeating ad nauseum (literally) tales of cannibalism, lingering on the stories of families devouring each other, children being lured away to be butchered, and bodies being stolen from gibbets and graveyards.[65] After several gruesome pages recounting how the Austrians and Croats (for Raumer, the words "Catholic" and "foreigner" are almost interchangeable) indulged in an orgy of mass rape and execution, immolation, mutilation, torture, and crucifixion after the battle of Liegnitz in 1634, Raumer takes the opportunity to remind his readers that Grimmelshausen's novel, far better than some dry documents from the archive, provides the best account of this terrible time. Atrocity is piled upon atrocity as Raumer paints his picture of a time of disorder and revolution divided in Manichean terms between victim and perpetrator, depravity and innocence: "In an impudent inversion of language, the maxim became all crimes were virtuous, all virtue was the work of the devil."[66] Heinrich Hecht also described a world turned upside down when the princes had lost their power, the nobleman his castle, the burgher his wealth, and the peasant his fields: "Cunning and deceit became universal. Loyalty and faith disappeared, and religion became disgraced in and out of church!"[67] The Mecklenburg historian Otto Krabbe recalled how the Thirty Years' War dissolved all distinctions and privileges that distinguished noble from commoner, priest from layman, burgher from peasant, man from woman, and lord from knight; all were hunted down and martyred, and the "word of God was exiled from the land."[68] These atrocity narratives recalled the effects of the war on morals and society by focusing on the overturning of order and the assaults on the "body" of Protestant Germany.[69] War, revolution, and civil war—the German collective remembrance of a seventeenth-century war commingled the apocalypse of religious war with more recent nineteenth-century terrors. Narratives of war, Elaine Scarry reminds us, reflect the physical unmaking of the world (and the anxieties caused by this destruction) as they use vocabularies of demonization to divide the world into victims and perpetrators. These vocabularies deny the authenticity of the enemy's beliefs and values and exalt one's own.[70] This is why, as Jill Lepore has pointed out in her study of the histories of King Philip's War, the remembrance and narration of war will always somehow be grounded in an original victimization or injustice that becomes central to the imagination of identity.[71]

Protestants who wrote general histories of the war, or examined the war within general German histories, always returned to the political, cultural, and economic achievements of Germany in the middle decades of the nineteenth century. This comparative perspective emphasized the all-consuming destruction of the war and its lasting impact on Germany's progress toward nationhood. Regional and municipal histories celebrated deliverance from death and destruction. Survival was usually attributed to an unwavering patriotism and religious faith. Local festivals of thanksgiving and commemoration also kept the past alive as a shared German experience. These local histories of the war create a vivid sense of a Germany stranded in time, caught between two eras of trial and possibility, but always shadowed by the ruins the war left on the national landscape. In 1818, three years after the final defeat of Napoleon, Jacob Unold wrote in his history of Memmingen that northern Germany was still marked by the ruins of villages that had been abandoned two hundred years earlier.[72] More than anything else, these local remembrances of the war, despite their unmistakable mourning of something lost, expressed a pride in German resilience, bravery, and loyalty and a consciousness of a unique German vitality created by war. These histories may have been written from the local perspective, but they also recalled a common German experience that any reader would recognize. The nineteenth-century histories of the war, regardless of their perspective, reached back to the catastrophic history of the seventeenth century in a tentative embrace of a shared national experience of suffering, perhaps not the most desirable foundation for national identity, but authentically and uniquely German for all that.[73]

C. B. Sommerlatt, a Freiburg bookseller, published a commemorative volume in 1824 that brought together different accounts of Tilly's battle with the Protestant forces of Friedrich V at Wimpfen in northern

Württemberg in May 1622. Sommerlatt hoped his book would stimu-
late similar projects which, strung together as "a string of pearls" har-
vested from the experiences of a common German "national history"
(*Volksgeschichte*), might inspire the present generation with the same
patriotic feelings that had moved the Protestant heroes of 1622.[74] Ernst
Munch, whose contribution opened the book, asserted that the primary
task of the German historian was to illustrate the basis of the German
national character. Accordingly, his account of the heroism of Margrave
Georg Friedrich of Baden-Durlach, that "bright, great star of German
honor," aimed at awakening "a new enthusiasm in all Germans for the
old masterful German race."[75] Wimpfen was celebrated in the popular memory of the war because of the legend of the "four hundred of
Pforzheim" who made up the Margrave's household guard, the famous
"White Regiment" of Colonel Helmstett. Their sacrifice for prince
and fatherland and the constitutional liberties that were "the founding pledge and protecting shield of German and European freedom"
was compared to that of the Spartans at Thermopylae and Hermann's
Teutons in the Teutoburgerwald.[76] Remembering the "yoke of slavery"
that Napoleon had imposed on Germany, the poet Dietrich Anton celebrated the patriotic sacrifice of Wimpfen's heroes:

> Everything—honor, wealth, and life—
> Oh! Everything, everything you have given us,
> You, our passionately loved and holy Fatherland;
> Here, where hope's last sparks dwindled,
> You shall not find us weak or ungrateful,
> Here we stand until our last breath.[77]

It is worth noting that two twentieth-century historians also remarked
on the legend of Wimpfen. In C. V. Wedgwood's classic 1939 history of
the war we find an account of a Catholic legend concerning Wimpfen
that tells of a "white-robed woman" who appeared over the battlefield to rally the imperial troops to victory. Forty-six years later, Günter
Barudio's history also discusses Wimpfen at some length as an example of steadfast loyalty to the Protestant cause. Barudio points out that
the legend of the four hundred was popular among republican-minded

Germans in the early nineteenth century, especially Georg Büchner, who preached revolution against the Restoration regimes during the 1830s by citing the choice the Pforzheimers had made between "freedom or serfdom."[78]

History, memory, and time, leading backward and forward, flowed together in these commemorations. Identity seemed to be more easily located in the past and more accessible in the certainty of memory than in the flux of the present. On New Year's Eve in 1829, a Lusatian historian, F. G. Fritsche, the rector at the *gymnasium* in Bautzen, took his audience back to the bitterly cold night two hundred years earlier when the Saxons had approached through the snow to plunder the town. Fritsche reminded his listeners of the power of the muse of history to unlock the mystery of the past and "throw off the chains of the present."[79] The sites of memory and sacrifice were preserved as places of patriotic instruction for a new generation in which a new kind of nationalism had been awakened, as a Nördlingen poet urged in his commemoration of the battle of the same name in 1634:

> That you comprehend the meaning of this day
> In which our fathers endured much suffering;
> That you grasp well the noble spirit
> Which they so loyally carried in pious breast;
> That you never abandon the precious struggle
> In which our fathers fought so bravely:
> A monument must be piously raised
> As eloquent witness to their deeds and aspirations![80]

These writers pointed to the ruins of villages, sunken foundations, and fallen walls, the overgrown traces of trenches and fortifications, as reminders of a time when the peaceful order of things was reversed, when, in the words of another Lusatian, Karl Zehme of Sonnewalde, Germany was ruled by the "iron scepter of the sword."[81] The still visible scars of the war that marked the landscape and the collective memory of Swedish atrocities preserved in the Saxon epithet "bloody Swedes!" (*Potz Schweden!*) constantly reminded nineteenth-century Germans of the consequences of political disunion and religious schism as well as the vitality and resilience of the German people. Zehme recommended his account as a "book of instruction" and hoped that the recently burned church in Sonnewalde might be rescued a second time from the flames in the expectation "that a special blessing will be bestowed on the present through the miraculous preservation of the past."[82]

Commemorations on the sites of old battlefields usually celebrated Protestant survival and deliverance from Catholic tyranny, as we saw in ceremonies at Magdeburg, Breitenfeld, and Lützen. We do see instances, however, where the common *German* experience of war was emphasized. There were recollections of the Thirty Years' War that called on all Germans to remember a common traumatic past as a spur to create a more united German future. As the commemorations of Gustavus Adolphus's death at Lützen demonstrated, the unifying patriotic "spirit of 1813" still had force in the 1830s and was the basis of appeals to a more ecumenical memory of the Thirty Years' War. In August 1832 the mayor of Nuremberg, Jakob F. Binder, announced in the local papers the groundbreaking ceremonies for a monument at the battlefield of the Old Fortress (Alte Veste) near the village of Zirndorff. "All who value the historical worth of the Alte Veste," the announcement ran, "and who believe that the remembrance of the past is a sacred duty, are invited."[83] On Friday, August 24, a procession of local elites, including the great-grandson of one of the Swedish combatants, marched under the flags of Bavaria, Sweden, Austria, and Saxony to the high ground of the old battlefield, the "Swedish Table" (*Schwedentisch*), where the monument's cornerstone was to be laid. Wilhelm von Kreß, the district judge, opened the ceremony by asking the audience to look around at the flourishing land all around them, where two hundred years earlier death, famine, and pestilence had ravaged the German fatherland. Binder followed Kreß with a speech formally dedicating the monument in which he emphasized the current generation's duty to build on the foundation of the past by understanding the impact of that past on the present. The mayor felt that a comparison to the momentous battle against Napoleon at Leipzig in 1813 was appropriate, because they were gathered on the site of the equally momentous clash between Gustavus Adolphus and Wallenstein to honor the sacrifices that had brought freedom of belief to Germany. The hollow cornerstone, which contained, among other things, a list of the monument fund's subscribers and a framed portrait of King Ludwig I, was set in the ground by a master mason while the assembly sang, "Let us now set this stone in the earth. The German race is not yet in decline!" In his closing prayer, Pastor Hilpert of Nuremberg praised what he called a "ceremony of reconciliation" because it reminded Germans of the dangers of hatred and fanaticism.[84]

Local festivals that commemorated the deliverance of the community through the sacrifice of heroic ancestors, because they had less obvious political or ideological axes to grind, also tended to deemphasize confessional differences. In Hesse-Kassel, the town of Hanau, like Rothenburg ob der Tauber in the Frankenhöhe, celebrated its survival in an annual festival of thanksgiving that went back two centuries.[85] The town of Hanau was besieged three times during the "Swedish War," which was also marked by the terrible plague winter of 1636–37 when, according to contemporary accounts collected by local historian E. F. Keller in 1854, the fields of Nassau and Hesse were littered with emaciated bodies that had become food for dogs and foxes. Keller hoped that his anthology would remind Germans of the terrible consequences of religious division and political fragmentation, which, he sadly noted, remained seemingly unresolved in "the renewed battles of the present day."[86] Playwright J. W. Großmann turned the story of the siege of Hanau by imperial forces under General Lomboy between September 11, 1635, and June 13, 1636, into an inspirational epic. Written in 1816 in the heady period following the defeat of Napoleon, Großmann's self-described "patriotic play" depicted a heroic citizenry fighting for "family and farm" in the name of their prince, Wilhelm V of Hesse-Kassel. When the Swedish commander calls for the town's surrender, Großmann has the mayor reply, in an obvious allusion to Magdeburg, that there is "enough powder in the city to blow the entire imperial camp into the air."[87] Adhering faithfully to the classical trope of sacrifice central to Magdeburg history, Großmann puts the most defiant words in the mouth of one of the city's women, who, in a plot device common in the patriotic dramas of the period, was in love with one of the doomed defenders. Warned that she faces certain rape and death at the hands of the Croats, she declares herself only "a weak woman" who is nevertheless loyal to her prince, and declaims: "You do not fight for your prince alone. You fight for hearth and home, for your wife and children, for God and Fatherland, and for your faith." Later, in a heavy-handed scene drawing on the imagery of the Pietà, the heroine's fiancé dies in the arms of his mother, who sobs, "My son! He died for Hanau! He died for his faith! Sweet death!"[88]

On June 13, 1636, the Swedes lifted the siege.[89] In gratitude for Hanau's survival, Wilhelm V declared June 22 a day of fasting, prayer, and atonement. By the nineteenth century, this thanksgiving observance had become an annual midsummer holiday and revel. Beginning in the morning with services in the churches of the old quarter, it concluded with a feast under the shade of the oaks and beeches outside the city walls. Weeks earlier, the streets had been cleaned, the children had practiced their music and modeled their new clothes, and historical lectures had been given. On the day of the festival, the men left their jobs early and, joined by their wives and children, strolled along the decorated paths to the tables and benches set up under the trees. Entertained by musicians, jugglers, and puppets, whole neighborhoods gathered at the long tables, which were well supplied with food, wine, and beer. Fathers explained to their children that the forest in which they sat was called the "Lomboy Wood" because it was here that the terrible imperial general was blown sky high. This climactic, possibly apocryphal, event of the siege was reenacted later that evening with a fireworks display, followed by dancing, drinking, and singing around the bonfires until dawn.[90] In 1836 one L. Weinrich, Hanau's town clerk, wrote a commemorative pamphlet for the bicentennial Lomboy Day. Weinrich wanted to pay tribute to the heroes of the Thirty Years' War because he believed that "sincere popular celebrations like this remain an elevating spectacle; they exalt the existence and warm the heart for humanity, one's fellow citizens, and for state and fatherland!"[91] His pamphlet was also intended to mark the anniversary of the successful resistance of Hanau against the incursions of Hesse-Kassel in 1736. Weinrich reminded Hanauers that the same love of fatherland manifested in the epic struggles of 1636 and 1736 had again been displayed in the noble sacrifice the sons of the city had made in the Battle of Hanau in 1813.

That Protestant Germany miraculously survived the Thirty Years' War was interpreted in the nineteenth century as a sign of the German nation's strength and a good omen for its ultimate destiny. The collective remembrance of a catastrophe that had devastated most of Germany was given new meaning in narratives of national resurrection and renewal. Defeat, the test of the chosen people, had to be endured before triumph. The modern recollection of the war experience as a patriotic "elevating spectacle" was strongly influenced by Schiller's view of history writing as the revelation of essential truths. Graphic tales of German victimization and Protestant martyrdom in the tradition of Magdeburg history not only rationalized German backwardness but also articulated a deep fear of the moral and social dissolution that accompanied revolution and civil war. Yet the expectation of divine justice, embodied in nationhood, as a reward for sacrifice counterbalanced this existential dread at the core of the modern German historical consciousness. This belief in the redemption of the national covenant was most apparent in the commemorative rituals and narratives that paused at the sites of memory to remember the shared German experience of the war. If "Germany" was an as-yet-unrealized possibility, the collective remembrance across Germany of heroism, loyalty, and resilience revealed a nation hopeful in the contemplation of its latent strength and the potential for renewal. In Protestant memory, the recollection of the suffering of the "Great German War" was, ultimately, a patriotic act: history as "elevating spectacle."

Catholic Dread

For Catholic Germany the collective remembrance of the Thirty Years' War did not offer the same "elevating spectacle" found in the Protestant stories of survival and promised triumph. Despite the preservation of the empire by the Treaty of Westphalia in 1648, and the maintenance of that sheltering institution (along with its successor, the German Confederation) for another 150 years, Catholic historians in the nineteenth century reacted to Protestant triumphalism with narratives of defeat suffused with a defiant and mournful pride in the lost cause and a dread of extinction. Popular memory of the terrible revenge visited on Bavaria after Magdeburg remained sharp, and after 1789 it became conflated with a fear of revolution. Writing in 1796 after five years of revolutionary war, the Munich archivist and historian Georg Karl von Sutner (1763–1836) explicitly compared the atrocities of the Thirty Years' War with the cruelties committed by the French revolutionaries in the name of liberty, equality, and fraternity. He noted that, as "wars of belief," they bore "striking similarities" with each other in the way that the antagonists sought not only conquest and territorial expansion but also the annihilation (*Vertilgung*) of their enemies.[92] Lamenting the "extraordinary abuses" of the Swedes that flooded Munich with refugees fleeing their burning villages, the famine and plague that followed in their wake, and the endless lines of wagons emptying the dead into mass graves, Sutner declared that the "spirit of revenge for Magdeburg was in the air" as Gustavus Adolphus advanced into Bavaria.[93] Casting an apprehensive eye on the armies of enlightenment advancing across the Rhine, Sutner feared that the age of mass murder in the name of belief was returning to Germany and Europe as the nineteenth century dawned. In 1856 Eugen von Sobbe (1834–1907) wrote a short pamphlet about the destruction of Salzkotten by the Swedes in December 1633. Although the event had already been commemorated in an annual religious service, Sobbe thought that the bicentennial brochure published in 1833 had not done full justice to the event. His account of three days of rape, torture, suicide, and arson, "the fruit of the partisan hatreds inflamed by the Reformation, before which even the most brutal man shudders," indulged in the same gruesome details that had been established as the norm in the Magdeburg histories.[94] In 1833 Franz Ferchel (in another stomach-turning account) christened this phase of the war the "time of annihilation." This was the "Swedish War" in Catholic and Bavarian memory, a trial compared to the Great Plague, when Gustavus Adolphus's war of Protestant liberation was vividly recalled as a time of horror, "nameless tortures," "cold-blooded crimes," and "contempt and disdain for the laws of humanity."[95] Albert Heising characterized it as "a period of lamentation in German history" that destroyed the wealth of a thousand years, transformed Germany into a rubble heap, and ushered in two hundred years of political weakness and foreign domination.[96] An Austrian history of the Swedish occupation of Iglau in Moravia in 1647, written in 1828, concluded with lines from a contemporary ballad that preserved the image of the "terrible Swede" (or the Protestant German in Swedish service) as it was passed down over the years:

> They put in charge a commandant
> Named Samuel Osterling,
> From Saxony, born in Halle,
> His like will never be seen again,
> As this godless devil,
> Cruel and terrible tyrant,
> So ruined the town and tortured the people
> That one would scarcely believe it.
> Attila's malice and fury,
> Even that which is heard of the Turks,
> Cannot compare to our torments,
> But must shrink before them.[97]

As shown in chapter 1, Catholic histories of the Thirty Years' War were essentially conservative in that they attempted to legitimate a vision of a unified Germany built on the foundation of a reformed Holy Roman Empire. But these histories were also inspired by a fear of revolution. In the Catholic atrocity narratives of the war, Protestant and Swedish cruelties were described as the inevitable and logical consequence of the incendiary and emancipatory rhetoric of the Reformation. From this position it was a short step to an interpretation of Protestant nationalism in the nineteenth century, which strove to overturn the political status quo in Germany, that labeled it as being as destabilizing and dangerous for Germany as the revolutionary ideas of 1789. This reasoning was at the core of Catholic historians' attempts to integrate the political and cultural legacy of the empire into a modern German national narrative. They mourned the lost cause of the imperial idea and the failure of Ferdinand II's project to restore a unitary empire. Catholic historians in the Rhineland invoked memories of the Napoleonic occupation in their descriptions of the Swedish War with assertions that the Swedes had merely been the instrument of Mazarin and Richelieu's plans to dismember Germany during the Thirty Years' War. In their view, just as the Protestant powers of Europe, in league with German princes, had turned back the Counter-Reformation idea of an imperial-Catholic German state in the seventeenth century, the secular idea of Protestant nationalism threatened to defeat the confederal idea in the nineteenth century. The mourning of the idealistic "lost cause" defeated by a barbarous and cynical enemy has long been a familiar theme in "loser's history."[98] In 1847, the *HpB* asked how Hessian historians could continue to maintain that Tilly's soldiers were solely responsible for the utter destruction of the wealth and culture accumulated over centuries. Had it been the Croats, the *HpB* wondered, who were responsible for the mutilations, crucifixions, tortures, quarterings, and mass executions of 1637? If this were true, notwithstanding the efforts of liberals like Karl von Rotteck (in his General History of the World) to rationalize the Swedish atrocities as the unfortunate but necessary means of pushing Germany toward political rationalization, why did Hessian mothers even today scold their children with the traditional rhyme:

> Say your prayers, children, say your prayers!
> In the morning comes the Swede,
> In the morning rises the Bull,
> To teach you well your prayers.[99]

For those living in western Germany and on the Rhine frontier, the collective remembrances of the plundering, vandalism, expulsions, and religious persecution inflicted by the Swedish armies were woven easily into the still fresh memory of the French occupation. For Franz Joseph Bodmann (1754–1820), professor of history in Mainz, the memory of his own experience of the French occupation, when he had witnessed the flight of many of the town's leading citizens and endured exile for publicly criticizing "republican" ideas, remarkably resembled an earlier time when, in November 1631, Gustavus Adolphus's army had approached, filling Mainz's citizens with "deathly fear and terror" as they fled into the night. According to Bodmann, who was writing in 1812, the next time

Mainz would see such general panic was in October 1792.[100] Bodmann described how Mainz became headquarters of the Swedish occupation of the Rhenish lands as it endured the extortion of 80,000 talers, a systematic plundering of everything that was not nailed down and much of what was, and finally a regime of terror, religious persecution, robbery, and murder that preyed on every citizen, regardless of estate or sex. It was during this "time of vandalism," Bodmann pointed out, that Gustavus Adolphus's "glittering court" had received the shameful homage of the German princes.[101] Bodmann was obviously confident that the French censors, on the alert for attacks on their administration, would overlook his history of the seventeenth-century Swedish occupation. His litany of Swedish tyrannies, especially the abuse of Catholic clergy, seemed to him to parallel exactly his own century's experience with the French occupiers.[102] Writing in the early 1840s, a period of renewed anti-French feeling across Germany that arose as a response to the Thiers government's bellicosity, the Würzburg historian Carl Gottfried Scharold, a legitimist in the mold of Westenrieder, Hurter, and Klopp, condemned the Swedes as tools of Richelieu in detailed descriptions of the robbery, murder, and torture of Würzburg's Catholics and the methodical plunder of churches, libraries, and museums. Making the same inferences as Bodmann, Scharold reserved his most stinging prose for an account of how a stream of "exultant" Protestants flowed into Würzburg to pay court to Gustavus Adolphus and turn the bishopric into a secular principality by expropriating church property and installing Lutheran clergy in the parishes.[103] The past was never far beneath the surface of the present in German historical consciousness.

After Napoleon's defeat in 1814, themes of revenge and liberation became more prominent in the Rhineland Catholic accounts of the Swedish War. In 1816, the playwright Carl Rabenalt immortalized the resistance of the citizens of Villingen in a romance "freely adapted from the true history."[104] The Swedish general Gustav Horn, a favorite villain in Rhenish lore, confronted a citizenry roused by cries of "revenge!" "retribution!" and "liberation!"[105] "Our loyalty to the Kaiser," one citizen declared, "and the fact that we remain true to our faith, enrages [the Swedes] so much they refuse to spare the elderly, the mothers, and the children," and threaten that "the name of Villingen will be wiped from the face of the earth and those set wandering from the ruins will loudly lament: here was the revenge of the Swedes!"[106] Rabenalt closed the play on a triumphant note with the Swedes in retreat and Villingen's citizens triumphant: "The enemy flees! Citizens, we are free! . . . God give us peace soon! . . . Peace for us and all of the nations that groan under the oppression of this disastrous war."[107] Beneath this celebration of Catholic survival, however, there was obviously still a fear of Protestant persecution and a dread of a biblical judgment of annihilation having been pronounced on Germany's Catholics as punishment for Magdeburg. A privately printed novel by an anonymous author from Überlingen, written sometime between 1830 and 1850, had an emissary of the fearsome General Horn announce this sentence after Überlingen refused to surrender in 1634: "You shall rue that, insolent townspeople! No stone shall remain atop another, and all the waters of the Bodensee shall not suffice to quench the fires that will rain down on you, and the seas of blood that our muskets and swords will let from your breasts shall not dry for a whole year."[108] In Catholic narratives this recurring biblical language of divine judgment, typical of Magdeburg history, does not, as is the case in Protestant usage, invoke martyrdom and redemption, but is instead an expression of the Catholic fear of exile and the loss of the security and community of the imperial polity. There is no reassuring claim of "chosenness," which ultimately elevated Protestant history writing about the war with a sense of hope, but rather a dread of persecution, dispossession, and annihilation. In the collective remembrance of the Thirty Years' War in Germany we have seen how narratives of defeat and victimization predominated. But Catholic recollection of the war could not point to the formation of a vital and resilient national character emerging out of collective suffering. Rather, Catholic narratives articulated an anxiety about the loss of identity and marginalization within the German nation.

The relative isolation of the Catholic communities in the Rhineland and Hesse accounts for a certain degree of paranoia. In comparison, Bavarian history writing about the Swedish War, which includes the work of Franconian and Swabian writers, was characterized less by this pervasive fear than by the same assertion of patriotic fortitude that we found in the Protestant histories. There are three probable reasons for this. Bavaria was a relatively large and territorially cohesive kingdom (except for the Palatinate), second only to Prussia among the states of the German Confederation. In the first half of the nineteenth century, Munich could boast of a cosmopolitan history and cultural patrimony that arguably surpassed Berlin's. And, finally, Bavarian historical consciousness was firmly anchored in the gravitas of the Catholic Wittelsbach dynasty and its claim to represent, in the nineteenth century, a sovereign counterweight to Prussian and Austrian influence in the Confederation. Bavarian histories of the Thirty Years' War, such as those by Westenrieder and Schmidt, had always idealized Maximilian's leadership of the Catholic League as the "Sword of the Counter-Reformation" and the protector and guarantor of the imperial constitution. Bavarian historians worked from a very strong sense of patriotism based on Catholic identity and the legitimist idea that Bavarian status and influence in Germany required the maintenance of the confederal constitutional structure. Although the Bavarian histories of the Swedish War did dwell on the considerable destruction wrought on Bavaria by Gustavus Adolphus's soldiers, their overall perspective is rather different than that found in the Rhenish histories. Bavaria is depicted as an invaded state, suffering not only because it was Catholic but also because it was the main defender and linchpin of the Holy Roman Empire. If the Swedish king could only defeat Bavaria, then the dream of the unified Protestant German Reich could be realized. Bavaria's trial during the Swedish War was interpreted in these nineteenth-century narratives as a patriotic sacrifice to preserve the empire. By focusing on the destruction wrought by a foreign army on German soil, Bavarian historians sought to undermine the claims of Protestant nationalism that glorified Gustavus Adolphus while elevating Bavaria's status as the true defender of German interests and independence.

Until the final acquiescence to the reality of Prussian power in 1871, the course of modern Bavarian history had been marked by the often adverse consequences of the attempt to pursue an independent policy that maintained her position within the Empire (and Confederation) against the ambitions of France, Austria, and Prussia. It is not surprising that the most prominent Bavarian historians who wrote about the Thirty Years' War in the first half of the nineteenth century—Westenrieder, Zschokke, Buchner, Soden, and Mussinan—should find in the events of the Swedish invasion and occupation between 1632 and 1634 much that was instructive for modern Bavaria (and Germany). These historians maintained that Bavaria, after the Catholic League's defeat at Rain in April 1632, had been abandoned by Wallenstein and the Kaiser and forced to carry on the fight for German independence against Sweden alone. It was a time, in the words of Westenrieder, when the lands between the Lech and Munich and from the Isar to the Danube were desolated and "emptied of man and beast . . . the distress of the country was indescribable."[109] The two sieges of Landshut in 1632 and 1634 stood out in Bavarian memory as particularly vivid examples of patriotic sacrifice. Westenrieder lamented the "martyrdom" of Landshut's citizens who, after the city's capture in July 1634, were "tortured for fourteen days with all manner of cruelties."[110] Franz Reithofer (1767–1819), a Cistercian monk and historian of Landshut, pointedly compared the destruction of 1632 and 1634 to the "blood-soaked and fire-scorched" April days of the Austrian-led uprising against Napoleon in 1809, when Bavaria was "invaded by a new war. Here in Landshut the first cannonades rang out, the first blood flowed, the first houses were burned down, the first dwellings were destroyed. It was the first to be plundered and humiliated; the city was stripped of provisions and threatened by friend and foe (France and Austria) alike with general destruction."[111] Returning his narrative to the seventeenth century, Reithofer listed those villages (Hofmarken, Achdorf, Berg, Aichach, and Schrobenhausen) that were plundered, burned, and ruined as the Swedish soldiers took their revenge on the "patriotic peasants" who stubbornly defended their land.[112] Gustavus Adolphus is described as a black-clad "Angel of Death" who stood by in Munich as widows and their daughters were dragged to the Swedish camp to be raped and murdered, their bodies thrown afterwards into the Isar. The more fortunate, according to Reithofer in one of the many references to Magdeburg, saved their honor or virginity by committing suicide. Citing "contemporary reports and local folklore," he described how the Swedish War, made unforgettable by the cruelties of the "northern barbarians," had swept over Bavaria like "a wild mountain flood," leaving the rich land forsaken by its inhabitants and covered with bitter weeds and, under hedges and stone walls, the corpses of those who had died from starvation with grass and leaves still in their mouths.[113] Reithofer portrayed the second siege, in July 1634, as a repeat of Magdeburg, the churches being a special target as the monks, Jesuits, and other clergy were tortured, the altars destroyed, the chalices defiled with excrement, and the holy vestments mocked. He claimed that over a thousand people lost their lives in this biblical ordeal, cut down with the words "That's for Magdeburg!"[114]

The Swiss polymath Heinrich Zschokke (1771–1848), a Magdeburg native and republican-inclined publicist, playwright, novelist, scientist, theologian, and historian, claimed in his controversial history of Bavaria that it was on the tenth of May 1632, a year to the day after Magdeburg was destroyed, that Gustavus Adolphus arrived at the gates of Munich, which had not seen an invading army for over a hundred years, let alone witnessed enemy soldiers within its walls. Zschokke noted that while Munich was largely spared the fury of the Swedes, the countryside from Landsberg to Landshut was turned into a wasteland in the months following the Swedish king's death: "Every atrocity was repeated again and again, so that Swede became a word of eternal horror in Germany."[115] The Swedish general Torstenson had a dread reputation in local lore on a par with Gustavus Adolphus's. Zschokke's description of his "terrible" assault on Landsberg in 1633 uses the vocabulary of Magdeburg histories: altars splashed with blood, infants killed on their mothers' breasts, mass rapes, and virgins leaping from the buildings to preserve their virtue.[116] The local historians of Bavaria, Franconia, and Swabia all had their own Magdeburgs to record. Father Endres of Hagenheim outside of Landsberg told of a great exodus of the peasants as they fled their burned and plundered villages into the woods, mountains, and holes in the earth, where they were hunted down like animals: "The terror which preceded the Swedes was frightful."[117] Plague and famine followed in the train of the enemy's revenge on Bavaria, the defender of the Kaiser, the Empire, and Germany and thus the "chief victim" of Sweden's barbaric cruelties, "which had not been practiced since the time of the Huns."[118] Like the narrators of Magdeburg's destruction, Endres provided his readers with page after page of unrestrained descriptions of the mass rape and torture of women and children, suicides, beheadings, hangings, disembowelings, crucifixions, mutilations, and immolations: "Not since the days of the Huns had a people suffered such cruelties. . . . Everything was smashed, torn down, and broken. Nothing remained whole."[119] For Catholic chroniclers, Bavaria's martyrdom for faith and fatherland, both in the scale of suffering and in the uniqueness of the tortures inflicted, matched and exceeded that of Magdeburg. Catholic accounts of the Swedish War, detailed catalogues of brutality and suffering, were offered as a counterweight to the tribulations glorified by Protestant nationalism. If, as the conventions of Magdeburg history asserted, suffering and sacrifice demonstrated the nation's covenant with God, then, the message seemed to be, Catholic Germany had endured an equivalent (or greater) martyrdom in defense of its own idea of the German nation.[120] Joseph Mussinan (1766–1819), a historian who would make his name with a four-volume history of the Wars of Liberation against Napoleon, described the siege of Straubing in 1633 from the perspective of a Germany united in the war against Napoleon, citing the city's resistance, and Bavarian suffering in general, as "proof of how much the Bavarian of any era rivaled other nations in love of prince and Fatherland and thus rightly competed for this distinction with other Germans. . . . Even if we can no longer, as before, mount the walls of the city and from the bastions deny the enemy entry, we are still prepared to meet that enemy, as we have met him when honor and Fatherland demanded, as when our king called to us on 28 October 1813: 'Arm yourselves for the Fatherland!'"[121] Another witness to the Wars of Liberation, the Regensburg historian Joseph Schuegraf (1790–1861), also appealed to the living memory of the war against Napoleon to celebrate the national character and loyalty of the Bavarians during the Thirty Years' War. In a series of sketches written for the journal *Eos* in 1825, Schuegraf described the guerrilla war in the Bavarian Forest and the patriotic exploits of the archdeacon of Cham who, in 1633, had taken up arms like a medieval cleric and, burning with "the holy fire of love of Fatherland and religion," continued the war with the free hunters of the forests against the "inhuman" enemy.[122]

By the 1880s historians had transformed the celebration of Bavarian patriotism found in earlier accounts of the sack of Landsberg into a paean to German fortitude and loyalty. As he explored the remains of the Swedish trenches that still could be found on the heights surrounding the town, Franz Zwerger mused that "the recollections of the terrible cruelty of [the Thirty Years' War] live so immediately in the consciousness of the people, that one cannot believe that it was so far back in time." Zwerger believed that the passage of time should not be allowed to obscure the many examples of "the courage of the Germans as they fought for prince and fatherland," as in the Swabian "guerrilla war," when the peasants took up arms against the foreign conqueror.[123] Remembering the time of annihilation offered Germany's Catholics an opportunity to express a type of patriotism that still honored loyalty to the old empire, which had, in their view, embraced all Germans. For over a century, the Franconian town of Kronach had gathered in a midsummer thanksgiving feast to celebrate the lifting of the Swedish siege in 1634. This "Festival of Liberation" began with cannonades and pealing bells as a colorful procession made its way to the old earthworks on the Rosenberg. Franz August Bauer, on the two hundredth anniversary of the siege, published an account of his participation in one of these festivals. Bauer fondly recalled his "passionate speech," which had paid homage to the old German virtues of strength and loyalty and had led his audience back through the centuries to a time when Gustavus Adolphus had approached Kronach through a countryside filled with flaming villages and forests and soil soaked in rivers of German blood. In their sacrifice for "Kaiser, Prince, and Fatherland," Bauer compared the citizens of Kronach to their Hussite forefathers and the warriors of Sparta and Carthage, who knew that it was "better to go under with sword in hand than to give in to such bloodthirsty tyranny!"[124]

The physical scars that the time of annihilation left on the Bavarian landscape were still visible well into the nineteenth century. Even as they inspired collective remembrance of Bavaria's sacrifices for the lost cause of imperial unity, they also reinforced the Bavarian sense of nation. Joseph von Mussinan recalled that "it was with tears our forefathers told these tales, and we still cannot look on the mournful traces of the cruelties without a shudder."[125] In similar mournful tones Joseph Schuegraf described his hikes up to the ruins of the fortress called the Donaustauf that defended Regensburg during the siege of 1634: "Today we climb the massif for pleasure, so that we might wonder at its ancient magnificence and, standing on its ruins, look on the past in all its glory. . . . Even Donaustauf, a work of German knights, sinks under the river of time, as any other miracle."[126] In an earlier work written in 1813, during the uprising against Napoleon, Mussinan reminded his readers that if they wanted confirmation that a new spirit of unity was animating the German nation, they need only seek out a stone in the church in the abbey of Oberalteich near Straubing inscribed with these words:

> In sixteen hundred and twenty-two,
> When this church was begun,
> Cries for war filled the whole empire;
> The Calvinists, together with the princes,
> Waged war on the emperor and his rule,
> Each side returned blow and counterblow,
> From which flowed plundering, murder, and death,
> Debased coin, oppression, dearth, and famine;
> Eight Kreutzer bought little bread.[127]

In focusing on Catholic martyrdom for a lost cause, Catholic historians argued for the legitimacy of their community's patriotic sacrifice for its idea of Germany. But a persistent dread of marginalization, expropriation, and even outright physical annihilation marked Catholic accounts of the Swedish War. Catholic historians, and Catholic memory, could not easily forget the time of annihilation that had bloodily thrown back the armies that had stood victorious on the Baltic in 1629, a defeat that seemed to be reenacted at many levels in the nineteenth century.[128] They remembered the threat of annihilation as a warning of the dire consequences of a revolutionary ideology that threatened legitimate political structures and institutions.

The histories of the Swedish War, both Catholic and Protestant, were "Gothic" narratives in the sense that they were obsessed with the violent dissolution of community, with decline and death, with the loss of identity and place, and with the possibility that the nation might not survive.[129] Both narratives were driven by the sense of a threat to identity arising out of the past that could not be overcome or avoided—a presence of the past that would always undermine the foundations of the German nation. But there was also a sense of hope, or at least defiance, in these stories of suffering and victimization. Both Protestant and Catholic wrote a history of sacrifice that was intended to confirm and strengthen their community's covenant with God, their membership in the one true church of the nation. Ultimately, they tried to find meaning in a long tortuous story of triumph and defeat, the multiple histories of an unrealized Germany.

Conclusion

War and the National Covenant

In the nineteenth century, German historians rediscovered the Thirty Years' War as the great conflict that created the foundations of the modern German nation. As they retold the story of the war, they uncovered, or so they believed, the meaning of centuries of defeat, territorial fragmentation, and political disunity. They also found clues they thought disclosed the shape of Germany's future and signposts indicating possible roads to unification. Interpreting the tribulations of the war as signs of God's covenant with the German nation, Protestant historians found in the story of the war an ideal platform from which to declare a new nationalist history that revealed the Germans as Europe's chosen people destined not only for unity but also for dominion. The Catholic recollection of the war found no such promise of redemption, only the threat of marginalization, dissolution, and expropriation. The euphoria over unification in 1871, that long-awaited entrance into the Promised Land, celebrated the fulfillment of this covenant while pushing the Catholic story of the nation, against fierce resistance, to the margins of the new unifying narrative. Conceived out of the enduring antagonism between Catholic and Protestant, the nineteenth-century histories of "The Great German War" were constructed around the five essential stories of German history: unification, liberation, revolution, martyrdom, and sacrifice. German historians used these narratives to connect the legacy of the Thirty Years' War to the fulfillment of their nation's destiny.

The Battle of the Teutoburgerwald, Luther's confrontation with the Catholic Church, the Thirty Years' War, and the Wars of Liberation against Napoleonic France were linked by nineteenth-century Protestant historians in a continuous and coherent history that identified the struggle with Rome and Catholicism as the defining conflict that shaped German identity. Faced with the Protestant charge that Catholics were less than authentic Germans, Catholic historians were compelled to challenge this interpretation of the war with vigorous assertions of the legitimacy (and viability) of the imperial-confederal idea of the German nation. In the clash between the Protestant and Catholic ideas of Germany, each side was seen by the other as determined to destroy or undermine the political and territorial conception that best protected German interests. But without this conflict, crystallized in the story of the Thirty Years' War, no idea of Germany, or what it meant to be German, was possible. Protestant identity in particular, and everything the Protestant idea of Germany stood for, was rooted in the experience of the war.

In almost any nationalist worldview, history is primarily the story of war, an elemental struggle to preserve the existence of the community. In particular, the waging of religious war elevates this battle for existence above all other rationales. But even in the secular conception of modern total war, we find this rationale still exerting a powerful influence on the articulation of war aims, in propaganda, and in the mobilization of the nation.[1] In the late seventeenth century, as European conflicts became less explicitly about God and more about dynasty and nation, the persuasive power of the religious cause remained latent in the continent's emerging nationalisms. Michael Walzer, in his study of the seventeenth-century civil war in Britain, labels religious war "Puritan war," which he defines as a "crusade [as a] struggle against external enemies as continuous and unrelenting as was the saints' war against sin."[2] Exile and servitude are the fate and punishment of man expelled from Eden, conditions that are the denial of nationhood, conditions that require the constant renewal of the exclusive covenant with God. Walzer believes that this is "an idea of great presence and power in Western political thought: the idea of deliverance from suffering and oppression: this-worldly redemption, liberation, revolution."[3] Protestant Germany came to believe that Luther's revolt against Rome in 1517 was the first chapter in the unfolding story of God's special plan for

Germany. Understanding the Reformation not only as a struggle against a corrupt Catholic Church but also as a struggle for German freedom made it possible to characterize the German aspiration to nationhood as an exclusively Protestant cause. Catholic historians strenuously tried to refute this definition of German identity, but it remained a powerful dynamic within German nationalism well into the twentieth century. World War I witnessed its apotheosis when German war aims were linked to the defense of *Kultur*, but it was not entirely absent from the millenarian ambitions of the Third Reich.

Of the five narratives that were used to tell the story of the Thirty Years' War in the nineteenth century, three—liberation, revolution, and sacrifice (necessary for redemption)—were perhaps the most central to the reinterpretation of the war and, it is clear, to the German understanding of their history, through the experience of the Thirty Years' War, as essentially a "narrative of covenants." To grasp at such a religiously inflected conception of a national history is not a peculiarity confined to the Germans, nor is it the only way they chose (or could choose) to read their history. But the clash between the Protestant and Catholic visions of the nation, revealed in the histories and commemorations that are the subject of this book, inevitably cast arguments about Germany's destiny in religious terms. In his study of religiously inspired violence, Mark Juergensmeyer describes how fundamentalist creeds use the narrative of covenants to justify war as a cosmic struggle to restore order (and thus the covenant) and defend the nation's (or group's) "basic identity and dignity" through violence and sacrifice.[4] In this struggle, the nation can only survive by inflicting (following God's command) on other nations the fate it fears most: annihilation.[5] This is the dread, so strongly present in the Catholic histories and transcended in Protestant nationalism through the idea of sacrifice, which emerges out of nineteenth-century Germany's rediscovery of the Thirty Years' War. The narrative of the war foretold the German rise to nationhood as a story that alternated between the extremes of defeat and victory, sacrifice and extermination, and covenants fulfilled and broken. The Promised Land was continually struck from the Germans' grasp, or they were driven from it into a metaphorical exile and captivity manifested in political and territorial fragmentation. Each time the covenant was broken, the promise of nationhood was elaborated in ever-grander terms in German history writing: the remaking of the medieval imperium in 1629, a unified Protestant Reich in 1632, a powerful central European kingdom in 1634, and then, after the long quiescence imposed by the Treaty of Westphalia, a unified nation-state in 1813, the dominant European power in 1871, *primus inter pares* in 1914, and, finally, a world empire in 1933. In this chronology of continually redefined national ambitions, defeat or the broken covenant has had a profound impact on the German historical consciousness, as Ulf Hedetoft points out in his conclusion that Germany's national narrative "is one of disruption and hiatuses, grandiose ideas and often less than grandiose implementations, of abortive revolution rather than evolution."[6]

It was through the matrix of three broken covenants in particular—1629, 1632, and 1634—that the Thirty Years' War was reinterpreted in the nineteenth century. It began as what contemporaries called "the great German civil war." Protestant historians argued that the war had its origins in a justified rebellion against the imperial violation of the civil religious peace. In the Catholic view, the war had indeed begun as a rebellion, but much more was at stake in this revolt than a restoration of the status quo of 1555. It was a revolution against the legitimate constitution of the empire. From the Catholic perspective, what was at issue was nothing less than the preservation and strengthening of the imperial constitutional polity, the guarantor of "German liberty" and the bastion of German culture and civilization. Catholic historians, especially anti-Prussian conservatives such as Onno Klopp and Friedrich von Hurter, explicitly compared the Reformation to the French Revolution because both, in their view, had unleashed uncontrollable forces that had threatened to overturn the established order. The magnitude of this threat legitimated the vision of a German nation that Catholic historians promoted and defended in their histories of the war. They saw the Thirty Years' War as that epochal moment when, out of the destruction of civil war, an opportunity to unify and reform the Holy Roman Empire had briefly beckoned. That moment had come in 1629 and 1630 when the armies of Tilly and Wallenstein stood victorious on the shores of the Baltic Sea. In trying to bring Germany back under the banner of the double eagle, these historians argued, Ferdinand II had made a bold bid to resurrect the glory and power of the medieval empire. More compelling still, from the nineteenth-century perspective, was Wallenstein's "Baltic project" in its vision of an economically and politically modernized Holy Roman Empire that could compete with England, France, the Netherlands, and Sweden.

Gustavus Adolphus's landing on the Baltic island of Rügen in 1631 ended these schemes. With Sweden's intervention, the German civil war became a larger war for a more grandly conceived German liberation. For Protestant historians, Gustavus Adolphus was the "savior of German Protestantism" who had arrived in Germany's darkest hour to free her from the tyranny of Rome and the "Spanish party" in Vienna. As with Wallenstein's dramatic push to the Baltic in 1629, Gustavus Adolphus's triumphal march through Germany in 1631 and 1632 had also promised to achieve much more than merely preserving the status quo. The Catholic empire would be demolished and remade. For Protestant historians, particularly those who were pro-Prussian, the epic of Gustavus Adolphus demonstrated the possibility of the fulfillment of the German destiny covenanted in 1517: an independent and unified Protestant Reich. Gustavus Adolphus's victory at Breitenfeld promised the establishment of a new notion of what it meant to be German as well: a Nordic German state purged of the domination of Rome, the corruption of the Catholic south, and the foreign tyranny of the imperial armies. But this covenant was broken in 1632 at Lützen.

The broken covenant was brought to light in the great debate that became known as the "trial of Wallenstein." Wallenstein's story was transformed into the history of an ambitious revolutionary warlord who had tried to remake the empire into a powerful secular state. From the Rankean perspective of mid-nineteenth-century historiography, Wallenstein was Germany's world-historical figure, a genius on a par with Cromwell and Napoleon, who had seen the future of a unified Germany and whose ambitions legitimated the power politics of Bismarck as he orchestrated Prussian leadership of German unification. As in the tantalizing mirage of 1629 and in the catastrophe of Lützen in 1632, the chorus behind the "tragedy" of Wallenstein's assassination in 1634 repeated a familiar lament of modern German history: "what might have been." Wallenstein's Catholic detractors in Austria condemned him as a traitor driven by personal ambition to deliver the empire into the hands of its enemies. Protestant German nationalists rejected this interpretation and praised Wallenstein as a visionary "bringer of peace," a German hero betrayed by an emperor under the influence of foreigners and Jesuits. In the Protestant view, the "catastrophe" of Wallenstein's murder in his castle in Eger in 1634 ended the most ambitious design for the German nation to emerge in the war: a powerful and unitary state stretching from the Alps to the Baltic and from the Rhine to the Prussian marches.

There was broad agreement that the Peace of Westphalia was the heavy price paid for the broken covenants of 1629, 1632, and 1634. In the view of most nineteenth-century historians, Protestant or Catholic, the settlement of 1648 confirmed 200 more years of Germany's subordinate status in Europe and left a divided and weakened Germany helpless prey for the great powers. Friedrich von Raumer's 1832 history of the war was presented to his fellow Germans as a "mirror in which we can recognize our sins." Raumer concluded with a pessimistic quote from a seventeenth-century lament, "Germany for Germans! Our scepter and eagle are no longer ours, our Reich is no longer ours."[7] Johann Sporschil also mourned the decline of the Reich as a dynamic national idea: "The German Reich was only a name and imperial authority a shadow. A few states arose out of Germany, which disappeared from the ranks of European powers and for a long time ceased to be regarded as their Fatherland by its sons."[8] For a brief moment, the revolution of 1848 was a hopeful interruption of the commemorations of the bicentennial of Westphalia. Konrad Rüdel saw that year's springtime promise of national unity (the broken covenant of 1848?) as closely connected to the significance of 1648: "in the eyes of the world the power and authority of Germany, and her inner unity, have significantly declined since 1648 and only now, after the humiliating oppression of the Napoleonic tyranny, has a small beginning been made to again uplift the German people, whose emperor once wielded the greatest power in Christendom."[9]

Even a Catholic historian like Franz Keym welcomed the renewal of the national covenant when he proclaimed that the humiliation of 1648 had been finally reversed by the triumph of 1871.[10]

A religiously inflected concept of war tends to see it as God's trial and judgment of the chosen people, without which the covenant has no binding force. The broken covenants of 1629, 1632, and 1634 (and 1813, 1848, 1871, 1917–18, 1941) could only be renewed, and the nation reborn, through continuing sacrifice. The histories of the Thirty Years' War turned the miseries of war into marks of divine grace. This belief became the foundation of the harsh faith of modern German nationalism. From the Protestant side, the atrocity narratives that described the destruction of Magdeburg and the cruelties of the Swedish War transcended the fear of destruction and annihilation with prophecies of Germany's rise from the ruins. Here we have an example of how the Old Testament injunction that remembrance ensures the survival of the group became a fundamental component of the Western historical consciousness. At least in the German case this consciousness, born in war, defeat, and victimization, was essential to the nationalist perspective that transformed the lamentations of exile, slavery, and tribulation into triumphant (and optimistic) stories of liberation. The Protestant histories of the sack of Magdeburg believed that the city's sacrifice must *eventually* be redeemed in German freedom, however near or distant that liberation was. But this liberation could only be conceived in terms of the founding of the Protestant nation. Conversely, the Catholic crime of Magdeburg would be punished with expulsion from the Promised Land. Forever marked with the sign of Cain, the city's Catholic destroyers were set apart from the true nation of the elect. It was a stigma that Catholic historians tried in vain to remove.

The tropes of Magdeburg histories are the essential context for understanding the message that Protestant and Catholic histories of the Swedish War were trying to deliver. In both narratives the extraordinary brutalities of the war were reconceived as sacrifices for opposed ideas of the German nation. For Protestant historians, the triumph of 1871 irrefutably demonstrated which sacrifice ultimately was accepted and which national covenant was consecrated. But there was no redemption to be found in the Catholic narratives of the Swedish War. We read in them a palpable dread of expropriation, expulsion, and extermination. Whether it was the seventeenth century or the nineteenth, the violent dissolution of Catholic membership in the nation always loomed.

For three hundred years the memory of the Thirty Years' War tormented the German historical imagination. It was remembered as the whirlwind out of which so much misfortune had come, yet there had also been so much unfulfilled promise glimpsed through the storm. As an epic cataclysm of fratricidal gore, it had no less an impact on the Germans' conception of their nation in the nineteenth and twentieth centuries than the seventeenth-century Civil War had on the British, the Revolution of 1789 on the French, and the Civil War on the Americans. But Germans were not able to construct a reconciling historical myth out of the experience of the Thirty Years' War that could confidently claim that a new nation had emerged from the conflict. But despite all this, the histories of the Thirty Years' War still offered the Germans hope, which was, ultimately, their purpose. Ironically, it is Walter Benjamin, who saw deeper into the "German problem" than most (and become one of its victims), who offers the clearest explanation for this nation's obsession with a traumatic past. The Germans believed, as Benjamin himself believed, that "to articulate the past historically does not mean to recognize it 'the way it really was.' It means to seize hold of a memory as it flashes up in a moment of danger."[11]

A Second Thirty Years' War? (1914–1945)

The survival of Protestantism after the Thirty Years' War did much to establish the "chosen people" narrative that made possible the great awakening of German nationalism in the nineteenth century. By 1893 Georg Winter could claim that the Protestant cause in the war was the beginning of a "genuine German-national Protestant idea," a revolutionary moment in German history when "a great unified spiritual movement went through all Germans in their political disunity."[12] The nineteenth-century histories of the Thirty Years' War expose the tangled roots of modern German nationalism that made Germany's bellicose self-righteousness largely incomprehensible to her enemies during World War I. They also help explain the widespread disbelief on the part of Germany's politicians and intellectuals that Britain and France would ally themselves with expansionist Russia, an alliance that the philosopher Max Scheler would condemn in 1916 as "a betrayal of Western culture."[13] For Scheler the war was not a "world war" but a "German war" waged not only for his country's "existence, independence, and freedom" but also for Europe and, indeed, for all of mankind.[14] Also prominent among German intellectuals was the view that this latest war with France was a renewal of the crusade of 1870–71 against French rationalism, materialism, and republicanism, which in itself was a renewal of the longer war against French expansionism that had begun in the Thirty Years' War.[15] The alliance of the Entente also mystified German theologians such as Ernst Troeltsch and Adolf von Harnack, who could not comprehend Britain's cynical abandonment of the German Protestant cause of defending European civilization.[16] That these views were pervasive among the intellectual elites and educated Germans is in no small part because of the emotional and psychological traction they found in the nineteenth-century histories of the Thirty Years' War.

The Protestant nationalism of the nineteenth century, in large part a product of the new interpretations of the war, was a key element of the "war theology" that Wilhelm Pressel sees emerging in World War I as an attempt by the church to justify the destruction of the war by preaching a "nationalist understanding of God." This idea, very similar to Scheler's hope that a new national consciousness would come out of the war, sanctified German war aims as a battle for a divinely ordained worldview, in this instance the creation of a new *Volksgemeinschaft* morally superior to that of Germany's apostate and decadent enemies. The history of the Great War, like those of the Thirty Years' War, the Wars of Liberation, and the Wars of Unification before it, was susceptible to a religious framing because it promised the "fulfillment" (*Vollendung*), in an eschatological sense, of German history. Because it was delivering divine judgment on which nation would survive to establish the righteous rule of God on earth, this war could only be defined as an apocalyptic battle between good and evil.[17] In 1911 the theologian Karl Holl looked back on the Thirty Years' War as the origin of "the [German] conviction of the ethical worth of the state [and] the commitment to the whole which was prepared even for heavy sacrifices. The inner resources of the state were thus greatly increased. Herein lies the reason why the Protestant lands recovered so quickly from the Thirty Years' War . . . why poor Prussia could become a great power."[18]

By the winter of 1917–18, three years of stalemate and mass slaughter had brought home to most Germans, if not to the annexationist politicians and the General Staff, that the grand designs of 1914 had very likely gone glimmering. A catastrophic defeat threatened the fulfillment of the covenant of 1871. The dread of enslavement and annihilation pressed heavily on Germany as the nation once again faced invasion, defeat, and partition. Nevertheless, another opportunity for rebirth, if not victory, could be glimpsed through the approaching storm. The looming collapse was yet another crisis in a longer struggle that had begun in 1618 (if not 1517), one more trial and judgment of the German nation by God. A collection of documents from the period of the Thirty Years' War published in 1917 opened with the foreword to the 1683 edition of Grimmelshausen's *Simplicissimus*. "To the Loyal German Reader" reminded Germans of the destruction of the Thirty Years' War: the burned villages, destroyed churches, raped women, and German blood that had "flowed like water"—all the sacrifices demanded in the defense of German liberty from the "tyranny of Byzantium."[19] In Vilna in 1916 Holl announced to an assembly of Lutheran missionaries and church leaders that the world war was a religious war that had come to test the "moral worth" (*sittliche Wert*) of the German people. He called on Germans to summon the spiritual power to prevail by recalling how the nation had twice fought a "battle for existence" (*Daseinskampf*): the Thirty Years' War and the Wars of Liberation. In Holl's view, the similarities between the Thirty Years' War and the world war were even more remarkable—both were wars of "to be or not to be" for German Protestantism.[20]

Michael Geyer has coined the expressive term "catastrophic nationalism" to describe the dread and pessimism that enveloped the German High Command toward the end of 1918 that went beyond fear of defeat on the battlefield. The military and civil collapse threatened the dissolution of the nation in Bolshevik-style revolution and barbarism. There seemed to be no alternative other than to embrace apocalypse and to call for a popular uprising (*Volksaufstand*) in the tradition of 1813—a Wagnerian "war unto destruction" (*Endkampf*) that promised national rebirth.[21] But reality soon overcame Ludendorff's hysterical visions of *Götterdämmerung*. Losing their nerve, the military leadership handed power to the civilians and, following their Kaiser, abandoned the field. They returned after the peace to fulminate against a world turned upside down in the wake of the epochal "world civil war" unleashed in 1917.[22] They preached the penance of German moral regeneration made necessary by conditions "reminiscent of the period after the Thirty Years' War."[23] Above all, the broken covenant of 1918 inspired violent fantasies of national redemption that in no small measure contributed to the rise of Adolf Hitler.

The Second Reich's disintegration in 1918 was yet another catastrophe in the long history of the unrealized nation. Peace brought neither harmony nor stability, only a reawakening of the dread of national dissolution and despair over another broken covenant, another failure to fulfill the national destiny. But modern German history was inconceivable as a narrative without the beginning story of defeat—indeed, the narrative in all its versions, Protestant and Catholic, was a *response* to defeat. This narrative, established as the defining national epic in the histories of the Thirty Years' War, was written in what Stefan-Ludwig Hoffman, in his study of the commemorations of the Battle of the Nations in 1813, perceptively identifies as the guilt-ridden "pietistic language of liberation": the crippling conviction that Germany history was an eternal cycle of subjection, sacrificial death, and rebirth.[24] Ultimately, it was impossible to reconcile a narrative of defeat with nationalist allegiance without recourse to Christian imagery that promised redemption in the covenant, the establishment of the Kingdom of God on earth.[25] This confluence of religious millenarian hope, sacral nationalism, and the trauma of mass death, first given concrete form as the fundamental elements of a German national history in the narratives of the Thirty Years' War, exerted a powerful influence on the conception of the German nation after the defeat of 1918.

How did post-1918 interpretations of the Thirty Years' War reflect these themes of degeneration, renewal, and revolution? In 1920 Ricarda Huch published a novelistic "character study" of Wallenstein that chronicled the Duke of Friedland's attempt to renew and unify a "degenerate and decadent" Reich through war and violent revolution.[26] In a defeated Germany, in which the nationalist themes of regeneration through violence swirled poisonously in public discourse, the environment was favorable to such reconsiderations of the career of Wallenstein. The only novel by Alfred Döblin that the Nazis did *not* ban was his *Wallenstein*, also published in 1920, which Harro Müller believes was less offensive to the Nazi worldview because it advanced a view of history as "war history [which] is the history of terror with strongly marked cyclical moments."[27] After the Nazi seizure of power in 1933, Walther Tritsch rhapsodized that "the theme of Wallenstein is in the air" as he compared Wallenstein's grasp of war as the means to create a new type of state to Hitler's vision of a revitalized Germany.[28] The Thirty Years' War, wrote Carl Rummel in 1941, had been sent by God so that Wallenstein, "a bridge between past and future," could attempt to "remold the Reich into a new form," a task, Rummel believed, that continued under the leadership of Hitler.[29]

Radicalized nationalism in interwar Germany used references to the enormous population losses (and forced migrations) of the Thirty Years' War, which were so deeply embedded in the German popular memory of the "Swedish War," to promote a vision of German recovery after World War I that was based on the regeneration of the race. Karl Brandi, a noted historian of the Holy Roman Empire, concluded in his 1927 history of the Thirty Years' War that the devastation of Germany, particularly the human losses, at the hands of foreigners only strengthened the "national soul" (*Volksseele*) and led to a "rediscovery of the national" that was much more profound and enduring than the national idea that had emerged during the first blossoming of German humanism.[30] Post-1918 German fears of national decline and dissolution also gave new life to the nineteenth-century ideas of Nordicism and racial renewal, which shaped the Nazi concept of the racially pure national community (*Volksgemeinschaft*). These particular anxieties also gave rise to new interpretations of the ambitions of Gustavus Adolphus. Johannes Paul, the Swedish king's most authoritative biographer in this period, argued that in light of the national humiliation of the Napoleonic occupation, surely it would have been better for Germany if a "racially kindred hero" (*Stammverwandter Held*) had reorganized the Holy Roman Empire as a "great Swedish-German Reich."[31] This interpretation was repeated by Ernst Kohlmeyer in 1940, who pointed out that a "strongly bound Germanic Reich" (*germanischen, festumgrenzten Reich*) under the rule of a "racially kindred blood relative" (*stammesnäher, blutsverwandter*) would certainly have been preferable to the tyranny of "the international, half-Spanish imperium with its Croats and Magyars."[32] A young Gerhard Ritter, writing in 1932 in his student newspaper *Wingolf's Herald* on the tercentenary commemoration of the king's death at Lützen, asserted that such a state would have created a bulwark defending German-Protestant culture from "Muscovite barbarism."[33] A similar position was taken by Richard Schmidt, who in February 1933 compared Gustavus Adolphus's failure to create a Swedish-German union to defend Protestant northern Europe with Alexander the Great's failure to unite the "Hellenistic-Asiatic world" against Persia.[34] In 1943, after four bloody years of a second world war, Günther Franz reminded war-weary Germans that the Thirty Years' War had created a more vital "German racial stock" (*deutschen Volkstämme*).[35]

Even before the Second World War began, an exegesis of the history of the Thirty Years' War that supported Adolf Hitler's new racial covenant received the imprimatur of the Nazi Party. In December 1937 Wilhelm Frick, the Nazi minister of the interior, gave a speech to the German-Swedish Society in which he promoted a plan to build a new national monument to Gustavus Adolphus on the site of the memorial chapel at Lützen. Frick believed that it was now time to acknowledge that the "true Germanic hero king" had been fighting, even if unconsciously, for the "Nordic-Germanic racial idea"—a battle which, if it had been lost, might have spelled defeat for "the entire Nordic-Germanic worldview" for which Hitler was fighting today.[36] Frick's speech was published as a foreword to a 1939 book by Hans Chilian that proposed

to answer for modern readers the question "What present-day significance does the king have for the racial consciousness of Sweden and
Germany?" The answer was to be found, according to Chilian, in the
recognition that Gustavus Adolphus's spirit "walks in the ranks of all
German freedom fighters, in the armies of Frederick the Great, the Wars
of Liberation, the Wars of Unification, and the World War . . . inspiring the racial comrades (*Volksgenossen*) of the Third Reich with new
energy [in the battle] against Bolshevism and imperialism." There is no
doubt, Chilian concludes, that there was "a direct line from Gustavus
Adolphus to Adolf Hitler."[37]

Hitler himself made repeated references to the "fifteen million dead"
of the Thirty Years' War as the great trial in which the German *Volk*
proved its worth. It is interesting to note that Hitler had originally
believed, as he wrote in *Mein Kampf*, that the war had brought on a
period of decline of the German race, when "poisonings of the blood"
had led to "a decomposition of . . . our soul."[38] Yet, once he was in
power, he came to point to the demographic recovery from losses of
the Thirty Years' War (always using the canonical figure of fifteen million dead) and Germany's rise to nationhood after 1648 as proof of
German racial vitality and superiority.[39] After 1939 these references
became a consistent theme in his wartime table talk.[40] In his last public speech before a civilian audience, on July 4, 1944, in Obersalzberg,
Hitler rallied himself and his audience of two hundred industrialists
after a catastrophic month in which the German army had lost over a
million men. He recalled the "numberless wars," including the Thirty
Years' War, which the German people had survived, "even as they
would survive this one," and reminded his listeners that "it is always
better that the birth certificate of a new Reich be written in blood, with
blood, and in crisis."[41]

The German nation, more than any other, had imagined its birth in
death and sacrifice, a gestation that many believed had begun in the
Thirty Years' War. This book has attempted to uncover and explain
the origins of this oft-repeated truism by examining the visions of the
German nation articulated in the nineteenth-century histories of that
war and make a claim for its essential validity. In the hands of German

historians, the story of the Thirty Years' War was fashioned into an idea of the nation rooted in the fear of annihilation. This morbid imagining of the nation was a conception of the German national narrative as thanatopsis, a meditation on death that was at the heart of what Norbert Elias sees as the German quest for "fulfillment in destruction." Ultimately, Elias reminds us, the word *Reich* came to stand for something that was lost, the elusive goal forever beyond the German grasp that was the reason for "the dream-like character of the German self-image."[42]

Notes

Abbreviations

ADB: Allgemeine Deutsche Biographie
AGO: Archiv für Geschichte und Alterthumskunde von Oberfranken
GbM: Geschichtsblätter für Stadt und Land Magdeburg
HpB: Historisch-politische Blätter für das katholische Deutschland
JMG: Jahrbücher des Vereins für meklenburgische Geschichte und
    Altherthumskunde
NDB: Neue Deutsche Biographie

Introduction

1. See Luise Mühlbach, *Die Opfer des religiösen Fanatismus: Historischer Roman aus dem dreißigjährigen Krieg*, 3 vols. (Prague: Sigmund Bensinger, 1871–72). Bensinger repackaged the novel as a six-volume offering in 1873 under the title *Der Dreißigjährigen Krieg*. Mühlbach also enjoyed considerable success in English translation. See Thea Ebersberger, ed., *Erinnerungsblätter aus dem Leben Luise Mühlbach's* (Leipzig: H. Schmidt & C. Günther, 1902).

2. There have been other exceptions. See Andrew Wolpert, *Remembering Defeat: Civil War and Civic Memory in Ancient Athens* (Baltimore: Johns Hopkins University Press, 2002).

3. See Thomas Mann, *Doktor Faustus* (Munich: S. Fischer, 1967), 638–39.

4. Bernhard Erdmannsdörffer, "Zur Geschichte und Geschichtschreibung des dreißigjährigen Krieges," *Historische Zeitschrift* 14 (Munich, 1865): 4–5. Erdmannsdörffer, a student of Sybel and Droysen, was Treitschke's successor at Heidelberg. His advocacy of a national German history deplored polemics and insisted on objective appraisals of both Habsburg and Hohenzollern accomplishments. See Fduard Fueter, *Geschichte der neueren Historiographie* (Munich and Berlin: R. Oldenbourg, 1911), 547–48; and Heinrich Ritter von Srbik, *Geist und Geschichte vom deutschen Humanismus bis zur Gegenwart* (Munich: F. Bruckmann, 1951), 2:4–6.

5. Nineteenth-century Britain underwent a similar process of self-reflection on its seventeenth-century past, but in this case to confirm the certainties of parliamentary liberalism. See J. W. Burrow, *A Liberal Descent: Victorian Historians and the English Past* (Cambridge: Cambridge University Press, 1983) and *Whigs and Liberals: Continuity and Change in English Political Thought* (New York: Oxford University Press, 1988).

6. Eugen Weber, *My France: Politics, Culture, Myth* (Cambridge: Harvard University Press, 1991), 23, quoted in Celia Applegate, "A Europe of Regions: Reflections on the Historiography of Sub-National Places in Modern Times," *American Historical Review* 104, no. 4 (October 1999): 1159.

7. See Srbik, *Geist und Geschichte*. See also the essays in Arnold Esch and Jens Petersen, eds., *Geschichte und Geschichtswissenschaft in der Kultur Italiens und Deutschlands* (Tübingen: Niemeyer, 1989); Heiner Timmermann, ed., *Geschichtschreibung zwischen Wissenschaft und Politik: Deutschland-Frankreich-Polen im 19. und 20. Jahrhundert* (Saarbrücken-Scheidt: R. Dadder, 1987); and Wolfgang Hardtwig, *Geschichtskultur und Wissenschaft* (Munich: DTV, 1990).

8. Georg G. Iggers, *The German Conception of History: The National Tradition of Historical Thought from Herder to the Present*, rev. ed. (Middletown CT: Wesleyan University Press, 1983). The literature on this subject is extensive and focuses on the manifestation of German philosophical idealism in German history writing. See also Peter Hanns Reill, *The German Enlightenment and the Rise of Historicism* (Berkeley: University of California Press, 1975); the essays in Horst W. Blanke and Jörn Rüsen, eds., *Von der Aufklärung zum Historismus: Zum Strukturwandel des historischen Denkens* (Paderborn: F. Schöningh, 1984); and in Otto Gerhard Oexele and Jörn Rüsen, eds., *Historismus in den Kulturwissenschaften* (Cologne: Böhlau, 1996); and Horst W. Blanke, *Historiographiegeschichte als Historik* (Stuttgart and Bad Canstatt: Frommann-Holzboog, 1991).

9. See Bernd Faulenbach, *Ideologie des deutschen Weges: Die deutsche Geschichte in der Historiographie zwischen Kaiserreich und Nationalsozialismus* (Munich: C. H. Beck, 1980). See also Stefan Berger, *The Search for Normality: National Identity and Historical Consciousness in Germany since 1800* (Providence RI: Berghahn Books, 1997). Berger focuses mainly on German historians' debates after 1945.

10. See Franz X. von Wegele, *Geschichte der deutschen Historiographie seit dem Auftreten des Humanismus* (Munich and Leipzig: R. Oldenbourg, 1885); Fueter, Geschichte der neueren Historiographie; Georg von Below, *Die deutsche Geschichtschreibung von den Befreiungskriegen bis zu unsern Tagen* (Munich and Berlin: R. Oldenbourg, 1924); and Moriz Ritter, Die Entwicklung der Geschichtswissenschaft an den führenden Werken betrachtet (Munich and Berlin: R. Oldenbourg, 1919). For an early, yet still useful, survey of the development of modern history writing in Europe, see G. P. Gooch, *History and Historians in the Nineteenth Century* (London: Longmans, Green, 1913).

11. The modern literature on individual historians of the nineteenth century, especially Ranke, is extensive. For important representative works, see Walther Hofer, *Geschichtschreibung und Weltanschauung: Betrachtungen zum Werk Friedrich Meineckes* (Munich: R. Oldenbourg, 1950); Walter Bußmann, *Treitschke, sein Welt- und Geschichtsbild* (Göttingen: Musterschmidt, 1952); Hellmut Seier, *Die Staatsidee Heinrich von Sybels in den Wandlungen der Reichsgründungszeit*

1862/1871 (Lübeck: Matthiesen, 1961); Andreas Dorpalen, *Heinrich von Treitschke* (New Haven: Yale University Press, 1957); Jörn Rüsen, *Begriffene Geschichte: Genesis und Begründung der Geschichtstheorie J. G. Droysens* (Paderborn: F. Schöningh, 1969); and Roger Chickering, *Karl Lamprecht: A German Academic Life (1856–1915)* (Atlantic Highlands NJ: Humanities Press, 1993). See also Hans-Ulrich Wehler, ed., *Deutsche Historiker* (Göttingen: Vandenhoeck & Ruprecht, 1971–82); Wolfgang Weber, *Priester der Klio: Historisch-sozialwissenschaftliche Studien zur Herkunft und Karriere deutscher Historiker und zur Geschichte der Geschichtswissenschaft, 1800–1970,* 2d ed. (Frankfurt: Peter Lang, 1987); and Roger Chickering, ed., *Imperial Germany: A Historiographical Companion* (Westport CT: Greenwood Press, 1996). On the Ranke literature, see chapter 3.

12. Otto Hintze, *Die Hohenzollern und ihr Werk: Fünfhundert Jahre vaterländische Geschichte* (Berlin: P. Parey, 1915), vi.

13. See Charles McClelland, *State, Society, and University in Germany, 1700–1914* (New York: Cambridge University Press, 1980); and Konrad H. Jarausch, *Students, Society, and Politics in Imperial Germany: The Rise of Academic Illiberalism* (Princeton: Princeton University Press, 1982). On the emergence of sociocultural critiques in the *Kulturwissenschaften* that took aim at the academic establishment, see Fritz K. Ringer, *The Decline of the German Mandarins: The German Academic Community, 1890–1933* (Hanover NH: University Press of New England, 1990); Woodruff D. Smith, *Politics and the Sciences of Culture in Germany, 1840–1920* (New York: Oxford University Press, 1991); and Friedrich Jaeger, *Bürgerliche Modernisierungskrise und historische Sinnbildung: Kulturgeschichte bei Droysen, Burckhardt, und Max Weber* (Göttingen: Vandenhoeck & Ruprecht, 1994).

14. On the debate over Fritz Fischer's tracing of continuities in German war aims between the Second and Third Reichs, see Immanuel Geiss, *Studien über Geschichte und Geschichtswissenschaft* (Frankfurt: Suhrkamp, 1972); and John A. Moses, *The Politics of Illusion: The Fischer Controversy in German Historiography* (London: Barnes & Noble Books, 1975). For a discussion of the *Historikerstreit* of the 1980s, see chapter 4.

15. Work on the interpretations of German unification and reunification is the notable exception. See the essays in Walter Pape, ed., *1870/71–1989/90: German Unifications and the Change of Literary Discourse* (Berlin: Walter de Gruyter, 1993) and Frank Becker, *Bilder von Krieg und Nation: Die Einigungskriege in der bürgerliche Öffentlichkeit Deutschlands, 1864–1913* (Munich: R. Oldenbourg, 2001). As even the *Historikerstreit* of the 1980s demonstrated, interest in methodological disputes as manifestations of ideology is closer to the norm. See the essays in Michael Geyer and Konrad Jarausch, eds., *German Histories: Challenges in Theory, Practice, Technique,* special issue of *Central European History* 22, nos. 3–4 (September–December 1989).

16. On the reconstruction of national histories as part of the process of state

building, see Anthony D. Smith, *National Identity* (Reno: University of Nevada Press, 1991); and Anthony W. Marx, *Faith in Nation: Exclusionary Origins of Nationalism* (New York: Oxford University Press, 2003).

17. There is a vast literature on the interpretation of the French Revolution. See, e.g., Ann Rigney, *The Rhetoric of Historical Representation: Three Narrative Histories of the French Revolution* (Cambridge: Cambridge University Press, 1990); Linda Orr, *Headless History: Nineteenth-Century French Historiography of the Revolution* (Ithaca NY: Cornell University Press, 1990); Steven L. Kaplan, *Farewell Revolution: Disputed Legacies: France, 1789/1989* (Ithaca NY: Cornell University Press, 1995); and the essays in Bernadotte Fort, ed., *Fictions of the French Revolution* (Evanston IL: Northwestern University Press, 1991) and James A. W. Heffernan, ed., *Representing the French Revolution: Literature, Historiography, and Art* (Hanover NH: University Press of New England, 1992). On the debates over the legacies of the English Civil War, see chapter 3. On the American Civil War, see David Montgomery, *The American Civil War and the Meanings of Freedom* (New York: Oxford University Press, 1987); and David W. Blight, *Race and Reunion: The Civil War in American Memory* (Cambridge: Harvard University Press, 2001). Carolyn P. Boyd examines the Spanish debate over the meaning of national history and identity in *Historia Patria: Politics, History, and National Identity in Spain, 1875–1975* (Princeton: Princeton University Press, 1997). On the Russian Revolution, see Orlando Figes and Boris Kolonitskii, *Interpreting the Russian Revolution: The Language and Symbols of 1917* (New Haven: Yale University Press, 1999). On Holocaust historiography and nationalist politics in Israel, see chapters 4 and 5.

18. See Hans Kellner, *Language and Historical Representation: Getting the Story Crooked* (Madison: University of Wisconsin Press, 1989), 1–74.

19. F. R. Ankersmit, "Historical Representation [1988]," in *History and Tropology: The Rise and Fall of Metaphor* (Berkeley: University of California Press, 1994), 101–2, 117. See also the essays in Frank Ankersmit and Hans Kellner, eds., *A New Philosophy of History* (Chicago: University of Chicago Press, 1995).

20. See J. G. A. Pocock, *The Machiavellian Moment: Florentine Political Thought and the Atlantic Republican Tradition* (Princeton: Princeton University Press, 1975), 3–30. See also his discussion on how historical explanation and political theory meet in philosophies of history in "Time, Institutions, and Action: An Essay on Traditions and Their Understanding," in *Politics, Language, and Time: Essays on Political Thought and History* (New York: Atheneum, 1971), 233–72. See also Raymond Aron, *Introduction to the Philosophy of History: An Essay on the Limits of Historical Objectivity*, trans. George J. Irwin (Boston: Beacon Press, 1961), 1–59; and Felix Gilbert, *Machiavelli and Guicciardini: Politics and History in Sixteenth-Century Florence* (New York: W. W. Norton, 1984), 219–38.

21. Michel de Certeau, *The Writing of History*, trans. Tom Conley (New York: Columbia University Press, 1988), 2, 6–14, 56–113.

22. Günter Grass, *The Meeting at Telgte*, trans. Ralph Mannheim (New York: Harcourt, 1981), 3.

1. The Great War

1. Compared with the voluminous literature on the "Prussian paradigm" in German historical thought, the body of works specifically on Catholic-großdeutsch historiography is relatively compact. One of the first analyses of the großdeutsch concept in German history writing can be found in Johann Paul Hassel, "Die Absetzung der Herzoge von Mecklenburg und die Einsetzung Wallensteins zum Fürsten des Landes: Ein Beitrag zur Politik des Hauses Habsburg im Dreißigjährigen Kriege," in *Historisches Taschenbuch*, 4th ser., 8 (Leipzig, 1867): 3–85; and "Zur Geschichte Gustav Adolf," in *Zeitschrift für Preußische Geschichte und Landeskunde*, no. 6 (1869): 370–79. Eduard Fueter, *Geschichte der neueren Historiographie* (Munich and Berlin: R. Oldenbourg, 1911); G. P. Gooch, *History and Historians in the Nineteenth Century* (London: Longmans, Green, 1913); and Heinrich Ritter von Srbik, *Geist und Geschichte vom deutschen Humanismus bis zur Gegenwart*, vol. 2 (Munich: F. Bruckmann, 1951) offer concise examinations of Catholic historiography. Most analyses of this theme in Catholic history writing focus on its utilization by conservative political and religious opinion, not as historical practice. See Friedrich Schneider, "Einleitung," in Friedrich Schneider, ed., *Universalstaat oder Nationalstaat: Macht und Ende des Ersten deutschen Reiches: Die Streitschriften von Heinrich v. Sybel und Julius Ficker zur deutschen Kaiserpolitik des Mittelalters*, 2d ed. (Innsbruck: Universitäts-Verlag Wagner, 1943); Franz Schnabel, *Deutsche Geschichte im neunzehnten Jahrhundert*, vol. 4, *Die religiösen Kräfte* (Freiburg im Breisgau, 1937; reprint, Munich: Deutscher Taschenbuch, 1987); Heinz Gollwitzer, "Zur Auffassung der mittelalterlichen Kaiserpolitik im 19. Jahrhundert," in Rudolf Vierhaus and Manfred Botzenhart, eds., *Dauer und Wandel der Geschichte* (Münster: Aschendorff, 1966); Karl-Hermann Lucas, "Joseph Edmund Jörg: Konservative Publizistik zwischen Revolution und Reichsgründung (1852–71)," PhD diss., Köln Universität, 1969; Bernhard Weber, *Die "Historisch-politische Blätter" als Forum für Kirchen- und Konfessionsfragen* (Munich: Ludwig-Maximilians-Universität München, 1983); Hans Schmidt, "Onno Klopp und die 'kleindeutschen Geschichtsbaumeister,'" in Albert Portmann-Tinguely, ed., *Kirche, Staat, und katholische Wissenschaft in der Neuzeit* (Paderborn: F. Schöningh, 1988); Lorenz Matzinger, *Onno Klopp (1822–1903): Leben und Werk* (Aurich: Ostfriesischelandschaft, 1993); Matthias Klug, *Rückwendung zum Mittelalter? Geschichtsbilder und historische Argumentation im politischen Katholizisimus des Vormärz* (Paderborn: F. Schöningh, 1995); and Holger T. Gräf, "Reich, Nation, und Kirche in der groß- und kleindeutschen Historiographie," *Historisches Jahrbuch* 116, no. 2 (Munich, 1996): 367–94. On recent work on the sociopolitical character of Catholic ideology and theology, see Margaret Lavinia Anderson, "Piety and Politics: Recent Work on German Catholicism," *Journal of*

Modern History 63, no. 4 (December 1991): 681–716; and Oded Heilbronner, "From Ghetto to Ghetto: The Place of German Catholic Society in Recent Historiography," *Journal of Modern History* 73, no. 2 (June 2000): 453–95.

2. Arnold Berney, "Reichstradition und Nationalstaatsgedanke (1789–1815)," *Historische Zeitschrift* 140, no. 1 (1929): 57–86; Helmut Tiedemann, *Der deutsche Kaisergedanke vor und nach dem Wiener Kongress* (Breslau: M. & H. Marcus, 1932); Friedrich Hermann Schubert, "Volkssouveränität und Heiliges Römisches Reich," *Historische Zeitschrift* 213, no. 1 (August 1971): 91–122; Rudolf Vierhaus, *Germany in the Age of Absolutism*, trans. Jonathan B. Knudsen (Cambridge: Cambridge University Press, 1988); Heinz Angermeier, *Das alte Reich in der deutschen Geschichte* (Munich: R. Oldenbourg, 1991); Otto Dann, *Nation und Nationalismus in Deutschland, 1770–1990* (Munich: C. H. Beck, 1993).

3. E. Klebel, "Reich und Reichsidee," in *Gibt es ein deutsches Geschichtsbild?* (Frankfurt: M. Diesterweg, 1955), 67–86; Geoffrey Barraclough, "The Medieval Empire: Idea and Reality," in *History in a Changing World* (Norman: University of Oklahoma Press, 1957), 105–30; Werner Conze, "Deutschland und deutsche Nation als historische Begriffe," in Otto Büsch and James Sheehan, eds., *Die Rolle der Nation in der deutschen Geschichte und Gegenwart* (Berlin: Colloquium, 1985), 21–38. See also Klaus Epstein, *The Genesis of German Conservatism* (Princeton: Princeton University Press, 1966) and John Gagliardo, *Reich and Nation: The Holy Roman Empire as Idea and Reality, 1763–1806* (Bloomington: Indiana University Press, 1980).

4. James Sheehan, "The Problem of the Nation in German History," in *Die Rolle der Nation*, 5. Sheehan notes, "One of the problems of the kleindeutsch triumph has been to reduce the historiography of the fifties and sixties to the story of its own creation, ignoring or pushing to one side the rich variety of historiographical—and, one might add, of political—alternatives that continued to exist."

5. On the Sybel-Ficker controversy, see Schneider, ed., *Universalstaat oder Nationalstaat*; James Sheehan, *German History, 1770–1866* (New York: Oxford University Press, 1993), 850–52; and Hans-Ulrich Wehler, *Deutsche Gesellschaftgeschichte* (Munich: C. H. Beck, 1995), 3:239–41. See also Matzinger, *Onno Klopp*, 52–54.

6. Lucas, "Joseph Edmund Jörg," 225–32.

7. Annekatrin Wacker, "Historisch-Politische Blätter für das katholische Deutschland," in Heinz-Dietrich Fischer, ed., *Deutsche Zeitschriften des 17. bis 20. Jahrhunderts* (Munich: Aufbau, 1973), 150; Klug, *Rückwendung zum Mittelalter?* 15–19; Heinz Gollwitzer, "Zur Auffassung der mittelalterlichen Kaiserpolitik im 19. Jahrhundert," in Rudolf Vierhaus and Manfred Botzenhart, eds., *Dauer und Wandel der Geschichte: Aspekte Europäischer Vergangenheit: Festgabe für Kurt von Raumer* (Münster: Aschendorff, 1966), 502–3.

8. For a conventional interpretation of the großdeutsch/kleindeutsch divide in

nineteenth-century German historiography that concentrates on the midcentury debate over the "national" legacy of the medieval empire, see Gräf, "Reich, Nation, und Kirche."

9. Hassel, "Zur Geschichte Gustav Adolf," 371–73. This article was a review of Gustav Droysen's biography of Gustavus Adolphus.

10. "For over a thousand years the imperial idea was the highest expression of all the political aspirations and goals of the German people." Felix Stieve, ed., foreword to *Die Deutsche Kaisergedanke in Laufe der Jahrhunderte* (Munich: M. Rieger, 1915), 5. For a general examination of how nineteenth-century European nationalism idealized medieval polities, see Patrick J. Geary, *The Myth of Nations: The Medieval Origins of Europe* (Princeton: Princeton University Press, 2001).

11. Hermann Schulz, *Vorschläge zur Reichsreform in der Publizistik von 1800–1806* (Giessen: Buchdruckerei Nitschkowski, 1926), 15–21; Wilhelm Mommsen, "Zur Bedeutung des Reichsgedankens," *Historische Zeitschrift* 174, no. 2 (1952): 386–94; Karl Otmar Freiherr von Aretin, *Heiliges Römisches Reich, 1776–1806: Reichsverfassung und Staatssouveränität* (Wiesbaden: F. Steiner, 1967), 10–11; Hanns Gross, *Empire and Sovereignty: A History of the Public Law Literature in the Holy Roman Empire, 1599–1804* (Chicago: University of Chicago Press, 1973), 484–85; Gerhard Benecke, *Society and Politics in Germany, 1500–1750* (London: Routledge and Kegan Paul, 1974), 6–23, 32. Benecke notes that postwar German constitutional history "magnified" the myth of the empire in order to accentuate the historical basis for a federal solution, a view that "distorts" the history of German state development. See also Leonard Krieger, *The German Idea of Freedom* (Boston: Beacon Press, 1957), 231–42; and Thomas Nipperdey, *Nachdenken über die deutsche Geschichte* (Munich: C. H. Beck, 1986), 60–109. For a fresh look at the constitutional issues central to the war's origins, see Brennan Pursell, *The Winter King: Frederick V of the Palatinate and the Coming of the Thirty Years' War* (Aldershot: Ashgate, 2003).

12. On how political consciousness is connected to, and shaped by, historical self-awareness (and how history writing is an instrument in that process), see J. G. A. Pocock, *The Machiavellian Moment: Florentine Political Thought and the Atlantic Republican Tradition* (Princeton: Princeton University Press, 1975); see also Sheehan, "The Problem of the Nation in German History," 12–13.

13. On the project of ultramontane Catholicism to rehabilitate the principle of authority, see Jacques Droz, *Europe between Revolutions, 1815–1848*, trans. Robert Baldick (New York: Harper & Row, 1967), 12–14.

14. *Allgemeine Deutsche Biographie* (*ADB*), 56 vols. (Munich, 1891; reprint, Berlin: Duncker & Humblot, 1971), 32:6–8.

15. Michael Ignaz Schmidt (1736–94), *Neuere Geschichte der Deutschen* (Frankenthal: L. B. F. Gegel, 1789), 7:13, 131–36.

16. *ADB*, 36:750–51.

17. Andreas Sebastian Stumpf, *Diplomatische Geschichte der teutschen Liga im siebzehnten Jahrhunderte* (Erfurt: Hoyer & Rudolphi, 1800), vi–ix.

18. Stumpf, *Diplomatische Geschichte der teutschen*, 17–20.

19. See Helmut Berding and Hans-Peter Ullmann, "Veränderungen in Deutschland an der Wende vom 18. zum 19. Jahrhundert," in Berding and Ullmann, eds., *Deutschland zwischen Revolution und Restauration* (Düsseldorf: Athenäum, 1981), 12–15.

20. Lorenz von Westenrieder, *Geschichte des dreyßigjährigen Kriegs* (Munich: J. Lindauer, 1804–6), 1:i–ii.

21. See August Kluckhohn, *Ueber Lorenz von Westenrieders Leben und Schriften* (Bamberg: Buchner, 1890) and Rolf Wünnenberg, *Lorenz von Westenrieder: Sein Leben, sein Werk, und seine Zeit* (Tutzing: H. Schneider, 1982).

22. Westenrieder, *Geschichte des dreyßigjährigen Kriegs*, 1:vi–vii, 14–15, 81. Westenrieder, a Bavarian patriot, regrets the "common and current error" that tends to see the Catholic League as the "blind instrument" of the Habsburgs. He argues in no uncertain terms that the Catholic League was intended to uphold the legal authority and prestige of the Kaiser.

23. Lorenz von Westenrieder, *Beytrage zur vaterländischen Historie, Geographie, Statistik* (Munich: J. Lindauer, 1806), 8:214–15.

24. See also Friedrich August Köthe, "Das Jahr 1616 oder die Lage Europa's vor dem Beginn des dreißigjährigen Krieges," in *Köthe's Historisches Taschenbuch auf das Jahr 1817* (Leipzig, 1817), 10–15. "The history of this time stands as a warning for what we should guard against, what we should avoid, and what consolation and good spirit can be derived from it. . . . The old misery is always renewed. Germany has once again bled in a twenty-five-year-long war. The same tragedy that characterized the seventeenth century is repeated again before our very eyes." Karl Adolf Menzel praised in similar terms Saxony and Brandenburg's opposition to the revolutionary tendencies of Calvinism in the decade before 1618. In his view, this loyalty to Kaiser, Reich, and constitution was a bulwark against the ambitions of France, Britain, and the Netherlands. The motivations behind the Habsburg attempt to preserve the unity of the empire in the face of this threat, he notes, should be very understandable to nineteenth-century readers. See Menzel, *Neuere Geschichte der Deutschen von der Reformation bis zur Bundes-Acte* (Breslau: Grass, Barth, 1833), 5:iii, ix–x.

25. On the political usages of the history of Maximilian I, see Heinz Gollwitzer, "Vom Funktionswandel Politischer Traditionen: Zum Bild Kurfürst Maximilians I. und Tillys in der bayerischen Überlieferung," in Andreas Kraus, ed., *Land und Reich, Stamm und Nation*, vol. 2, *Frühe Neuzeit* (Munich: C. H. Beck, 1984), 51–80.

26. Karl Kristian von Mann, *Kaiser Ludwig IV., genannt der Baier, und Maximilian I. Kurfürst von Baiern, eine historische Parallele* (Munich: J. Lindauer, 1806), 70–71.

27. Peter Philipp Wolf, *Geschichte Maximilians I. und seiner Zeit* (Munich: J. Lindauer, 1807), 1:vii–ix, xiv.

28. Wolf, *Geschichte Maximilians I.* (1807), 2:288–91.

29. *ADB*, 1:519–20.

30. Aretin's work was highly praised in the German Catholic world. A review in the leading Catholic journal enthusiastically agreed with the conclusions that Aretin drew from his "valuable and new material." In particular, it was Aretin's historical justification of the common duty of Bavaria and Austria to preserve Germany and the balance of power in Europe from the common enemy, France, that impressed the anonymous reviewer. See review of *Bayerns auswärtige Verhältniße seit dem Anfang des sechszehnten Jahrhunderts,* by Karl Maria von Aretin, in *Historisch-politische Blätter für katholische Deutschland* 3 (1839): 433–39, 507–8.

31. Karl Maria Freiherr von Aretin, *Bayerns auswärtige Verhältniße seit dem Anfang des sechszehnten Jahrhunderts* (Passau: F. Winkler, 1839), 1:vi–vii, 75–80.

32. On Bavarian patriotism, see Anton Grassl, *Westenrieder's Briefwechsel mit einer darstellung seiner innern Entwicklung* (Munich: Verlag der Kommission für bayerische Landesgeschichte, 1934), 53–67.

33. Karl Maria Freiherr von Aretin, *Geschichte des bayerischen Herzogs und Kurfürsten Maximilian des Ersten,* vol. 1 (Passau: F. Winkler, 1842), vi–xi. For a Protestant argument that similarly claims that the Protestant Union was intended to preserve the imperial constitution and defend it against Habsburg violations, see Johann Michael von Söltl, *Der Religionskrieg in Deutschland,* vol. 1 (Hamburg: J. A. Meissner, 1840), 39–40.

34. See Wacker, "Historisch-politische Blätter," 144–50; Franz Rhein, *Zehn Jahre "Historisch-politische Blätter"* (Obercassel: E. Heeg, 1916), 45–48; Weber, *Die "Historisch-politischen Blätter,"* 105–6; and Klug, *Rückwendung zum Mittelalter?* 27.

35. [Jodok Stülz], "Kaiser Ferdinand II. im Kampfe gegen die protestantischen Stände Oesterreichs," in *Historisch-politische Blätter für das katholische Deutschland (HpB)* 3 (1839): 673. Stülz (1799–1872) was a *Reichshistoriograph* and archivist in Austrian service.

36. [Stülz], "Kaiser Ferdinand II," 673–75, 745.

37. Friedrich von Hurter, *Geschichte Kaiser Ferdinands II. und seiner Eltern bis zu dessen Krönung in Frankfurt: Personen-Haus- und Landesgeschichte* (Schaffhausen: Fr. Hurter'sche Buchhandlung, 1857), 1:vii–xiv, 56–57, 188, 231.

38. *ADB*, 13:431–44; on Müller, see Sheehan, *German History, 1770–1866,* 22.

39. For the Protestant response to Hurter, see Karl Gustav Helbig, "Herr Hofrath v. Hurter als Historiker," in *Historische Zeitschrift* 4 (1860): 174–83; and Johann Michael von Söltl, "Kaiser Ferdinand II und sein Geschichtschreiber Hurter," in *Historische Zeitschrift* 4 (1860): 366–437; 5 (1861): 1–45. Söltl was contemptu-

ously dismissive of Hurter's intellectual qualifications and style. Helbig accused him of being the representative of an increasingly powerful faction that damaged the true interests of Germany by portraying them as incompatible with Austria's. Hurter's obituary in the *HpB* praised his demonstration that Ferdinand had sincerely sought to heal the divisions within the Reich and make Germany a great European power. See "Charakterbild Kaiser Ferdinand's II. Nach Fr. von Hurters Geschichtswerk," in *HpB* 56 (1865): 905.

40. See Klug, *Rückwendung zum Mittelalter?* 50 ff.

41. Lucas, "Joseph Edmund Jörg," 196–97.

42. Matzinger, *Onno Klopp*, 46. See also Hans Schmidt, "Onno Klopp and die 'kleindeutschen Geschichtsbaumeister,'" 381–95.

43. Onno Klopp, "Das Restitutions-Edikt im nordwestlichen Deutschland," in *Forschungen zur Deutschen Geschichte* 1 (1862): 81–82; [Onno Klopp], *Wer ist der wahre Erbfeind von Deutschland?* (Munich: J. G. Weiss, 1868), 22–24. Klopp condemned a centralized federal union of the German states as a "foreign idea."

44. Onno Klopp, *Der König Friedrich II. von Preußen und die deutsche Nation* (Schaffhausen: Fr. Hurter'sche Buchhandlung, 1860), 499–503; and Klopp, *Erbfeind*, 4–6. Klopp shared these misgivings with Gervinus. See Georg G. Iggers, *The German Conception of History*, rev. ed. (Middletown CT: Wesleyan University Press, 1983), 121; and Matzinger, *Onno Klopp*, 145.

45. Matzinger, *Onno Klopp*, 41–43. A few years later, Klopp wrote a more direct, vituperative, and comprehensive attack on Friedrich as a cynical betrayer of German interests. See Klopp, *Der König Friedrich II. von Preußen und die deutsche Nation*.

46. [Onno Klopp], *Studien über Katholizismus, Protestantismus, und Gewissensfreiheit in Deutschland* (Schaffhausen: Fr. Hurter'sche Buchhandlung, 1857), 256–62.

47. Onno Klopp, *Tilly im dreißigjährigen Kriege* (Stuttgart: J. G. Cotta'scher, 1861), 1:25. Klopp attacks the "Slavic" aspirations of the Bohemian nobility that aimed to create "another Poland." Another famous Catholic historian echoed Klopp's chauvinism, describing the Bohemian revolt as "a Slavo-Czech movement of the Bohemian aristocracy against those German elements who ruled as representatives of the Habsburgs." See Johannes Janssen, *Frankreich's Rheingelüste und deutsch-feindliche Politik in früheren Jahrhunderten*, 2d ed. (Freiburg im Breisgau: Herder'sche, 1863), 34.

48. Klopp, "Das Restitutions-Edikt im nordwestlichen Deutschland," 81–82, 96–98. The editors prefaced this article with an apologetic note to the effect that they were under a scholarly obligation to present such opinions, even if they did not share them.

49. See Sheehan, *German History, 1770–1866*, 848–49, 864–69. Sheehan notes

a remark of Joseph Edmund Jörg, editor of the *HpB* during this period, to the effect that Prussia had "only a stomach for Germany, never a heart."

50. Onno Klopp, *Kleindeutsche Geschichtsbaumeister* (Freiburg im Breisgau: Herder'sche, 1863), v. This quote is from Klopp's foreword to this collection of a series of reviews of the works of Häusser, Droysen, and Sybel that appeared in the *HpB* in 1861 and 1862. Klopp goes on to say that, at the same time and for the same reasons, he turned his attention to Friedrich II. On the controversy that followed Sybel's lecture, see G. P. Gooch, *History and Historians*, 117–20.

51. See Gooch, *History and Historians*, 510–13; and Sheehan, *German History, 1770–1866*, 557–59.

52. Carl Adolph Cornelius, *Zur Geschichte der Gründung der deutschen Liga* (Munich: F. Straub, 1863), 20–29. Austrian scholarship on this topic, while not backing away from defending the sanctity of the *Reichsverfassung*, was noticeably sharper in its condemnation of the Union's ties to France and other foreign powers, such as "proud Albion." See Karl Haselbach, *Die Politik der "Union" gegenüber dem Hause Habsburg* (Krems: M. Pammer, 1862), 4–9.

53. Moriz Ritter, *Geschichte der deutschen Union von den Vorbereitungen des Bundes bis zum Tode Kaiser Rudolphs II* (Schaffhausen: Fr. Hurter'sche Buchhandlung, 1867), 34, 269–70. Julius Krebs, the leading Protestant authority on Palatine politics in the decade before 1618, saw both confessional alliances, in their opportunistic attempts to "reconfigure" the imperial constitution, as setting themselves against both the empire and the "national conception" (*nationale Gedanke*). See his *Christian von Anhalt und die Kurpfälzische Politik am Beginn des Dreißigjährigen Krieges (23. Mai – 3. October 1618)* (Leipzig: Bär & Hermann, 1872), 1–2.

54. See Gräf, "Reich, Nation, und Kirche," 374–81, 392.

55. See Alfred Altmann, "Zur Erinnerung an Felix Stieve," in Felix Stieve, *Der oberösterreichische Bauernkrieg*, 2d ed. (Linz: E. Maries, 1904), xvii–xxx; also Hans Zwiedineck-Südenhorst, foreword to Felix Stieve, *Abhandlungen, Vorträge, und Reden* (Leipzig: Duncker & Humblot, 1900), i–x.

56. Felix Stieve, *Der Kampf um Donauwörth im Zusammenhänge der Reichsgeschichte*, vol. 1, *Der Ursprung des dreißigjährigen Krieges, 1607–1619* (Munich: M. Rieger, 1875), 82, 246; Stieve, *Die Politik Baierns, 1591–1607* (Munich: M. Rieger, 1878), 7–13, 259–60; Stieve, *Churfürst Maximilian I. von Bayern* (Munich: Verlag der k. b. Akademie, 1882), 23–26; Stieve, *Abhandlungen*, 176–77.

57. Stieve, *Abhandlungen*, 179–80.

58. As the Sybel-Ficker debate showed, Protestant historians were skeptical of the medieval ideal as a useful framework for the articulation of the German nation's place in Central Europe. But the idea of a German-dominated Mitteleuropa, with its links to a hegemonic "imperial idea" (*Reichsidee*) remained a key ideological reference point in modern German historiography. It has its origins in the großdeutsch school of the nineteenth century under discussion. See Conze, "Deutschland und

deutsche Nation als historische Begriffe," 21–38; Heinrich Ritter von Srbik, *Das Österreichische Kaisertum und das Ende des Heiligen Römischen Reiches, 1804–1806* (Berlin: Deutsche Verlagsgesellschaft für Politik und Geschichte, 1927), 70–73; and his *Deutsche Einheit: Idee und Wirklichkeit vom Heiligen Reich bis Königgrätz* (Munich: F. Bruckmann, 1935), 1:6. On Srbik's justification of Germany's imperial role in Central Europe, see Helmut Reinalter, "Heinrich Ritter von Srbik," in Hans-Ulrich Wehler, ed., *Deutsche Historiker*, vol. 8 (Göttingen: Vandenhoeck & Ruprecht, 1982), 86–87. On the "Reichsidee" of the German medieval emperors, see Hans K. Schulze, *Hegemoniales Kaisertum: Ottonian und Salier* (Berlin: Siedler, 1991), 15–16.

59. Lorenz von Westenrieder, *Geschichte des dreyßigjährigen Kriegs*, vol. 1 (Munich: J. Lindauer, 1804), 1:ii.

60. Westenrieder, *Geschichte des dreyßigjährigen Kriegs*, 1:vi–vii.

61. *ADB*, 44:188–90. See also Karoline von Woltmann, *Karl Ludwig und Karoline von Woltmann* (New York: n.p., 1870). Woltmann, an enthusiastic supporter of the revolution as a student at Göttingen, became an ardent German patriot after Jena. He was a chargé for Bremen and Hamburg when he became associated with Stein. "Biographische Skizze: Karl Ludwig von Woltmann," in *Meyer's Groschen Bibliothek der Deutschen Klassiker für alle Stände*, vol. 294 (New York: H. I. Meyer, 1870): 5–6.

62. Karl Ludwig von Woltmann, *Politische Blicke und Berichte* (Leipzig and Altenburg: F. A. Brockhaus, 1816), 1:7, 23–30, 54–56.

63. On Vogt, see chapter 2.

64. Woltmann, *Politische Blicke*, 194–202, 211.

65. Karl Ludwig von Woltmann, *Friedrich Schiller's Geschichte des dreyßigjährigen Krieges*, vols. 3–4, *Geschichte des Westphälischen Friedens* (Leipzig: Göschen, 1816), 18–19, 30.

66. Karl Ludwig von Woltmann, *Oesterreichs Politik und Kaiserhaus* (Frankfurt: n.p., 1815), 174–75.

67. Karl Adolf Menzel, *Neuere Geschichte der Deutschen von der Reformation bis zur Bundes-Acte* (Breslau: Grass, Barth, 1833), 6:454; (1837), 7:110–11, 172–73, 228–30. In his discussion of Bohemia, Menzel observed that German historians had always been more solicitous of other people's national aspirations than their own. On Menzel, see *ADB*, 21:380–81; and Christoph Prignitz, *Vaterländsliebe und Freiheit: Deutscher Patriotismus von 1750 bis 1850* (Wiesbaden: Steiner, 1981), 139–56. See also Karl August Müller, *Fünf Bücher vom Böhmischen Krieg in den Jahren 1618 bis 1621* (Dresden and Leipzig: G. Fleischer, 1841), viii–ix, xix–xx. Müller acknowledges the service Menzel did Germany by opening up the possibilities of interpreting the war from a "German-national historical viewpoint." On the significance of 1629 for the unitary "Habsburg project" of Ferdinand II as the successor of Charles V, see Ottokar Lorenz, *Oesterreich's Stellung in Deutschland*

während der ersten Hälfte des dreißigjährigen Krieges (Vienna: C. G. Gerold's Sohn, 1858), 3. Lorenz claimed, "In a decisive moment the concept of imperial unity had developed new force and new life." On the role that the nonnational territorial state conception played in shaping German nationalist thinking, see Abigail Green, *Fatherlands: State-Building and Nationhood in Nineteenth-Century Germany* (Cambridge: Cambridge University Press, 2001).

68. See Adolf M. Birke, "Nation und Konfession: Varianten des politischen Katholizismus im Europa des 19. Jahrhunderts," in *Historisches Jahrbuch* 116, no. 2 (1996): 395–416. Birke maintains that the overriding concern for German Catholics was the structure of the church-state relationship. Therefore, there was no basis for the development of a "national Catholicism," as occurred in Ireland, for example.

69. Onno Klopp, *Die gothaische Auffassung der deutschen Geschichte und der Nationalverein* (Hanover: F. Klindworth, 1862), 8.

70. Klopp, *Tilly,* 1:336–37.

71. Klopp, *Tilly,* 1:272.

72. Klopp, *Die gothaische Auffassung,* 14–16.

73. Klopp, *Die gothaische Auffassung,* 27–30, 62. According to Klopp, it was the gradual "paralysis of the central power," which started in the thirteenth century and which was a direct consequence of French policy, that had destroyed the basis for a "German national history." Charles V and his successor, Ferdinand II, had tried to reverse this process in their attempts to restore the political and moral power of the Habsburg tradition. Klopp further maintained that Catholic historiography had always been hostile to France, but this had been ignored by the Protestant tradition for obvious reasons, particularly after 1871. See Onno Klopp, *Deutschland und die Habsburger,* ed. Leo König (Graz and Vienna: Verlags-Buchhandlung Styria, 1908), 1, 254. Johannes Janssen dissented, claiming that Maximilian I (1493–1519) had been the last imperial representative of the "national feeling" that united peasant, burger, and nobleman against the French threat to Germany and Europe. See Janssen, *Frankreich's Rheingelüste,* 13. Julius Opel went further than Klopp in making a virtue of necessity in conceiving the policies of Ferdinand and the Counter-Reformation as a forward-looking "new idea of universal Romanism" that attempted to unite Germany against the "authoritiarian and dogmatic tendencies" of Protestantism. See Julius Otto Opel, *Der niedersächsisch-dänische Kriege* (Halle: Verlag der Buchhandlung des Waisenhauses, 1872–78), 1:2–3, 591–93.

74. On these documents, see "Zur Vorgeschichte des dreißigjährigen Krieges," in *HpB* 26 (1851): 73–77.

75. Wolf, *Geschichte Maximilians,* 2:533–42.

76. Aretin, *Bayerns auswärtige Verhältniße,* 87–88, 100–101. One Protestant historian saw the "great plans and beautiful hopes" of Henry IV substantially fulfilled by the Peace of Westphalia because it established a stable "*Staatenverein.*"

See Severin Ewald, *Der dreißigjährigen Krieg nebst dem westphälischen Frieden: Nach Schiller, Galletti, und anderen Geschichtschreibern dargestellt für die Jugend und zum Selbstunterrichte* (Berlin: C. F. Amelang, 1830), 38, 53–54.

77. See Nipperdey, *Nachdenken über die deutsche Geschichte*, 28; Schulz, *Vorschläge zur Reichsreform*, 15; and Franz Schnabel, *Deutsche Geschichte im neunzehnten Jahrhundert*, vol. 1, *Die Grundlagen* (Freiburg im Breisgau, 1929; reprint, Munich: Deutscher Taschenbuch, 1987), 562–64. See also Edmund H. Dickerman and Anita M. Walker, "The Choice of Hercules: Henry IV as Hero," in *Historical Journal* 39, no. 2 (1996): 325–32; and Charles Irenee Castel de Saint-Pierre, *A Project for Settling an Everlasting Peace in Europe* [*Projet pour rendre la paix perpetuelle en Europe*] (London: Ferdinand Burleigh, 1714).

78. Menzel, *Neuere Geschichte der Deutschen*, 5:272–75, 372–73; Müller, *Böhmischen Kriege*, xxx. The difference, in Müller's view, was that in 1813 Germany had the "national spirit" to resist.

79. Aretin, *Bayerns auswärtige Verhältnisse*, 87–88.

80. Johann Sporschil, *Der Dreißigjährigen Krieg* (Braunschweig: G. Westermann, 1843), 57–58. See ADB, 35:77–78. Johann Wilhelm Richter, a Prussian historian, deplored the violation of the constitution by Ferdinand, but argued at the same time for the preservation of the "inner structure" of Europe that was endangered by French meddling. Johann Wilhelm Daniel Richter, *Geschichte des dreißigjährigen Krieges*, vol. 2 (Leipzig and Erfurt: A. F. Böhme, 1849), 137–38; vol. 4 (1851), 372.

81. Janssen, *Frankreich's Rheingelüste*, 37–39. On Janssen, see Gräf, "Reich, Nation, und Kirche," 383–89.

82. See Hans Rosenberg, *Bureaucracy, Aristocracy, and Autocracy: The Prussian Experience, 1660–1815* (Boston: Beacon Press, 1966), 226–28; Berding and Ullmann, "Veränderungen"; Reinhart Koselleck, *Preußen zwischen Reform und Revolution: Allgemeines Landrecht, Verwaltung, und Soziale Bewegung von 1791 bis 1848* (Munich: Klett-Cotta in Deutscher Taschenbuch Verlag, 1989), 245–55, 388.

83. See Georg Philipp Anton Neubur, *Beytrag zu der Geschichte des dreißigjährigen Krieges* (Leipzig and Stralsund: n.p., 1772), 14, 20, 27–36; cf. Westenrieder, *Geschichte des dreyßigjährigen Kriegs*, 2:48–52. Westenrieder remarked that Wallenstein's campaign to take Stralsund revealed a new, unexpected, and "highly significant" goal that showed "unlimited vision": the conquest of Denmark to gain the trade of the Baltic and North seas. See also Christoph Ziemssen, *Das Wallensteins-Fest: Gebete und Predigten zur Feier des vier und zwanzigsten Julius 1819 and 1820 in der St. Marien-Kirche zu Stralsund* (Stralsund: n.p., 1821), 15–17; Ernst Heinrich Zober, *Geschichte der Belagerung Stralsunds durch Wallenstein, im Jahre 1628* (Stralsund; W. Trinius, 1828), 5–7.

84. See Lawrence Sondhaus, "Mitteleuropa zur See? Austria and the German Navy Question, 1848–52," *Central European History* 20, no. 2 (June 1987): 125–44.

85. Some Protestant historians saw in Wallenstein's maritime ambitions evidence

of a "Spanish" conspiracy to ensure that the Hansa never recovered its independence. See K. D. Hüllmann, "Gustaf Adolf in Beziehung auf die evangelischen Fürsten Deutschlands," *Zeitschrift für Geschichtswissenschaft* 1 (1844): 283–88; Hassel, "Die Absetzung der Herzoge von Mecklenburg"; and Theodor Bischoff, *Tilly: Ein Zeitbild* (Rothenburg ob der Tauber: Schneider'schen Buchdruckerei, 1881), 9.

86. Johann Gottlob Böhmen, notes to *Das Leben Gustav Adolphs des Großen, Königs von Schweden*, by Walther Harte, trans. Georg Heinrich Martini (Leipzig: J. G. Dyck, 1760), 176–77.

87. Karl Ludwig von Woltmann, *Leben, Thaten, und Schicksale Wallensteins* (Zofingen: n.p., 1804), 40–49.

88. Johann Michael von Söltl, *Der Religionskrieg in Deutschland*, vol. 2 (Hamburg: J. A. Meissner, 1840), 9. See also Heinrich August Hecht, *Der dreißigjährigen Krieg und der westphälische Friede* (Altenburg: Julius Helbig, 1848), 151–54; and Heinrich W. J. Thiersch, *Luther, Gustav Adolf, und Maximilian I. von Bayern: Biographische Skizzen* (Nördlingen: C. H. Beck, 1869), 109.

89. Karl Adolf Menzel, *Neuere Geschichte der Deutschen*, 7:231. A student of Menzel's, the rabid pan-German nationalist Wolfgang Menzel (who confessed to großdeutsch sympathies), recalled his thoughts in 1848: "Germany must have her old borders again . . . she must have a navy and colonies." Wolfgang Menzel, *Wolfgang Menzel's Denkwürdigkeiten*, ed. Konrad Menzel (Bielefeld and Leipzig: Velhagen & Klasing, 1877), 409. On Menzel's nationalist thinking, see Prignitz, *Vaterlandsliebe und Freiheit*, 171.

90. Sporschil, *Der Dreißigjährige Krieg*, 283–84.

91. Gustav Droysen, *Gustav Adolf* (Leipzig: Veit, 1869), 1:285–87.

92. See Carl du Jarrys La-Roche, *Der dreißigjährigen Krieg, von militärischen Standpunkte ausgeleuchtet* (Schaffhausen: Fr. Hurter'sche Buchhandlung, 1848), 1:218–19; August Friedrich Gfrörer, *Gustav Adolph, König von Schweden und seine Zeit*, 3d ed. (Stuttgart: A. Krabbe, 1852), 521–29; Johannes Janssen, *Gustav Adolf in Deutschland*, Katholischer Broschüren-Verein 1, no. 8 (Frankfurt: G. Hamacher, 1865), 9; and F. A. Wilhelm Schreiber, *Maximilian I. der Katholische, Kurfürst von Bayern und der dreißigjährigen Krieg* (Munich: Fleischmann, 1868), 408.

93. Friedrich von Hurter, *Zur Geschichte Wallensteins* (Schaffhausen: Fr. Hurter'sche Buchhandlung, 1855), 179–80.

94. Klopp, *Studien über Katholizismus*, 275–76.

95. Klopp, *Tilly*, 1:377–78. Friedrich Hurter also maintained that a key element in Ferdinand's plan to restore the Reich's "honor, greatness, and welfare" was the goal of making Germany a "trading state" to compete with Britain and the Netherlands. *Geschichte Kaiser Ferdinands II* (1861), 10:13.

96. Otto Krabbe, *Zur Geschichte Wallensteins und des dreißigjährigen Krieges: Aus dem kirchlichen und wissenschaftlichen Leben Rostocks* (Berlin: G. Schlawitz, 1863), 107–9.

97. Konrad Reichard, *Die maritime Politik der Habsburger im siebzehnten Jahrhundert* (Berlin: W. Hertz, 1867), 25, 48, 118; Carl Wittich, "Wallenstein und die Spanier," *Preußische Jahrbücher* 22, no. 3 (1868): 331, 335; Krebs, *Christian von Anhalt*, 13–15. A final rebuttal from a German expatriate in Switzerland, addressed to the "bigots and hypocrites," "so lacking in historical awareness," of the Gustav-Adolf Verein, is worth noting: "Had the counsel that Wallenstein gave the Kaiser in this period been followed, then truly the German Reich would have gone down another road in the last two centuries and not have been the laughingstock of the other powers." Carl Lempens, *Pragmatische Geschichte des Dreißigjährigen Krieges* (Zurich: Frick-Vogel, 1881), 7, 127, 136.

98. See Lothar Gall, *Bismarck: The White Revolutionary*, trans. J. A. Underwood (Boston: Allen & Unwin, 1986), 1:236–38.

99. Franz Keym, *Geschichte des Dreißigjährigen Krieges*, 2 vols. (Freiburg im Breisgau: Herder'sche, 1873), 1:iii–iv. See George G. Windell, *The Catholics and German Unity, 1866–1871* (Minneapolis: University of Minnesota Press, 1954).

2. The War of Protestant Liberation

1. Friedrich Salamo Moser, *Gustav Adolph und die dankbare Nachwelt* (Zwickau: n.p., 1844), 12–13, 50, 77–80.

2. On Gustavus Adolphus as literary subject, see Eduard Willig, *Gustav II: Adolf, König von Schweden im deutschen Drama: Ein literär-historischer Versuch* (Parchim: H. Freise, 1908); and Werner Milch, *Gustav Adolf in der deutschen und schwedischen Literatur* (Breslau: M. & H. Marcus, 1928). Both contain comprehensive bibliographies beginning in the seventeenth century.

3. On the "tragic" content of historical narrative as analyzed by Hegel, see Hayden White, *Metahistory: The Historical Imagination in Nineteenth-Century Europe* (Baltimore: Johns Hopkins University Press, 1973), 89–92.

4. See Hartmut Lehmann, "Martin Luther as a National Hero in the Nineteenth Century," in J. C. Eade, ed., *Romantic Nationalism in Europe* (Canberra: Humanities Research Center, Australian National University, 1983), 194–95.

5. Hartmut Lehmann, "Martin Luther als Deutscher Nationalheld im 19. Jahrhundert," *Luther: Zeitschrift der Luther-Gesellschaft* 55, no. 2 (1984): 57–59.

6. See John Breuilly, "Nation and Nationalism in Modern German History," *Historical Journal* 33, no. 3 (1990): 659–75; and "Sovereignty and Boundaries: Modern State Formation and National Identity in Germany," in Mary Fulbrook, ed., *National Histories and European History* (Boulder: Westview Press, 1993), 94–140. For an attempt at rectification, see the essays in William R. Hutchinson and Hartmut Lehmann, eds., *Many Are Chosen: Divine Election and Western Nationalism*, Harvard Theological Studies, no. 38 (Minneapolis: Fortress Press, 1994).

7. Joel F. Harrington and Helmut Walser Smith, "Confessionalization, Community, and State Building in Germany, 1555–1870," *Journal of Modern History* 69, no. 1 (March 1997): 77; see also the essays in Helmut Walser Smith, ed., *Protestants, Jews, and Catholics in Germany, 1800–1914* (New York: Berg, 2001).

8. Hartmut Lehmann, "Pietism and Nationalism: The Relationship between Protestant Revivalism and National Renewal in Nineteenth-Century Germany," *Church History* 51, no. 1 (March 1992): 40.

9. Hans Rothfels, "Zur Krise des Nationalstaats," and Wolfgang Sauer, "Das Problem des deutschen Nationalstaats," in Helmut Böhme, ed., *Probleme der Reichsgründungszeit, 1848–1879* (Cologne: Kiepenhauer & Witsch, 1968), 369–83, 448–80; M. Rainer Lepsius, "The Nation and Nationalism in Germany," *Social Research* 52, no. 1 (Spring 1985): 43–64; Ernst Gellner, *Nations and Nationalism* (Ithaca: Cornell University Press, 1983).

10. Benedict Anderson, *Imagined Communities: Reflections on the Origin and Spread of Nationalism* (London: Verso, 1983); Werner Conze, "Deutschland und deutsche Nation als historische Begriffe," in Otto Büsch and James Sheehan, eds., *Die Rolle der Nation in der deutschen Geschichte und Gegenwart* (Berlin: Colloquium, 1985), 21–38; Otto Dann, *Nation und Nationalismus in Deutschland, 1770–1990* (Munich: C. H. Beck, 1993); and Wolfgang Hardtwig, *Nationalismus und Bürgerkultur in Deutschland, 1500–1914* (Göttingen: Vandenhoeck & Ruprecht, 1994). Hardtwig discusses the "intellectual" formation of national myths in the early modern period, as well as cultural and socioeconomic determinants. See also David Blackbourn, *Marpingen: Apparitions of the Virgin Mary in Bismarckian Germany* (New York: Oxford University Press, 1993); and James Sheehan, "Nation und Staat: Deutschland als 'imaginierte Gemeinschaft,'" in Manfred Hettling and Paul Nolte, eds., *Nation und Gesellschaft in Deutschland* (Munich: C. H. Beck, 1996), 33–45.

11. The concept of the nation "was still a vague force in which old and new mingled": Friedrich Meinecke, *The Age of German Liberation, 1795–1815*, trans. Peter Paret (Berkeley: University of California Press, 1977), 124. See Dieter Langewiesche, "Kulturelle Nationsbildung im Deutschland des 19. Jahrhunderts," in Manfred Hettling and Paul Nolte, eds., *Nation und Gesellschaft in Deutschland: Historische Essays* (Munich: C. H. Beck, 1996), 46–64.

12. On the metaphorical importance of war as national trauma and crusade, see Leon Stein, "Religion and Patriotism in German Peace Dramas during the Thirty Years' War," *Central European History* 4, no. 2 (June 1971): 132; and Christoph Prignitz, *Vaterländsliebe und Freiheit: Deutscher Patriotismus von 1750 bis 1850* (Wiesbaden: Steiner, 1981), 118. On the cult of the "warrior-king" in German mythology, see Carlo Ginzburg, "Germanic Mythology and Nazism: Thoughts on an Old Book by Georges Dumezil," in his *Clues, Myths, and the Historical Method*, trans. John and Anne C. Tedeschi (Baltimore: Johns Hopkins University Press, 1989),

126–45. See also my essay, "Religious Conflict as History: The Nation as the One True Church," in Michael Geyer and Hartmut Lehmann, eds., *Religion und Nation: Beiträge zu einer unbewältigte Geschichte* (Göttingen: Wallstein, 2004), 23–38.

13. Salo Wittmayer Baron, *Modern Nationalism and Religion* (New York: Harper, 1947), 3–6, 46, 141; see also Fritz Fischer, "Der deutsche Protestantismus und die Politik im 19. Jahrhundert," *Historische Zeitschrift* 171, no. 3 (1951): 473–518; Reinhard Wittram, "Kirche und Nationalismus in der Geschichte des Deutschen Protestantismus im 19. Jahrhundert," in Wittram, ed., *Das Nationale als europäisches Problem* (Göttingen: Vandenhoeck & Ruprecht, 1954), 109–48; Manfred Jacobs, "Die Entwicklung des deutschen Nationalgedankens von der Reformation bis zum deutschen Idealismus," in Horst Zillessen, ed., *Volk-Nation-Vaterland: Der deutsche Protestantismus und der Nationalismus* (Gütersloh: Gütersloher Verlagshaus G. Mohn, 1970), 51–110; Gerhard Kaiser, *Pietismus und Patriotismus im literarischen Deutschland: Ein Beitrag zum Problem der Säkularisation*, 2d ed. (Frankfurt: Athenäum, 1973), 39; Arlie J. Hoover, *The Gospel of Nationalism* (Stuttgart: F. Steiner, 1986), 3, 43, 79; and Hartmut Lehmann, "'God Our Old Ally': The Chosen People Theme in Late-Nineteenth- and Early-Twentieth-Century German Nationalism," in William R. Hutchinson and Hartmut Lehmann, eds., *Many Are Chosen: Divine Election and Western Nationalism*, Harvard Theological Studies, no. 38 (Minneapolis: Fortress Press, 1994), 85–108.

14. Horst Zillessen, *Protestantismus und politische Form: Eine Untersuchung zum protestantischen Verfassungsverständnis* (Gütersloh: Gütersloher Verlagshaus G. Mohn, 1971), 42–45. Gerlach is quoted in Robert Bigler, "The Rise of Political Protestantism in Nineteenth-Century Germany," *Church History* 34, no. 4 (December 1965): 440.

15. Wolfgang Altgeld, *Katholizismus, Protestantismus, Judentum* (Mainz: M. Grunewald, 1992), 4, 22, 64–65, 125–36, 160.

16. Helmut Walser Smith, *German Nationalism and Religious Conflict: Culture, Ideology, and Politics, 1870–1914* (Princeton: Princeton University Press, 1995), 11; cf. Altgeld, *Katholizismus*, 75–78; and Lepsius, "The Nation and Nationalism in Germany," 43–64.

17. Smith, *German Nationalism*, 20–24, 33.

18. Peter Herbst, "Myth as the Expression of Collective Consciousness in Romantic Nationalism," in J. C. Eade, ed., *Romantic Nationalism in Europe* (Canberra: Humanities Research Centre, Australian National University, 1983), 17, 24–26; and Jan Bialostocki, "The Image of the Defeated Ruler in Romantic Art," in *Romantic Nationalism*, 64–71; Bernard Willms, *Idealismus und Nation: Zur Rekonstruktion des politischen Selbstbewußtseins der Deutschen* (Paderborn: F. Schöningh, 1986), 149–51; Thomas Nipperdey, "Auf der Suche nach der Identität: Romantischer Nationalismus," in *Nachdenken über die deutsche Geschichte* (Munich: C. H. Beck, 1986), 120–24. See also Hermann Timm, *Die heilige Revolution: Das religiöse*

Totalitätskonzept der Frühromantik (Frankfurt: Syndikat, 1978), 80–84; and Susanne Zantop, "Re-presenting the Present: History and Literature in Restoration Germany," *MLN* 102, no. 3 (April 1987): 581–83.

19. Dietrich von Engelhardt, "Romanticism in Germany," in Roy Porter and Mikulas Teich, eds., *Romanticism in National Context* (New York: Cambridge University Press, 1988), 116.

20. Engelhardt, "Romanticism in Germany," 110–19; Peter Hohendahl, *Building a National Literature: The Case of Germany, 1830–1870,* trans. Renate B. Franciscono (Ithaca NY: Cornell University Press, 1989), 159; Frederick C. Beiser, *Enlightenment, Revolution, and Romanticism: The Genesis of Modern German Political Thought, 1790–1800* (Cambridge: Harvard University Press, 1992), 5–6, 224, 237–38; Hinrich Seeba, "'Germany—a Literary Concept': The Myth of a National Literature," *German Studies Review* 17, no. 2 (May 1994): 354–57; and Stephen Bann, *Romanticism and the Rise of History* (New York: Twayne, 1995), 5, 10, 27.

21. Heinz Duchhardt, *Protestantisches Kaisertum und Altes Reich* (Wiesbaden: Steiner, 1977), 147.

22. Johannes Paul, *Gustaf Adolf,* vol. 1, *Schwedens Aufsteig zur Großmachtstellung* (Leipzig: Quelle & Meyer, 1927), 5–9; and *Gustaf Adolf,* vol. 3, *Von Breitenfeld bis Lützen* (Leipzig: Quelle & Meyer, 1932), 148–50; see also Paul's "Gustaf Adolf in der deutschen Geschichtsschreibung," *Historische Vierteljahrschrift* 25, no. 3 (September 1930): 415–29; Richard Schmidt, "Gustav Adolf: Die Bedeutung seiner Erscheinung für die europäische Politik und für den deutschen Volksgeist," *Zeitschrift für Politik* 22, no. 11 (February 1933); 701–19. Paul and Schmidt were of a decided right-wing orientation, implying that Gustavus Adolphus's Swedish-German alliance was an example of an "imperialistic *Weltpolitik*" based on common racial-cultural origins. See also Gerhard Ritter, "Gustav Adolf, Deutschland und das nordische Luthertum," in *Die Weltwirkung der Reformation,* 2d ed. (Munich: R. Oldenbourg, 1959), 134–45. Ritter praised the Scandinavian-German alliance as a model for erecting a bulwark against "Muscovite barbarism." Ernst Ekman, "Three Decades of Research on Gustavus Adolphus," *Journal of Modern History* 38, no. 3 (September 1966): 243–55; Werner Buchholz, "Der Eintritt Schwedens in den Dreißigjährigen Krieg in der Schwedischen und Deutschen Historiographie des 19. und 20. Jahrhunderts," *Historische Zeitschrift* 245, no. 2 (1987): 291–314; and Sverker Oredsson, *Geschichtsschreibung und Kult: Gustav Adolf, Schweden, und der Dreißigjährigen Krieg,* trans. Klaus Böhme (Berlin: Duncker & Humblot, 1994). Oredsson only cursorily focuses on the Gustavus Adolphus phenomenon before 1914.

23. Johannes Willms, *Nationalismus ohne Nation: Deutsche Geschichte von 1789 bis 1914* (Düsseldorf: Classen, 1983), 113.

24. On the formative impact of the Wars of Liberation on nascent German nationalism, see Willms, *Nationalismus ohne Nation,* 107–14; Anthony Stephens, "Kleist's

Mythicisation of the Napoleonic Era," in Eade, *Romantic Nationalism*, 165–80; Jost Hermand, "Dashed Hopes: On the Painting of the Wars of Liberation," in Seymour Drescher, David Sabean, and Allan Sharlin, eds., *Political Symbolism in Modern Europe: Essays in Honor of George L. Mosse* (New Brunswick: Rutgers University Press, 1982), 218 ff.; Engelhardt, "Romanticism in Germany," 117; Dieter Düding, "Das deutsche Nationalfest von 1814: Matrix der deutschen Nationalfeste im 19. Jahrhundert," in Dieter Düding, Peter Friedemann, and Paul Munch, eds., *Öffentliche Festkultur: Politische Feste in Deutschland von der Aufklärung bis zum Ersten Weltkrieg* (Hamburg: Rowohlt, 1988), 67–88; Dann, *Nation und Nationalismus*, 56–69; Seeba, "'Germany—A Literary Concept,'" 360; and Christopher Clark, "The Wars of Liberation in Prussian Memory: Reflections on the Memorialization of War in Early-Nineteenth-Century Germany," *Journal of Modern History* 68, no. 3 (September 1996): 550–76.

25. Heinz Gollwitzer, *Europabild und Europagedanke* (Munich: C. H. Beck, 1964), 53–66, 81–82.

26. Gollwitzer, *Europabild und Europagedanke*, 83–84, 119.

27. Ursula Berg, *Niklas Vogt (1756–1836): Weltsicht und Politische Ordnungsvorstellungen zwischen Aufklärung und Romantic*, Beiträge zur Geschichte der Universität Mainz, 16 (Stuttgart: F. Steiner, 1992), 138–42, 236–47, 262–64.

28. Nicolaus Vogt, *Ueber die Europäische Republik*, 2 vols. (Frankfurt: Varrentrapp & Werner, 1787), 1:7, 95, 127.

29. See Bogislav Philipp von Chemnitz, *Belli Sueco-Germanici* (Stettin: Georg Rethen, 1648).

30. Nicolaus Vogt, *Gustav Adolph, König in Schweden, als Nachtrag zur europäischen Republik* (Frankfurt: Varrentrapp & Werner, 1790), 1–11, 24–28. See Magdelene Hermann, *Niklas Vogt, eine Historiker der Mainzer Universität aus der 2. Hälfte des 18. Jahrhunderts* (Giessen: O. Kindt, 1917), 89–91.

31. Steven A. Stargardter, *Niklas Vogt, 1756–1836: A Personality of the Late German Enlightenment and Early Romantic Movement* (New York: Garland, 1991), 68. Stargardter notes that Metternich had been a pupil of Vogt in Mainz.

32. Nicolaus Vogt, *Historische Darstellung des europäischen Völkerbundes* (Frankfurt: Fr. Andreäischen Buchhandlung, 1808), 1:3, 49, 235–37.

33. Vogt, *Gustav Adolph*, 10.

34. On Vogt's praise for the "limited monarchies" of north Germany, especially the "well-ordered" state and *"bürgerliche Gesellschaft"* of Prussia, see Hermann, *Niklas Vogt*, 48–49, 63–65.

35. Christoph Friedrich Rühs, *Geschichte Schwedens* (Halle: J. J. Gebauer, 1810), 4:226, 244; Heinrich von Hungerkhausen, *Epaminondas und Gustav Adolph: Eine Parallele* (Munich: Gedruckt mit Zängl'schen Schriften, 1813), 44, 51–52; Ludwig Flathe, *Geschichte des Kampfes zwischen dem alten und dem neuen Verfassungsprincip der Staaten der neuesten Zeit seit dem Auftreten des Humanismus, 1789–1791*

(Leipzig: Göschen, 1813), 1:22–23. On Rühs, see Franz X. von Wegele, *Geschichte der Deutschen Historiographie* (Munich and Leipzig: R. Oldenbourg, 1885), 1023. Flathe published a biography of Gustavus Adolphus in 1847.

36. Friedrich von Raumer, *Geschichte Deutschlands von der Abdankung Karls V bis zum westphälischen Frieden* (Leipzig: F. A. Brockhaus, 1832), 3:3, 60, 95–96. Raumer also noted that, had Gustavus Adolphus lived, he would inevitably have been forced to establish strong Swedish rule in Germany. On Raumer, see Hans Herzfeld, "Friedrich von Raumer," in *Mitteldeutsche Lebensbilder*, vol. 3, *Lebensbilder des 18. und 19. Jahrhunderts* (Magdeburg, 1928), 318–61. On Raumer's service in the Prussian administration during the Reform era, see Werner Friedrich, *Friedrich von Raumer als Historiker und Politiker* (Leipzig: F. A. Brockhaus, 1930), 13–18. Raumer strongly supported Prussian leadership of a united Germany. See his *Friedrich von Raumer an Rudolf Köpke: Ein historisch-politischer Brief* (Berlin: E. S. Mittler & Sohn, 1866).

37. See Dann, *Nation und Nationalismus*, 92–101.

38. Dieter Düding, "Das Deutsche Nationalfest von 1814," in *Öffentliche Festkultur*, 71 ff. In the same volume, see Peter Brandt, "Das Studentische Wartburgfest vom 18./19. Oktober 1817," 89–112; and Cornelia Foerster, "Das Hambacher Fest 1832," 113–31. The Luther tercentenary in 1817 fell just two years after Friedrich Wilhelm III had promulgated the Union of the Lutheran and Calvinist confessions. The students of the Wartburg consciously linked the anniversary to the victory of 1813. For a contemporary observation, see Gerhard Friederich, *Geistesblick auf die Bedeutung des heutigen Jubelfestes der christlichen Kirchenverbesserung und das Verdienst ihres Stifters* (Frankfurt: Ferdinand Boselli, 1817), 5. See also Hartmut Lehmann, "Martin Luther als deutscher Nationalheld," 58–63. On the Union, see Paul W. Schroeder, *The Transformation of European Politics, 1763–1848* (New York: Oxford University Press, 1994), 594.

39. To compare the "popular" character of the German political festival with the state-sanctioned revolutionary variety in France, see Mona Ozouf, *Festivals and the French Revolution*, trans. Alan Sheridan (Cambridge: Harvard University Press, 1988).

40. In the aftermath of Hambach, the official crackdown on overtly democratic demonstrations and polemical literature was codified in the "Ten Articles" passed by the Confederation Diet in July 1832. This act reaffirmed the rules on censorship and the policing of public political activity established by the Karlsbad Decrees of 1819. See Edda Ziegler, *Literarische Zenzur in Deutschland, 1819–1848* (Munich: C. Hanser, 1983), 133–34; and Frederick Ohles, *Germany's Rude Awakening: Censorship in the Land of the Brothers Grimm* (Kent OH: Kent State University Press, 1992), 612–13.

41. The emancipatory dynamic of the Reformation and German Protestantism was never a completely comfortable fit with more conservative ideas of the state.

See Klaus Siblewski, *Rittlicher Patriotismus und romantischer Nationalismus in der deutschen Literatur, 1770–1830* (Munich: Fink, 1981), 178; Schnabel, *Deutsche Geschichte in neunzehnten Jahrhundert*, vol. 2, *Monarchie und Volkssouveranität* (Freiburg im Breisgau, 1933; reprint, Munich, Deutscher Taschenbuch, 1987), 246–47; and Brandt, "Das Studentische Wartburgfest," 106–7.

42. See Anderson, *Imagined Communities*, 26.

43. Patrick H. Hutton, *History as an Art of Memory* (Hanover VT: University Press of New England, 1993), 79–80.

44. See Paul Connerton, *How Societies Remember* (Cambridge: Cambridge University Press, 1989), 42–43; Maurice Halbwachs, *On Collective Memory*, trans. and ed. Lewis A. Coser (Chicago: University of Chicago Press, 1992), 51–52, 63; and Rudy J. Koshar, "Building Pasts: Historic Preservation and Identity in Twentieth-Century Germany," in John R. Gillis, ed., *Commemorations: The Politics of National Identity* (Princeton: Princeton University Press, 1994), 222–23.

45. Friedrich Ludwig von Rango, *Denkmal der verhängnißvollen Jahre 1813 und 1814 jedem deutschen Biedermann gewidmet: Ein Taschenbuch, zum besten der im heiligen Freiheitskampf verstummelten Königl. Preuß Krieger* (Berlin: n.p., 1815), v.

46. Friedrich Ludwig von Rango, *Gustav Adolph der Große König von Schweden: Ein historisches Gemälde* (Leipzig: C. H. F. Hartmann, 1824), i–viii. A second edition of this book was issued for the *Säcularfeier* of 1832. As an indication of the devotional reverence with which the author regarded the Swedish king's memory, note his observation of the "unusual size" of Gustavus Adolphus's heart revealed at the embalming (a favorite detail from the folklore) and his sober description of the king's "magic sword" (*Zauberschwert*), said to be covered with talismanic signs and figures. In common with the history of such relics, the magic weapon was reported to have resided in multiple locations: Stockholm, Aix la Provence, and the Book Hall in Leipzig. See 386 and "Anhang," 127–28. Another familiar element was the persistent rumor that the king had been assassinated. The treacherous deed had been variously attributed to the machinations of Richelieu, Wallenstein, and Ferdinand II, but the most popular suspect was the traitor Franz Albrecht of Sachsen-Lauenburg. Although C. J. Jahn decisively debunked this theory in his *Ueber den Tod Gustav Adolph's, Königs in Schweden* (Weissenfels: J. F. Leyckham, 1806), the guilt of Franz Albrecht was still a hot topic of debate well into the 1840s.

47. Otto von Ravensberg [Otto Jacobi], *Gustav Adolph und Wallenstein: Tragödie in fünf Akten* (Berlin: Georg Reimer, 1840), 8. This work was the last part of a dramatic trilogy set during the Thirty Years' War that began with *Der böhmische Krieg* (1836) and continued with *Mansfeld und Tilly* (1840). On Jacobi, see Willig, *Gustav II*, 51–53. Willig states erroneously that the first part was published in 1856.

48. In 1815 the Kingdom of Saxony was forced to cede Lützen to Prussia.

49. *Erinnerung an die Schlacht bei Breitenfeld am 7ten September and deren Feier am 7. September 1831* (Leipzig: n.p., 1831), 5, 15–44.

50. A wrought iron fence later was built around the stele. See Otto Lerche, *Gustav Adolf: Deutsche Bilder und Stätten*, Das Bild zum Wort, vol. 1 (Hamburg: Agentur des Rauhen Hauses, 1932), 67, plate 20.

51. Ernst Ortlepp, *Gustav Adolph: Eine lyrische Phantasie zu dem zweihundertjährigen Jubiläum der Breitenfelder-Leipziger Schlacht am 7ten September 1631* (Leipzig: Wilhelm Zirges, 1831), 8–9.

52. Horst Denkler, "Zwischen Julirevolution (1830) und Märzrevolution (1848/49)," in Walter Hinderer, ed., *Geschichte der politischen Lyrik in Deutschland* (Stuttgart: Reclam, 1978), 183, 187–88; and *ADB*, 24:447. On the evolution of the political poem from the cosmopolitan tropes of the Enlightenment to the celebration of the *bürgerlich-liberalen* national state in this period, see in the same volume Jürgen Wilke, "Vom Sturm und Drang bis zur Romantik," 169. On Ortlepp, see Joachim Köhler, *Nietzsche and Wagner: A Lesson in Subjugation*, trans. Ronald Taylor (New Haven: Yale University Press, 1998), 16–18.

53. Carl Freiherr von Vincke, *Die Schlacht bei Lützen den 6ten November 1632: Historisches Fragment zur Erinnerung an Gustav Adolph am zweihundertjährigen Jahrestage seines Todes* (Berlin: Nauckschen Buchhandlung, 1832), 2–5.

54. J. C. Pfister, *Geschichte der Teutschen* (Hamburg: F. Perthes, 1833), 4:537.

55. The dedicatory language that accompanied the consecration of the monuments at Breitenfeld and Lützen tends to contradict Christopher Clark's assertion that the "patriot memory" of the Wars of Liberation found no representation in public monuments in the immediate postwar decades. See his "The Wars of Liberation in Prussian Memory," 576.

56. *Die Schlacht bei Lützen, am 6. November 1632* (Naumburg: K. A. Klassenbach, 1832), 3–4. Gerhard Friederich, *Gustav Adolf's Heldentod für Teutschlands Freiheit: Ein historisches Gedicht in vier Gesängen*, 2d ed. (Frankfurt: Sauerländer, 1834), 72–78. Friederich was a participant in the ceremonies at Lützen and a lifelong advocate of the reunification of the confessions and the Protestant mission to safeguard the "*Humanitätsbildung*" of Europe. See his *Luther: Ein historisches Gedicht in vier Gesängen* (Frankfurt: Sauerländer, 1855), 5; and *ADB*, 7:389–90. In 1706 another Swedish king, Charles XII, was similarly greeted by the people of Silesia as his forces pursued the Saxon army. The popular memory of the Protestant liberator from the north was still strong. See R. M. Hatton, *Charles XII of Sweden* (London: Weybright and Talley, 1968), 212, 226.

57. See Friederich, *Gustav Adolf's Heldentod*, 92–95.

58. Dietrich Freiherr von Bülow, *Gustav Adolph in Deutschland: Kritische Geschichte seiner Feldzüge* (Berlin: Himburg, 1808), 2:111–14; Andreas Buchner, *Geschichte von Bayern während des dreißigjährigen Krieges* (Munich: Lindauer'schen, 1851), 169.

59. *ADB*, 7:185–89. On Förster as playwright, see Willig, *Gustav II*, 47–48. Förster had been an officer in the Lützow Freikorps and received the Iron Cross after being severely wounded at the Battle of La Belle Alliance in 1815.

60. Friedrich Förster, *Gustav Adolph: Ein historisches Drama* (Berlin: Friedrich Maurer'schen Buchhandlung, 1832), 140, 161–63.

61. Hartmut Mai and Kurt Schneider, "Die Stadtkirche St. Viti und die Gustav-Adolf-Gedenkstätte," *Das Christliche Denkmal*, ed. Fritz Loffler, no. 115 (Berlin: Evangelische, 1981), 23–24. The exact location of the place of death was open to dispute. C. J. Jahn, who identified the marker as an old milestone, questioned Joseph de Francheville's placing of the actual spot some 700 paces from the stone. In fact, according to Jahn, the king had died exactly 83 paces from the traditional location. See his *Ueber den Tod Gustav Adolph's*, 3. See also Joseph Du Fresene de Francheville, *La Mort de Gustave-Adolphe* (Breslau: Theodor Korn, 1799).

62. Hermann Wolfgang Beyer, *Die Geschichte des Gustav-Adolf-Verein in ihren kirchen-und geistesgeschichtlichen Zusammenhängen* (Göttingen: Vandenhoeck & Ruprecht, 1932), 5.

63. Moser, *Gustav Adolph und die dankbare Nachwelt*, 70–71.

64. Pfister, *Geschichte der Teutschen*, 4:537.

65. Beyer, *Die Geschichte des Gustav-Adolf-Verein*, 5.

66. C. H. F. Hartmann, *Der Schwedenstein: Die Zweite Säcularfeier der Schlacht bei Lützen am 6. November 1632 in allen ihren An-und Nachklängen: Ein Denkmal für Gustav Adolph, den Retter Deutschlands von geistlichen und weltlichem Sclavenjoche* (Leipzig: C. H. F. Hartmann, 1833), 56–57. The possible consequences of such sparks apparently concerned the Prussian minister of culture and the interior, who stipulated that the ceremony must remain purely local in character and avoid any excessively martial flourishes.

67. In January 1832 Captain Philippi had discovered, beneath a mural of the Swedish coat of arms, a decomposed oaken urn beneath the flooring of the west nave. He conjectured, based on local tales, that the urn had contained the viscera of Gustavus Adolphus, removed by the embalmers. The table on which the king had lain could still be found in a nearby home. Philippi's great-grandfather, who was the village carpenter and schoolmaster, had made the royal coffin. See F. C. F. Philippi, "Der Tod Gustav Adolph's, Königs von Schweden, in der Schlacht bei Lützen am 6. November 1632: Zur Erinnerung bei der zweiten Säcularfeier [1832]," in Hartmann, *Der Schwedenstein*, 62–64. The church was renovated in 1855 and 1856. In 1912, during more extensive renovations, the urn was sealed in a lead cylinder and interred in its original location. On November 6, 1912, the church was reconsecrated. In 1913 it was renamed the *König-Gustav-Adolf-Gedächtniskirche* by imperial decree. See Mai and Schneider, *Die Stadtkirche St. Viti*, 29–31.

68. Philippi, "Der Tod," 65–67.

69. Friederich, *Gustav Adolf's Heldentod*, 197; Hartmann, *Der Schwedenstein*,

58–61, 102–3. On the ceremony, see also Moser, *Gustav Adolph und die dank-bare Nachwelt*, 71–75.

70. Hartmann, *Der Schwedenstein*, 121–22. See also Beyer, *Die Geschichte des Gustav-Adolf-Verein*, 13; and Hermann von Criegern, *Geschichte des Gustav-Adolf-Vereins* (Hamburg: F. A. Perthes, 1903), 10.

71. C. A. W. Schild, "Ausforderung zu einer Sechser-Subscription, zur Errichtung eines Denkmals," *Leipziger Tageblatt*, December 7, 1832 (no. 160), in Hartmann, *Der Schwedenstein*, 123–25; Criegern, *Geschichte des Gustav-Adolf-Vereins*, 11–12.

72. Emil Reiniger, "Die Schlacht bei Lützen, den 6. November 1632," in Hartmann, *Der Schwedenstein*, 84.

73. Hartmann, *Der Schwedenstein*, 136–38.

74. Mai and Schneider, *Die Stadtkirche St. Viti*, 25. On November 6, 1907, a memorial chapel was built behind the site. For a guide to the various sites and monuments connected to Gustavus Adolphus's campaign in Germany, see Lerche, *Gustav Adolf*.

75. F. Treumund [Eduard Sparfeld], *Gustav Adolf König von Schweden, der helden-müthige Kämpfer für Deutschlands Religionsfreiheit: Ein Volksbuch für alle Stände* (Leipzig: Freise, 1845), 460–62. See Hayden White's reference to Memnon's column, which spoke when touched by the sun, in *The Content of the Form* (Baltimore: Johns Hopkins University Press, 1990), 3.

76. Beyer, *Die Geschichte des Gustav-Adolf-Verein*, 6. On the ceremony see also Moser, *Gustav Adolph und die dankbare Nachwelt*, 77–82.

77. Schild, Grossmann, and Goldhorn, among others, called for the establishment of such a foundation in an article in the *Tageblatt* that appeared in December 1832. It is probable that the idea originated with Grossmann during the convocation at Lützen. The monument fund had a surplus of some 200,000 talers, which were used to put the foundation on a firm financial basis. For a full account of the founding of the GAV, its goals, organizational structure, and subsequent history, see Criegern, *Geschichte des Gustav-Adolf-Vereins*; and Beyer, *Die Geschichte des Gustav-Adolf-Verein*. For a biographical register of its leadership, a listing of its regional committees, and a glossary of programmatic religious, social, and political positions, among which can be found, under the entry "National Questions," an explicit statement supporting unification but rejecting chauvinism, see Otto Lerche, *Hundert Jahre Arbeit an der Diaspora*, vol. 1 (Leipzig: Verlag des Centralvorstandes des Evangelischen Vereins der Gustav-Adolf Stiftung, 1932). On the evolution toward a more militant expression of Protestant nationalism, see Heiner Grote, "Konfessionalistische und unionistische Orientierung am Beispiel des Gustav-Adolf-Vereins und des Evangelischen Bundes," in Wolf-Dieter Hauschild, ed., *Das deutsche Luthertum und die Unionsproblematik im 19. Jahrhundert* (Gütersloh: Gütersloher Verlagshaus G. Mohn, 1991), 110–30.

78. Gellner's definition of "diaspora nationalism" cannot be applied here.

Germany's Protestants might have seen themselves historically as a "pariah" group on a Catholic continent, but in "choosing nationalism" they certainly were not seeking to legitimate a self-conceived minority status or specialized socioeconomic function. See his *Nations and Nationalism*, 101–9.

79. Halbwachs, *On Collective Memory*, 63–65; Jacques Le Goff, *History and Memory*, trans. Steven Rendall and Elizabeth Claman (New York: Columbia University Press, 1992), 59.

80. George L. Mosse, *The Nationalization of the Masses: Political Symbolism and Mass Movements in Germany from the Napoleonic Wars through the Third Reich* (New York: Howard Fertig, 1975), 50–51.

81. Thomas Nipperdey, "Nationalidee und Nationaldenkmal in Deutschland im 19. Jahrhundert," *Historische Zeitschrift* 206, no. 3 (June 1968): 530–38; Hermann Beenken, *Das Neunzehnte Jahrhundert in der Deutschen Kunst* (Munich: F. Bruckmann, 1944), 449–52; Hubert Schrade, *Das Deutsche Nationaldenkmal* (Munich: Albert Langen, 1934), 5, 44–46; Hans-Gerhard Evers, "Denkmalplastik," in Rudolf Zeitler, ed., *Die Kunst des 19. Jahrhunderts* (Berlin: Propyläen, 1966), 158; Gerhard Kapner, "Skulpturen des 19. Jahrhunderts als Dokumente der Gesellschaftsgeschichte," in Hans-Ernst Mittig und Volker Plagemann, eds., *Denkmaler im 19. Jahrhundert: Deutung und Kritik* (Munich: Prestel, 1972), 12. On the construction of a secular pantheon, see Wilhelm Hansen, *Nationaldenkmaler und Nationalfeste im 19. Jahrhundert* (Luneburg: Niederdeutscher Verband für Volks- & Altertümskunde, 1976), 6–9.

82. See Zantop, "Re-presenting the Present," 584.

83. See Gollwitzer, *Europabild und Europagedanke*, 250–51; Hohendahl, *Building a National Literature*, 74–76, 84–85, 104–5; and Wolfgang Hardtwig, *Geschichtskultur und Wissenschaft* (Munich: DTV, 1990), 103–12. See also Georg G. Iggers, *The German Conception of History: The National Tradition of Historical Thought from Herder to the Present*, rev. ed. (Middletown CT: Wesleyan University Press, 1983), 63–109.

84. Fischer, "Der deutsche Protestantismus," 489.

85. Pfister, *Geschichte der Teutschen*, 4:539, 545–48. J. C. Pfister served in the Württemberg Diet. See *ADB*, 25:667–68; Johann Michael von Söltl, *Der Religionskrieg in Deutschland* (Hamburg: J. A. Meissner, 1840), 2:126, 144–45; and Carl August Mebold, *Der dreißigjährige Krieg, und die Helden desselben: Gustav Adolf, König von Schweden, und Wallenstein, Herzog von Friedland* (Stuttgart: Comptoir, 1840), 2:275. Mebold was a liberal journalist and adherent of Heinrich von Gagern who had been expelled from seminary for membership in the *Burschenschaften*. See *ADB*, 21:151–52.

86. Friedrich Schiller, *Geschichte des dreißigjährigen Krieges* (1791–93; reprint, Zurich: Manesse, 1985), 278–79, 402–5.

87. Karl Adolf Menzel, *Geschichte des dreißigjährigen Krieges in Deutschland* (Breslau: Grass, Barth, 1839), 2:319–20.

88. Menzel, *Geschichte des dreißigjährigen Krieges in Deutschland*, 321.

89. Menzel, *Geschichte des dreißigjährigen Krieges in Deutschland*, 343–44, 350–51. For an early twentieth-century musing on Gustavus Adolphus's plans for creating a "Protestant constitutional alliance under the aegis of a Swedish protectorate," see M. Doeberl, "Das Kaiserprojekt und die letzten Absichten König Gustav Adolfs von Schweden nach bayerischer Auffassung," *Forschungen zur Geschichte Bayerns. Vierteljahreschrift* 15, no. 3 (1907): 202–8.

90. See Friedrich, *Friedrich von Raumer als Historiker und Politiker*, 41–43.

91. Friedrich Wilhelm Barthold, *Geschichte des großen deutschen Krieges vom Tode Gustav Adolfs ab mit besonderer Rücksicht auf Frankreich*, 2 vols. (Stuttgart: S. G. Liesching, 1842–43), 1:vii–x.

92. On Barthold, see *ADB*, 2:104–5; and Wegele, *Geschichte der Deutschen Historiographie*, 1039–40.

93. Barthold, *Geschichte des großen deutschen Krieges*, 1:29. In a reference to Vogt, Barthold dismisses the "great plan" of the Swedish king as "essentially fraudulent." See 1:9–10. Here Barthold anticipates Klopp by over a decade.

94. Barthold, *Geschichte des großen deutschen Krieges*, 2:vi.

95. Gottlieb Mohnike, "Gustav Adolph, gezeichnet von Erich Gustav Geijer," *Zeitschrift für die historische Theologie* 3 (Leipzig, 1844): 59–61. This was a review of a major Swedish biography.

96. Hans-Ulrich Wehler, *Deutsche Gesellschaftgeschichte* (Munich: C. H. Beck, 1987), 2:419. On the distinction in German political thought between "constitutional monarchy" ("English model") and the absolutist "monarchichal-constitutional" system ("Prussian model") as stages in modern state development, see Otto Hintze, "Das monarchische Prinzip und die konstitutionelle Verfassung [1911]," in Gerhard Oestreich, ed., *Staat und Verfassung*, 2d ed. (Göttingen: Vandenhoeck & Ruprecht, 1962), 359–89; and Horst Dreitzel, *Monarchiebegriffe in der Fürstengesellschaft: Semantik und Theorie der Einherrschaft in Deutschland von der Reformation bis zum Vormärz*, vol. 2, *Theorie der Monarchie* (Cologne, Weimar, and Vienna: Böhlau, 1991), 827–49.

97. Johann Sporschil, *Der Dreißigjährige Krieg* (Braunschweig: G. Westermann, 1843), 410–15.

98. Treumund, *Gustav Adolph König von Schweden*, 390–93.

99. Wilhelm Bötticher, *Gustav Adolph, König von Schweden: Ein Buch für Fürst und Volk* (Kaiserswerth am Rhein: B. Fliebner, 1845), vii, 2, 68–69, 171–75.

100. Ludwig Flathe, *Geschichte Gustav Adolf's und des dreißigjährigen Krieges*, 2d ed. (Leipzig: B. G. Teubner, 1847), 1:1–5.

101. Flathe, *Geschichte Gustav Adolf's und des dreißigjährigen Krieges*, 1:1, 2:675–76.

102. On the importance of Schmidt in defining this new direction, see Wegele, *Geschichte der deutschen Historiographie*, 912–13; and Eduard Fueter, *Geschichte der neueren Historiographie* (Munich and Berlin: R. Oldenbourg, 1911), 371–77. See also Mack Walker, *Johann Jakob Moser and the Holy Roman Empire of the German Nation* (Chapel Hill: University of North Carolina Press, 1981).

103. Lorenz von Westenrieder, *Beyträge zur vaterländischen Historie, Geographie, Statistik* (Munich: J. Lindauer, 1806), 8:243–55. See also Michael Ignaz Schmidt, *Neuere Geschichte der Deutschen* (Frankenthal: L. B. F. Gegel, 1791), 9:132–36.

104. Lorenz von Westenrieder, *Geschichte des dreyßigjährigen Krieges* (Munich: J. Lindauer, 1805), 2:136–37, 233.

105. See John E. Acton, "German Schools of History," *Historical Review* 1 (January 1886): 17–18; *ADB*, 9: 139–41; Hans Fenske, "Gelehrtenpolitik im liberalen Südwesten, 1830–1880," in Gustav Schmidt and Jörn Rüsen, eds., *Gelehrtenpolitik und politische Kultur in Deutschland, 1830–1930* (Bochum: N. Brockmeyer, 1986), 39–41; and Oredsson, *Geschichtsschreibung und Kult*, 50–53.

106. L. F. Rieger in Stuttgart published the first edition in two volumes in 1835–36.

107. Wegele, *Geschichte der Deutschen Historiographie*, 1039–41. See also Karl August Müller, *Forschungen auf dem Gebiete der neueren Geschichte*, vol. 3, *Fünf Bücher vom Böhmischen Kriegen in der Jahren 1618–1621* (Dresden and Leipzig: G. Fleischer, 1841).

108. August Friedrich Gfrörer, *Gustav Adolph, König von Schweden, und seine Zeit*, 3d ed. (Stuttgart: A. Krabbe, 1852), 149–50, 580–81.

109. Gfrörer, *Gustav Adolph*, 749–50.

110. Gfrörer, *Gustav Adolph*, 891, 897.

111. Klopp's obvious dissatisfaction with Gfrörer's failure to adequately address contemporary political issues and contexts is clear in his introduction, emendations, and notes. See Christian d'Elvert, *Beiträge zur Geschichte der Rebellion, Reformation, des dreißigjährigen Krieges und der Neugestaltung Mährens im siebzehnten Jahrhunderts* (Brünn: R. Rohrer, 1867), vi.

112. [Onno Klopp], *Studien über Katholizismus, Protestantismus, und Gewissensfreiheit in Deutschland* (Schaffhausen: Fr. Hurter'schen Buchhandlung, 1857), 298–300; Klopp, *Der König Friedrich II. von Preussen und die deutsche Nation* (Schaffhausen: Fr. Hurter'sche Buchhandlung, 1860), 4–5; Klopp, *Tilly im dreißigjährigen Kriege* (Stuttgart: J. G. Cotta'scher, 1861), 2:59–64; Friedrich von Hurter, *Geschichte Kaiser Ferdinands II. und seiner Eltern bis zu dessen Krönung in Frankfurt* (Schaffhausen: Fr. Hurter'sche Buchhandlung, 1861), 3:427–32, 592.

113. See Karl Helbig's attack on the "Hurter-Klopp clique" of "falsifiers of history" in "Stimmungen in Deutschland vor Gustav Adolf's Landung," *Die Grenzboten* 24, no. 2 (1865): 173–79. See also J. Venedey, "Tilly und Gustav Adolf nach Onno Klopp," *Historische Zeitschrift* 7 (1862): 381–444. Among other things, Venedey accuses Klopp of "tilting at windmills" in pursuing his legitimist agenda.

114. Klopp called the Restoration period after 1817 the "Third Phase of Protestantism," in which the "powerful Protestant party," in fundamental opposition to the rationalist principles of the Second Phase, attempted to restore the revolutionary orthodoxy of the First Phase. See *Studien über Katholizismus*, 417.

115. "Gustav Adolf und Kurfürst Georg Wilhelm," *HpB* 1 (1838): 81, 88–89.

116. "Wie Gustav Adolph die religiöse Freiheit der Katholiken verstand," *HpB* 11 (1844): 580–84. It is acidly noted that the Gustavus Adolphus Association should properly have been called the "Richelieu Association."

117. See chapter 4.

118. Albert Heising, *Magdeburg nicht durch Tilly zerstört. Gustav Adolph in Deutschland. Zwei historische Abhandlüngen* (Berlin: Eyßenhardt, 1846). See also Heising, *Magdeburg nicht durch Tilly zerstört: Die Politik Gustav Adolph's in Deutschland*, 2d ed. (Berlin: Schneider, 1854). In the foreword to the second edition, Heising recalled the polemic with which the first edition was "honored." He noted that it was interpreted erroneously as an attack on the Gustavus Adolphus Association. Heising admitted that the title was unfortunately provocative, the first work of a younger man. It had been intended as a warning against the damage that confessional divisions inflicted on the German national sensibility. For the heated Protestant response, see Johann Valerius Kutscheit, *Herr Albert Heising für Tilly und gegen Gustav Adolph, oder wie die ehrlichen Deutschen mit Ruthen gestrichen werden wegen bisher geübter lügnerischer Geschichtschreibung* (Magdeburg: Creutz, 1847), 6. "The German nation is awake and prepared as never before. The current battle will be more decisive and enduring in its consequences than it was two hundred years ago, when it was purely religious in nature. If this war should again give rise to a Tilly in the enemy camp, instead of the petty skirmishers and partisan hangers-on of today, then we will again summon a Gustavus Adolphus."

119. Heising, *Magdeburg*, 137–40.

120. Heising, *Magdeburg*, 141, 177–87. See also Heising, *Notwendigkeit und Geist einer katholischen Universal-Encyklopädie* (Regensburg: G. Joseph Manz, 1857), 4–20. "Because German history, like the history of the Church, has been falsified, and generations have been imbued by these falsifications with a hostility toward everything Catholic, history will be the main component of the encyclopedia." Klopp also supported this project, though he despaired of making it a reality.

121. Johannes Janssen, *Gustav Adolf in Deutschland*, Katholischer Broschüren-Verein, 1, no. 8 (Frankfurt: Verlag für Kunst und Wissenschaft, G. Hamacher, 1865), 3–4.

122. Janssen, *Gustav Adolf in Deutschland*, 12, 32.

123. Zillessen, *Protestantismus und politische Form*, 159–60.

124. On the formation of the nation-state and national identity as contingent on a "modernization" of the concept of sovereignty, see Breuilly, "Sovereignty and Boundaries," 99–102, 127–31. Breuilly relies on a functionalist analysis of the

process of state building. In comparing the German experience to the French and British, it might be useful to examine the "geopolitical" definition of the German nation that partially identified the German national mission with its position in central Europe. A "philosophic geography," to use Larry Wolff's term, positioned the German nation as a bulwark against the decadent Catholic south and the barbarous Russian empire to the east. The figure of Gustavus Adolphus represented this heroic and historical German role perfectly. See Larry Wolff, *Inventing Eastern Europe: The Map of Civilization on the Mind of the Enlightenment* (Stanford: Stanford University Press, 1994), 4–8. See also Henry Cord Meyer, *Mitteleuropa in German Thought and Action, 1815–1945* (The Hague: Martinus Nijhoff, 1955), 9–26.

125. Ludwig August von Rochau, *Grundsätze der Realpolitik* [1853], ed. Hans-Ulrich Wehler (Frankfurt: Ullstein, 1972), 41.

126. See Friedrich Veit, *Gustav-Adolfs Vermächtnis: Vortrag bei der Schlußfeier des Gustav-Adolf Jahres 1932* (Nuremberg: Agentur des Rauhen Hauses, 1932).

127. Friedrich Karl Wild, *Leben Gustav Adolfs des Grossen, König von Schweden: Zur Belehrung, Verehrung, und Erbauung für das Volk* (Basel: Dr. Marriott, 1852), 37. Despite the Swiss imprint, Wild was German and the author of several "moral tales" set in the Schmalkaldic and Thirty Years' War and the Wars of Liberation. He had been politically active as a publicist in 1848 as a member of the *Protestantische Freunde* or *Lichtfreunde* movement and was celebrated by contemporaries in the 1850s and 1860s as "one of our best popular folklorists." See Klaus Müller-Salget, *Erzählungen für das Volk: Evangelische Pfarrer als Volksschriftsteller im Deutschland des 19. Jahrhunderts* (Berlin: E. Schmidt, 1984), 25–28, 160–61.

128. Wolfgang Menzel, *Deutschlands auswärtige Politik* (Stuttgart and Tübingen: J. G. Cotta, 1848), 5.

129. Wolfgang Menzel, *Die Aufgabe Preußens* (Stuttgart: J. B. Metzler, 1854), 16–18. Menzel's democratic radicalism combined with a passionately intolerant nationalism that rejected anything that was "un-German." See Prignitz, *Vaterländsliebe und Freiheit*, 164–67. See also Ludwig Börne, *Menzel, der Franzosenfresser* (Paris: T. Barrois fils, 1837).

130. Franz Mauritius, *Gustav Adolf, König von Schweden: Ein Lebensbild*, Unterhaltende Belehrungen zur Förderung allgemeiner Bildung, no. 26 (Leipzig: F. A. Brockhaus, 1856), 1–6, 66–72. Johann Preuß, the prolific and popular chronicler of the Hohenzollerns, strained to portray Friedrich II as an ardent admirer of the Swedish king. See his "Friedrichs des Großen Wohlgefallen an Gustav Adolph," *Zeitschrift für Preußische Geschichte und Landeskunde* 5 (1868): 209–16. On Preuß, see *ADB*, 26:581–84.

131. *Das Staats-Lexikon: Encyclopädie der sämmtlichen Staatswissenschaften für alle Stände*, ed. Karl von Rotteck and Karl Welcker, 3d ed., vol. 17 (Leipzig: F. A. Brockhaus, 1862), s.v. "Gustav II. Adolf," by Karl Biedermann. On Biedermann see Richard J. Bazillion, *Modernizing Germany: Karl Biedermann's Career in the Kingdom of Saxony, 1835–1901* (New York: Peter Lang, 1990).

132. G. Trauttwein, *Der dreißigjährige Krieg und der westfälische Friede* (Berlin: Georg Reimer, 1866), 14–15.

133. Heinrich W. J. Thiersch, *Luther, Gustav Adolf, und Maximilian I. von Bayern: Biographische Skizzen* (Nördlingen: C. H. Beck, 1869), 110, 145–46, 169–70. Thiersch updated seventeenth-century concerns in comparing the seventeenth-century fear of the Habsburg universal monarchy to nineteenth-century apprehensions regarding Russia.

134. On Droysen the elder and the "Prussian School," see Iggers, *The German Conception of History*, 104–23. On Gustav Droysen, see Hans Schulz, "Gustaf Droysen," in *Mitteldeutsche Lebensbilder*, vol. 3, *Lebensbilder des 18. und 19. Jahrhunderts* (Magdeburg, 1928), 481–96; Buchholz, "Der Eintritt Schwedens," 294; Oredsson, *Geschichtsschreibung und Kult*, 64

135. Gustav Droysen, *Gustav Adolf* (Leipzig: Veit, 1869), 1:viii. Gustavus Adolphus was closely identified with "Nordic" Europe, an emphasis that by an easy transference, and the traditional animus toward Catholic and southern Europe, allowed the identification with Prussia. As Wolfgang Menzel expressed it: "The unifying force of the German nation, or the strivings toward this goal, have always come from the north, all divisive tendencies from the south." Wolfgang Menzel, *Was hat Preußen für Deutschland geleistet?* (Stuttgart: A. Kröner, 1870), 3.

136. Droysen, *Gustav Adolf*, 2:423–24.

137. According to one reviewer, all historical judgments (Catholic and Protestant) about the Thirty Years' War came down to answering one "political question": "Whether in the German *Reich* the monarchical principle or the sovereignty of the princes would win out." See Johann Paul Hassel, "Zur Geschichte Gustav Adolf," *Zeitschrift für Preußische Geschichte und Landeskunde* 6 (1869): 370–79.

138. Hermann Hoffmeister, *Gustav Adolf der Retter deutscher Glaubensfreiheit* (Berlin: n.p., 1870), 106.

139. Franz Keym, *Geschichte des Dreißigjährigen Krieges*, 2 vols. (Freiburg im Breisgau: Herder'sche, 1873), 2:32–34; Otto von Schaching, *Maximilian I., der Große, Kurfürst von Bayern* (Freiburg im Breisgau: Herder'sche, 1876), 215; Carl Lempens, *Pragmatische Geschichte des Dreißigjährigen Krieges* (Zurich: Frick-Vogel, 1881), 3–10; and Felix Stieve, "Gustav Adolf [1886]," in *Abhandlungen, Vorträge, und Reden* (Leipzig: Duncker & Humblot, 1900), 195–207.

140. Gustav Droysen, "Brandenburgische Audienzen bei Gustav Adolf," *Zeitschrift für Preußische Geschichte und Landeskunde* 15 (1878): 21–35.

141. Julius Otto Opel, *Zur Erinnerungen an Gustav Adolf* (Leipzig: T. O. Weigel, 1894), 36–41. Franz Keym also saw the opportunity to diminish Gustavus Adolphus by praising the much maligned Schwarzenberg's efforts to secure Brandenburg's neutrality and Saxony's attempt to create a "Third Power" in Germany through the Leipzig Covenant of 1631. See Keym, *Dreißigjährigen Krieges*, 1:270–72.

142. Heinrich von Treitschke, "Gustav Adolf und Deutschlands Freiheit [1894],"

in *Historische und Politische Aufsätze*, 2d ed. (Leipzig: S. Hirzl, 1920), 35. A year later, in a letter to Max Lehmann, Treitschke confessed, "The cautious Realpolitik of the younger Droysen has always repelled me. I believe simply that the Swede was above all a Scandinavian ruler, but also a true hero of our faith." See *Heinrich von Treitschkes Briefe*, ed. Max Cornicelius (Leipzig: S. Hirzl, 1920), 3:637–38.

3. Wallenstein's Revolution

1. Friedrich Schiller, *Geschichte des Dreißigjährigen Krieges* (Leipzig, 1791–93; reprint, Zurich: Manesse, 1985), 470.

2. Golo Mann notes that in 1879 [*sic*] a standard bibliography of Wallenstein literature listed 780 titles. By 1911, it listed 2,574. See his *Wallenstein: Sein Leben erzählt* (Frankfurt: S. Fischer, 1971), 994 ff. The bibliography to which Mann refers was published in 1878. See Georg Schmid, "Die Wallenstein Literatur," *Mittheilungen des Vereins für Geschichte der Deutschen in Böhmen* 17, no. 1 (1878): 68–137. Schmid lists pamphlets published as early as 1626. Updated by Viktor Loewe, this bibliography appeared in five later editions.

3. On the idea of "coherence" in nineteenth-century historical writing, see Leonard Krieger, *Time's Reasons: Philosophies of History Old and New* (Chicago: University of Chicago Press, 1989), 52–106.

4. Golo Mann, "Foreword to the English-Language Edition," *Wallenstein: His Life Narrated*, trans. Charles Kessler (New York: Holt, Rinehart & Winston, 1976), 7–8. Hereafter, all citations to Mann refer to the English-language edition.

5. See Helmut Diwald, foreword to *Geschichte Wallensteins*, by Leopold von Ranke (Leipzig: Duncker & Humblot, 1869; reprint, Kronberg: Athenäum, 1978), 7–30.

6. As indicated, the secondary literature on Wallenstein is enormous. On the modern historiographical debate and for an overview of the pre-1945 preoccupation with Wallenstein's "national-political realism" as an innovative "German solution" in Central Europe, see Paul Schweizer, *Die Wallenstein-Frage in der Geschichte und Drama* (Zurich: Fäsi & Beer, 1899), 340–54; Moriz Ritter, "Der Untergang Wallensteins," *Historische Zeitschrift* 97, no. 2 (1906): 237–88; and, primarily, Heinrich Ritter von Srbik, *Wallensteins Ende: Ursachen, Verlauf, und Folgen der Katastrophe* [1920], 2d ed. (Salzburg: O. Müller, 1952), esp. 20–36, 278–80. The National Socialist viewpoint is enthusiastically expressed in A. Tiefenbach, *Wallenstein: Ein deutscher Staatsmann* (Oldenburg: G. Stalling, 1932). For more on the Nazi hagiography on Wallenstein, see my conclusion. The postwar literature approached the *Fragenkomplex* of Wallenstein with an eye toward his "progressive" secular politics and ideas on state building. See Gerhard Hoehne, "Das religiöse Charakterbild Wallensteins," *Zeitschrift für Kirchengeschichte* 3, no. 3 (1950/51): 268–90; Adam Wandruszka, *Reichspatriotismus und Reichspolitik zur Zeit des Prager Friedens von 1635: eine Studie zur Geschichte des deutschen*

Nationalbewusstseins (Graz and Cologne: H. Böhlaus, 1955), 7–28; Christfried Coter, "Zwischen Habsburg und dem Reich: Ein Versuch über Albrecht von Wallenstein," *Zeitschrift für Geschichtswissenschaft* 4, no. 4 (1956): 713–34; Friedrich Hermann Schubert, "Wallenstein und der Staat des 17. Jahrhunderts [1965]," in Hans-Ulrich Rudolf, ed., *Der Dreißigjährige Krieg: Perspektiven und Strukturen* (Darmstadt: Wissenschaftliche Buchgesellschaft, 1977), 185–207; Friedrich Prinz, "Wallenstein, Das Reich und Europa," in Andreas Kraus, ed., *Land und Reich, Stamm und Nation: Probleme und Perspektiven bayerischen Geschichte*, vol. 2, *Frühe Neuzeit* (Munich: C. H. Beck, 1984), 81–90; and Christoph Kampmann, *Reichsrebellion und kaiserliche Acht: Politische Strafjustiz im Dreißigjährigen Krieg und das Verfahren gegen Wallenstein 1634* (Münster: Aschendorff, 1992), 1–8. For a bibliography of the recent literature on Wallenstein, see Gottfried Lorenz, ed., *Quellen zur Geschichte Wallensteins* (Darmstadt: Wissenschaftliche Buchgesellschaft, 1987).

7. On the impact of the French Revolution on German politics and society, see T. C. W. Blanning, *The French Revolution in Germany: Occupation and Resistance in the Rhineland, 1792–1802* (Oxford: Clarendon Press, 1983); Reinhart Koselleck, *Preußen zwischen Reform und Revolution: Allgemeines Landrecht, Verwaltung, und Soziale Bewegung von 1791 bis 1848* (Munich: Klett-Cotta im Deutschen Taschenbuch, 1989), 163–216; Otto Dann, *Nation und Nationalismus in Deutschland, 1770–1990* (Munich: C. H. Beck, 1993), 45–72. See also Horst Dippel, *Germany and the American Revolution, 1770–1800: A Sociohistorical Investigation of Late Eighteenth-Century Political Thinking*, trans. Bernhard A. Uhlendorf (Chapel Hill: University of North Carolina Press, 1977), 329–64; and the essays in Helmut Berding and Hans-Peter Ullmann, eds., *Deutschland zwischen Revolution und Restauration* (Düsseldorf: Athenäum, 1981).

8. To get a sense of the hovering specter of a "public hanging" in postrevolutionary Europe during the first decades of the century, see Paul Johnson, *The Birth of the Modern: World Society, 1815–1830* (New York: HarperCollins, 1991), 356–443. On the impetus behind social modernization, see the essays in Charles Tilly et al., eds., *The Rebellious Century, 1830–1930* (Cambridge: Harvard University Press, 1975).

9. See Pieter Geyl, *Napoleon, For and Against*, trans. Olive Renier (New Haven: Yale University Press, 1949); and Stuart Semmel, "Napoleon in British Political Culture: Early-Nineteenth-Century Conceptions of National Character, Legitimacy, and History" (PhD diss., Harvard University, 1997). On a comparable New World revolutionary iconography, see Merrill D. Peterson, *The Jefferson Image in the American Mind* (New York: Oxford University Press, 1960); and Barry Schwartz, *George Washington: The Making of an American Symbol* (New York: Free Press, 1987).

10. Tim W. Mason, "Nineteenth-Century Cromwell," *Past and Present* 40 (July 1968): 187–91.

11. On the debate over the "revolutionary" legacy of Cromwell and its impact on the evolution of modern British political structures, see Olive Anderson, "The Political Uses of History in Mid-Nineteenth-Century England," *Past and Present* 36 (April 1967): 87–105; J. P. D. Dunbabin, "Oliver Cromwell's Popular Image in Nineteenth-Century England," in J. S. Bromley and E. H. Kossmann, eds., *Britain and the Netherlands*, vol. 5, *Some Political Mythologies* (The Hague: Martinus Nijhoff, 1975), 141–63; J. S. A. Adamson, "Eminent Victorians: S. R. Gardiner and the Liberal as Hero," *Historical Journal* 33, no. 3 (1990): 641–57; and the essays by Roger Howell in R. C. Richardson, ed., *Images of Oliver Cromwell: Essays for and by Roger Howell Jr.* (Manchester: Manchester University Press, 1993). For discussions of the debate and overviews of the historiography within the larger context of the argument over the reality of the "English Revolution," see Christopher Hill, *God's Englishman: Oliver Cromwell and the English Revolution* (New York: Harper & Row, 1972), esp. 253–75; and R. C. Richardson, *The Debate on the English Revolution* (London: Methuen, 1977), esp. 53–73. See also Alan Smith, "The Image of Cromwell in Folklore and Tradition," *Folklore* 79 (Spring 1968): 17–39; Martine W. Brownley, *Clarendon and the Rhetoric of Historical Form* (Philadelphia: University of Pennsylvania Press, 1985), 149–73; Ian Green, "'Repulsives vs. Wromantics': Rival Views of the English Civil War," in Brady Ciaran, ed., *Ideology and the Historians* (Dublin: Lilliput Press, 1991), 146–67; Beth S. Wright, "An Image for Imagining the Past: Delacroix, Cromwell, and Romantic Historical Painting," *Clio* 21, no. 3 (1992): 243–63; and Blair Worden, *Roundhead Reputations: The English Civil Wars and the Passions of Posterity* (London: Allen Lane, 2002).

12. Christoph Martin Wieland, foreword to Schiller, *Dreißigjährigen Krieges*, 7.

13. On the nationwide public commemoration of his birth in 1859, see Rainer Noltenius, "Schiller als Führer und Heiland: Das Schillerfest 1859 als nationaler Traum von der Geburt des zweiten deutschen Kaiserreichs," in Dieter Düding, Peter Friedemann, and Paul Munch, eds., *Öffentliche Festkultur: Politische Fest in Deutschland von der Aufklärung bis zum Ersten Weltkrieg* (Hamburg: Rowohlt, 1988), 237–58.

14. Schiller on "universal history": "Fruitful and comprehensive is the realm of history; within its compass lies the whole moral world." Friedrich Schiller, "Was heißt und zu welchem Ende studiert man Universalgeschichte?" in Jost Perfahl, ed., *Sämtliche Werke*, vol. 4, *Historische Schriften* (Munich: Winkler, 1968), 703.

15. This theme of the hero representing the revolutionary imperative as expressed in the tragic plot is developed in Walter Benjamin, *The Origin of German Tragic Drama*, trans. John Osborne (London: NLB, 1977), 57–158. See also Oskar Seidlin, "Schiller: Poet of Politics," in A. L. Wilson, ed., *A Schiller Symposium: In Observance of the Bicentennary of Schiller's Birth* (Austin: Department of Germanic Languages, University of Texas, 1960), 31–50; Edward McInnes, "Drama as Protest and

Prophecy: The Historical Drama of the *Jungdeutschen*," in *Maske und Kothurn: Internationale Beiträge zur Theaterwissenschaft* 17, no. 3 (1971): 191–202; John P. Farrell, *Revolution as Tragedy: The Drama of the Moderate from Scott to Arnold* (Ithaca: Cornell University Press, 1980), 19–42; Jeffrey N. Cox, *In the Shadow of Romance: Romantic Tragic Drama in Germany, England, and France* (Athens: Ohio University Press, 1987), 53–71; and Brian Murdoch, *The Germanic Hero: Politics and Pragmatism in Early Medieval Poetry* (Rio Grande OH: Hambledon Press, 1996), 3–12. See also the essays, esp. of Benno von Weise, in Elfriede Neubuhr, ed., *Geschichtsdrama* (Darmstadt: Wissenschaftliche Buchgesellschaft, 1980). For Schiller as a poet of Marxist politics, see Johannes R. Becher, "Denn er ist Unser: Friedrich Schiller: Der Dichter der Freiheit [1955]," in Ilse Siebert, ed., *Gesammelte Werke*, vol. 18, *Publizistik IV. 1952–1958* (Berlin and Weimar: Aufbau, 1981), 408–34; and Alexander Abusch, *Schiller: Größe und Tragik eines deutschen Genius* (Berlin: Aufbau, 1955), among many others.

16. See Karl Grün, *Friedrich Schiller als Mensch, Geschichtschreiber, Denker, und Dichter* (Leipzig: F. A. Brockhaus, 1844), 10–19.

17. Hermann F. W. Hinrichs, *Schiller's Dichtungen nach ihren historischen Beziehungen und nach ihrem inneren Zusammenhänge* (Leipzig: J. C. Hinrichs, 1837–39), 1:v–vii; 2, pt. 2:13–27, 55, 77–80.

18. See Karl Tomaschek, *Schiller's Wallenstein: Ein Vortrag gehalten am 31. März 1858* (Vienna: C. G. Gerold's Sohn, 1858), 8–13. As an Austrian defending the legitimacy of the German Confederation, Tomaschek stressed Wallenstein's "cosmopolitan" variety of patriotism. A discussion of Wallenstein's "world-historical" parallels with Napoleon can be found in Frantisek Thomas Bratranek, *Goethes Egmont und Schillers Wallenstein: Eine Parallele der Dichter* (Stuttgart: Cotta, 1862), 96, 179.

19. Johann Eduard Hess, *Biographien und Autographen zu Schiller's Wallenstein* (Jena: F. Mauke, 1859), vii. For more of the nineteenth-century appropriation of the "patriotic" in Schiller, see also Karl Gustav Helbig, foreword to *Wallenstein*, by Friedrich Schiller (Stuttgart: Cotta, 1856), 1–36; Heinrich Düntzer, *Schiller's Wallenstein* (Leipzig: E. Wartig, 1877); and J. G. Rönnefahrt, *Schillers dramatische Gedicht Wallenstein aus seinem Inhalt erklärt*, 2d ed. (Leipzig: Byk'sche Buchhandlung, 1886). Twentieth-century views of the trilogy did not substantially revise the view that Wallenstein was intended by Schiller to symbolize powerful forces immanent in modern German history. In the shadow of the Third Reich, however, they were inclined to see his symbolism in "Faustian" terms: history as nemesis and as a confrontation between power and principle. See Thomas Mann, "Schillers Wallenstein," *Die Neue Rundschau* 66, no. 3 (1955): 281–92; Rolf Linn, "Wallenstein's Innocence," *Germanic Review* 34, no. 3 (October 1959): 200–207; W. F. Mainland, "Schiller and Shakespeare—Some Points of Contact," in R. W. Last, ed., *Affinities: Essays in German and English Literature* (London: Leonard

Wolff, 1971), 19–33; John Neubauer, "The Idea of History in Schiller's *Wallenstein*," *Neophilologus* 56, no. 4 (October 1972): 451–63. In Fritz Hauer and Werner Keller, eds., *Schillers Wallenstein* (Darmstadt: Wissenschaftliche Buchgesellschaft, 1977), see these essays: Reinhold Schneider, "Wallensteins Verrat [1965]," 119–38; Oskar Seidlin, "Wallenstein: Sein und Zeit [1963]," 237–53; and Horst Hartmann, "Wallenstein: Geschichte und Dichtung [1969]," 311–27. See also Maria Wolf, "Wallenstein als Dramenheld" (PhD diss., Heidelberg Universität, 1992). One critic notes the "epic" historiographical perspective drawn from the plot of the *Iliad*: Wallenstein as Achilles, Ferdinand II as Agamemnon, and Gustavus Adolphus as Hector. See Gisela N. Berns, *Greek Antiquity in Schiller's Wallenstein* (Chapel Hill: University of North Carolina Press, 1985), 13–45.

20. For a still useful account of this process in an earlier century, see Felix Gilbert, *Machiavelli and Guicciardini: Politics and History in Sixteenth-Century Florence* (New York: W. W. Norton, 1984), esp. 105–235. See also the commentary on the creation, manipulation, and staging of the historical figure in Michel de Certeau, *The Writing of History*, trans. Tom Conley (New York: Columbia University Press, 1988).

21. For the history of this period, conventionally bracketed between the intervention of Sweden in 1630 and the Peace of Prague in 1635, see the discussions in Günter Barudio, *Der Teutsche Krieg, 1618–1648* (Frankfurt: S. Fischer, 1985), 329–475; and Geoffrey Parker, *The Thirty Years' War* (London: Routledge and Kegan Paul, 1987), 111–55.

22. For examples of the early Schillerian revolutionary hero, see his *Don Karlos, Infant von Spanien* (Leipzig: Göschen, 1787); the figure of Karl Moor in *Die Räuber* (Frankfurt and Mannheim: Tobias Löffler, 1782); and the figures of William of Orange and Count Egmont in *Geschichte des Abfalls der vereinigten Niederlande von der spanischer Regierung* (Leipzig: Siegfried Lebrecht Crusius, 1788).

23. The fascination with Wallenstein in this period can also be found in music inspired by Schiller. Cf. Franz A. Maurer, *Lied der Thecla: Aus Schillers Wallenstein in Musik Gesetzt* (Munich, ca. 1796–1800); Bernhard A. Weber, *Marche et Sinfonie Guerrière sur le second Acte de la Mort de Wallenstein* (Berlin, 1803); and Ludwig van Beethoven, *Grande Sonate pour le Pianoforte, Op. 53, composée et dédièe à Monsieur le Comte de Waldstein* (Bonn and Cologne, 1805).

24. The collation, annotation, and publication of what remained of Wallenstein's scattered papers, by two generations of scholars, would take the better part of the century.

25. Erdmann F. Bucquoi (1750–1821), *Leben und Thaten des General Wallenstein* (Bunzlau and Breslau: Weisenh. Buchdruckerei, 1783), 5, 105, 162. Intended as a "character study of a great man," this work was based primarily on Guillaume-Hyacinthe Bougeant's influential *Histoire des guerres et des negotiations qui précéderent le traite de Westphalie sous le regne de Louis XIII et le ministere du car-*

dinal de Richelieu et du cardinal Mazarin: Composée sur les memoires du Comte d'Avaux (Paris: Chez Pierre-Jean Mariette, 1744). The first German translation was published in 1758.

26. *ADB*, 12:51.

27. Johann Christian Herchenhahn, *Geschichte Albrechts von Wallenstein, des Friedländers* (Altenburg: n.p., 1790), 1:173, 215–16; 2:40–53.

28. See chapter 2.

29. Michael Ignaz Schmidt, *Neuere Geschichte der Deutschen* (Frankenthal: L. B. F. Gegel, 1791), 9:211–52. On Schmidt, see *ADB*, 32:6–8; and Eduard Fueter, *Geschichte der neueren Historiographie* (Munich and Berlin: R. Oldenbourg, 1911), 376–77. Schmidt, who served as director of the *Staatsarchiv* in Vienna, nevertheless claimed that Wallenstein put very little of his plans on paper. As it turned out, the paper trail of Wallenstein's negotiations and secret correspondence with the Swedes and Saxons, though exiguous, was there to be found in the collection *Papiere aus Wallensteins Nachlaße*, located in the military archives in Vienna. Extracts from this holding were first published in the *Neuen Militärischen Zeitschrift* (Vienna) between 1811 and 1813, with a new edition published in 1834–35. This was the first significant (and eye-opening) offering of new archival material in the nineteenth century. For the full bibliography of this series, see Schmid, "Die Wallenstein Literatur," 86–87.

30. Johann Georg August Galletti, *Geschichte des dreyßigjährigen Krieges und des westphälischen Friedens* (Halle: J. J. Gebauer, 1791), 1:254; 2:321–29. On Galletti, see *ADB*, 8:332–33; and Franz X. von Wegele, *Geschichte der deutschen Historiographie seit dem Auftreten des Humanismus* (Munich and Leipzig: R. Oldenbourg, 1885), 942.

31. Friedrich Schiller, *Geschichte des Dreißigjährigen Krieges*, 436–37, 469. On the planned Spanish intervention from Italy, see C. V. Wedgwood, *The Thirty Years' War* (New Haven: Yale University Press, 1939), 342–45.

32. For biographical sketches on Rebmann, see *ADB*, 27:483–85; and Hedwig Voegt, introduction to *Werke und Briefe*, by Andreas Georg Friedrich Rebmann, ed. Wolfgang Ritschel (Berlin: Rütten & Loening, 1990), 1:5–52.

33. Rebmann fled to France after provoking the Erfurt authorities with his outspoken advocacy for the imprisoned members of the Jacobin Club of Mainz, which included Georg Forster. See Jürgen Wilke, "Vom Sturm und Drang bis zur Romantik," in Walter Hinderer, ed., *Geschichte der politischen Lyrik in Deutschland* (Stuttgart: Reclam, 1978), 149; and James Sheehan, *German History, 1770–1866* (New York: Oxford University Press, 1993), 258.

34. Andreas Georg Friedrich Rebmann, *Albrecht der Friedländer, Hochverräther durch Cabale: Halb Geschichte einer mißlungenen Revolution des siebzehnden Jahrhunderts, halb Roman* (Leipzig: Wilhelm Heinsius, 1794), 17–22, 49.

35. Rebmann, *Albrecht der Friedländer*, 43, 52.

36. Andreas Georg Friedrich Rebmann, "Wahrheiten ohne Schminke: Bei Gelegenheit des Werks von Arthur Young: Die französische Revolution, ein warnendes Beispiel für andre Reiche [1794]," in *Werke und Briefe*, 1:265. Benjamin Constant also wrote, and left unfinished, a belletristic work about Wallenstein. See his *Wallstein: tragédie en cinq actes et en vers: Précédee de quelques réflexions sur le théâtre allemand, et suivie de notes historiques* (Paris: Paschoud, 1809).

37. Andreas Georg Friedrich Rebmann, "Einige Ideen über Revolutionen in Deutschand [1797]," in *Werke und Briefe*, 3:24–25.

38. See Falko Schneider, *Aufklärung und Politik: Studien zur Politisierung der deutschen Spätaufklärung am Beispiel A. G. F. Rebmanns* (Wiesbaden: Akademische Verlagsgesellschaft, 1978), 10, 50–56; Rainer Kawa, *Georg Friedrich Rebmann (1768–1824): Studien zu Leben und Werk eines deutschen Jakobiners* (Bonn: Bouvier, 1980), 119, 172–75; and Maria Anna Sossenheimer, *Georg Friedrich Rebmann und das Problem der Revolution* (Frankfurt: Peter Lang, 1988), 95–134, 181, 297.

39. *Albrechts von Wallenstein Herzogs von Friedland wahre, bisher immer verfälschte Lebensgeschichte* (Berlin: F. Maurer, 1797), i–ii, 36–70. See also another much-cited work in the same vein from this period, Christoph Gottlieb Murr, *Die Ermordung Albrechts, Herzogs von Friedland* (Halle: Hendel, 1806). Murr was the first to examine, if not very systematically, the Wallenstein material in the archives in Vienna. On Murr, see *ADB*, 23:76–80.

40. Friedrich Schiller, *Wallenstein: Ein dramatisches Gedicht* [1798–99], in *Sämtliche Werke*, vol. 1, *Dramen I*, ed. Jost Perfahl (Munich: Winkler, 1968), 679, 758–59, 833.

41. Schiller, *Wallenstein*, 686, 695, 812–13.

42. Karl Ludwig von Woltmann, *Leben, Thaten, und Schicksale Wallensteins* (Zofingen: n.p., 1804), 35–60. Woltmann had written a "supplement" to Schiller's history of the war.

43. See Heinrich Ritter von Srbik, *Geist und Geschichte vom deutschen Humanismus bis zur Gegenwart* (Munich: F. Bruckmann, 1950), 1:232–33. On Woltmann, see also Wegele, *Deutschen Historiographie*, 922–23; *ADB*, 44:188–90; Karoline von Woltmann, *Karl Ludwig und Karoline von Woltmann* (New York: n.p., 1870); and "Biographische Skizze: Karl Ludwig von Woltmann," *Meyer's Groschen Bibliothek der Deutschen Klassiker für alle Stände* 294 (New York: H. I. Meyer, 1870): 5–6.

44. See Nicolaus Vogt, *Ueber die Europäische Republik*, 2 vols. (Frankfurt: Varrentrapp & Werner, 1787); Vogt, *Gustav Adolph, König in Schweden, als Nachtrag zur europäischen Republik* (Frankfurt: Varrentrapp & Werner, 1790); and Vogt, *Historische Darstellung des europäischen Völkerbundes*, vol. 1 (Frankfurt: Fr. Andreäischen Buchhandlung, 1808). For the discussion of Vogt's interpretation of the aims of Gustavus Adolphus, see chapter 2. On Vogt, see Magdelene Hermann, *Niklas Vogt, eine Historiker der Mainzer Universität aus der 2. Hälfte*

des 18. Jahrhunderts (Giessen: O. Kindt, 1917); Ursula Berg, *Niklas Vogt (1756–1836): Weltsicht und Politische Ordnungsvorstellungen zwischen Aufklärung und Romantic* (Stuttgart: F. Steiner, 1992); and Steven A. Stargardter, *Niklas Vogt, 1756–1836: A Personality of the Late German Enlightenment and Early Romantic Movement* (New York: Garland, 1991). See also Heinz Gollwitzer, *Europabild und Europagedanke* (Munich: C. H. Beck, 1964).

45. Nicolaus Vogt, *Europäische Staats-Relationen* (Frankfurt: n.p., 1805), 3:231–38.

46. For a similar meditation, written during the period of French occupation, on the lost "German warrior spirit willing to fight for the independence of the nation," inspired by a visit to the "honored soil" of Wallenstein's Egerland, see L.C., "Wallensteins Revolte und Tod; nach der Handschrift eines seiner Zeitgenossen. Bruchstück aus dem Tagebuch eines Reisenden," *Minerva* 4 (October–December 1811): 100–125. This "patriotic" historical journal of liberal orientation, which was viewed with suspicion by the French authorities and German conservatives alike (among them Friedrich Perthes, who accused it, along with Woltmann, of Jacobin sympathies) was edited and published by Johann Wilhelm von Archenholz (1743–1812). See Friedrich Rucf, *Johann Wilhelm von Archenholtz: Ein deutscher Schriftsteller zur Zeit der Französischen Revolution und Napoleons (1741–1812)* (Berlin: E. Ebering, 1915); and Wegele, *Deutschen Historiographie*, 960. See also Charles E. McClelland, *The German Historians and England: A Study in Nineteenth-Century Views* (Cambridge: Cambridge University Press, 1971), 30–33, 239.

47. On the reforms undertaken during the occupation and the Wars of Liberation, see the discussions in Koselleck, *Preußen zwischen Reform und Revolution*; and Manfred Botzenhart, *Reform, Restauration, Krise: Deutschland, 1789–1847* (Frankfurt: Suhrkamp, 1985). See also Sheehan, *German History*, 425–41.

48. On the "materialist ethos" of the bureaucratic-political order of this period, particularly in Prussia, see Thomas Nipperdey, *Deutsche Geschichte, 1800–1866: Bürgerwelt und starker Staat* (Munich: C. H. Beck, 1987), 320–37. Karl Mannheim also noted the German tendency to turn problems of politics into problems of administration, resulting in political analyses that were "*de facto* treatises on administration." See Karl Mannheim, *Ideology and Utopia: An Introduction to the Sociology of Knowledge*, trans. Louis Wirth and Edward Shils (Bonn, 1929, reprint, London: K. Paul, Trench, Trubner, 1936), 118.

49. On cameralist theory, see Friedrich-Wilhelm Henning, *Landwirtschaft und ländliche Gesellschaft in Deutschland* (Paderborn: F. Schöningh, 1979), 1:221–59; and Keith Tribe, *Governing Economy: The Reformation of German Economic Discourse, 1750–1840* (New York: Cambridge University Press, 1988). See also Leonard Krieger, *Kings and Philosophers, 1689–1789* (New York: W. W. Norton, 1970).

50. See Henri Brunschwig, *Enlightenment and Romanticism in Eighteenth-Century*

Prussia, trans. Frank Jellinek (Chicago: University of Chicago Press, 1974), 22, 45–48; Hans Rosenberg, *Bureaucracy, Aristocracy, and Autocracy: The Prussian Experience, 1660–1815* (Boston: Beacon Press, 1966), 226–28; Reinhart Koselleck, "Staat und Gesellschaft in Preußen, 1815–1848," in Werner Conze, ed., *Staat und Gesellschaft im deutschen Vormärz, 1815–1848* (Stuttgart: Klett-Cotta, 1962), 94–105; Koselleck, *Preußen zwischen Reform und Revolution*, 245–55, 388; Jacques Droz, *Europe between Revolutions, 1815–1848*, trans. Robert Baldick (New York: Harper & Row, 1967), 17, 31–33, 54–55; and Helmut Berding and Hans-Peter Ullmann, "Veränderungen in Deutschland an der Wende vom 18. zum 19. Jahrhundert," in *Deutschland zwischen Revolution und Restauration*, 12–22.

51. For a detailed discussion of Förster, the Berlin Hegelians, and the ideological underpinnings of "Hegelian politics" in the 1820s, see John Edward Toews, *Hegelianism: The Path toward Dialectical Humanism, 1805–1841* (Cambridge: Cambridge University Press, 1980), 71–121. Toews notes that Förster's dramatic falling away from subversive enthusiasm for constitutional reform, which cost him his teaching post in 1818, was such that, by 1823, when he received a state-supported position, he had become known as the "court demagogue" because of his advocacy for the Prussian state. See also Georg G. Iggers, *The German Conception of History: The National Tradition of Historical Thought from Herder to the Present*, rev. ed. (Middletown CT: Wesleyan University Press, 1983), 39, 66. On Hegel and constitutionalism, see the selections from *Philosophy of Right* and *Philosophy of Mind* in G. W. F. Hegel, *Hegel: The Essential Writings*, ed. Frederick G. Weiss (New York: Harper & Row, 1974), 284–307.

52. G. W. F. Hegel, *The Philosophy of History*, trans. J. Sibree (New York, 1899; reprint, New York: Dover Books, 1956), 9–32. 427–37. Hegel defined the "world-historical" figure as follows: "It was theirs to know this nascent principle; the necessary, directly sequent step in progress, which their world was to take; to make this their aim, and to expend their energy in promoting it. . . . They die early like Alexander; they are murdered, like Caesar; transported to St. Helena, like Napoleon. . . . They are *great* men, because they willed and accomplished something great; not a mere fancy, a mere intention, but that which met the case and fell in with the needs of the age."

53. See Linda Orr, *Headless History: Nineteenth-Century French Historiography of the Revolution* (Ithaca: Cornell University Press, 1990), esp. 1–36; Stanley Mellon, *The Political Uses of History: A Study of Historians in the French Restoration* (Stanford: Stanford University Press, 1958); and Alice Gérard, *La Révolution française, mythes, et interprétations* (1789–1970) (Paris: Flammarion, 1970), 29–47. On the "recuperative" agenda of French Restoration historiography, see also Lionel Gossman, *Between History and Literature* (Cambridge: Harvard University Press, 1990), 83–200.

54. Friedrich Förster, *Kunst und Leben*, ed. Hermann Kletke (Berlin: Paetel, 1873),

15–33. See also *ADB*, 7:185–89; and Ernst Förster, *Aus der Jugendzeit* (Berlin: W. Spemann, 1887).

55. Friedrich Förster, Albrechts von Wallenstein, des Herzogs von Friedland und Mecklenburg, ungedrückte, eigenhändige vertrauliche Briefe und amtliche Schreiben aus den Jahren 1627 bis 1634 an Arnheim, Aldringer, Gallas, Piccolomini, und andrere Fürsten und Feldherrn seiner Zeit: Mit einer Charakteristik des Lebens und der Feldzüge Wallensteins (Berlin: Georg Reimer, 1828–29), 1:xii–xvi; 2:148. This was an epistolary history of diplomatic correspondence between Wallenstein, Vienna, Paris, Stockholm, and Dresden. Förster found this material in the same Habsburg military archive in Vienna that Murr had used and which was the source of the documents published in 1811–13. The tenacity of the Wallenstein myth, he claimed, was demonstrated by its perpetuation by Michael Ignaz Schmidt, who, as director of the archive, had long had access to the very same material.

56. Förster, *Albrechts von Wallenstein*, 2:xi–xv, 5, 60, 169, 246–52; 3:vii–ix, 89–103, 167, 450–54.

57. Johann Sporschil, *Wallenstein: Historischer Versuch* (Leipzig: J. F. Fischer, 1828), iii–vi, 52–55, 135–36.

58. Joseph von Hormayr, "Versuch Albrecht's von Waldstein, eine ständische Verfassung in seinem Herzogthume Friedland einzuführen," *Taschenbuch für vaterländische Geschichte* 1 (Stuttgart, 1830): 29. The French royalist Joseph Fiévée had occasion to observe in 1818: "Our century is singular in that it apprehends by memories, as it makes politics with memories." Quoted in Mellon, *Political Uses of History*, 1–2.

59. Hormayr, "Versuch," 30–44.

60. Srbik, *Geist und Geschichte*, 1:231–32. Hormayr had been a member of the insurrectionary *Alpenbund*. See also André Robert, *L'Idée Nationale Autrichienne et les Guerres de Napoléon: L'Apostolat du Baron de Hormayr et Le Salon de Caroline Pichler* (Paris: F. Alcan, 1933), 216–302. Caroline Pichler was the author of two fictional works about the Thirty Years' War. See Pichler's *Ferdinand der Zweyte, König von Ungarn und Böhmen: Ein historisches Schauspiel in fünf Aufzügen* (Augsburg: Gerhard Fleischer, 1817) and *Die Schweden in Prag* (Vienna: August Liebstind, 1827). On Hormayr, see also Kurt Adel, ed., introduction to *Joseph Freiherr von Hormayr and die "vaterländische Romantik" in Österreich* (Vienna: Bergland, 1969), 7–41.

61. Hormayr, "Versuch," 34–39.

62. Julius Max Schottky, *Ueber Wallensteins Privatleben* (Munich: G. Franz, 1832), 78–79, 107–10. Schottky taught art history in Munich. See *ADB*, 32:418–19.

63. Friedrich Förster, "Wallenstein als regierender Herzog und Landesherr," *Historisches Taschenbuch* 5 (Leipzig, 1834): 3–29, 52–62. This journal was edited and published by the pro-Prussian Friedrich von Raumer, who had earlier dismissed Förster's conclusions based on Wallenstein's correspondence, noting only

that Wallenstein had gone against "the temper of his times." See Friedrich von Raumer, *Geschichte Deutschlands von der Abdankung Karls V bis zum westphälischen Frieden: Zweite Hälfte von 1630–1648* (Leipzig: F. A. Brockhaus, 1831–32), 3:128–36. Förster's 1834 biography of Wallenstein consisted primarily of standard anti-Habsburg and anti-Catholic boilerplate, portraying Wallenstein as the victim of Bavarian particularism and an "Italian-Catholic conspiracy" against the Germans. See his *Wallenstein Herzog zu Mecklenburg, Friedland und Sagan, als Feldherr und Landesfürst in seinem öffentlichen und Privat-Leben: Eine Biographie* (Potsdam: F. Reigel, 1834). Nineteenth-century Mecklenburg historians, chafing under the grand duke's unreconstructed absolutism, guardedly endorsed Wallenstein's constitutional and administrative innovations. The ducal archivist and librarian noted that, in pursuing "the separation of administration from justice," Wallenstein had attempted a program of modernization in Mecklenburg that remained unfinished two centuries later: "Wallenstein was born two hundred years before his time." See G. C. F. Lisch, "Plau während des dreißigjährigen Krieges," *Jahrbücher des Vereins für meklenburgische Geschichte und Altherthumskunde [JMG]* 17 (1852): 196–226; Lisch, "Wallensteins Abzug aus Meklenburg im Jahre 1629," and "Wallensteins Armenversorgungs-Ordnung für Meklenburg," *JMG* 25 (1870): 45–59, 80–92; and Lisch, "Ueber Wallensteins Regierungsform in Meklenburg," *JMG* 27 (1871): 3–31. See also Otto Krabbe, *Zur Geschichte Wallensteins und des dreißigjährigen Krieges: Aus dem kirchlichen und wissenschaftlichen Leben Rostocks* (Berlin: G. Schlawitz, 1863).

64. On the prioritizing of unity over liberty in a "pragmatic" historiography as represented by Menzel, see Srbik, *Geist und Geschichte*, 1:172–73. On Menzel, see *ADB*, 21:380–81; Wegele, *Deutschen Historiographie*, 1011–12; and Christoph Prignitz, *Vaterländsliebe und Freiheit: Deutscher Patriotismus von 1750 bis 1850* (Wiesbaden: Steiner, 1981), 139–56.

65. Karl Adolf Menzel, *Geschichte des dreißigjährigen Krieges in Deutschland* (Breslau: Grass, Barth, 1837), 2:377–409. On the famous "Pilsen oath," which was frequently submitted as evidence against Wallenstein, see Golo Mann, *Wallenstein*, 762–69. Mann dismisses its "treasonous" intent and states it was sworn on the officers' initiative, to keep Wallenstein from resigning and thus foiling their mercenary designs.

66. Friedrich Wilhelm Barthold, *Geschichte des großen deutschen Krieges vom Tode Gustav Adolfs ab mit besondere Rücksicht auf Frankreich* (Stuttgart: S. G. Liesching, 1842), 1:1–79, 123–29. On Barthold, see *ADB*, 2:104–5; and Wegele, *Deutschen Historiographie*, 1039–40. The Austrian historian Johann Mailath (1786–1855) believed Menzel's interpretation absolved Ferdinand II of the base charge of ordering Wallenstein's "assassination" (*Meuchelmord*). However, Mailath denied French involvement in Wallenstein's downfall, instead attributing it to the "labyrinthine web of his own ignoble intrigues." See Johann Grafen Mailath, *Geschichte des österreichischen Kaiserstaates* (Hamburg: F. Perthes, 1842), 3:334–88. On Mailath, see *ADB*, 20:101–5.

67. Friedrich Förster, *Wallensteins Prozess vor den Schranken des Weltgerichts und des k.k. Fiscus zu Prag* (Leipzig: B. G. Teubner, 1844), iii–vi, 191–216. Förster directed his response in particular to Menzel, Barthold, and Mailath, dating his foreword "Berlin, 25. Feb. 1844, on the 210th anniversary of the murder of the Duke of Friedland."

68. See Karl Maria Freiherr von Aretin, *Wallenstein: Beiträge zur nähreren Kenntniß seines Charakters, seiner Pläne, seines Verhältnisses zu Bayern* (Regensburg: G. Joseph Manz, 1846), 23–29, 92–94; Albert Heising, *Magdeburg nicht durch Tilly zerstört: Gustav Adolph in Deutschland: Zwei historische Abhändlungen* (Berlin: Eyßenhardt, 1846), 198; and Georg Thomas Rudhart, *Einige Wort über Wallensteins Schuld* (Munich: J. G. Weiss, 1850), 3–18. One Catholic journal enthusiastically drew attention to the "salutary reaction" of Protestant historians like Menzel and Barthold to the "fanatical partisan scribbler" (*fanatischen Partheiscribenten*) Förster. See "Wallensteins Tod," *HpB* 14 (1844): 703–10. On the Baltic ploject, see chapter 1.

69. Richard Roepell, "Der Verrath Wallenstein's an Kaiser Ferdinand II.," *Historisches Taschenbuch* n.s., 6 (1845): 239–306. This article was originally published in 1834 as Roepell's inaugural dissertation at Halle under the title *De Alberto Waldsteino, Friedlandiae duce Proditore*. On Roepell, see *Schlesische Lebensbilder* (Breslau: W. G. Korn, 1922), 1:471.

70. See J. H. Krönlein, *Wallenstein und seine neuesten historischen Ankläger und Vertheidiger* (Leipzig: O. Wigand, 1845), 3–7, 104–15. Wallenstein's reputed religious toleration was a key factor that commended him to many Restoration historians: "Religion had meant nothing to him. If he had only founded a kingdom, Catholics and Protestants would have lived together!" See Heinrich August Hecht, *Der dreißigjährige Krieg und der westphälische Friede* (Altenburg: Julius Helbig, 1848), 373.

71. See Nipperdey, *Deutsche Geschichte, 1800–1866*, 684–87.

72. On Helbig, see *ADB*, 11:677–78. While in Warsaw in 1830, Helbig was caught up in the Polish Revolt and became an ardent supporter of Polish national self-determination, whose inspiration he compared to the German idealism of 1813. See C. G. Freimund [Karl Gustav Helbig], *Bemerkungen über den Zustand Polens unter russischer Herrschaft im Jahre 1830* (Leipzig: Arnold, 1831). On the attempt to create a "national" conservative-liberal consensus politics during the 1850s, see Nipperdey on the so-called "*Wochenblattpartei*," *Deutsche Geschichte*, 682–83. On the Polish Revolt of 1830–31, see Paul W. Schroeder, *The Transformation of European Politics, 1763–1848* (New York: Oxford University Press, 1994), 705–9.

73. Karl Gustav Helbig, *Wallenstein und Arnim, 1632–1634: Ein Beitrag zur Geschichte des dreißigjährigen Kriegs* (Dresden: Adler & Dietze, 1850), v–viii, 12–14, 25–31.

74. Beda Dudik, *Forschungen in Schweden für Mährens Geschichte* (Brünn: C.

Winiker, 1852), 288–90, 430–44. Cf. Karl Gustav Helbig, *Der Kaiser Ferdinand und der Herzog von Friedland während des Winters 1633–34* (Dresden: Adler & Dietze, 1852). See also the collection of Wallenstein's correspondence in Beda Dudik, *Waldstein von seiner Enthebung bis zur abermaligen Uebernahme des Armee Ober-Kommandos, vom 15. August 1630 bis 15. April 1632* (Vienna: C. G. Gerold's Sohn, 1858). On Dudik, see [Matthias Koch], *Der mährische Landeshistoriograph Dr. Beda Dudik* (Brünn: n.p., 1890).

75. See Otto Urban, *Die tschechische Gesellschaft 1848 bis 1918*, trans. Henning Schlegel (Vienna and Cologne: Böhlau, 1994), 1:141–55.

76. On the evolution of Bohemian national thinking, see Oscar Jászi, *The Dissolution of the Habsburg Monarchy* (Chicago: University of Chicago Press, 1929), 388–89; A. J. P. Taylor, *The Habsburg Monarchy, 1809–1918* (London, 1941; reprint, Chicago: University of Chicago Press, 1976), 238–39; Arthur J. May, *The Habsburg Monarchy, 1867–1914* (Cambridge: Harvard University Press, 1951), 27–28, 195–200, 325–26; Hans Raupach, *Der tschechische Frühnationalismus* (Essen, 1939; reprint, Darmstadt: Darmstadt Wissenschaftliche Buchgesellschaft, 1969), 9–25, 90–114; the essays, esp. Plaschka and Lemberg, in Ernst Birke and Kurt Oberdorffer, eds., *Das böhmische Staatsrecht in der deutsch-tschechischen Auseinandersetzungen des 19. und 20. Jahrhunderts* (Marburg and Lahn: N. G. Elwert, 1960); Eugenie T. von Falkenstein, *Der Kampf der Tschechen um die historischen Rechte der böhmischen Krone im Spiegel der Presse, 1861–1879* (Wiesbaden: Harrossowitz, 1982), 11–19, 136–37, 205, 217; John F. N. Bradley, *Czech Nationalism in the Nineteenth Century* (Boulder CO: East European Monographs, 1984), 2–24, 46, 50; Wolfgang Menzel, *Die nationale Entwicklung in Böhmen, Mähren, und Schlesien* (Nuremberg: H. Preussler, 1985), 19, 52, 64–84; Hugh Agnew, *Origins of the Czech National Renascence* (Pittsburgh: University of Pittsburgh Press, 1993), 26–37, 251; Zdenek Suda, *The Origins and Development of the Czech National Consciousness and Germany* (Prague: Central European University Press, 1995), 5–27.

77. See Johann Nepomuk Komareck, *Albrecht Waldstein, Herzog von Friedland: Ein Trauerspiel in fünf Akten* (Leipzig: K. F. Kohler, 1793); Franz Aloysius Wacek, "Beitrag zu Charakteristik des berühmten Albrecht von Waldstein, Herzogs von Friedland," *Hesperus: Ein Nationalblatt für gebildete Leser* 59 (October 1814): 385–90; 60 (December 1814): 478–80; 61 (December 1814): 482–84; Franz Nemethy, *Das Schloß Friedland in Böhmen und die Monumente in der Friedländer Stadtkirche* (Prague: n.p., 1818); Franz Palacky, "Jugendgeschichte Albrechts von Waldstein, Herzog von Friedland," *Jahrbücher des böhmischen Museums für Natur- und Ländeskunde, Geschichte, Kunst, und Literatur* 1, no. 2 (Prague, 1831): 78–89; Anton Krombholz, *Die Stiftung des Böhmisch-Leipper Gymnasiums durch Albrecht von Waldstein, Herzog von Friedland* (Leitmeritz: n.p., 1834); and F. C. von Watterich, *Kreigsgeschichtsphilosophische Ehrengebuhr dem helden-Charakter und Feldherrnstabe Albrecht Waldstein's* (Prague: C. W. Medau, 1843).

78. For further discussion of the problematic place of Wallenstein in modern Czech nationalist literature, see Eugen Rippl, "Wallenstein in der tschechischen Literatur," *Germanoslavica* 2, no. 4 (1932–33): 521–44; Josef Pekar, *Wallenstein, 1630–1634: Tragödie einer Verschwörung* (Berlin: A. Metzner, 1937); Srbik, *Wallensteins Ende*, 13–38; and Josef Polisensky, "Zur Problematik des Dreißigjährigen Krieges und der Wallensteinfrage," in Karl Obermann and Josef Polisensky, eds., *Aus 500 Jahren deutsch-tschechoslowakischer Geschichte* (Berlin: Rütten & Loening, 1958), 99–136.

79. Karl Gustav Helbig, "Über das historische in Schillers Wallenstein," *Morgenblatt für gebildete Leser* 30 (July 25 1852): 607–701; 31 (August 1, 1852): 726–29.

80. August Friedrich Gfrörer, *Gustav Adolph, König von Schweden und seine Zeit*, 3d ed. (Stuttgart: A. Krabbe, 1852), 529, 678, 843–44, 892. A Bavarian historian noted, "The Kaiser was not convinced of Wallenstein's guilt and was only persuaded by the Guelph party." See Andreas Buchner, *Geschichte von Bayern während des dreißigjährigen Krieges* (Munich: Lindauer'sche, 1851), 284. The Catholic military historian Carl du Jarrys La-Roche was convinced that Wallenstein was pushed into negotiations with the German princes in order to preempt massive French intervention. See his *Der dreißigjährigen Krieg, vom militärischen Standpunkte beleuchtet* (Schaffhausen: Fr. Hurter'sche Buchhandlung, 1851), 2:337–40.

81. Karl Gustav Helbig, "Die Resultate der neuesten Forschungen über Wallensteins Verrath," *Allgemeine Monatsschrift für Wissenschaft und Literatur* (Braunschweig, September 1853): 715–25.

82. Friedrich von Hurter, *Zur Geschichte Wallensteins* (Schaffhausen: Fr. Hurter'sche Buchhandlung, 1855), vi–xi, 149–51, 342. In one passage, Hurter unfavorably contrasts Wallenstein's inaction in the winter of 1633 to the initiative "the hero Radetzky" displayed in saving the Habsburg monarchy in 1848. On Hurter's "romantic" legitimist-conservative theory of the Christian state and its derivation from the ideas of Haller, see Srbik, *Geist und Geschichte*, 2:55–57.

83. [Onno Klopp], *Studien über Katholizismus, Protestantismus, und Gewissensfreiheit in Deutschland* (Schaffhausen: Fr. Hurter'sche Buchhandlung, 1857), 280–81.

84. Onno Klopp, *Tilly im dreißigjährigen Kriege* (Stuttgart: J. G. Cotta'scher, 1861), 1:474–77; 2:1, 10, 25–27, 147–48. See also Klopp's claim that Wallenstein had made Gustavus Adolphus an offer of "open rebellion" in 1631, in the expanded second edition, *Der dreißigjährige Krieg bis zum Tode Gustav Adolfs 1632*, vol. 3, part 2, *Die Jahre 1631 bis Ende 1632* (Paderborn: F. Schöningh, 1896), 429–31. On the Catholic League as the legitimate defender of the princes' interests, see Joseph Würdinger, "Johann Tzerklas Graf von Tilly, bayerischer Heerführer," *Bayerischer Militär-Almanach* 4 (Munich, 1859): 75–275. On Klopp's rejection of Protestant historiography's self-proclaimed "realism" and his projection of a "fantasy picture" (*Wunschbild*) of the present and future onto the past as a warning against Prussian

despotic militarism, see Srbik's analysis in *Geist und Geschichte*, 2:71–73. See also Hans Schmidt, "Onno Klopp und die 'kleindeutschen Geschichtsbaumeister,'" in Albert Portmann-Tinguely, ed., *Kirche, Staat, und katholische Wissenschaft in der Neuzeit* (Paderborn: F. Schöningh, 1988), 381–95; and Lorenz Matzinger, *Onno Klopp (1822–1903): Leben und Werk* (Aurich: Ostfriesischelandschaft, 1993).

85. Friedrich von Hurter, *Wallensteins vier letzte Lebensjahre* (Vienna: Wilhelm Braumueller, 1862), 1, 96–115, 226–27, 241–45, 353–54, 484–85; and *Geschichte Kaiser Ferdinands II. und seiner Eltern bis zu dessen Krönung in Frankfurt: Personen-Haus- und Landesgeschichte* (Schaffhausen: Fr. Hurter'sche Buchhandlung, 1864), 4:118–21. Hurter also noted that the imperial commission that investigated the charges against Wallenstein had been "impartial and honest."

86. Cited in Helmut Diwald, foreword to *Geschichte Wallensteins*, 26.

87. See Rudolf Vierhaus, "Historiography between Science and Art," in Georg G. Iggers and James M. Powell, eds., *Leopold von Ranke and the Shaping of the Historical Discipline* (Syracuse NY: Syracuse University Press, 1990), 61–69.

88. Srbik, *Geist und Geschichte*, 1:275–79.

89. See Friedrich Meinecke, *Machiavellism: The Doctrine of Raison d'État and Its Place in Modern History*, trans. Douglas Scott (Munich, 1924; reprint, London: Routledge and Kegan Paul, 1957), 377–91; Iggers, *German Conception of History*, 63–89; Peter Gay, *Style in History: Gibbon, Ranke, Macaulay, Burckhardt* (New York: Basic Books, 1974), 59–60; Karl-Heinz Metz, *Grundformen historiographischen Denkens: Wissenschaft als Methodologie: Dargestellt an Ranke, Treitschke, und Lamprecht* (Munich: W. Fink, 1979), 131–33; and Ernst Schulin, "Universal History and National History, Mainly in the Lectures of Leopold von Ranke," in Iggers and Powell, 70–81. See also Friedrich Meinecke, *Cosmopolitanism and the National State*, trans. Robert B. Kimber (Princeton: Princeton University Press, 1970), 215–18.

90. Leopold von Ranke, *Geschichte Wallensteins* (Leipzig: Duncker & Humblot, 1869), 242–43, 273.

91. Ranke, *Geschichte Wallensteins*, 151, 267–73.

92. Ranke, *Geschichte Wallensteins*, 314–15, 383–84, 434, 450–51.

93. Helbig praised Ranke's "balanced portrait" of a Cromwell-like statesman who had attempted a "regeneration of the Reich" by pragmatic means. See his review in *Historische Zeitschrift* 22 (1869): 195–202. That same year the Jena historian Karl Wittich (1840–1916) wrote of Wallenstein's "patriotism and national passion" in pursuing "German-national interests" in his confrontation with Spain. See his "Wallenstein und die Spanier," *Preußische Jahrbücher* 22, no. 3 (1868): 329–44; 23, no. 1 (1869): 19–62. A few years after unification, another historian noted Wallenstein's historical significance for "our Germany," remarking that his "martyrdom," in allowing further French intervention, "was a heavy loss for Protestantism and the German nation." See Bernhard Kugler, *Wallenstein* (Berlin: Lüderitz, 1873), 4, 12, 37.

94. Otto von Schaching, *Maximilian I., der Große, Kurfürst von Bayern* (Freiburg im Breisgau: Herder'sche, 1876), 166–67. See also Felix Stieve, "Zur Geschichte Wallensteins," in *Abhandlungen, Vorträge, und Reden* (Leipzig: Duncker & Humblot, 1900), 228–88; and Franz Keym, *Geschichte des Dreißigjährigen Krieges* (Freiburg im Breisgau: Herder'sche, 1873), 1:236–39; 2:64, 130. One Protestant historian vehemently objected to the attempt to make Wallenstein, the leader of an army of Croats, Spaniards, and Italians, a "German hero," in that such an interpretation devalued the "national" meaning of the war. See H. Zwiedineck-Südenhorst, *Die neueste Wallenstein-Forschung* (n.p., 1886), 30–31. Cf. Georg M. Thomas, *Hans Ulrich Schaff-gotsch* (Hirschberg: C. W. J. Krahn, 1820); and Julius Krebs, *Hans Ulrich Freiherr von Schaffgotsch* (Breslau: W. G. Korn, 1890), for two "particularist" (and somewhat unlikely) views of Wallenstein as the champion of Silesian autonomy.

95. On the background of Bohemian-Czech disputes over the realization of their national aspirations during the period of the *Ausgleich*, see Edvard Benes, "The Unreconciled Czechs [1908]," in Harold J. Gordon and Nancy M. Gordon, eds., *The Austrian Empire: Abortive Federation?* (Lexington MA: D. C. Heath, 1974); and Urban, *Die tschechische Gesellschaft*, 205–307. For a discussion of the "nationalist turn" in German domestic politics during this period, see Andreas Beifang, "National-preußisch oder deutsch-national? Die Deutsche Fortschrittspartei in Preußen, 1861–1867," *Geschichte und Gesellschaft* 23, no. 3 (1997): 360–83.

96. Srbik, *Geist und Geschichte*, 2:111–12. See also Richard Georg Plaschka, *Von Palacky bis Pekar: Geschichtswissenschaft und Nationalbewußtsein bei dem Tschechen* (Graz and Cologne: H. Böhlaus, 1955), 35–42; and *Neue Deutsche Biographie* [NDB] (Berlin: Duncker & Humblot, 1963), 6:402.

97. On Hallwich, see NDB (1975), 7:566–67; and *Deutsche Arbeit: Monatschrift für das Geistige Leben der Deutschen in Böhmen* 7 (Prague, October 1907–September 1908), s.v. "Hofrat Dr. Hermann Hallwich," 628–30. Hallwich was a founding member of the influential nationalist Association for the History of the Germans in Bohemia.

98. Hermann Hallwich, "Zur Geschichte Wallensteins im Jahre 1633," *Archiv für die Sächsische Geschichte* n.s., 3, no. 1 (1876): 289–311, 339–49.

99. Vinzenz Prökl, *Waldstein, Herzogs von Friedland letzte Lebensjahre und Tod in Eger* (Falkenau an den Eger: Müller & Weiser, 1879), 46–47.

100. Otto Kaemmel, "Wallenstein's Ausgang," *Die Grenzboten* 37, no. 2 (1878): 6–18. Kaemmel noted that Eger had been the scene of "the greatest historical tragedy in German literature."

101. Martin Philippson, *Wallenstein*, Neue Volks-Bibliothek, series 2, nos. 11–12 (Stuttgart: Levy & Müller, 1876), 46–47.

102. Ottokar Lorenz, "Zur Wallenstein-Literatur," *Historische Zeitschrift* n.s., 3 (1878): 22–24. On Lorenz, see NDB (1986), 15:170–72; Srbik, *Geist und*

Geschichte, 2:105–7; and Fueter, *Geschichte der neueren Historiographie*, 548–49. See also Ottokar Lorenz, *Leopold von Ranke: Die Generationenlehre und der Geschichtsunterricht* (Berlin: W. Hertz, 1891).

103. See Hans Schleier, "Ranke in the Manuals on Historical Methods of Droysen, Lorenz, and Bernheim," in Iggers and Powell, 111–23. Schleier notes that Lorenz was heavily influenced by the thinking of one of his contemporaries at Kiel, Wilhelm Dilthey, who identified the "intuitive" component of historical cognition: "There never *is* a present: what we experience as present always contains memory of what has just been present . . . the recalling of the past replaces immediate experience." See Wilhelm Dilthey, "Draft for a Critique of Historical Reason," in Kurt Mueller-Vollmer, ed., *The Hermeneutics Reader: Texts of the German Tradition from the Enlightenment to the Present* (New York: Continuum, 1989), 148–52.

104. Lorenz, "Zur Wallenstein-Literatur," 24–26, 32–33, 44–45.

105. Hermann Hallwich, *Wallenstein's Ende: Ungedrückte Briefe und Akten* (Leipzig: Duncker & Humblot, 1879), 1:iii–xi, lvi–lvii. Hallwich notes that most of the material came from the State Archives in Vienna and acknowledges the diligence of the archivists, who helped to "bring justice to an undeniably significant man."

106. Hallwich, *Wallenstein's Ende*, 2:cxxviii; and Hermann Hallwich, *Über Wallenstein's Verrath* (Prague, Leipzig, and Vienna: F. Tempsky & F. A. Brockhaus, 1879), 5–10, 14. Hallwich cited as an appropriate epitaph for Wallenstein a contemporary Italian poem that contained the line: "I am not a traitor, but I am well betrayed." In yet another monograph from his prolific year of 1879, Hallwich maintained that it had been "insufficiently recognized" by historians that Maximilian, who had engineered Wallenstein's disgrace, was the real traitor to imperial and German interests, demonstrated by the conclusion of the Franco-Bavarian treaty of neutrality in May 1631. See Hermann Hallwich, *Wallenstein und Arnim im Frühjahre 1632* (Prague: F. Tempsky, 1879), 3–10.

107. Edmund Schebek, *Die Lösung der Wallensteinfrage* (Berlin: T. Hoffmann, 1881), vi.

108. The primary documents in question were the *Alberti Fridlandi perduellionis chaos* (the so-called Bamberg text) and the notorious *An Expediat*, which was presented as an anonymous opinion at a secret meeting of the Imperial War Council in late 1633. They accused Wallenstein of atheism, royal ambitions, disaffection and treason, and collusion with the Bohemian rebels. For a discussion of the pamphlet campaign against Wallenstein during this period, see Mann, *Wallenstein*, 753–57. For a bibliography of the accusatory contemporary literature against Wallenstein, see Schmid, "Die Wallenstein Literatur," 70–74.

109. Schebek, *Die Lösung der Wallensteinfrage*, 8–9, 19–42, 155, 214, 241–42, 521–30. One anonymous reviewer, while acknowledging Schebek's "valuable and highly interesting" contribution to the debate, was skeptical that he had found, in an isolated piece of documentary evidence, proof that a 250-year-old tradition

stemmed from a solitary literary fabrication. See "Die Lösung der Wallensteinfrage," *Die Grenzboten* 40, no. 35 (August 25, 1881): 357–72.

110. Edmund Schebek, *Kinsky und Feuquières: Nachtrag zur "Lösung der Wallensteinfrage"* (Berlin: T. Hoffmann, 1882), v–vi.

111. Schebek, *Kinsky und Feuquières*, 34, 89–91, 169. Schebek did point out the political affinity of the visions of Richelieu and Wallenstein, represented in the *Staatsidee* and the *Reichsidee*, respectively. One commentator was warmly approving of the great diligence with which modern historical scholarship had been applied to the "burning issue" of Wallenstein's "guilt," even as he condemned Schebek's deductions as based on a dubious source. See Fritz Skowronnek, *Quellenkritische Beiträge zur Wallensteinfrage* (Königsberg: Kommissionsverlag von Th. Nürmberger's Buch-und Verlagshandlung, 1882), 5–19.

112. Hermann Hallwich, ed., foreword to *Heinrich Matthias Thurn als Zeuge im Prozess Wallenstein: Ein Denkblatt zur Dritten Säcularfeier Wallenstein's* (Leipzig: Duncker & Humblot, 1883), xvii–xviii. Hallwich lamented the destruction of a significant part of the Wallenstein papers, particularly the correspondence with his wife: "Everything, absolutely everything, disappeared, apparently without a trace!" This volume presents, in a beautifully bound vellum facsimile, the so-called (and possibly apocryphal) *Thurn'schen Apologie*, or *Defension Schrifft*, written in 1636, in which the leader of the Bohemian rebels exonerates Wallenstein. Given the later hostile exchanges between the two historians, Hallwich records that it was Gindely who first apprised him of the document's location in the state archive in Gotha.

113. Hallwich, foreword, v, xv–xvi.

114. Richard Wapler, *Wallensteins lezte Tage: Ein historisch-kritisches Gedenkenblatt zum 25. Februar 1884* (Leipzig: G. Höfler, 1884), v–viii. This book was largely a recapitulation of Schebek's arguments. Another historian also sharply criticized the "unhistorical considerations" that drove Catholic work on Wallenstein, especially in comparison to the judgment by Ranke of Wallenstein the "statesman," who was the first to attempt the fulfillment of that "great idea," a unified and reconciled Germany. See Hans Held, *Wallensteins Katastrophe nach den neuesten Publikationen: Beilage zum Programm der Realschule bei St. Johann zu Straßburg* (Strasbourg: G. Fischbach, 1884), 3–7.

115. See Anton Gindely, *Geschichte des Dreißigjährigen Krieges*, 3 vols. (Prague: F. Tempsky, 1869–80). This work remained incomplete at Gindely's death. See A. W. Ward, "Anton Gindely," *English Historical Review* 8, no. 31 (July 1893): 500–514.

116. See Moriz Ritter, *Deutsche Geschichte im Zeitalter der Gegenreformation und des Dreißigjährigen Krieges* (Stuttgart: J. G. Cotta, 1889–1908).

117. Anton Gindely, *History of the Thirty Years' War*, 2 vols., trans. Andrew Ten Brook (New York: G. P. Putnam & Sons, 1883), 1:x–xi. This is the authorized English translation of Gindely's *Geschichte des dreißigjährigen Krieges*, 3 vols.

(Leipzig: G. Freytag, 1882–84), which was a shorter work intended for a general audience that covered the entire war.

118. Gindely, *History*, 2:159–73, 186–87. Emil Hildebrand's work in the Swedish archives in Stockholm was cited in confirmation of Gindley's essential point that Wallenstein's treasonous contacts with the Swedes, through the intermediary of Thurn, dated back as early as 1632, after the battle of the Old Fortress outside Nuremberg. See Emil Hildebrand, ed., *Wallenstein und seine Verbindungen mit den Schweden* (Frankfurt: Rütten & Leoning, 1885), v–viii.

119. Arnold Gaedeke, *Wallenstein's Verhandlungen mit den Schweden und Sachsen, 1631–1634* (Frankfurt: Rütten & Leoning, 1885), 1–13, 24–27, 42–52, 100–109.

120. Anton Gindely, *Waldstein während seines ersten Generalats im Lichte der gleichzeitigen Quellen, 1625–1630* (Prague and Leipzig: T. Tempsky, 1886), 1: iii, 1–8.

121. Gindely, *Waldstein während seines ersten Generalats*, 2:22–27, 184, 384–85.

122. Hermann Hallwich, "Gindely's 'Waldstein,'" *Mittheilungen des Vereins für Geschichte der Deutschen in Böhmen* 25, no. 2 (1886–87): 98, 102, 107, 120–33. Hallwich was also disdainful of Gindely's credulous overreliance on diplomatic documents, asking whether a modern biographer of Friedrich II or Bismarck would be well served in relying exclusively on the reports of Austrian or French envoys.

123. Hallwich, "Gindely's 'Waldstein,'" 133–37.

124. Hermann Hallwich, *Wallenstein und Waldstein: Ein offener Brief an Dr. Gindely* (Leipzig: Duncker & Humblot, 1887), iv–vi.

125. Hallwich, *Wallenstein und Waldstein*, 7–11.

126. Hallwich, *Wallenstein und Waldstein*, 16–21, 68. On the confessional division and its influence on a Protestant definition of a rationalist and secular civil society which in this instance, as was commonly the case, was used to denigrate Catholic historiography as methodologically suspect, see the discussion in Jürgen Kocka, "The European Pattern and the German Case," in Jürgen Kocka and Allen Mitchell, eds., *Bourgeois Society in Nineteenth-Century Europe*, trans. Gus Fagan (Oxford: Berg, 1993), 3–39. On German liberalism's blunt wielding of Enlightenment rationalism to consign "Catholic" perspectives beyond the pale of educated discourse, see also David Blackbourn, *Marpingen: Apparitions of the Virgin Mary in Bismarckian Germany* (New York: Oxford University Press, 1993), 282–300. The uproar over the appointment of the Catholic medievalist Martin Spahn to the new chair of history at the University of Strasbourg in 1900 is a good example of this prevalent intellectual prejudice. See Gordon Craig, *Germany, 1866–1945* (New York: Oxford University Press, 1978), 200–201.

127. Anton Gindely, *Zur Beurtheilung des kaiserlichen Generals im 30-jährigen Kriege, Albrechts von Waldstein, oder Gegen die Waldsteinbewunderer: Zweite*

Antwort an Dr. Hallwich (Prague and Leipzig: F. Tempsky, 1887), 3, 7–12, 18, 28, 44–48.

128. Max Lenz, "Zur Kritik Sezyma Rascins," *Historische Zeitschrift* 59, no. 3 (1888): 477–78. The gist of the article was to confirm that Wallenstein had indeed secretly negotiated with the empire's enemies, a fact that Lenz obviously thought irrelevant. See also the similar views of the Anglophobe Georg Irmer (1853–1931), *Die Verhandlungen Schwedens und seiner Verbündeten mit Wallenstein und den Kaiser von 1631 bis 1634*, pt. 1, *1631 und 1632* (Leipzig: S. Hirzl, 1888), xvii–xix, xxxvi–xxxviii, xli–xliii; and the Ranke protégé Georg Winter (1856–1912), *Geschichte des Dreißigjährigen Krieges* (Berlin: G. Grote, 1893), 488–89. On Lenz, see *NDB* (1984), 14:231–33; Srbik, *Geist und Geschichte*, 2:6–8; McClelland, *German Historians and England*, 207–11, 246; McClelland, "Berlin Historians and German Politics," in Walter Laqueur and George L. Mosse, eds., *Historians and Politics* (Beverly Hills: Sage, 1974), 191–222; and John L. Herkless, "Ein Unerklärtes Element in der Historiographie von Max Lenz," *Historische Zeitschrift* 222, no. 1 (1976): 81–104. On Lenz and the "Ranke Renaissance" and the "Neo-Rankean" school, see Hans-Heinz Krill, *Die Ranke Renaissance: Max Lenz und Erich Marcks* (Berlin: Walter de Gruyter, 1962); Wolfgang J. Mommsen, "Ranke and the Neo-Rankean School in Imperial Germany," in Iggers and Powell, 124–40; and Jens Nordalm, *Historismus und Moderne Welt: Erich Marcks (1861–1938) in der deutschen Geschichtswissenschaft* (Berlin: Duncker & Humblot, 2003).

129. Gerhard Ritter, "Machiavelli und der Ursprung des modernen Nationalismus," in *Vom sittlichen Problem der Macht: Fünf Essays* (Bern: A. Francke, 1948), 42.

130. See also Gerhard Ritter, "Politische Ethik: Vom historischen Ursprung ihrer Problematik," in *Vom sittlichen Problem der Macht*, 11, 33–38; and H. Stuart Hughes, *Consciousness and Society: The Reorientation of European Social Thought, 1890–1930* (New York: Vintage Books, 1977), 229–48.

131. Max Weber's observations, in the course of his own study of "Machiavellianism," provide useful context here: "Normally, Protestantism, however, absolutely legitimated the state as a divine institution and hence violence as a means. Protestantism, especially, legitimated the authoritarian state." Max Weber, "Politics as a Vocation [1918]," in H. H. Gerth and C. Wright Mills, trans., *From Max Weber: Essays in Sociology* (New York: Oxford University Press, 1958), 124.

132. Meinecke, *Machiavellism*, 50–51, 130. Meinecke introduced his subject with this reflection: "Those that interest us most will be the thinkers and politicians, in whom Machiavellism and anti-Machiavellism touch closely upon one another. For, as they are themselves divided, they mirror the tragic duality which came into historical life through the medium of Machiavellism—that indivisible and fateful combination of poison and curative power, which it contained." Cf. the post-1945 judgment of Thomas Mann, in the words of the fictional Serenus Zeitblom: "For was this government, in word and deed, anything but the distorted, vulgarized,

besmirched symbol of a state of mind, a notion of world affairs which we must recognize as both genuine and characteristic?" in H. T. Lowe-Porter, trans., *Doctor Faustus* (New York: Vintage Books, 1948), 482. See also J. G. A. Pocock, *The Machiavellian Moment: Florentine Political Thought and the Atlantic Republican Tradition* (Princeton: Princeton University Press, 1975), 462–505. On the "rediscovery" and nationalist reinterpretation of Machiavelli by German political thinkers in the early nineteenth century, see Martin Thom, *Republics, Nations, and Tribes* (London: Verso, 1995), 160–68.

4. The Martyrdom of Magdeburg

1. Tilly, a great hero of Bavarian military history, is one of the commanders immortalized in the Feldherrnhalle in Munich.

2. See C. R. Friedrichs, "The War and German Society," in Geoffrey Parker, ed., *The Thirty Years' War* (London: Routledge & Kegan Paul, 1987), 211. See the accounts of the siege in C. V. Wedgwood, *The Thirty Years' War* (New Haven: Yale University Press, 1939), 286–89; and Günter Barudio, *Der Teutsche Krieg, 1618–1648* (Frankfurt: S. Fischer, 1985), 363–71.

3. Otto Schmidt, *Geschichte des dreißigjährigen Krieges* (Weimar: Rauschke & Schmidt, 1853), 136.

4. R. E. Clements, *Isaiah and the Deliverance of Jerusalem: A Study of the Interpretation of Prophecy in the Old Testament*, supplement series, vol. 13 (Sheffield: Journal for the Study of the Old Testament Press, 1980), 40, 72–80.

5. Friedrich Richter, *Magdeburg, die wieder empor-gerichtete Stadt Gottes auf Erben: Denkschrift zur zweiten Säcularfeier der Zerstörung Magdeburgs* (Zerbst: G. A. Kummer, 1831), 69–71.

6. *Letzte Belagerung und jämmerliche Erober- und Zerstörung der alten Stadt Magdeburg* (Magdeburg: n.p., 1719), 4–5. In 1812 Gottfried Becker repeated the story of the buildings streaming blood and added the detail of women giving birth to "monsters." See Gottfried Wilhelm Becker, "Die Eroberung von Magdeburg, 1631: Historisches Basrelief," *Der Verkundiger*, May 12, 1812, 376–77.

7. See Erich Auerbach, *Mimesis: The Representation of Reality in Western Literature*, trans. Willard R. Trask (Princeton: Princeton University Press, 1953), 16, 38, 445, 555; and Meir Sternberg, *The Poetics of Biblical Narrative: Ideological Literature and the Drama of Reading* (Bloomington: Indiana University Press, 1985), 36–48.

8. On the centrality of the "Jerusalem tradition" for the theopolitics of Old Testament narrative, see Ulrike Berger, Ursula Bohn, et al., *Jerusalem: Symbol und Wirklichkeit* (Berlin: Institüt für Kirch & Judentum, 1976), 5–7; Regina M. Schwartz, "Monotheism and the Violence of Identities," *Raritan* 14, no. 3 (Winter 1995): 131–34; Ben C. Ullenberger, *Zion: The City of the Great King: A Theological Symbol of the Jerusalem Cult*, supplement series, vol. 41 (Sheffield: Journal for the Study of the Old Testament Press, 1987), 48–55, 152; Yair Hoffmann, "Reflections on the

Relationship between Theopolitics, Prophecy, and Historiography," in Henning Graf Reventlow, Yair Hoffmann, and Benjamin Uffenheimer, eds., *Politics and Theopolitics in the Bible and Postbiblical Literature,* supplement series, vol. 171 (Sheffield: Journal for the Study of the Old Testament, 1994), 92–96; and in the same volume, Benjamin Uffenheimer, "Isaiah's and Micah's Approaches to Policy and History," 182; and Klaus Wengst, "Babylon the Great and the New Jerusalem: The Visionary View of Political Reality in the Revelation of John," 197–201. On one usage of Old Testament models in creating a "national" narrative, see Peter Brown, *The Rise of Western Christendom: Triumph and Diversity, AD 200–1000* (New York: Oxford University Press, 1996), 91–92, on Gildas's *On the Ruin of Britain* (ca. 520). Until the early seventeenth century, allegorical dramas depicting the destruction of Jerusalem were second in popularity only to Passion plays. See Stephen K. Wright, *The Vengeance of Our Lord: Medieval Dramatizations of the Destruction of Jerusalem* (Toronto: Pontifical Institute of Medieval Studies, 1989), 1–2, 6–24.

9. René Girard, *Violence and the Sacred,* trans. Patrick Gregory (Baltimore: Johns Hopkins University Press, 1977), 39–67. See also Jürgen Wertheimer, ed., *Ästhetik der Gewalt: Ihre Darstellung in Literatur und Kunst* (Frankfurt: Athenäum, 1986), 125, 179; Mary K. Dahl, *Political Violence in Drama: Classical Models, Contemporary Variations,* Theater and Dramatic Studies 36 (Ann Arbor: UMI Research Press, 1987), 57–67; and Francis Huxley, *The Way of the Sacred* (London: Aldus Books, 1974), 107.

10. William Blake, *Jerusalem: The Emanation of the Giant Albion* [1820], in Alicia Ostriker, ed., *The Complete Poems* (New York: Penguin Books, 1977), 685.

11. The founding myth of Rome was based in part on a genealogy arising from the Trojan heroes, and the Stuart kings in England had commonly been given a Trojan ancestry legitimated through "improved" translations of Virgil's *Aeneid.* See Lawrence Venuti, "*The Destruction of Troy:* Translation and Royalist Cultural Politics in the Interregnum," *Journal of Medieval and Renaissance Studies* 23, no. 2 (Spring 1993): 197–219. The Serbian nationalist founding myth of Kosovo also was based on this idea of "triumph in defeat," which foretold redemption in unity. See Rebecca West, *Black Lamb and Grey Falcon: A Journey through Yugoslavia* (New York: Viking Press, 1943), 835–44. For use of the Jerusalem metaphor, see "The Fall of the Serbian Empire," in *Kossovo: Heroic Songs of the Serbs,* trans. Helen Rotham (New York: Houghton Mifflin, 1920), 25–31. On Masada, see Nachman Ben-Yehuda, *The Masada Myth: Collective Memory and Mythmaking in Israel* (Madison: University of Wisconsin Press, 1995).

12. On the siege, see *Appian's Roman History,* trans. Horace White (New York: Macmillan, 1912), 1:271–95. The first modern critical edition of this work was published in Germany in 1785. See also Carlos Fuentes, *The Buried Mirror: Reflections on Spain and the New World* (Boston: Houghton Mifflin, 1992), 36–38.

13. Miguel de Cervantes, "The Siege of Numantia," trans. Roy Campbell, in Eric Bentley, ed., *The Classic Theater*, vol. 3, *Six Spanish Plays* (New York: Doubleday, 1959), 97–160. On the play's sacrificial and "nationalist" imagery, see Edward H. Friedman, *The Unifying Concept: Approaches to the Structure of Cervantes' Comedias* (York SC: Spanish Literature Publications, 1981), 47–52.

14. On the reception and influence of the play, and Cervantes in general, in early nineteenth-century Germany, see J. A. Bertrand, *Cervantes et le Romantisme Allemand* (Paris: F. Alcan, 1914), 86–97, 143–150, 370–416; and Leinhard Bergel, "Cervantes in Germany," in Angel Flores and M. J. Bernadete, eds., *Cervantes across the Centuries* (New York: Gordian Press, 1969), 315–52. German archaeologists were the first to systematically uncover the ruins of Numancia in the late nineteenth century. Adolf Schulten's account, which also includes a map of Masada, of his work at the site is prefaced with a comparison to the twentieth century's impending battle with the "Bolshevik threat." See his *Geschichte von Numancia* (Munich: Piloty & Loehle, 1933), esp. 3–4, 156–61. Outside of Spain, the history and legend of the city seemed to attract the most scholarly attention in Germany.

15. For a discussion of the "sexualization" of the conquest of cities in the early modern period, see Ulinka Rublack, "Wench and Maiden: Women, War, and the Pictorial Function of the Feminine in German Cities in the Early Modern Period," *History Workshop Journal* 44 (Autumn 1997): 1–21.

16. M. Seth-Henrico Calvisio [Calvisius], *Das zerstöhrete und wieder aufgerichtete Magdeburg* (Magdeburg: Christian Leberecht Faber, 1727). The engraving appears between the foreword and page 1. This caption presumably refers to one of the first miracles of Jesus narrated in Mark, when his touch brought Jairus's dead daughter back to life: "Why do you make such a commotion and weep? The child is not dead but sleeping." See Mark 5:21–43 (New Revised Standard Version).

17. Susan Brownmiller, *Against Our Will* (New York: Simon & Schuster, 1975), see chapter 3: "War," esp. 34–38; Erika M. Hoerning, "The Myth of Female Loyalty," *Journal of Psychohistory* 16, no. 1 (Summer 1988): 19–45; and Elizabeth Heineman, "The Hour of the Woman: Memories of Germany's 'Crisis Years' and West German National Identity," *American Historical Review* 101, no. 2 (April 1996): 354–95. Conversely, the use of the "rape narrative" can serve an ideological purpose in setting up the heroic vengeance of the chivalric male. See Susan Jeffords, "Culture and National Identity in U.S. Foreign Policy," *Diplomatic History* 18, no. 1 (Winter 1994): 92–96; and Evelyn B. Vitz, "Rereading Rape in Medieval Literature," *Partisan Review* 63, no. 2 (1996): 280–91.

18. Wolfgang Lederer, *The Fear of Women* (New York: Grune & Stratton, 1968), 112–13; George L. Mosse, *Nationalism and Sexuality: Middle-Class Morality and Sexual Norms in Modern Europe* (Madison: University of Wisconsin Press, 1988), 93–113; Patricia K. Joplin, "The Voice of the Shuttle Is Ours," in Lynn A. Higgins and Brenda R. Silver, eds., *Rape and Representation* (New York: Columbia University

Press, 1991), 41–49; Georg Doblhofer, *Vergewaltigung in der Antike* (Stuttgart and Leipzig: B. G. Teubner, 1994), 37–39; Jean B. Elshtain, *Women and War* (Chicago: Basic Books, 1995), 58, 93–102; and Ruth Seifert, "The Second Front: The Logic of Sexual Violence in Wars," *Women's Studies International Forum* 19, nos. 1–2 (1996): 35–43. On the symbolism of the rape of Lucretia, see Michael Platt, "*The Rape of Lucrece* and the Republic for Which It Stands," *Centennial Review* 19, no. 2 (Spring 1975): 59–79; Ian Donaldson, *The Rapes of Lucretia: A Myth and Its Transformations* (New York: Oxford University Press, 1982), 8–10, 103–18; Leonard Tennenhouse, *Power on Display: The Politics of Shakespeare's Genres* (New York: Methuen, 1986), 107–10; and Coppelia E. Kahn, "Lucrece: The Sexual Politics of Subjectivity," in *Rape and Representation*, 141–59.

19. Ruth Harris, "The 'Child of the Barbarian': Rape, Race, and Nationalism in France during the First World War," *Past and Present* 141 (November 1993): 170–206; Nancy L. Paxton, "Mobilizing Chivalry: Rape in British Novels about the Indian Uprising of 1857," *Victorian Studies* 36, no. 1 (Fall 1992): 5–30; and Katherine Binhammer, "The Sex Panic of the 1790s," *Journal of the History of Sexuality* 6, no. 3 (1996): 409–34. See also Marina Warner, *Alone of All Her Sex: The Myth and Cult of the Virgin Mary* (New York: Alfred A. Knopf, 1976), 70–74.

20. Immanuel Geiss, "Zum Historiker-Streit," in Rudolf Augstein et al., *"Historikerstreit": Die Dokumentation der Kontroverse um die Einzigartigkeit der nationalsozialistischen Judenvernichtung* (Munich: R. Piper, 1987), 380.

21. See Geoff Eley, "Nazism, Politics, and Public Memory: Thoughts on the West German *Historikerstreit*," *Past and Present*, no. 121 (November 1988): 172–80.

22. Amos Funkenstein, "History, Counterhistory, and Narrative," in Saul Friedländer, ed., *Probing the Limits of Representation* (Cambridge: Harvard University Press, 1992), 66–81.

23. Dominick LaCapra, "Representing the Holocaust: Reflections on the Historians' Debate," in Friedländer, ed., *Probing the Limits of Representation*, 108–27.

24. Charles S. Maier, *The Unmasterable Past: History, Holocaust, and German National Identity* (Cambridge: Harvard University Press, 1988), 13–16, 164–70; Richard J. Evans, *In Hitler's Shadow* (New York: Pantheon Books, 1989), 116–19; and Peter Baldwin, "The *Historikerstreit* in Context," in Peter Baldwin, ed., *Reworking the Past: Hitler, the Holocaust, and the Historians' Debate* (Boston: Beacon Press, 1990), 3–37. Ernst Nolte's article "Die Vergangenheit, die nicht vergehen will" (The past that will not pass) appeared in the *Frankfurter Allgemeine Zeitung* on June 6, 1986. An English-language translation appears in James Knowlton and Truett Cates, trans., *Forever in the Shadow of Hitler?* (Atlantic Highlands NJ: Humanities Press, 1993), 18–23.

25. Henry Rousso, *The Vichy Syndrome: History and Memory in France since 1944*, trans. Arthur Goldhammer (Cambridge: Harvard University Press, 1991), 219–

22; Hans Mommsen, "Reappraisal and Repression: The Third Reich in West German Historical Consciousness," in Baldwin, ed., *Reworking the Past*, 173–83.

26. See Friedrich Spanheim, *Le Soldat Suedois, ou Histoire véritable de ce qui s'est passé depuis l'avenue du roy de Suede en Allemagne jusques a sa mort* (Paris: Chez Olivier de Varennes, 1642). The book appeared in three editions in 1633 and 1634: Bogislav Philipp von Chemnitz, *Königlichen Schwedischen in Teutschland geführten Krieges*, 4 vols. (Stettin and Stockholm: Georg Rethen, 1648–55); Samuel Pufendorf, *Commentariorum de rebus Suecicis; libri xxvi ab expeditione Gustavi Adolfi regis in Germaniam ad abdicationem usque Christinae* (Ultrajecti: Apud Johannem Ribbium, 1686); and Walter Harte, *The History of the Life of Gustavus Adolphus, King of Sweden*, 2d ed. (London: J. Hinton and R. Baldwin, 1767). The first German edition of Harte appeared in two volumes in 1760–61.

27. Johann Georg August Galletti, *Geschichte des dreyßigjährigen Krieges und des westphälischen Friedens* (Halle: J. J. Gebauer, 1791), 1:181–88. On Galletti, see *ADB*, 8:332–33; and Franz X. von Wegele, *Geschichte der Deutschen Historiographie seit dem Auftreten des Humanismus* (Munich and Leipzig: R. Oldenbourg, 1885), 942. The wholesale slaughter of civilians was shocking even by contemporary standards. See Friedrichs, "The War and German Society," 211.

28. *King Henry V*, Cambridge Text Edition, ed. William Aldis Wright (New York: Garden City, 1940), 3.27–43.

29. Friedrich Schiller, *Geschichte des Dreißigjährigen Krieges* (Leipzig, 1791–93; reprint, Zurich: Manesse, 1985), 238–40. The history originally appeared in installments in the *Historischen Calender für Damen für die Jahre 1791–1793*. "Zur Gustav-Adolf Literatur," *HpB* 35 (1855): 129–30.

30. See Friedrich Ludwig Schmidt, *Der Sturm von Magdeburg: Ein väterländisches Schauspiel in fünf Aufzügen* (Magdeburg: n.p,. 1799), v–vii. On the "pamphlet war," see Werner Lahne, *Magdeburgs Zerstörung in der Zeitgenössischen Publizistik* (Magdeburg: Verlag des Magdeburger Geschichtsvereins, 1931).

31. Friedrich Lampert, "Des Thürmers Töchterlein von Rothenburg: Eine Erzählung aus dem Jahre 1631," *Deutsche Volks-u. Jugendschriften*, no. 9 (1873): 90–91. On the Meistertrank festival in the nineteenth century, see Theodor Kutschmann, *Rothenburg ob der Tauber und sein Historisches Festspiel* (Rothenburg ob der Tauber: F. W. Klein, 1881); and *Historisches Festspiel mit historischen Festzug: Pfingstmontag den 29. Mai und Kirchweihmontag den 12. Juni 1882* (Rothenburg ob der Tauber: n.p., 1882). See also A. Hörber, *Der Meistertrank oder Tilly in Rothenburg: Schauspiel in zwei Aufzügen* (Rothenburg ob der Tauber: F. W. Klein, 1899).

32. Theodor Bischoff, *Tilly: Ein Zeitbild* (Rothenburg ob der Tauber: Schneider'schen Buchdruckerei, 1881). For a graphic catalog of imperial atrocities in Lower Saxony, see G. Lichtenstein, *Die Schlacht bei Lutter am Barenberge* (Braunschweig: Oehme & Müller, 1850), esp. 37–53, 111–12. Lichtenstein records

the castration of clergymen, multiple rapes and mutilations, including the cutting off of women's breasts, and the roasting alive of children. He recalled that when Munden fell in 1626, the Weser "ran red for days." Cf. the strikingly similar descriptions of the Russian advance into eastern Germany in 1945 in Johannes Kaps, *The Martyrdom of Silesian Priests 1945/46: Scenes from the Passion of Silesia* (Munich: Kirchliche Hilfsstelle, 1950), esp. 108; and Kaps, ed., *The Martyrdom and Heroism of the Women of East Germany: An Excerpt from the Silesian Passion, 1945–1946*, trans. Gladys H. Hartinger (Munich: Christ Unterwegs, 1955), esp. 94–104, 142–44.

33. Lorenz von Westenrieder, *Geschichte des dreißigjährigen Kriegs* (Munich: J. Lindauer, 1805), 2:169.

34. Lorenz von Westenrieder, *Beyträge zur vaterländische Historie, Geographie, Statistik* (Munich: J. Lindauer, 1806), 8:234–39.

35. See also Karl Maria von Aretin, *Tilly und Wrede: Zur Feier des 8. Octobers 1844* (Munich: n.p., 1844), written for the dedication of the Feldherrnhalle.

36. Jürgen Wilke, "Vom Sturm und Drang bis zur Romantik," in Walter Hinderer, ed., *Geschichte der politischen Lyrik in Deutschland* (Stuttgart: Reclam, 1978), 168–70.

37. *ADB*, 29:240–41.

38. Wilke, "Vom Sturm und Drang bis zur Romantik," 150–51, 161–63; in the same volume, see Peter Pütz, "Aufklärung," 130–31. See also Gerhard Kaiser, *Pietismus und Patriotismus im literarischen Deutschland: Ein Beitrag zum Problem der Säkularisation*, 2d ed. (Frankfurt: Athenäum, 1973), 124–38.

39. See Isa. 23.13–17 (New Revised Standard Version): "They destined Tyre for wild animals. They erected their siege towers, they tore down her palaces, they made her a ruin." For an earlier reference to Magdeburg's "poor Trojans," see Johann Georg Schummel, *Die Eroberung von Magdeburg: Ein Schauspiel in fünf Aufzügen*, Theater der Deutschen, no. 15 (Königsberg and Leipzig: Johann H. Rudiger, 1776): 516.

40. Johann Karl August Rese, *Die Zerstörung Magdeburgs durch Tilly: Ein streng historisches Gemählde* (Magdeburg: W. Heinrichshofen, 1809), 1–3, 67–71, 90–110.

41. Rese, *Die Zerstörung Magdeburgs durch Tilly*, 119–21. See also the two-page description of the women's self-sacrifice in Dietrich Freiherr von Bülow, *Gustav Adolf in Deutschland* (Berlin: Himburg, 1808), 1:216–18.

42. Becker, "Die Eroberung von Magdeburg," *Der Verkündiger*, May 10, 1812, 374–76.

43. Cf. the commemorative accounts of the siege of Stralsund: Christoph Ziemssen, *Das Wallensteins-Fest: Gebete und Predigten zur Feier des vier und zwanzigsten Julis 1819 und 1820 in der St. Marien-Kirche zu Stralsund* (Stralsund: n.p., 1821); Ernst Heinrich Zober, *Geschichte der Belagerung Stralsunds durch Wallenstein,*

im Jahre 1628 (Stralsund: W. Trinius, 1828); and Friedrich Förster, *Albrechts von Wallenstein, des Herzogs von Friedland und Mecklenburg*, 2 vols. (Berlin: Georg Reimer, 1828–29).

44. On the idealization of cities in this period as strongholds of liberal values and constitutional and civil freedoms, see René Trautmann, *Die Stadt in der deutschen Erzählungskunst des 19. Jahrhunderts (1830–1880)* (Winterthur: P. G. Keller, 1957), 35–41; James Sheehan, "Liberalism and the City in Nineteenth-Century Germany," *Past and Present* 51 (May 1971): 116–37; Reinhart Koselleck, *Preußen zwischen Reform und Revolution* (Stuttgart: Klett-Cotta im Deutscher Taschenbuch, 1989), 560–85; and Andrew Lees, *Cities Perceived: Urban Society and American Thought, 1820–1940* (Manchester: Manchester University Press, 1985), 86–88.

45. See F. Treumund [Eduard Sparfeld], *Gustav Adolf König von Schweden, der heldenmüthige Kämpfer für Deutschlands Religionsfreiheit: Ein Volksbuch für alle Stände* (Leipzig: Freise, 1845), 177–87; and Heinrich August Hecht, *Der dreißigjährige Krieg und der westphälische Friede* (Altenburg: Julius Helbig, 1848), 209.

46. Wilhelm Bötticher, *Gustav Adolf, König von Schweden: Ein Buch für Fürst und Volk* (Kaiserswerth am Rhein: B. Fliebner, 1845), 208; Severin Ewald, *Der dreißigjährigen Krieg nebst dem westphälischen Frieden: Nach Schiller, Galletti, und anderen Geschichtschreibern dargestellt für die Jugend und zum Selbstunterrichte* (Berlin: C. F. Amelang, 1830), 210; G. F. Gerloff, *Vortrag auf dem Rathause der Stadt Magdeburg am 10. Mai 1831 dem zweihundertjährigen Gedächtnißtage ihrer Zerstörung durch Tilly* (Magdeburg: Creutz, 1831), 3–5, 12–17, 28–31; Heinrich Rathmann, *Der zehnte Mai 1631: Ein Fragment aus der Geschichte Magdeburgs* (Magdeburg: Creutz, 1831), 295.

47. Dante Alighieri, *The Divine Comedy*, vol. 1, *Inferno*, trans. Mark Musa (New York: Penguin Books, 1984), 89.

48. Ulrich Raulff, "Herz der Finsternis: Daniel Jonah Goldhagens Ästhetik des Grauens," *Frankfurter Allgemeine Zeitung*, August 19, 1996.

49. Lam. 1.10 (New Revised Standard Version).

50. On the seventeenth-century "pamphlet war" over responsibility, see Lahne, *Magdeburgs Zerstörung*.

51. Johannes Rammelt, *Die Frage nach dem Urheber der Zerstörung Magdeburgs* (Halle: E. Karras, 1897), 1.

52. For an overview of these documents and their provenance, see Gustav Droysen, "Studien über die Belagerung und Zerstörung Magdeburgs 1631," *Forschungen zur Deutschen Geschichte* 3 (January 1863): 435–69.

53. Karl Menzel, *Geschichte des dreißigjährigen Krieges in Deutschland* (Breslau: Grass, Barth, 1839), 2:292–312.

54. Menzel, *Geschichte des dreißigjährigen Krieges in Deutschland*, 295–96; [Albert Heising], "Brand Magdeburgs im Jahre 1631," *HpB* 3 (1839): 43–51.

55. See Johann Michael von Söltl, *Der Religionskrieg in Deutschland* (Hamburg: J. A. Meissner, 1842), 2:105–13; and Johann Sporschil, *Der Dreißigjährige Krieg* (Braunschweig: G. Westermann, 1843), 385–90. Sporschil asserted that Falkenberg was a "born German."

56. See George Landau, "Dietrich von Falkenberg, Schwedischer Commandant von Magdeburg," *Allgemeines Archiv für die Geschichtskunde des Preußischen Staates* 15 (1834): 177–80.

57. Johann Grafen Mailath, *Geschichte des österreichischen Kaiserstaates* (Hamburg: F. Perthes, 1842), 3:vi, 227–42. On Mailath, see *ADB*, 20:101–5.

58. Albert Heising, *Magdeburg nicht durch Tilly zerstört: Gustav Adolph in Deutschland: Zwei historische Abhandlungen* (Berlin: Eyßenhardt, 1846), 11–14.

59. Heising, *Magdeburg nicht durch Tilly zerstört*, 58–60.

60. Heising, *Magdeburg nicht durch Tilly zerstört*, 65–66, 80–81.

61. Heising, *Magdeburg nicht durch Tilly zerstört*, 102–8.

62. Johann Valerius Kutscheit, *Herr Albert Heising für Tilly und gegen Gustav Adolph, oder wie die ehrlichen Deutschen mit Ruthen gestrichen werden wegen bisher geübter lügnerischer Geschichtschreibung* (Magdeburg: Creutz, 1847), 6, 33–38; Friedrich Wilhelm Hoffmann, Geschichte der Stadt Magdeburg (Magdeburg: A. Rathke, 1850), 3:116–25, 158–64; and Albert Heising, *Magdeburg nicht durch Tilly zerstört: Die Politik Gustav Adolph's in Deutschland*, rev. 2d ed. (Berlin: Schneider, 1854), 143–49. This second edition also provided more detailed identification and citation of sources, which mainly came from Calvisius.

63. "Zur Gustav-Adolf Literatur," *HpB* 35 (1855): 129–33.

64. [Onno Klopp], *Studien über Katholizismus, Protestantismus, und Gewissensfreiheit in Deutschland* (Schaffhausen: Fr. Hurter'sche Buchhandlung, 1857), 289–99.

65. Heinrich W. Bensen, *Der Verhängniß Magdeburgs: Eine Geschichte aus dem großen Zweispalt der teutschen Nation im 16ten und 17ten Jahrhundert* (Schaffhausen: Fr. Hurter'sche Buchhandlung, 1858), 505–28. A reviewer called Bensen's book "dilettantism at its worst" based on Karl Menzel's "nonsense" that distilled all his "poisonous hatred" of the Reformation. See the review in *Historische Zeitschrift* 2 (1859): 521–29. See also Heinrich W. Bensen, *Teutschland und die Geschichte: Eine Denkschrift* (Stuttgart: Franckh, 1844), 7–8, 11–13, 40. On Bensen, see *ADB*, 2:341–43.

66. Onno Klopp, "Magdeburg, Tilly, und Gustav Adolf," *HpB* 46 (1860): 849–53, 860, 866. Cf. Friedrich von Hurter, *Geschichte Kaiser Ferdinands II* (Schaffhausen: Fr. Hurter'sche Buchhandlung, 1861), 3:363. Hurter claims that the favored toast of the city's council became "Now we are good Swedes!"

67. Klopp, "Magdeburg, Tilly, und Gustav Adolf," *HpB* 47 (1861): 84–91, 99–100, 106–11, 116–17, 247–53. Bandhauer was the main source for the accu-

sation that Falkenberg had determined that the city be destroyed rather than be taken intact. See an early reference in [P. Carlick], "Der Brand Magdeburgs im Jahre 1631," *HpB* 14 (1844): 296–308. Klopp was first acquainted with the so-called "Tepler manuscript" of Bandhauer's diary from this article and an abstract published in 1855. See Philipp Klimesch, ed., "Zacharias Bandhauer's deutsches Tagebuch der Zerstörung Magdeburgs 1631," *Archives für die Kunde österreichischer Geschichtsquellen* 14 (Vienna, 1855): 239–319.

68. Klopp, "Magdeburg, Tilly, und Gustav Adolf," *HpB* 47 (1861): 263.

69. Onno Klopp, *Tilly im dreißigjährigen Kriege* (Stuttgart: J. G. Cotta'scher Verlag, 1861), 2:280–81. See also Klopp, *Der dreißigjährige Krieg bis zum Tode Gustav Adolfs 1632*, 4 vols. (Paderborn: F. Schöningh, 1891–96). The book on Tilly did as much for Klopp's notoriety in scholarly Protestant circles as did his earlier denunciation of the Hohenzollerns. See Jacob Venedey, "Tilly und Gustav Adolf nach Onno Klopp," *Historische Zeitschrift* 7 (1862): 381–444. On Venedey, see *ADB*, 39:600–604; and Julius Otto Opel, *Onno Klopp and die Geschichte des dreißigjährigen Krieges* (Halle: Verlag der Buchhandlung des Waisenhauses, 1862), 83.

70. See Georg G. Iggers, *The German Conception of History*, rev. ed. (Middletown CT: Wesleyan University Press, 1983), 90–123.

71. Droysen, "Studien über die Belagerung und Zerstörung Magdeburgs 1631," 435, 438.

72. See David Blackbourn, "Progress and Piety: Liberalism, Catholicism, and the State in Imperial Germany," *History Workshop Journal* 26 (Autumn 1988): 63–65, 72–73. The ideological and intellectual triumphalism behind the Kulturkampf, a result of the prevalent interpretation of the Reformation as a "German revolution," relied in part on evoking a nostalgia that played on "liberation themes." See Winfried Becker, "Der Kulturkampf als Europäisches und als Deutsches Phänomen," *Historisches Jahrbuch* 101 (1981): 432–33. See also Johannes Rammelt, *Wer hat Magdeburg zerstört? (1631)* (Wittenberg: Wattrodt, 1910), 7. In 1901, Friedrich Meinecke notoriously remarked, "Catholic professors of history are and remain a monstrosity." Cited in Blackbourn, "Progress and Piety," 74.

73. See Iggers, *The German Conception of History*, 128–31.

74. Gustav Droysen, "Studien über die Belagerung und Zerstörung Magdeburgs," 442, 450–57, 579, 582. The Halle historian Julius Otto Opel (1829–95) presented manuscript evidence that Calvisius, from patriotic motives, had probably altered some of the accounts to conceal pro-imperial authorship. See his "Einige Notizen Eroberung Magdeburgs durch Tilly," *Neue Mittheilungen aus dem Gebiet historisch-antiquarischer Forschungen* 11 (Halle and Nordhausen, 1867): 175–81. See also Opel, *Eine Flugschrift über die Zerstörung Magdeburgs* (Halle: n.p., 1874), 1–3.

75. Rudolf Usinger, "Die Zerstörung Magdeburgs," *Historische Zeitschrift* 13 (1865): 378–405. Usinger, a close acquaintance of Johannes Miquel, also displayed the usual marked distaste for the treachery of those historians who had crossed the

confessional line, notably Bensen and the converts Hurter and Klopp. On Usinger, see *ADB*, 39:378–81.

76. See Karl Wittich, "Wallenstein und die Spanier," *Preußische Jahrbücher* 22, no. 3 (1868): 329–44; 23, no. 1 (1869): 19–62.

77. Karl Wittich, "Kritische Erläuterungen über die Zerstörung Magdeburgs," *Zeitschrift für Preußische Geschichte und Landeskunde* 6 (1869): 317–18. On the perils of unconventionality for successful advancement up the academic ladder in nineteenth-century Germany, see Johannes Conrad, *The German Universities for the Last Fifty Years*, trans. John Hutchison (Glasgow: David Bryce, 1885), 195; and Konrad H. Jarausch, *Students, Society, and Politics in Imperial Germany: The Rise of Academic Illiberalism* (Princeton: Princeton University Press, 1982), 167–70.

78. Wittich, "Kritische Erläuterungen, 319–25, 330–34, 352–53.

79. Karl Wittich, *Die Zerstörung Magdeburgs im Jahre 1631* (Berlin: J. Sittenfeld, 1870), 1.

80. Wittich, *Die Zerstörung Magdeburgs im Jahre 1631*, 10, 15.

81. See Otto von Guericke, *Geschichte der Belagerung, Eroberung, und Zerstörung Magdeburgs*, ed. Friedrich W. Hoffmann (Magdeburg: Emil Baensch, 1860).

82. Wittich, *Die Zerstörung Magdeburgs*, 26–28.

83. On Droysen, see Hans Schulz, "Gustaf Droysen," in *Mitteldeutsche Lebensbilder*, vol. 3, *Lebensbilder des 18. und 19. Jahrhunderts* (Magdeburg, 1928), 480–96.

84. Karl Wittich, *Magdeburg, Gustav Adolf, und Tilly*, 2 vols. (Berlin: Carl Duncker, 1874), 1:36–45. The "unpublished sources" that Wittich offered as proof of this thesis were the reports of the Dutch Hansa agent Foppe van Aitzema (who, Wittich claimed, interviewed several refugees in the aftermath of the disaster), the various imperial and Catholic League military reports, and the *Originalbericht Guericke's*, or the "Berlin specimen." See the section "New Sources," 46–66, and *Magdeburg, Gustav Adolf, und Tilly*, 2:3 ff.

85. Wittich, *Magdeburg, Gustav Adolf, und Tilly*, 1:62–63. "Saguntum" was a Spanish ally of Rome that was besieged and conquered by Hannibal in 219–18 BC during the Second Punic War. Livy commemorated the Saguntine "reverence for principle" and loyalty, "even if such loyalty should involve their own destruction." See Livy, *The War with Hannibal: Books XXI–XXX of the History of Rome from Its Foundation*, ed. Betty Radice, trans. Aubrey de Selincourt (Baltimore: Penguin Books, 1965), 26–38.

86. Wittich, *Magdeburg, Gustav Adolf, und Tilly*, 1:74–84, 100–101, 113, 143, 148–49, 777.

87. See Onno Klopp, *Die Katastrophe von Magdeburg 1631: Auszug aus dem Tagebuch von Zacharias Bandhauer mit einer kritisch-historischen Uebersicht* (Freiburg im Breisgau: Herder'sche, 1874), 19–26, 52–56; Klopp, *Tilly, Gustav Adolf, und die Zerstörung von Magdeburg, Katholische Flugschriften zur Wehr*

und Lehr, no. 94 (Berlin: Germania, 1895): 9–15; and Hermann Haag, "Tilly," *Jahrbuch der Militärischen Gesellschaft München* (1875/76): 145–47, 166.

88. Wittich, *Magdeburg, Gustav Adolf, und Tilly*, 1:642–43, 650. On the initially favorable Protestant response to Wittich's interpretation of a "great *German* event*,*" see F. Winter, "Magdeburg, Gustav Adolf, und Tilly," *Geschichtsblätter für Stadt und Land Magdeburg (GbM)* 10 (1875): 199; Julius Opel in the *Literarisches Zentralblatt* (1875), cited in Hans Teitge, *Frage nach dem Urheber der Zerstörung Magdeburgs* (Halle: M. Niemeyer, 1904), 19; Friedrich Hülße, "Historische Tradition der Katastrophe der Stadt Magdeburg im Jahre 1631," *Jahrbuch des Pädagogiums zum Kloster Unser Lieben Frauen* 41 (1877): 1–36; and "Gustav Adolf und der Brand Magdeburg," *Die Grenzboten* 39, no. 12 (March 18, 1880): 497–506.

89. Franz Keym, *Geschichte des Dreißigjährigen Krieges* (Freiburg im Breisgau: Herder'sche, 1873), 1:296–317.

90. Max Dittmar, *Beiträge zur Geschichte der Stadt Magdeburg in den Ersten Jahren nach Ihrer Zerstörung 1631* (Halle: M. Niemeyer, 1884), 5, 17.

91. Dittmar, *Beiträge zur Geschichte der Stadt Magdeburg*, 21–22, 28–29.

92. Karl Wittich, "Zur Katastrophe des 10./20. Mai 1631," *GbM* 22 (1887): 411–12, 417; 23 (1888): 22–25, 124–26.

93. Karl Wittich, "Magdeburg als katholisches Marienburg: Eine Episode aus dem Dreißigjährigen Krieg," *Historische Zeitschrift* 65, no. 1 (1890): 431–40.

94. Karl Wittich, *Dietrich von Falkenberg, Oberst und Feldmarschall Gustav Adolfs* (Magdeburg: Verlag der Schäfers'schen Buchhandlung, 1892), 76–79. This book combined a series of articles that had appeared in the *GbM* in 1890–91. Wittich expressed a rather condescending sympathy for Dittmar's anxiety to defend the traditions of his hometown. See vi–vii.

95. Wittich, *Dietrich von Falkenberg, Oberst und Feldmarschall Gustav Adolfs*, 165–66, 173–215. The Leipzig historian Wilhelm Arndt praised the book as "a hero's life of a truly classical magnitude and power." See his review, "Die Zerstörung Magdeburgs 1631," *Blätter für literarische Unterhaltung* 50 (December 15, 1892): 785.

96. Stieve thought Wittich's comparisons with Moscow somewhat overdrawn and naive. See Stieve's lecture "Die Zerstörung Magdeburgs [1891]," in *Abhandlungen, Vorträge, und Reden* (Leipzig: Duncker & Humblot, 1900), 184, 192.

97. Robert Volkholz, *Die Zerstörung Magdeburgs (1631) im Lichte der neuesten Forschung* (Magdeburg: Faber, 1892), 22–23, 39–40, 48–50, 89–91.

98. Karl Wittich, *Pappenheim und Falkenberg: Ein Beitrag zu Kennzeichnung der lokalpatriotischen Geschichtsschreibung Magdeburgs* (Berlin: W. Baensch, 1894), v.

99. Wittich, *Pappenheim und Falkenberg*, 3, 12, 38–39.

100. Wittich, *Pappenheim und Falkenberg*, 4, 64.

101. Max Dittmar, "Die Zerstörung Magdeburgs im Jahre 1631: Offene Antwort an Herrn Professor Dr. Wittich," *GbM* 29 (1894): 303–6.

102. Dittmar, "Die Zerstörung Magdeburgs im Jahre 1631," 311–16, 324, 334.

103. Dittmar, "Die Zerstörung Magdeburgs im Jahre 1631," 348–54, 373, 398. See Wittich's reply, citing Otto Devrient's research on folk songs of the Thirty Years' War, in which he defends the significance that contemporaries attached to the example of Saguntum in "Noch einmal die Zerstörung Magdeburgs," *GbM* 30 (1895): 76–117.

104. Robert Volkholz, *Jürgen Ackermann, Kapitän beim Regiment Alt-Pappenheim, 1631* (Halberstadt: J. Schimmelburg, 1895), 5–8, 12–21, 57–58.

105. Karl Wittich, *Dietrich von Falkenbergs Ende: Entgegnung auf die Schrift "Jürgen Ackermann, Kapitän beim Regiment Alt-Pappenheim, 1631"* (Leipzig: n.p., 1895), 4.

106. Wittich, *Dietrich von Falkenbergs Ende*, 21.

107. See Teitge, *Frage nach dem Urheber*, 18–19; Rammelt, *Die Frage nach dem Urheber der Zerstörung Magdeburgs*, 3–9; and Rammelt, *Wer hat Magdeburg Zerstört?* 6–8. The consensus of twentieth-century scholarship on the Magdeburg question is that, while Pappenheim's troops started the fire at the Hohe Pforte, and probably others after breaking into the city, the other, simultaneous outbreaks remain unexplained. See Wedgwood, *Thirty Years' War*, 289; Barudio, *Der Teutsche Krieg*, 371–72; and Geoffrey Parker, ed., *The Thirty Years' War*, 125.

108. Eduard Marcour, "Wer hat Magdeburg zerstört?" *Frankfurter zeitgemäße Broschüren* n.s., 10, no. 1 (Frankfurt, 1884–85): 258–59, 280–82. At the time of writing Marcour was editor of the *Koblenzer Volkszeitung* and director of the Görresdrückerei. Teitge, writing in 1904, accused Marcour of writing a "partisan pamphlet" (*Tendenzschrift*) based on Wittich that was "saturated with ultramontane zealotry." See Teitge, *Zerstörung Magdeburgs*, 12.

5. German Gothic

1. For a discussion of the debate over how contemporaries made the sufferings of the war intelligible with a "plausible vocabulary of suffering," see John Theibault, "The Rhetoric of Death and Destruction in the Thirty Years' War," *Journal of Social History* 27, no. 2 (Winter 1983): 271–90. Cf. Thomas Hobbes's commentary on the English Civil War of the same period, "the war of everyman against everyman," a time of "no knowledge of the face of the earth; no account of time; no arts; no letters; no society; and, which is worst of all, continual fear and danger of violent death," in *Leviathan* [1651], ed. Herbert W. Schneider (New York: Liberal Arts Press, 1958), 107–8. Hobbes's use of extreme metaphorical rhetoric was intended to portray chaos, as in the narratives under discussion, to justify his scheme of political reconstruction. See David Johnston, *The Rhetoric of Leviathan: Thomas Hobbes and the Politics of Cultural Transformation* (Princeton: Princeton University Press, 1986), 66–91, 185–89. Apocalyptic language in political and cultural discourse

served similar ideological objectives in post-1918 Germany. See Jürgen Brokoff, *Die Apokalypse in der Weimarer Republik* (Munich: W. Fink, 2001). On the horrified English reaction to the German "war of reprisal," see Barbara Donagan, "Atrocity, War Crime, and Treason in the English Civil War," *American Historical Review* 99, no. 4 (October 1994): 1137–66.

2. Robert Ergang, *The Myth of the All-Destructive Fury of the Thirty Years' War* (Pocono Pines PA: Craftsmen, 1956), 6–16. See also S. H. Steinberg, *The "Thirty Years' War" and the Conflict for European Hegemony, 1600–1660* (London: E. Arnold, 1966).

3. "If simply compiling the terrifying reports would give far too negative an impression, by the same token, statistics for the Empire as a whole cannot come close to revealing the actual catastrophic losses that took place in a particular city or region." See Rudolf Vierhaus, *Germany in the Age of Absolutism*, trans. Jonathan B. Knudsen (Cambridge: Cambridge University Press, 1988), 1–30. See also Theodore K. Rabb, *The Struggle for Stability in Early Modern Europe* (New York: Oxford University Press, 1975), 76–99; and C. R. Friedrichs, "The War and German Society," in Geoffrey Parker, ed., *The Thirty Years' War* (London: Routledge and Kegan Paul, 1987), 208–15. For a summary of the modern German debate on the impact of the war between the "earlier decline" school of scholarship and the "disastrous war" theory, see Theodore K. Rabb, "The Effects of the Thirty Years' War on the German Economy," *Journal of Modern History* 34 (March 1962): 40–51.

4. Hans Jacob Christoffel von Grimmelshausen, *Der Abentheurliche Simplicissimus Teutsch*, in Dieter Breuer, ed., *Werke* (Frankfurt: Deutscher Klassiker Verlag, 1989), 1:28–29, 55. See the reproductions of Jacques Callot's *Large Miseries of War* [1633] accompanying the essay "The Revenge of the Peasants" in Peter Paret, *Imagined Battles* (Chapel Hill: University of North Carolina Press, 1997), 31–45.

5. See Barbara Salditt, *Das Werden des Grimmelshausensbildes im 19. und 20. Jahrhundert* (Chicago: University of Chicago Libraries, 1933), 3–21.

6. Peter Paret, *Art as History: Episodes in the Culture and Politics of Nineteenth-Century Germany* (Princeton: Princeton University Press, 1988), 18–52, 79–119. On Paret's evidence, it seems probable that Menzel supplied the allegorical chapter titles and illustrations for Johann Sporschil's *Der dreißigjährige Krieg* (Braunschweig: G. Westermann, 1843). On Baroque war art and its influence on Goya and the "artists of the barricade" in nineteenth-century France, see Paret, *Imagined Battles*, 65–82; and T. J. Clark, *The Absolute Bourgeois: Artists and Politics in France, 1848–1851* (Princeton: Princeton University Press, 1982), 9–30. Clark also cites the influence of Holbein's *Dance of Death*.

7. See Michael S. Shapiro, *Violent Cartographies: Mapping Cultures of War* (Minneapolis: University of Minnesota Press, 1997), 41–49. For a discussion of the twentieth-century experience, see Liisa H. Malkki, *Purity and Exile: Violence,*

Memory, and National Cosmology among Hutu Refugees in Tanzania (Chicago: University of Chicago Press, 1995), 53–66, 90–97.

8. Julius von Voß, *Krieg und Liebe, oder romantische Erzählungen, von dreißigjährigen Kriege bis auf unsre Zeiten* (Berlin: J. W. Schmidt, 1813), 1:12–14. On Voß, see Leif Ludwig Albertsen, *Die Eintagsliteratur in der Goethezeit: Proben aus Werken von Julius von Voß* (Bern: H. Lang, 1975).

9. Friedrich Karl Wild, *Erhard Daubitz: Aus der Belagerung von Nördlingen 1634* (Stuttgart: n.p., 1866), 97. On Wild, see chapter 3 and Klaus Müller-Salget, *Erzählungen für das Volk: Evangelische Pfarrer als Volksschriftsteller im Deutschland des 19. Jahrhunderts* (Berlin: E. Schmidt, 1984), 25–28, 160–61. Many of these works of "lamentation," both historical and literary, were written by clergymen and published regionally.

10. Otto Schmidt, *Geschichte des dreißigjährigen Krieges* (Weimar: Rauschke & Schmidt, 1853), 405; Franz Keym, *Geschichte des Dreißigjährigen Krieges* (Freiburg im Breisgau: Herder'sche, 1873), 2:184–86.

11. Friedrich Karl Wild, *Geschichte des westphälischen Friedens nebst einem kürzen Abriß des dreißigjährigen Krieges* (Nördlingen: C. H. Beck, 1848), 1. This was published to commemorate the bicentennial of the signing of the Peace of Westphalia.

12. On identifying the collective and social memory "function" in historiography, see Maurice Halbwachs, *On Collective Memory*, trans. and ed. Lewis A. Coser (Chicago: University of Chicago Press, 1992), 47–51, 92–98, 171–88; Peter Burke, "History as Social Memory," in Thomas Butler, ed., *Memory: History, Culture, and the Mind* (New York: Oxford University Press, 1989), 97–113; and James Fentriss and Chris Wickam, *Social Memory* (New York: Oxford University Press, 1992), 56–58, 72–73. See also Pierre Nora, "Mémoire collectivè," in Jacques Le Goff, ed., *La nouvelle histoire* (Paris: Retz, 1978); and Barry Schwartz, "The Social Context of Commemoration," *Social Forces* 61, no. 2 (December 1982): 374–97.

13. On the commemorative nexus between history and memory, see Patrick H. Hutton, *History as an Art of Memory* (Hanover VT: University Press of New England, 1993), 79–80; Jacques Le Goff, *History and Memory*, trans. Steven Rendall and Elizabeth Claman (New York: Columbia University Press, 1992); Paul Connerton, *How Societies Remember* (Cambridge: Cambridge University Press, 1989), 42–43; and David Lowenthal, *The Past Is a Foreign Country* (New York: Cambridge University Press, 1985), 235.

14. Edward S. Casey, *Remembering: A Phenomenological Study* (Bloomington: Indiana University Press, 1987), 182–210. On the ideological evocation of place in the creation of an artificial "historical" landscape such as the Teutoburger wald, see Simon Schama, *Landscape and Memory* (New York: Alfred A. Knopf, 1995), 75–134. The mnemonic power of landscape and place, particularly in remembering a ruinous war, was also an important element in the post–Civil War litera-

ture of the American South. Albion W. Tourgée wrote in 1888: "Because of the exceeding woefulness of the not too recent past, therefore, and the abiding horror of unavoidable conditions which are the sad inheritance of the present, we may confidently look for the children of "the South' to advance American literature to the very front rank of that immortal procession whose song is the eternal refrain of remembered agony." Quoted in Edmund Wilson, *Patriotic Gore: Studies in the Literature of the American Civil War* (New York: Oxford University Press, 1962), 604–16. In this American literature of lamentation, Jonathan Morse identifies the main trope of narratives of defeat: remembering the past without being able to change it. See his *Word by Word: The Language of Memory* (Ithaca: Cornell University Press, 1990), 38–43.

15. Ernest Renan, "Qu'est-ce qu'une nation?" trans. Ida Mae Snyder, in John Hutchinson and Anthony D. Smith, eds., *Nationalism* (New York: Oxford University Press, 1994), 18.

16. Cathy Carruth, "Unclaimed Experience: Trauma and the Possibility of History," *Yale French Studies*, no. 79 (1991): 181–92; and Eric L. Santner, "History beyond the Pleasure Principle: Some Thoughts on the Representation of Trauma," in Saul Friedländer, ed., *Probing the Limits of Representation: Nazism and the "Final Solution"* (Cambridge: Harvard University Press, 1992), 143–54. Dominick LaCapra, in his critique of Lawrence Langer's idea of "heroic memory," has expressed reservations about the compatibility between the "fetishistic" mode of the "ideologically saturated, redemptive narrative" and the historiographic "working through" of critical and comparative history. See his *Representing the Holocaust: History, Theory, Trauma* (Ithaca: Cornell University Press, 1994), 169–204. Cf. Deborah Jenson, *Trauma and Its Representations: The Social Life of Mimesis in Post-Revolutionary France* (Baltimore: Johns Hopkins University Press, 2001). This argument has been renewed in the recent debate on German suffering during the Allied bombing campaign in World War II generated by W. G. Sebald and Jörg Friedrich.

17. Iwona Irwin-Zarecka, *Frames of Remembrance: The Dynamics of Collective Memory* (New Brunswick NJ: Rutgers University Press, 1994), 5–9, 47–78.

18. The "consensual reality" of one group almost always provokes oppositional narratives from other "communities of memory." See Yael Zerubavel, "The Multivocality of a National Myth: Memory and Counter-Memories of Masada," in Robert Wistrich and David Ohana, eds., *The Shaping of Israeli Identity: Myth, Memory, and Trauma* (London: F. Cass, 1995), 110–28. See also Laurence J. Kirmayer, "Landscapes of Memory: Trauma, Narrative, and Disassociation," in Paul Antze and Michael Lambek, eds., *Tense Past: Cultural Essays in Trauma and Memory* (New York: Routledge, 1996), 173–98.

19. Michael Lambek, "The Past Imperfect: Remembering as Moral Practice," in *Tense Past*, 235–54. On the normative "conventionalization" of the past in the construction of "political memory," see the essays in James W. Pennebaker,

Dario Puez, and Bernard Rimé, eds., *Collective Memory of Political Events: Social Psychological Perspectives* (Mahwah NJ: Lawrence Erlbaum, 1997).

20. See Kali Tal, *Worlds of Hurt: Reading the Literatures of Trauma* (Cambridge: Cambridge University Press, 1996), 6–8. On the "scar literature," or "literature of the wounded," written by the survivors of the Cultural Revolution in Communist China, see Anne F. Thurston, "Victims of China's Cultural Revolution: The Invisible Wounds," in *Pacific Affairs* 57, no. 4 (Winter 1984–85): 599–620.

21. Jacob Neusner, "The Birth of History in Christianity and Judaism," in Neusner, ed., *The Christian and Judaic Invention of History* (Atlanta: Scholars Press, 1990), 3–18. The idea of a "prosaic" and "historiographic" tradition arising out of a reflective "Deuteronomistic history" (and preceding the nonlinear and prophetic "Isaianic" mode) is formulated by Gerhard Rad. See his *Old Testament Theology*, vol. 1, *The Theology of Israel's Historical Traditions*, trans. D. M. G. Stalker (New York: Harper, 1962), 108–17.

22. Yosef Hayim Yerushalmi, *Zakhor: Jewish History and Jewish Memory* (New York: Schocken Books, 1989), 5–21.

23. Jacob Neusner, *History and Torah: Essays on Jewish Learning* (London: Schocken Books, 1965), 17–29. On Midrashic exegesis as the basis of the Christian tendency to find scriptural revelation actualized in historical events, see Renée Bloch, "Midrash," in William S. Green, ed., *Approaches to Ancient Judaism: Theory and Practice* (Missoula MT: Scholars Press, 1978), 29–50.

24. Yerushalmi, *Zakhor*, 9–10; Daniel Boyarin, "'Language Inscribed by History on the Bodies of Living Beings': Midrash and Martyrdom," *Representations* 25 (Winter 1989): 139–51. Cf. Michael S. Roth on the antagonistic and "parasitic" relationship between modern historical consciousness and collective memory preserved within self-consciously "metahistorical" traditions, in *The Ironist's Cage: Memory, Trauma, and the Construction of History* (New York: Columbia University Press, 1995), 177–84.

25. William Pierson, *Preußische Geschichte*, 7th ed. (Berlin: Gebrüder Paetel, 1878), 1:132–33.

26. Karl Schmidt, *Geschichte des dreißigjährigen Krieges zur zweihundert Jubelfeier des westphälischen Friedens im Jahre 1648* (Jena: F. Fromann, 1848), 104–5. According to Schmidt, "Germany rebuilt so quickly, however, that a greater example of German industry can scarcely be found."

27. Wilhelm Scherer, *A History of German Literature*, 3d ed. [1885], trans. F. C. Conybeare (New York: Charles Scribner's Sons, 1899), 317–18. Josef Walter deplored the "barbarization" (*Bewilderung*) of the pure language of Luther and the creation of a "mongrel language" (*Mischsprache*) combining French and the coarse language of the camp. According to Walter, this "deathblow" delivered by the war affected the whole cultural life of Germany and led to "the despairing devotion to astrology and chiromancy, witchcraft, and all the various tales of ghosts and

demons." See Josef Walter, "Über den Einfluß des dreißigjährigen Krieges auf die deutsche Sprache und Literatur," *Programm des k.k. Kleinseitner Gymnasiums zu Prag*, pt. 1 (1871): 5–26; pt. 2 (1873): 39. For a more recent discussion of the effect of the war on cosmopolitan, humanist, and secular high culture in Germany, see R. J. W. Evans, "Culture and Anarchy in the Empire, 1540–1680," *Central European History* 18, no. 1 (March 1985): 14–30.

28. Alain Corbin, *The Village of Cannibals: Rage and Murder in France, 1870*, trans. Arthur Goldhammer (Cambridge: Harvard University Press, 1992), 88–97. See also Frank Lestringant, "Catholiques et cannibales: Le thème du cannibalisme dans le discours protestant au temps des guerres de religion," in Jean-Claude Margolin and Robert Souzet, eds., *Pratiques et Discours Alimentaires a la Renaissance* (Paris: G. P. Maisoneuve et Larose, 1982), 233–45. Writing in the shadow of the French Wars of Religion, Montaigne interpreted cannibalism among the native peoples of the New World as an extreme form of revenge. See "On the Cannibals," in Michel de Montaigne, *The Complete Essays*, trans. M. A. Screech (London: Penguin Books, 1991), 228–41. A member of the cathedral chapter in Augsburg discovered a contemporary report in 1839 from the famine winter of 1634–35, the details of which were reproduced in various forms in other histories. According to the document found in the archives of the Augsburg bishopric, four women of the village of Agawang cooked and ate the bodies of five men who had lain unburied in their houses. The curious pastor who interviewed them, asking how they had tasted, received the reply that they were "very good," the best parts being the brain, heart, and kidneys. See J. Baader, "Zwey merkwürdige Aktenstücke über die zur Zeit des Schwedenkriegs im Winter des jahrs 1634–35 zu Agawang geherrschte gräßliche Hungersnot," *Jahrs-Bericht des historischen Vereins für den Regierungs-Bezirk von Schwaben und Neuburg*, nos. 5–6 (Augsburg, 1839–40): 71–72.

29. Ulf Hedetoft, *War and Death as Touchstones of National Identity* (Aalborg: Department of Languages and Intellectual Studies, University of Aalborg, 1990), 66–78; and Michael Geyer, "The Place of the Second World War in German Memory and History," *New German Critique* 71 (Spring/Summer 1997): 5–40.

30. For a discussion of modern vocabularies of bereavement and narratives of disorder, see J. M. Winter, "The Great War and the Persistence of Tradition: Language of Grief, Bereavement, and Mourning," and Harro Müller, "War and Novel: Alfred Döblin's 'Wallenstein' and 'November 1918,'" in Bernd Hüppauf, ed., *War, Violence, and the Modern Condition* (Berlin: Walter de Gruyter, 1997), 33–45, 240–99. See also John W. Dower, "The Bombed: Hiroshimas and Nagasakis in Japanese Memory," in Michael J. Hogan, ed., *Hiroshima in History and Memory* (Cambridge: Cambridge University Press, 1996), 116–42.

31. Friedrich Schiller, *Geschichte des Dreißigjährigen Krieges* [1791–93] (Zurich: Manesse, 1985), 401–2.

32. F. R. Ankersmit, *History and Tropology: The Rise and Fall of Metaphor* (Berkeley: University of California Press, 1994), 75–94.

33. Ulrich Muhlack, "Schillers konzept der Universalgeschichte zwischen Aufklärung und Historismus," in Otto Dann, Norbert Oellers, and Ernst Osterkamp, eds., *Schiller als Historiker* (Stuttgart and Weimar: J. B. Metzlar, 1995), 5–28.

34. See Karl Pestalozzi, "Ferdinand II. in Schillers *Geschichte des Dreißigjährigen Kriegs*: Die Rechtfertigung eines Übel," in *Schiller als Historiker*, 179–90. For a discussion of the late Enlightenment notion of a "secular" theodicy that explained evil as an incidental but necessary product of historical and social processes, see Jean Starobinski, *Jean-Jacques Rousseau: Transparency and Obstruction*, trans. Arthur Goldhammer (Chicago: University of Chicago Press, 1988), 19–21.

35. See Ernst Schulin, "Schillers Interesse an Aufstandgeschichte," in *Schiller als Historiker*, 137–48. "It is upon the barbarous foundation of feudal anarchy that Germany erected her system of political and ecclesiastical liberty." See Friedrich Schiller, "Was heißt und zu welchem Ende studiert man Universalgeschichte?" in *Sämtliche Werke*, vol. 4, *Historische Schriften*, ed. Jost Perfahl (Munich: Winkler, 1968), 711.

36. *Correspondence of Schiller with Körner*, ed. and trans. Leonard Simpson (London: R. Bentley, 1849), 1:48.

37. Schiller, *Geschichte des Dreißigjährigen Krieges*, 321–22. Cf. Grimmelshausen's description: "[Each soldier] had invented his own unique way of torturing the peasant, just as each peasant had a special torment," in *Simplicissimus*, 29. For an almost verbatim appropriation of Schiller's description, see Heinrich August Hecht, *Der dreißigjährige Krieg und der westphälische Friede* (Altenburg: Julius Helbig, 1848), 272.

38. On Schiller's preservation of tradition within narrative, and his ambivalence toward source-oriented historiography, see Otto Dann, "Schiller, der Historiker und die Quellen," in *Schiller als Historiker*, 109–26.

39. Ankersmit, *History and Tropology*, 81, 90–94.

40. Thomas Carlyle, "State of German Literature [1827]," *Critical and Miscellaneous Essays* (London, 1899; reprint, New York: AMS Press, 1969), 1:85.

41. Christoph Martin Wieland, foreword to Schiller, *Dreißigjährigen Krieges*, 10–11.

42. Karl Hoffmeister, *Schiller's Leben: Geistesentwicklung und Werke in Zusammenhange* (Stuttgart: P. Balz, 1838–42), 2:201; and Karl Grün, *Friedrich Schiller als Mensch, Geschichtschreiber, Denker, und Dichter* (Leipzig: F. A. Brockhaus, 1844), 147–48.

43. See Peter Hanns Reill, *The German Enlightenment and the Rise of Historicism* (Berkeley: University of California Press, 1975), 29, 37–42.

44. Emil Palleske, *Schiller's Life and Works* [1858], trans. Grace Wallace (London:

Longman, Green, Longman and Roberts, 1860), 178. On the admiration for Schiller's accessible "artistic-historic style," see Johannes Scherr, *Schiller and His Times* [1859], trans. Elisabeth McClellan (Philadelphia: I. Kohler, 1880), 203. Cf. the puzzlement of an Austrian critic on the "oddity" that such a book, based on a few well known and recognizably biased sources, could have such an influence on modern opinion in Karl Tomaschek, *Schiller in seinem Verhältniße zur Wissenschaft* (Vienna: C. G. Gerold's Sohn, 1862), 105.

45. Julian Schmidt, *Schiller und seine Zeitgenossen* (Leipzig: F. W. Grunow, 1863), 241. See also [Julian Schmidt], "Schiller als Historiker," *Die Grenzboten* 18, no. 25 (June 17, 1859): 441–505. For a discussion of Schiller's influence on a Protestant historiography as a German variety of "Whig history," see Golo Mann, "Schiller als Geschichtsschreiber," afterword to *Geschichte des Dreißigjährigen Krieges*, 563–88. Cf. Theodor Schieder's view that Schiller's most important legacy, in that he intuitively pursued history's "essential truths," was to the hermeneutic theory of Dilthey and the "stirring rhetoricians" (*wortgewaltigen Rhetoriker*) of nineteenth-century political history such as Droysen and Treitschke. Schieder, *Begegnungen mit der Geschichte* (Göttingen: Vandenhoeck & Ruprecht, 1962), 56–79.

46. Johannes Janssen, *Schiller als Historiker* (Freiburg im Breisgau: Herder'sche, 1863), vii, 81–91. See also Carl Twesten, *Schiller in seinem Verhältniß zur Wissenschaft* (Berlin: J. Gutenberg, 1863), 105–12; and Adalbert Kuhn's analysis of the psychological and "patriotic-national" imperatives of "pragmatic history" to impose order and unity on the representations of "memoir history," in *Schiller's Geistiger Entwicklung*, 3d ed. (Berlin: E. Schweigger, 1867), 154–69, 180–90.

47. Gustav Freytag, *Erinnerungen aus meinem Leben* (Leipzig: S. Hirzl, 1887), 319–26. Freytag's library was of impressive proportions. The largest section was devoted to the pamphlet literature of the Reformation and the war, of which he had amassed over one thousand examples. See Paul Hohennemser, ed., *Flugschriftensammlung Gustav Freytag* (Frankfurt: Frankfurter Societäts-Druckerei, 1925), 307–88.

48. Freytag, *Erinnerungen*, 215, 226, 246, 310.

49. Eduard Fueter observed that Freytag "remained fundamentally rooted in the unpolitical conceptions of the German Romantics." See Fueter, *Geschichte der neueren Historiographie* (Munich and Berlin: R. Oldenbourg, 1911), 569–71. Cf. Srbik's judgment of Freytag's kleindeutsch "bourgeois liberal-national" tendencies as being compatible with his admiration for the "Whig history" of Macaulay. See Heinrich Ritter von Srbik, *Geist und Geschichte vom deutschen Humanismus bis zur Gegenwart* (Munich: F. Bruckmann, 1951), 2:138–42.

50. See Kurt Classe, *Gustav Freytag als politischer Dichter* (Hildesheim: A. Lax, 1914), 51–78; and Franz Kunkel, *Gustav Freytags "Bilder aus der deutschen Vergangenheit" als schriftstellerische, künstlerische, und dichterische Leistung gewürdigt* (Aschaffenburg: Dr. J. Kirsch, 1926), 6–35.

51. Nancy A. Kaiser, *Social Integration and Narrative Structure: Patterns of*

Realism in Auerbach, Freytag, Fontane, and Raabe (New York: Peter Lang, 1986), 35–47. Kaiser cites Hermann Kinder on the "anticipatory" nature of this realism in literature (which manifests itself as the teleological imperative in historiography) that aimed at the "accomplishment of the remaining historical synthesis between an anticipated future state and present reality."

52. Gabriele Büchler-Hauschild, *Erzählte Arbeit: Gustav Freytag und die soziale Prosa des Vor- und Nachmärz* (Paderborn: F. Schöningh, 1987), 67–71, 90–93. Büchler-Hauschild asserts that the aim of Freytag's histories was to demonstrate the "civilizing contribution of the liberal work ethic of the middle classes."

53. See Kunkel, *Gustav Freytags "Bilder aus der deutschen Vergangenheit,"* note 50.

54. Gustav Freytag, "Bilder aus der deutschen Vergangenheit: Die Dörfer und ihre Geistlichen im dreißigjährigen Kriege," *Die Grenzboten* 17, no. 1 (January 2, 1858): 3–7.

55. Freytag, "Bilder aus der deutschen Vergangenheit," 9–17.

56. Gustav Freytag, *Bilder aus der deutschen Vergangenheit*, vol. 4, *Aus dem Jahrhundert des großen Krieges* (Leipzig: P. List, 1924–25), 8, 15.

57. Freytag, *Bilder aus der deutschen Vergangenheit*, 79–87, 119–57.

58. Freytag, *Bilder aus der deutschen Vergangenheit*, 204–6.

59. Quoted in G. P. Gooch, *History and Historians in the Nineteenth Century* (London: Longmans, Green, 1913), 528.

60. Ergang, *Myth of the All-Destructive Fury*, 11–13.

61. Carl Georg Lentz, Geschichte des dreißigjährigen Glaubenskrieges in Deutschland: Erzählt zum Verständnisse der Gegenwart (Quedlinburg and Leipzig: Gottfried Basse, 1853), 163–64.

62. Friedrich Karl Biedermann, *Deutschlands trübste Zeit, oder der dreißigjäh-rige Krieg in seinen Folgen für das deutsche Culturleben*, 2d ed. (Berlin: F. Henschel, 1872), 41.

63. Ergang, *Myth of the All-Destructive Fury*, 12. On Raumer, see also Hans Herzfeld, "Friedrich von Raumer," in *Mitteldeutsche Lebensbilder* (Magdeburg, 1928), 3:318–61; and Werner Friedrich, *Friedrich von Raumer als Historiker und Politiker* (Leipzig: F. A. Brockhaus, 1930).

64. Friedrich von Raumer, *Geschichte Deutschlands von der Abdankung Karls V bis zum westphälischen Frieden* (Leipzig: F. A. Brockhaus, 1831–32), 3:25–26. Raumer went on to describe soldiers mockingly wearing holy vestments pushing ten children into a burning cellar. Lentz, citing only a "contemporary report," repeats this description word for word. See *Geschichte des dreißigjährigen Glaubenskrieges*, 130–31. The Catholic historian Franz Keym also includes this tale in his history, adding the mitigating detail that Götz sacked the town only after it was occupied by a Swedish detachment. See his *Geschichte des Dreißigjährigen Krieges*, 1:263.

65. Raumer, *Geschichte Deutschlands*, 3:168–69. A student of Raumer's who

taught at Berlin University, the archconservative advocate for the Hohenzollerns, Ernst Helwing (1803–75), repeated the story of corpses being exhumed and consumed in his history of Brandenburg-Prussia. See his *Geschichte des Brandenburgisch-Preußischen Staats während des dreißigjährigen Krieges und im Zeitalter des großen Kurfürsten* (Lemgo and Detmold: Meyer'sche Hof-Buchhandlung, 1846), 192–93. On Helwing, see *ADB*, 50:182–83.

66. Raumer, *Geschichte Deutschlands*, 3:182–83.

67. Hecht, *Der dreißigjährige Krieg*, 382–84.

68. Otto Krabbe, *Zur Geschichte Wallensteins und des dreißigjährigen Krieges: Aus dem kirchlichen und wissenschaftlichen Leben Rostocks* (Berlin: G. Schlawitz, 1863), 215–22.

69. In this deluxe modern edition of Freytag's work, published in the Weimar Republic, there is a reproduction of a seventeenth-century series of satirical woodcuts, entitled "The World Turned Upside Down," showing, among other things, the master serving the servant, the blind leading the sighted, the lamb eating the wolf, castles built on clouds, sheep shearing the shepherd, fish flying, and birds swimming. See Gustav Freytag, *Bilder aus der deutschen Vergangenheit*, vol. 4.

70. Elaine Scarry, *The Body in Pain: The Making and Unmaking of the World* (New York: Oxford University Press, 1985), 126–29.

71. Jill Lepore, *The Name of War: King Philip's War and the Origins of American Identity* (New York: Alfred A. Knopf, 1998), ix–xxi, 72–74, 117–19.

72. Jacob Friedrich Unold, *Geschichte der Stadt Memmingen im dreißigjährigen Kriege* (Memmingen: J. Rehm, 1818), 4.

73. On this "incremental definition of German nationality," see Geoff Eley, "State Formation, Nationalism, and Political Culture in Nineteenth-Century Germany," in Raphael Samuel and Gareth Stedman Jones, eds., *Culture, Ideology, and Politics* (London: Routledge and Kegan Paul, 1982), 287. For a discussion of the reconciliation of "local" and "national" memory through the "process of remembrance and forgetfulness in the Heimat idea" during a later period, see Alon Confino, *The Nation as a Local Metaphor: Württemberg, Imperial Germany, and National Memory, 1871–1918* (Chapel Hill: University of North Carolina Press, 1997), 3 ff.

74. C. B. Sommerlatt, foreword to his *Erinnerungen an die Schlacht bei Wimpfen und den Tod der vierhundert Pforzheimer* (Freiburg im Breisgau: F. X. Wangler, 1824), i–ii.

75. Ernst Munch, "Die Schlacht bei Wimpfen. 1622," in *Erinnerungen an die Schlacht bei Wimpfen*, 1–2. Munch was the author of biographies of Rotteck and Franz von Sickingen and the two-volume *Pantheon der Geschichte des Teutschen Volkes* (Freiburg am Breisgau: F. X. Wangler, 1825–33).

76. Ludwig Posselt, "Dem Vaterlandstod der vierhundert Bürger von Pforzheim: Eine Rede, gehalten den 29. Januar 1788," in *Erinnerungen an die Schlacht bei Wimpfen*, 18–23. See also Ernst L. Deimling, *Die Vierhundert Pforzheimer Burger*,

oder die Schlacht bey Wimpfen (Pforzheim and Augsburg: Klett & Franckh, 1788).

77. Anton Dietrich, "Heldentod der vierhundert Bürger von Pforzheim, in der Schlacht bei Wimpfen am 6. Mai 1622," in *Erinnerungen an die Schlacht bei Wimpfen*, 40–41.

78. C. V. Wedgwood, *The Thirty Years' War* (New Haven: Yale University Press, 1939), 152–53; and Günter Barudio, *Der Teutsche Krieg, 1618–1648* (Frankfurt: S. Fischer, 1985), 208–11.

79. F. G. Fritsche, *Budissin im Jahre 1629: Rede am Sylvesterabend 1829 in der Societät zu Budissin* (Budissin: Ernst Gottlob Monse, 1829), 4 ff.

80. Karl Rehlen, *Zur Säkularfeier der Schlacht bei Nördlingen (am 27 August 1834)* (Nördlingen: n.p., 1841), 11, stanza 18, lines 153–60.

81. Karl Adolph Zehme, *Die Einnahme und Einascherung der Stadt Sonnewalde durch die Schweden* (Leipzig: B. G. Teubner, 1841), 8.

82. Zehme, *Die Einnahme und Einascherung der Stadt Sonnewalde*, iii–iv, 9–12.

83. Jakob F. Binder, *Die Feier der Grundsteinlegung zu einem Thürme auf der Alten Veste bei Zirndorff als Andenken an die am 24. August 1632 Schlacht zwischen Gustav Adolf und Wallenstein vorgefallene Schlacht* (Nuremberg: Friedrich Campe, 1832), 7–10.

84. Binder, *Die Feier der Grundsteinlegung*, 12–38. The estimated cost of the monument was three thousand florins.

85. On the Rothenburg festival, see chapter 4.

86. E. F. Keller, *Die Drangsale des Nassauischen Volkes und der angrenzenden Nachbarländer in den Zeiten des dreißigjährigen Krieges, seine Helden, Staatsmänner, und andere berühmte Zeitgenossen* (Gotha: F. A. Perthes, 1854), iii–vi, 266–78. For a general account of the siege, see Richard Wille, *Hanau im dreißigjährigen Kriege* (Hanau: G. M. Alberti, 1886).

87. J. W. Großmann, *Die Belagerung der Stadt Hanau und deren Befreiung am 13. Junius 1636: Ein vaterländisches Schauspiel in fünf Aufzügen*, Deutsche Schaubühne; oder dramatische Bibliothek der neuesten Lust-Schau-Sing-und Trauerspiele, vol. 16 (Augsburg and Leipzig: n.p., 1816), 128–32.

88. Großmann, *Die Belagerung der Stadt Hanau*, 136–44.

89. Großmann had the heroic mayor point out to the "despairing" Swedish commander that never before in history had four thousand men kept twenty thousand at bay for so long. See ibid., 146.

90. Bernhard Hundeshagen, *Die Belagerung und Entfetzung der Stadt Hanau im dreißigjährigen Kriege: Ein Beitrag zur Geschichte jener Zeiten, nebst einer Schilderung des Jahrfestes dieser Begebenheiten vom 13ten Juni 1811* (Hanau: n.p., 1812), 78–99.

91. L. Weinrich, *Die Aufhebung der Blockade der Stadt Hanau im Jahre 1636*

("und zur Feieren des zweihundertjährigen Jubiläum") (Hanau: F. König, 1836), 80–81, 87.

92. Georg Karl von Sutner, *München während des dreyßigjährigen Krieges* (Munich: Joseph Lindauer, 1796), 5. Sutner, who served as mayor of Munich in 1804, was a member of the Munich academy of sciences and a respected amateur historian who was compared to Westenrieder, Zschokke, and Mussinan. On Sutner, see *ADB*, 37:201–2.

93. Sutner, *München*, 21–37.

94. Eugen von Sobbe, *Die Erstürmung der Stadt Salzkotten am 22. Dezember 1633 durch die Schweden und Hessen* (Salzkotten: n.p., 1856), 16–20.

95. Franz Maria Ferchel, ed., foreword to *Chronik von Erling und Heiligenberg während dem dreißigjährigen Kriege,* by Maurus Freisenegger (Munich: Montmorillion, 1833), i–ii.

96. Albert Heising, *Magdeburg nicht durch Tilly zerstört: Die Politik Gustav Adolph's in Deutschland,* 2d ed. (Berlin: Schneider, 1854), 255.

97. Andreas Sterly, *Drangsale der Stadt Iglau unter der schwedischen Zwingherrschaft besonders während ihrer Belagerung im Jahre 1647* (Iglau: Babian Beynhauer, 1828), 115. For three other accounts of the Swedish invasion of the Habsburg crown lands late in the war, which celebrate the preservation of the legitimate "unitary Austrian state" (*Österreichischen Gesammtstaat*), see Joseph Hormayr, "Die Schweden vor Brünn 1645," *Archiv für Geographie, Historie, Staats- und Kriegskunst* 7, nos. 1–2, 5–6, 11–12, 17–18 (January/February 1816): 1–4, 22, 64; Christian d'Elvert, *Der Schweden vor Brünn: Ein Abschnitt des dreißigjährigen Krieges: Zur Jubel-Feier der Vertheidigung Brünns gegen die Schweden vor zwei hundert Jahren* (Brünn: R. Rohrer, 1845); and Polykarp Koller, *Die Belagerung von Brünn durch die Schweden im Jahre 1645: Das denkwürdigste Jahr aus Brünns Vorzeit: Ein historischer Versuch* (Brünn: R. Rohrer, 1845). For a revisionist account of Ferdinand III's campaign against Torstenson in this period, introduced as a corrective to the ignorance and "partisanship" of modern historians, see Joseph Feil, *Die Schweden in Nieder-Oesterreich in den Jahren 1645 und 1646* (Vienna: C. G. Gerold's Sohn, 1865).

98. For an excellent discussion of this phenomenon in American history, see David W. Blight, *Race and Reunion: The Civil War in American Memory* (Cambridge: Harvard University Press, 2001).

99. "Die Schweden in Hessen," *Historisch-politische Blätter für das katholische Deutschland* 19 (1847): 513–21.

100. Franz Joseph Bodmann, *Die Schweden zu Mainz* (Mainz: Florian Kupferberg, 1812), 10–11. On Bodmann, see *ADB*, 3:15–17; and Franz X. von Wegele, *Geschichte der deutschen Historiographie seit dem Auftreten des Humanismus* (Munich and Leipzig: R. Oldenbourg, 1885), 938–39.

101. Bodmann, *Die Schweden zu Mainz*, 31, 47–70.

102. For a discussion of the Napoleonic occupation and administration of the Rhineland and the varieties of German cooperation, resistance, and resentments, see David Blackbourn, *The Fontana History of Germany, 1780–1918: The Long Nineteenth Century* (London: Fontana Press, 1997), 70–75. See also Thomas Mergel, *Zwischen Klasse und Konfession: Katholisches Bürgertum im Rheinland, 1794–1914* (Göttingen: Vandenhoeck & Ruprecht, 1994), 70–93.

103. Carl Gottfried Scharold, *Geschichte der kön. schwedischen und herzogl. sachsen-weimarischen Zwischenregierung in eroberten Fürstbisthume Würzburg i. J. 1631–1634* (Würzburg: Vogt & Mocker, 1844–45), 1:i, 1–11, 29–47, 159–80. Scharold adhered to the Catholic legitimist interpretation of the war's origins, accusing the Protestant Union of being in rebellion against the constitutionally appointed ruler of the German empire. See his "Zur Geschichte des 30jährigen Kriegs in Beziehung auf das Hochstift Würzburg," *Archiv des historischen Vereins für den Untermainkreis 1*, no. 2 (Würzburg, 1833): 107–23.

104. The siege lasted from January 1633 to August 1635 and was conducted with the help of German troops led by Duke Julius Friedrich of Württemberg. The town was praised for its loyalty and bravery in an imperial proclamation in 1635. See Christian Roder, *Beiträge zur Geschichte der Stadt Villingen während des dreißigjährigen Krieges* (Tübingen: H. Lang'sche Buchdruckerei, 1880). The cruelty of the Württemberg soldiers was remembered in local lore in the song "Die Metzelei zu Hüsingen" (The Slaughter in Hüsingen), which related how a Colonel Rau ordered all the men in the village shot. See K. H. von Schreckenstein, *Ein gleichzeitiger Bericht über das vom wirtembergischen Kriegsvolke am 15. Oktober 1632 in Hüsingen angerichtete Blutbad* (Freiburg im Breisgau: J. C. B. Mohr, 1867).

105. Carl Theodor Rabenalt, *Die Schweden vor Villingen im Jahre 1634: Ein romantisches Schauspiel in 4 Aufzügen*, Deutsche Schaubühne; oder dramatische Bibliothek der neuesten Lust-Schau-Sing-und Trauerspiel (Augsburg and Leipzig, 1816), 28:143–45.

106. Rabenalt, *Die Schweden vor Villingen im Jahre 1634*, 197–98, 222.

107. Rabenalt, *Die Schweden vor Villingen im Jahre 1634*, 265–66.

108. *Die Schweden am Bodensee: Bilder aus dem dreißigjährigen Kriege* (n.p.: author, n.d.), 119–20. The author's name on the title page is given as "W. R——ch."

109. Lorenz Westenrieder, *Geschichte des dreyßigjährigen Kriegs* (Munich: J. Lindauer, 1805), 2:265.

110. Westenrieder, *Geschichte des dreyßigjährigen Kriegs*, 264.

111. Franz Reithofer, *Denkwürdige Geschichte der Stadt Landshut in Baiern im dreyßigjährigen Kriege* (Landshut in Baiern: n.p., 1810), 3, 11.

112. Reithofer, *Denkwürdige Geschichte der Stadt Landshut in Baiern*, 20–24. A play from 1783 described the siege of Landshut as a test of the loyalty of the citizens to prince and fatherland as they heard reports of the fate of Altdorf, where

"the raped cried to heaven for revenge." See Maximilian Blaimhofer, *Die Schweden in Baiern, oder die Bürgertreu: Ein Schauspiel in fünf Aufzügen* (Munich, 1783; reprint, Landshut: Andreas Schlittmeier, 1989).

113. Reithofer, *Denkwürdige Geschichte der Stadt Landshut in Baiern*, 20, 27–38.

114. Reithofer, *Denkwürdige Geschichte der Stadt Landshut in Baiern*, 47–57. A manuscript from 1631–33, reportedly discovered in the archives of the abbey at Plankstetten in Franconia, described the "fury" with which the Swedes tortured Catholic clergy, especially monks. See Friedrich Anton Mayer, "Ein kleiner Beitrag zur Geschichte des dreißigjährigen Krieges aus einem Manuscripte des Klosters Plankstetten," *Jahresbericht des historischen Vereins in Mittelfranken* 18 (Ansbach, 1849): 97–99.

115. Heinrich Zschokke, *Der Baierischen Geschichten* (Aarau: H. R. Sauerländer, 1816), 3:271–84. Zschokke had fled the Austrian police to settle in the Aargau, where he supported the establishment of the Helvetian Republic in 1798. He was invited to write his Bavarian history by Schlichtegroll at the Munich Academy, a project that had the support of Montgelas as well. Zschokke remained "in opposition" in the Restoration period, although he was named an honorary citizen of Magdeburg in 1830. His rationalist contempt for the "revival of outward piety" he observed in the war-torn Europe of 1807, his pro-French inclinations, and his preference for Swiss exile provoked a hostile response to his work in Bavaria, where his critics labeled him a foreigner and a "free-thinking republican" whose scholarly credentials could not match those of Bavaria's "great patriotic historians" such as Westenrieder. See K. A. Kelteger, *Bemerkungen über die baierischen Geschichten* (Rauschenberg: n.p., 1818); Altomanus Bavaricus [pseud.], *Patriotische Betrachtungen über des Herrn Heinrich Zschokke's drey Bände baierischer Geschichten* (n.p., 1818); Jeremias Schwarzrock, *Frage: Hat Hr. Heinrich Zschokke eine Nationalgeschichte für Baiern schreiben können und wollen?* (Kautzopolis: n.p., 1818); and Jeremias Schwarzrock, *Theses wider Herrn Heinrich Zschokke's baierischen Geschichten* (Aarau: n.p., 1818). On Zschokke, see *ADB*, 44:449–65; and Heinrich Zschokke, *Eine Selbstschau* (Aarau: H. R. Sauerländer, 1842).

116. Zschokke, *Der Baierischen Geschichten*, 3:287–88.

117. A. W. Endres, *Die Stadt Landsberg und der Markt Bayerdiessen während des schwedischen Krieges von 1632 bis 1648* (Dillingen: K. Kränzle, 1862), 14, 21.

118. Endres, *Die Stadt Landsberg und der Markt Bayerdiessen*, 10, 24.

119. Endres, *Die Stadt Landsberg und der Markt Bayerdiessen*, 38–47.

120. The two major comprehensive histories of the war in Bavaria written in the middle decades of the century did nothing to alter the established tradition of Swedish atrocities as set down by Westenrieder, Zschokke, and the local chroniclers. They did earnestly attempt to provide the reader with additional detailed accounts, drawn from regional archives and numbing in their repetitions, of the gruesome fate

of every village and town in southern Germany. See Andreas Buchner (1776–1854), *Geschichte von Bayern während des dreißigjährigen Krieges* (Munich: Lindauer'schen Verlagshandlung, 1851); and Franz von Soden (1790–1869), *Gustav Adolph und sein Heer in Süddeutschland von 1631 bis 1635: Zur Geschichte des dreißigjährigen Krieges*, vol. 2, *Von Gustav Adolphs Tode bis zur Eroberung von Ungarn und Böhmen* (Erlangen: Deichert, 1867). Soden, who was a veteran of the campaign of 1812–15, was a military historian from Nuremberg. The most original claim his book made, and in which he took some pride, was his confirmation of the notion that Germans learned smoking from the Swedes during the war, hence the saying, "He smokes like a Swede." He referred the interested reader to two appendices on the cultivation of tobacco in Germany for "an interesting contribution to the history of customs." It is also interesting to note that smoking was condemned by many historians as evidence of the decline of morals caused by the war.

121. Joseph von Mussinan, *Befestigung und Belagerung der baierischen Haupt-Stadt Straubing in den Jahren 1633, 1704, und 1742* (Straubing: F. S. Lerno, 1816), iv–v, 174–75. Mussinan had been a jurist in Straubing from 1802 to 1813 and was later made an honorary citizen. After 1815, he became an upper-level bureaucrat in the finance ministry in Munich and a member of the Academy. See also his *Geschichte der französischen Kriege in Deutschland, besonderes auf baierischen Boden*, 4 vols. (Sulzbach: J. E. Seidel, 1822–29). On Mussinan, see ADB, 23:101–2.

122. Joseph R. Schuegraf, "Auszüge aus der Geschichte des 30jährigen Krieges in baierischen Wald," *Eos: Zeitschrift aus Baiern*, 57–59 (April 1825): 229–30, 233–34, 237–38. On Schuegraf, see ADB, 32:653.

123. Franz Zwerger, *Ein Beitrag zur Geschichte der Stadt Landsberg während des dreißigjährigen Krieges* (Landsberg: X. Kraus, 1882), 4–5, 16.

124. Franz August Bauer, *Die höhen Bürgertugenden der Stadt Kronach bei ihrer Belagerung im dreißigjährigen Kriege* (Erlangen: F. Büberlein, 1835), 5–22.

125. Mussinan, *Befestigung und Belagerung Schicksale*, 53–54.

126. Joseph R. Schuegraf, *Belagerung, Eroberung, und Zerstörung der Veste Donaustauf durch die Schweden im Jahre 1634* (Regensburg: G. Joseph Manz, 1831), 13.

127. Joseph von Mussinan, *Ueber das Schicksal Straubings und des baierischen Waldes während des dreyßigjährigen Krieges vom Oktober 1633 bis April 1634* (Straubing: F. S. Lerno, 1813), xxii.

128. On Catholic Germany's state of mind in the annus horribilis of 1866, see Hugo Lacher, "Das Jahr 1866," *Neue Politische Literatur* 14 (1969): 83–99, 214–31.

129. For a discussion of this idea of invoking the spirits of the dead to bolster a marginalized Irish national identity in Yeats's "Protestant Gothic," see R. F. Foster, "Protestant Magic: W. B. Yeats and the Spell of Irish History," in *Paddy and Mr. Punch: Connections in Irish and English History* (London: A. Lane, 1993), 212–32.

Conclusion

1. See Allen J. Frantzen, *Bloody Good: Chivalry, Sacrifice, and the Great War* (Chicago: University of Chicago Press, 2004).

2. Michael Walzer, *The Revolution of the Saints: A Study in the Origins of Radical Politics* (New York: Atheneum, 1973), 279–84. Walzer cites the influence of the Thirty Years' War on the development of English revolutionary Protestantism. See 288–90. This definition of war has not been confined to the West. In Kyoto in 1941, an assembly of prominent Japanese intellectuals called for a "holy war" against the West. See Ian Baruma and Avishai Margalit, "Occidentalism," in *New York Review of Books* 49, no. 1 (January 17, 2002): 4–7.

3. Michael Walzer, *Exodus and Revolution* (New York: Basic Books, 1985), ix, 91–92. See also Anthony W. Marx, *Faith in Nation: Exclusionary Origins of Nationalism* (New York: Oxford University Press, 2003).

4. Mark Juergensmeyer, *Terror in the Mind of God: The Global Rise of Religious Violence* (Berkeley: University of California Press, 2001), 157–61.

5. See David Stannard, *American Holocaust: The Conquest of the New World* (New York: Oxford University Press, 1992), 175–79.

6. Ulf Hedetoft, "National Identity and Mentalities of War in Three EC Countries," *Journal of Peace Research* 30, no. 3 (August 1993): 287.

7. Friedrich von Raumer, *Geschichte Deutschlands von der Abdankung Karls V bis zum westphälischen Frieden: Zweite Hälfte von 1630–1648* (Leipzig: F. A. Brockhaus, 1831–32), 207–18.

8. Johann Sporschil, *Der Dreißigjährige Krieg* (Braunschweig: G. Westermann, 1843), 700.

9. Konrad Rüdel, *Der Westphälische Friede: Eine Festgabe zur zweiten Säkularfeier desselben für das deutsche Volk evangelischen Bekenntnißes* (Nuremberg: J. P. Raw, 1848), 57.

10. Franz Keym, *Geschichte des Dreißigjährigen Krieges* (Freiburg im Breisgau: Herder'sche, 1873), 2:299.

11. Walter Benjamin, "Theses on the Philosophy of History," in Hannah Arendt, ed., *Illuminations*, trans. Harry Zohn (New York: Schocken Books, 1969), 255.

12. Georg Winter, *Geschichte des Dreißigjährigen Krieges* (Berlin: G. Grote, 1893), 4–6.

13. Max Scheler, "Der Genius des Krieges und der Deutschen Krieg [1916]," in Manfred S. Frings, ed., *Politisch-Pädagogische Schriften* (Bern and Munich: Francke, 1982), 141.

14. Max Scheler, *Krieg und Aufbau* (Leipzig: Verlag der Weissen Bücher, 1916), 14; and "Genius des Krieges," 137–39.

15. Martin Greschat, "Krieg und Kriegsbereitschaft im deutschen Protestantismus," in Jost Düffler and Karl Holl, eds., *Bereit zum Krieg: Kriegsmentalität in Wilhelmischen Deutschland, 1890–1914* (Göttingen: Vandenhoeck und Ruprecht, 1986), 35. See

also Christian Rak, *Krieg, Nation, und Konfession: Die Erfahrung des deutsch-französischen Krieges von 1870/71* (Paderborn: Ferdinand Schöningh, 2004).

16. Hew Strachan, *The First World War*, vol. 1, *To Arms* (New York: Oxford University Press, 2001), 1116. In 1916 the art critic Karl Sheffler invidiously compared Protestant culture with Catholic, noting that Catholicism "lacked the spirit of Protestantism, that is to say: the readiness to go into depth." Quoted in John Updike, "New Worlds: German and Austrian Art, 1840–1940," *New York Review of Books* 49 (February 14, 2002): 27.

17. Wilhelm Pressel, *Die Kriegspredigt 1914–1918 in der evangelischen Kirche* (Göttingen: Vandenhoeck & Ruprecht, 1967), 21–26, 51, 81–83, 140–53.

18. Karl Holl, *The Cultural Significance of the Reformation* [1911], trans. Karl and Barbara Hertz and John H. Lichtblau (New York: Meridian Books, 1959), 57. Cf. Hegel's reference, in *The Philosophy of Right*, to "the necessity of war from time to time to bring man back to the universal idea of the state." Quoted in Charles Taylor, *Hegel* (Cambridge: Cambridge University Press, 1975), 155–56; and Carl Schmitt's definition of war in "Totaler Feind, totaler Krieg, totaler Staat [1937]": "War can be total in the sense of the utmost effort and the utmost employment of all available means." Quoted in Eberhard Demm, *Ostpolitik und Propaganda im Ersten Weltkrieg* (Frankfurt: Peter Lang, 2002), 27–52.

19. Johann Jonathan Felßecker, "Teutsch-treugesinnter Leser," in Hans Karl Schulz, ed., *Der Dreißigjährige Krieg*, vol. 1, *Bis zum Tode Gustav Adolfs* (Leipzig and Berlin: B. G. Teubner, 1917), 1–2.

20. Karl Holl, *Die Bedeutung der großen Kriege für das religiöse und kirchliche Leben innerhalb des deutschen Protestantismus* (Tübingen: J. C. B. Mohr, 1917), 4–5. Hermann Oncken, Erich Marcks, Johannes Haller, and Rudolf Eucken also compared the Thirty Years' War and the Great War. See Steffen Bruendel, *Volksgemeinschaft oder Volksstaat: Die "Ideen von 1914" und die Neuordnung Deutschlands im Ersten Weltkrieg* (Berlin: Akademie, 2003), 204–6.

21. Michael Geyer, "Insurrectionary Warfare: The German Debate about a *Levée en Masse* in October 1918," *Journal of Modern History* 73, no. 3 (September 2001): 467, 473–76, 509–14.

22. Dan Diner and Bill Templar, "European Counter-Images: Problems of Periodization and Historical Memory," *New German Critique*, no. 53 (Spring/Summer 1991): 165–66.

23. Richard Bessel, *Germany after the First World War* (New York: Oxford University Press, 1995), 220, 243. Cf. Daniel W. Stowell, *Rebuilding Zion: The Religious Reconstruction of the South* (New York: Oxford University Press, 1998).

24. Stefan-Ludwig Hoffmann, "Mythos und Geschichte: Leipziger Gedenkfeieren der Völkerschlacht in 19. und 20. Jahrhundert," in Etienne Françoise, Hannes Siegrist, and Jakob Vogel, eds., *Nation und Emotion: Deutschland und Frankreich*

in Vergleich 19. und 20. Jahrhundert (Göttingen: Vandenhoeck & Ruprecht, 1995), 114.

25. Annette Maas, "Der Kult der toten Krieger: Frankreich und Deutschland nach 1870/71," in *Nation und Emotion*, 227.

26. Ricarda Huch, *Wallenstein: Eine Charakterstudie* (Leipzig: Insel, 1920), 5–6, 12.

27. Harro Müller, "War and Novel: Alfred Döblin's 'Wallenstein' and 'November 1918,'" in Bernd Hüppauf, ed., *War, Violence, and the Modern Condition* (New York: Walter de Gruyter, 1997), 293–97.

28. Walther Tritsch, *Wallenstein: Herr des Schicksal—Knechte der Sterne* (Leipzig: J. Kittl, 1936), 11, 22–25.

29. Carl Johannes Rummel, *Kaiser, Gott, und Reich* (Berlin: Vier Falken, 1941), 5–6, 820.

30. Karl Brandi, *Die Deutsche Reformation und Gegenreformation*, vol. 2, *Gegenreformation und Religionskriege* (Leipzig: Quelle & Meyer, 1930), 306–9.

31. Johannes Paul, *Gustav Adolf*, vol. 1, *Schwedens Aufsteig zur Großmachtsstellung* (Leipzig: Quelle & Meyer, 1927), 6. In 1930 Paul referred to this as a "North German-Scandinavian Unity Front." See Johannes Paul, "Gustav Adolf in der deutschen Geschichtsschreibung," *Historische Viertaljahrschrift* 25, no. 3 (September 1930): 429.

32. Ernst Kohlmeyer, *Gustav Adolf und Deutschland* (Bonn: Bonner Universitäts-Buchdruckerei, 1940), 11–13.

33. Gerhard Ritter, "Gustav Adolf, Deutschland, und das nordische Luthertum [1932]," in *Die Weltwirkung der Reformation*, 2d ed. (Munich: R. Oldenbourg, 1959), 137–38, 144–45.

34. Richard Schmidt, "Gustav Adolf: Die Bedeutung seiner Erscheinung für die europäische Politik und für den deutschen Volksgeist," *Zeitschrift für Politik* 22, no. 11 (February 1933): 719.

35. Günther Franz, *Der Dreißigjährige Krieg und das deutsche Volk: Untersuchungen zur Bevölkerungs- und Agrargeschichte*, 2d ed. (Jena: G. Fischer, 1943), 100.

36. Wilhelm Frick, foreword to *"Geknechtete befreite er!" Gustav Adolfs nordischer Freiheitskampf im Lichte unserer Zeit*, by Hans Chilian (Leipzig: G. Kummer, 1939), vii–xv.

37. Hans Chilian, *"Geknechtete befreite er!"* 211, 213, 220–21.

38. Adolf Hitler, *Mein Kampf*, trans. Ralph Mannheim (Boston: Houghton Mifflin, 1971), 396.

39. Adolf Hitler, "Rede vor dem Industrieklub in Düsseldorf [1932]," "Regensburger Rede [1937]," and "Aufbau und Organisation der Volksführung [1937]," in Max Domarus, ed., *Hitler: Reden und Proklamationen, 1932–1945*, vol. 1, *Triumph, 1932–1938* (Neustadt: Verlagsdruckerei Schmidt, 1962), 71, 699, 761.

40. Adolf Hitler, "Tischgespräche, Juli 1941–August 1942," in Max Domarus, ed., *Hitler: Reden und Proklamationen, 1932–1945*, vol. 2, *Untergang, 1939–1945* (Neustadt: Verlagsdruckerei Schmidt, 1963), 1744.

41. Adolf Hitler, "Tagung von Wirtschaftführern [1944]," in *Untergang, 1939–1945*, 2115.

42. Norbert Elias, *The Germans: Power Struggles and the Development of Habitus in the Nineteenth and Twentieth Centuries*, ed. Michael Schröter, trans. Eric Dunning and Stephen Mennell (New York: Columbia University Press, 1996), 208, 320–21.

Bibliography

Libraries and Special Collections

Bavarian State Library, Munich
Bodleian Library, Oxford University, Oxford
British Library, British Museum, London
University Library, Ludwig Maximilian University, Munich
University Library, Georg August University, Göttingen
University Library, University of Freiburg im Breisgau
Widener Library, Harvard University:
    Harvard College Library Collection on the Thirty Years' War, Gift of Helen
    Bigelow Merriman and Roger Bigelow Merriman
    Hohenzollern Collection
    Library of Konrad von Maurer of Munich
    Library of Philipp Pfister of Munich
    Library of Rodolphe Reuss of Strasbourg

Primary Sources

Albrechts von Wallenstein Herzogs von Friedland wahre, bisher immer verfälschte Lebensgeschichte. Berlin: F. Maurer, 1797.

Altomanus Bavaricus. *Patriotische Betrachtungen über des Herrn Heinrich Zschokke's drey Bände baierische Geschichten*. N.p., 1818.

Aretin, Karl Maria Freiherr von. *Bayerns auswärtige Verhältniße seit dem Anfang des sechszehnten Jahrhunderts*. Passau: F. Winkler, 1839.

———. *Geschichte des bayerischen Herzogs und Kurfürsten Maximilian des Ersten*. Vol. 1. Passau: F. Winkler, 1842.

———. *Tilly und Wrede: Zur Feier des 8. Octobers 1844*. Munich: n.p., 1844.

———. *Wallenstein: Beiträge zur näheren Kenntniß seines Charakters, seiner Pläne, seines Verhältnisses zu Bayern*. Regensburg: G. Joseph Manz, 1846.

Arndt, Wilhelm. "Die Zerstörung Magdeburgs 1631." *Blätter für literarische Unterhaltung* 50 (December 15, 1892): 785–87.

Baader, J. "Zwey merkwürdige Aktenstücke über die zur Zeit des Schwedenkriegs im Winter des jahrs 1634–35 zu Agawang geherrschte graßliche Hungersnot." *Jahrs-Bericht des historischen Vereins für den Regierungs-Bezirk von Schwaben und Neuburg*, nos. 5–6 (Augsburg, 1839–40): 71–72.

Barthold, Friedrich Wilhelm. *Geschichte des großen deutschen Krieges vom Tode Gustav Adolfs ab mit besonderer Rücksicht auf Frankreich*. 2vols. Stuttgart: S. G. Liesching, 1842–43.

Bibliography

Bauer, Franz August. *Die höhen Bürgertugenden der Stadt Kronach bei ihrer Belagerung im dreißigjährigen Kriege.* Erlangen: F. Büberlein, 1835.

"Bayerns auswärtige Verhältniße seit dem Anfange des sechzehn Jahrhunderts, von Karl Maria von Aretin." *Historisch-politische Blätter für das katholische Deutschland* 3 (1839): 433–39, 507–8.

Beck, Friedrich Adolf. *Auszug aus der Osnabrücker Friedensurkunde vom Jahre 1648.* Darmstatdt: C. W. Leske, 1844.

Becker, Gottfried Wilhelm. "Der Eroberung von Magdeburg, 1631: Historisches Basrelief." *Der Verkundiger* (Nuremberg), May 10, 12, 1812.

Bensen, Heinrich W. *Teutschland und die Geschichte: Eine Denkschrift.* Stuttgart: Franckh, 1844.

———. *Der Verhängniß Magdeburgs: Eine Geschichte aus dem großen Zweispalt der teutschen Nation im 16ten und 17ten Jahrhundert.* Schaffhausen: Fr. Hurter'sche Buchhandlung, 1858.

Biedermann, Friedrich Karl. *Deutschlands trübste Zeit, oder der dreißigjährigen Krieg in seinen Folgen für das deutsche Culturleben.* 2d ed. Berlin: F. Henschel, 1872.

Binder, Jacob F. *Die Feier der Grundsteinlegung zu einem Thürme auf der Alten Veste bei Zirndorff als Andenken an die am 24. August 1632 Schlacht zwischen Gustav Adolf und Wallenstein vorgefallene Schlacht.* Nuremberg: Friedrich Campe, 1832.

Bischoff, Theodor. *Tilly: Ein Zeitbild.* Rothenburg ob der Tauber: Schneider'schen Buchdruckerei, 1881.

Blaimhofer, Maximilian. *Die Schweden in Baiern, oder die Bürgertreu: Ein Schauspiel in fünf Aufzügen.* Munich, 1783; reprint, Landshut: Andreas Schlittmeier, 1989.

Bodmann, Franz Joseph. *Die Schweden zu Mainz.* Mainz: Florian Kupferberg, 1812.

Börne, Ludwig. *Menzel, der Französenfresser.* Paris: T. Barrois fils, 1837.

Bötticher, Wilhelm. *Gustav Adolph, König von Schweden: Ein Buch für Fürst und Volk.* Kaiserswerth am Rhein: B. Fliebner, 1845.

Bougeant, Guillaume-Hyacinthe. *Histoire des guerres et des negotiations qui précéderent le traite de Westphalie sous le regne de Louis XIII et le ministre du cardinal de Richelieu et du cardinal Mazarin: Composée sur les memoires du Comte d'Avaux.* Paris: Chez Pierre-Jean Mariette, 1744.

Brandi, Karl. *Die Deutsche Reformation und Gegenreformation,* vol. 2, *Gegenreformation und Religionskriege.* Leipzig: Quelle & Meyer, 1930.

Bratranek, Frantisek Thomas. *Goethes Egmont und Schillers Wallenstein: Eine Parallele der Dichter.* Stuttgart: Cotta, 1862.

Buchner, Andreas. *Geschichte von Bayern während des dreißigjährigen Krieges.* Munich: Lindauer'schen, 1851.

Bucquoi, Erdmann F. *Leben und Thaten des General Wallenstein*. Bunzlau and Breslau: Weisenh. Buchdruckerei, 1783.

Bülow, Dietrich Freiherr von. *Gustav Adolph in Deutschland: Kritische Geschichte seiner Feldzüge*. 2 vols. Berlin: Himburg, 1808.

Calvisio, M. Seth-Henrico. *Das zerstörte und wieder aufgerichtete Magdeburg*. Magdeburg: Christian Leberecht Faber, 1727.

[Carlick, P.]. "Der Brand Magdeburgs in Jahre 1631." *Historisch-politische Blätter für das katholische Deutschland* 14 (1844): 296–308.

"Charakterbild Kaiser Ferdinand's II. nach Fr. von Hurters Geschichtswerk." *Historisch-politische Blätter für das katholische Deutschland* 56 (1865): 899–915.

Chemnitz, Bogislav Philipp von. *Belli Sueco-Germanici*. Stettin: Georg Rethen, 1648.

———. *Königlichen Schwedischen in Teutschland geführten Krieges*. 4 vols. Stettin and Stockholm: Georg Rethen, 1648–55.

Chilian, Hans. *"Geknechtete befreite er!" Gustav Adolfs nordischer Freiheitskampf im Lichte unserer Zeit*. Leipzig: G. Kummer, 1939.

Constant, Benjamin. *Wallstein: tragédie en cinq actes et en vers: Précédee de quelques réflexions sur le théâtre allemand, et suivie de notes historiques*. Paris: Paschoud, 1809.

Cornelius, Carl Adolph. *Zur Geschichte der Gründung der deutschen Liga*. Munich: F. Straub, 1863.

Coste, David. "Die vierhundert Pforzheimer." *Historische Zeitschrift* 16, no. 3 (1874): 23–48.

Deimling, Ernst Ludwig. *Die Vierhundert Pforzheimer Bürger, oder die Schlacht bey Wimpfen*. Pforzheim and Augsburg: Klett & Franckh, 1788.

Dietrich, Anton. "Heldentod der vierhundert Bürger von Pforzheim, in der Schlacht bei Wimpfen an 6. Mai 1622." In *Erinnerungen an die Schlacht bei Wimpfen und den Tod der vierhundert Pforzheimer*, ed. C. B. Sommerlatt, 36–92. Freiburg im Breisgau: F. X. Wangler, 1824.

Dittmar, Max. *Beiträge zur Geschichte der Stadt Magdeburg in den Ersten Jahren nach Ihrer Zerstörung 1631*. Halle: M. Niemeyer, 1884.

———. "Die Zerstörung Magdeburgs in Jahre 1631: Offene Antwort an Herrn Professor Dr. Wittich." *Geschichtsblätter für Stadt und Land Magdeburg* 29 (1894): 303–400.

Droysen, Gustav. "Studien über die Belagerung und Zerstörung Magdeburgs 1631." *Forschungen zur Deutschen Geschichte* 3 (January 1863): 435–69.

———. *Gustav Adolf*. 2 vols. Leipzig: Veit, 1869–70.

———. "Brandenburgische Audienzen bei Gustav Adolf." *Zeitschrift für Preußische Geschichte und Landskunde* 15 (1878): 21–35.

Dudik, Beda. *Forschungen in Schweden für Mährens Geschichte.* Brünn: C. Winiker, 1852.

———. *Waldstein von seiner Enthebung bis zur abermaligen Uebernahme des Armee Ober-Kommandos, vom 15. August 1630 bis 15. April 1632.* Vienna: C. G. Gerold's Sohn, 1858.

Düntzer, Heinrich. *Schiller's Wallenstein.* Leipzig: E. Wartig, 1877.

d'Elvert, Christian. *Der Schweden vor Brünn: Ein Abschnitt des dreißigjährigen Krieges: Zur Jubel-Feier der Vertheidigung Brünns gegen die Schweden vor zwei hundert Jahren.* Brünn: R. Rohrer, 1845.

———. *Beiträge zur Geschichte der Rebellion, Reformation, des dreißigjährigen Krieges und der Neugestaltung Mährens im siebzehnten Jahrhunderte.* Brünn: R. Rohrer, 1867.

Endres, A. W. *Die Stadt Landsberg und der Markt Bayerdiessen während des schwedischen Krieges von 1632 bis 1648.* Dillingen: K. Kränzle, 1862.

Erdmannsdörffer, Bernhard. "Zur Geschichte und Geschichtsschreibung des dreißigjährigen Krieges." *Historische Zeitschrift* 14 (1865): 1–44.

Erinnerung an die Schlacht bei Breitenfeld am 7ten September und deren Feier am 7. September 1831. Leipzig: n.p., 1831.

Ewald, Severin. *Der dreißigjährigen Krieg nebst dem westphälischen Frieden: Nach Schiller, Galletti, und anderen Geschichtschreibern dargestellt für die Jugend und zum Selbstunterrichte.* Berlin: C. F. Amelang, 1830.

Feil, Joseph. *Die Schweden in Nieder-Oesterreich in den Jahren 1645 und 1646.* Vienna: C. G. Gerold's Sohn, 1865.

Felßecker, Johann Jonathan. "Teutsch-treugesinnter Leser." In *Der Dreißigjährige Krieg,* vol. 1, *Bis zum Tode Gustav Adolfs,* ed. Hans Karl Schulz, 1–2. Leipzig and Berlin: Teubner, 1917.

Flathe, Ludwig. *Geschichte des Kampfes zwischen dem alten und dem neuen Verfassungsprincip der Staaten der neuesten Zeit seit dem Auftreten des Humanismus, 1781–1791.* Vol. 1. Leipzig: Göschen, 1813.

———. *Geschichte Gustav Adolf's und des dreißigjährigen Krieges.* 2 vols. 2d ed. Leipzig: B. G. Teubner, 1847.

Förster, Friedrich. *Albrechts von Wallenstein, des Herzogs von Friedland und Mecklenburg, ungedrückte, eigenhändige vertrauliche Briefe und amtliche Schrieben aus den Jahren 1627 bis 1634 an Arnheim, Aldringer, Gallas, Piccolomini und andrere Fürsten und Feldherrn seiner Zeit: Mit einer Charakteristik des Lebens und der Feldzüge Wallensteins.* 2 vols. Berlin: Georg Reimer, 1828–29.

———. *Gustav Adolph: Ein historisches Drama.* Berlin: Friedrich Maurer'schen Buchhandlung, 1832.

———. "Wallenstein als regierender Herzog und Landesherr." *Historisches Taschenbuch* 5 (Leipzig, 1834): 1–62.

————. *Wallenstein Herzog zu Mecklenburg, Friedland und Sagan, als Feldherr und Landesfürst in seinem öffentlichen und Privat-Leben: Eine Biographie.* Potsdam: F. Reigel, 1834.

————. *Wallensteins Prozess vor den Schranken des Weltgerichts und des k.k. Fiscus zu Prag.* Leipzig: B. G. Teubner, 1844.

————. *Kunst und Leben.* Edited by Hermann Kletke. Berlin: Paetel, 1873.

Francheville, Joseph du Fresne de. *La Mort de Gustave-Adolphe.* Breslau: Theodor Korn, 1799.

Franz, Günther. *Der Dreißigjährige Krieg und das deutsche Volk: Untersuchungen zur Bevölkerungs- und Agrargeschichte.* 2d ed. Jena: G. Fischer, 1943.

Freimund, C. G. [Karl Gustav Helbig]. *Bemerkungen über den Zustand Polens unter russischer Herrschaft im Jahre 1830.* Leipzig: Arnold, 1831.

Freisenegger, Maurus. *Chronik von Erling und Heiligenberg während dem dreißigjährigen Kriege.* Edited by Franz Maria Ferchel. Munich: Montmorillon, 1833.

Freytag, Gustav. "Bilder aus der deutschen Vergangenheit: Die Dörfer und ihre Geistlichen im dreißigjährigen Kriege." *Die Grenzboten* 17, no. 1 (January 2, 1858): 3–21.

————. *Bilder aus der deutschen Vergangenheit,* vol. 4, *Aus dem Jahrhundert des großen Krieges.* Leipzig: S. Hirzl, 1859–60; reprint, Leipzig: P. List, 1924–25.

————. *Erinnerungen aus meinem Leben.* Leipzig: S. Hirzl, 1887.

Frick, Wilhelm. Foreword to *"Geknechtete befreite er!" Gustav Adolfs nordischer Freiheitskampf im Lichte unserer Zeit,* by Hans Chilian. Leipzig: G. Kummer, 1939.

Friederich, Gerhard. *Geistesblick auf die Bedeutung des heutigen Jubelfestes der christlichen Kirchenverbesserungen und das Verdienst ihres Stifters.* Frankfurt: Ferdinand Boselli, 1817.

————. *Luther: Ein historisches Gedicht in vier Gesängen.* Frankfurt: Sauerländer, 1855.

————. *Gustav Adolf's Heldentod für Teutschlands Freiheit: Ein historisches Gedicht in vier Gesängen.* 2d ed. Frankfurt: Sauerländer, 1834.

Friedrichs, C. R. "The War and German Society." In *The Thirty Years' War,* ed. Geoffrey Parker. London: Routledge & Kegan Paul, 1984.

Fritsche, F. G. *Budissin in Jahre 1629: Rede an Sylvesterabend 1829 in der Societät zu Budissin.* Budissin: Ernst Gottlob Monse, 1829.

Gaedeke, Arnold. *Wallenstein's Verhandlungen mit den Schweden und Sachsen, 1631–1634.* Frankfurt: Rütten & Loening, 1885.

Galletti, Johann Georg August. *Geschichte des dreyßigjährigen Krieges und des westphälischen Friedens.* 2 vols. Halle: J. J. Gebauer, 1791.

Gerloff, G. F. *Vortrag auf dem Rathause der Stadt Magdeburg an 10. Mai 1831 den zweihundertjährigen Gedächtnißtage ihrer Zerstörung durch Tilly.* Magdeburg: Creutz, 1831.

Gfrörer, August Friedrich. *Gustav Adolph, König von Schweden, und seine Zeit.* 3d ed. Stuttgart: A. Krabbe, 1852.

Gindely, Anton. *Geschichte des Dreißigjährigen Krieges.* 4 vols. Prague: F. Tempsky, 1879–80.

———. *Geschichte des dreißigjährigen Krieges.* 3 vols. Leipzig: G. Freytag, 1882–84.

———. *History of the Thirty Years' War.* 2 vols. Translated by Andrew Ten Brook. New York: G. P. Putnam & Sons, 1883.

———. *Waldstein während seines ersten Generalats im Lichte der gleichzeitigen Quellen, 1625–1630.* Prague and Leipzig: F. Tempsky, 1886.

———. *Zur Beurtheilung des kaiserlichen Generals im 30-jährigen Kriege, Albrechts von Waldstein, oder Gegen die Waldsteinbewunderer: Zweite Antwort an Dr. Hallwich.* Prague and Leipzig: F. Tempksy, 1887.

Grimmelshausen, Hans Jacob Christoffel von. *Der Abentheurliche Simplicissimus Teutsch* [1669]. Vol. 1 of *Werke,* ed. Dieter Breuer. Frankfurt: Deutscher Klassiker Verlag, 1989.

Großmann, J. W. *Die Belagerung der Stadt Hanau und deren Befreiung an 13. Junius 1636: Ein vaterländisches Schauspiel in fünf Aufzügen.* Deutsche Schaubühne, oder dramatische Bibliothek der neuesten Lust-Schau-Sing-und Trauerspiele, vol. 16. Augsburg and Leipzig: n.p., 1816.

Grün, Karl. *Friedrich Schiller als Mensch, Geschichtsschreiber, Denker, und Dichter.* Leipzig: F. A. Brockhaus, 1844.

Guericke, Otto von. *Geschichte der Belagerung, Eroberung, und Zerstörung Magdeburgs.* Edited by Friedrich W. Hoffmann. Magdeburg: Emil Baensch, 1860.

Gundling, Nicolai H. *Gründlicher Discours über den Westphälischen Frieden.* Frankfurt and Leipzig: Wolfgang Ludwig Spring, 1736.

"Gustav Adolf und der Brand Magdeburg." *Die Grenzboten* 39, no. 12 (March 18, 1880): 497–506.

"Gustav Adolf und Kurfürst Georg Wilhelm." *Historisch-politische Blätter für das katholische Deutschland* 1 (Munich, 1838): 80–89.

Haag, Hermann. "Tilly." *Jahrbuch der Militärischen Gesellschaft München* (1875/76): 145–66.

Hallwich, Hermann. "Zur Geschichte Wallensteins im Jahre 1633." *Archiv für die sächsische Geschichte* n.s., 3, no. 1 (Leipzig, 1876): 289–311, 339–49.

———. *Über Wallenstein's Verrath.* Prague, Leipzig, and Vienna: F. Tempsky & F. A. Brockhaus, 1879.

———. *Wallenstein und Arnim im Frühjahre 1632.* Prague: F. Tempsky, 1879.

———. *Wallenstein's Ende: Ungedrückte Briefe und Akten.* 2 vols. Leipzig: Duncker & Humblot, 1879.

————, ed. *Heinrich Matthias Thurn als Zeuge im Prozess Wallenstein: Ein Denkblatt zur Dritten Säcularfeier Wallenstein's.* Leipzig: Duncker & Humblot, 1883.

————. "Gindely's 'Waldstein.'" *Mittheilungen des Vereins für Geschichte der Deutschen in Böhmen* 25, no. 2 (Prague and Leipzig, 1886–87): 98–133.

————. *Wallenstein und Waldstein: Ein offener Brief an Dr. Gindely.* Leipzig: Duncker & Humblot, 1887.

Harte, Walter. *Das Leben Gustav Adolphs der Grossen, Königs von Schweden.* Translated by Georg Heinrich Martini. Leipzig: J. G. Dyck, 1760.

————. *The History of the Life of Gustavus Adolphus, King of Sweden.* 2d ed. London: J. Hinton and R. Baldwin, 1767.

Hartmann, C. H. F. *Der Schwedenstein: Die Zweite Säcularfeier der Schlacht bei Lützen am 6. November 1632 in allen ihren An-und Nachklängen: Ein Denkmal für Gustav Adolph, den Retter Deutschlands von geistlichen und weltlichem Sclavenjoche.* Leipzig: C. H. F. Hartmann, 1833.

Haselbach, Karl. *Die Politik der "Union" gegenüber dem Hause Habsburg.* Krems: M. Pammer, 1862.

Hassel, Johann Paul. "Die Absetzung der Herzoge von Mecklenburg und die Einsetzung Wallensteins zum Fürsten des Landes: Ein Beitrag zur Politik des Hauses Habsburg im Dreißigjährigen Kriege." *Historisches Taschenbuch*, 4th ser., 8 (Leipzig, 1867): 3–85.

————. "Zur Geschichte Gustav Adolf." *Zeitschrift für Preußische Geschichte und Landeskunde* 6 (1869): 370–79.

Hecht, Heinrich August. *Der dreißigjährige Krieg und der westphälischen Friede.* Altenburg: Julius Helbig, 1848.

"Heinrich W. Bensen's Der Verhängniß Magdeburgs." *Historische Zeitschrift* 2 (1859): 521–29.

Heising, Albert. "Brand Magdeburgs im Jahre 1631." *Historisch-politische Blätter für das katholische Deutschland* 3 (1839): 43–51.

————. *Magdeburg nicht durch Tilly zerstört: Gustav Adolph in Deutschland: Zwei historische Abhändlungen.* Berlin: Eyßenhardt, 1846.

————. *Magdeburg nicht durch Tilly zerstört: Die Politik Gustav Adolph's in Deutschland.* 2d ed. Berlin: Schneider, 1854.

————. *Notwendigkeit und Geist einer katholischen Universal-Encyklopädie.* Regensburg: G. Joseph Manz, 1857.

Helbig, Karl Gustav. *Wallenstein und Arnim, 1632–1634: Ein Beitrag zur Geschichte des dreißigjährigen Kriegs.* Dresden: Adler & Dietze, 1850.

————. *Der Kaiser Ferdinand und der Herzog von Friedland während des Winters 1633–34.* Dresden: Adler & Dietze, 1852.

————. "Über das historische in Schillers Wallenstein." *Morgenblatt für gebildete Leser*, July 25, August 1, 1852.

————. "Die Resultate der neuesten Forschungen über Wallensteins Verrath." *Allgemeine Monatsschrift für Wissenschaft und Literatur* (Braunschweig, September 1853): 715–25.

————. "Herr Hofrath v. Hurter als Historiker." *Historische Zeitschrift* 4 (1860): 174–83.

————. "Stimmungen in Deutschland vor Gustav Adolf's Landung." *Die Grenzboten* 24, no. 2 (Leipzig, 1865): 173–79.

————. "Leopold von Rankes Geschichte Wallensteins." *Historische Zeitschrift* 22 (1869): 195–202.

Held, Hans. *Wallensteins Katastrophe nach den neuesten Publikationen: Beilage zum Programm der Realschule bei St. Johann zu Straßburg.* Strasbourg: G. Fischbach, 1884.

Helwing, Ernst. *Geschichte des Brandenburgisch-Preußischen Staats während des dreißigjährigen Krieges und im Zeitalter des großen Kurfürsten.* Lemgo and Detmold: Meyer'sche Hof-Buchhandlung, 1846.

Herchenhahn, Johann Christian. *Geschichte Albrechts von Wallenstein, des Friedländers.* 2 vols. Altenburg: n.p., 1790.

Hess, Johann Eduard. *Biographien und Autographen zu Schiller's Wallenstein.* Jena: F. Mauke, 1859.

Hildebrand, Emil, ed. *Wallenstein und seine Verbindungen mit den Schweden.* Frankfurt: Rütten & Loening, 1885.

Hinrichs, Hermann F. W. *Schiller's Dichtungen nach ihren historischen Beziehungen und nach ihren inneren Zusammenhänge.* Vols. 1 and 2. Leipzig: J. C. Hinrichs, 1837–39.

Hintze, Otto. *Die Hohenzollern und ihr Werk: Fünfhundert Jahre vaterländische Geschichte.* Berlin: P. Parey, 1915.

————. "Deutschland und das Weltenstaatensystem." In *Deutschland und der Weltkrieg,* 2d ed., ed. Otto Hintze et al., 3–52. Leipzig and Berlin: B. G. Teubner, 1916.

Historisches Festspiel mit historischen Festzug: Pfingstmontag den 29. Mai und Kirchweihmontag den 12. Juni 1882. Rothenburg ob der Tauber: n.p., 1882.

Hitler, Adolf. *Hitler: Reden und Proklamationen, 1932–1945,* vol. 1, *Triumph (1932–1938).* Edited by Max Domarus. Neustadt: Verlagsdruckerei Schmidt, 1962.

————. *Hitler: Reden und Proklamationen, 1932–1945,* vol. 2, *Untergang (1939–1945).* Edited by Max Domarus. Neustadt: Verlagsdruckerei Schmidt, 1963.

————. *Mein Kampf.* Translated by Ralph Mannheim. Boston: Houghton Mifflin, 1971.

Hoffmann, Friedrich Wilhelm. *Geschichte der Stadt Magdeburg.* Magdeburg: A. Rathke, 1850.

Hoffmeister, Hermann. *Gustav Adolf der Retter deutscher Glaubensfreiheit.* Berlin: n.p., 1870.

Hoffmeister, Karl. *Schiller's Leben: Geistesentwicklung und Werke in Zusammenhänge.* Vol. 2. Stuttgart: P. Balz, 1838–42.

Holl, Karl. *Die Bedeutung der großen Kriege für das religiöse und kirchliche Leben innerhalb des deutsche Protestantismus.* Tübingen: J. C. B. Mohr, 1917.

——. *The Cultural Significance of the Reformation* [1911]. Translated by Karl and Barbara Hertz and John H. Lichtblau. New York: Meridian Books, 1959.

Hörber, A. *Der Meistertrank oder Tilly in Rothenburg: Schauspiel in 2 Aufzügen.* Rothenburg ob der Tauber: F. W. Klein, 1899.

Hormayr, Joseph. "Die Schweden vor Brünn 1645." *Archiv für Geographie, Historie, Staats- und Kriegskunst,* January 3, 12, 26, February 9, 14, 1816.

——. "Versuch Albrecht's von Waldstein, eine Ständische Verfassung in seinem Herzogthume Friedland einzuführen." *Taschenbuch für vaterländische Geschichten* n.s., 1 (1830): 29–45.

Huch, Ricarda. *Der große Krieg in Deutschland.* Leipzig: Insel-Verlag, 1912.

——. *Wallenstein: Eine Charakterstudie.* Leipzig: Insel, 1920.

Hüllmann, K. D. "Gustav Adolf in Beziehung auf die evangelischen Fürsten Deutschlands." *Zeitschrift für Geschichtswissenschaft* 1 (1844): 283–88.

Hülße, Friedrich. "Historische Tradition der Katastrophe der Stadt Magdeburg in Jahre 1631." *Jahrbuch des Pädagogiums zum Kloster Unser Lieben Frauen* 41 (Magdeburg, 1877): 1–36.

Hundeshagen, Bernhard. *Die Belagerung und Entfetzung der Stadt Hanau im dreißigjährigen Kriege: in Beitrag zur Geschichte jener Zeiten, nebst einer Schilderung des Jahrfestes dieser Begebenheiten von 13ten Juni 1811.* Hanau: n.p., 1812.

Hungerkhausen, Heinrich von. *Epaminondas und Gustav Adolph: Eine Parallele.* Munich: Gedruckt mit Zängl'schen Schriften, 1813.

Hurter, Friedrich von. *Geschichte Kaiser Ferdinands II. und seiner Eltern bis zu dessen Krönung in Frankfurt: Personen-Haus- und Landesgeschichte.* 11 vols. Schaffhausen: Fr. Hurter'sche Buchhandlung, 1850–64.

——. *Zur Geschichte Wallensteins.* Schaffhausen: Fr. Hurter'sche Buchhandlung, 1855.

——. *Wallensteins vier letzte Lebensjahre.* Vienna: Wilhelm Braumueller, 1862.

Irmer, Georg. *Die Verhandlungen Schwedens und seiner Verbündeten mit Wallenstein und den Kaiser von 1631 bis 1634,* pt. 1, *1631 und 1632.* Leipzig: S. Hirzl, 1888.

Jahn, Carl Johann. *Ueber den Tod Gustav Adolph's, Königs in Schweden.* Weissenfels: J. F. Leyckham, 1806.

Janssen, Johannes. *Frankreich's Rheingelüste und deutsch-feindliche Politik in früheren Jahrhunderten.* 2d ed. Freiburg im Breisgau: Herder'sche Verlagshandlung, 1863.

Bibliography

———. *Schiller als Historiker.* Freiburg im Breisgau: Herder'sche Verlagshandlung, 1863.

———. *Gustav Adolf in Deutschland.* Katholischer Broschüren-Verein 1, no. 8. Frankfurt: G. Hamacher, 1865.

Kaemmel, Otto. "Wallenstein's Ausgang." *Die Grenzboten* 37, no. 2 (Leipzig, 1878): 6–18.

Kelteger, K. A. *Bermerkungen über die baierischen Geschichten.* Rauschenberg: n.p., 1818.

Keller, E. F. *Die Drangsale des nassauischen Volkes und der angrenzenden Nachbarländer in den Zeiten des dreißigjährigen Krieges, seine Helden, Staatsmänner, und andere berühmte Zeitgenossen.* Gotha: F. A. Perthes, 1854.

Keym, Franz. *Geschichte des Dreißigjährigen Krieges.* 2 vols. Freiburg im Breisgau: Herder'sche Verlagshandlung, 1873.

Klimesch, Philipp, ed. "Zacharias Bandhauer's deutsches Tagebuch der Zerstörung Magdeburgs 1631." *Archives für die Kunde österreichischer Geschichtsquellen* 14 (1855): 239–319.

Klopp, Onno. *Studien über Katholizismus, Protestantismus, und Gewissensfreiheit in Deutschland.* Schaffhausen: Fr. Hurter'sche Buchhandlung, 1857.

———. *Der König Friedrich II. von Preußen und die deutsche Nation.* Schaffhausen: Fr. Hurter'sche Buchhandlung, 1860.

———. "Magdeburg, Tilly, und Gustav Adolf." *Historisch-politische Blätter für das katholische Deutschlands* 46 (1860): 845–78, 913–42; 47 (1861): 72–118, 193–212, 245–69.

———. *Tilly im dreißigjährigen Kriege.* 2 vols. Stuttgart: J. G. Cotta'scher, 1861.

———. "Das Restitutions-Edikt im nordwestlichen Deutschland." *Forschungen zur Deutschen Geschichte* 1 (1862): 75–128.

———. *Die gothaische Auffassung der deutschen Geschichte und der Nationalverein.* Hanover: F. Klindworth, 1862.

———. *Kleindeutsche Geschichtsbaumeister.* Freiburg im Breisgau: Herder'sche Verlagshandlung, 1863.

———. *Wer ist der wahre Erbfeind von Deutschland?* Munich: J. G. Weiss, 1868.

———. *Die Katastrophe von Magdeburg 1631: Auszug aus dem Tagebuch von Zacharias Bandhauer mit einer kritisch-historischen Uebersicht.* Freiburg im Breisgau: Herder'sche Verlagshandlung, 1874.

———. *Der dreißigjährigen Krieg bis zum Tode Gustav Adolfs 1632.* 4 vols. Paderborn: F. Schöningh, 1891–96.

———. *Tilly, Gustav Adolf, und die Zerstörung von Magdeburg.* Katholische Flugschriften zur Wehr und Lehr, no. 94. Berlin: Germania, 1895.

———. *Deutschland und die Habsburger.* Edited by Leo König. Graz and Vienna: Verlags-Buchhandlung Styria, 1908.

Kohlmeyer, Ernst. *Gustav Adolf und Deutschland*. Bonn: Bonner Universitäts-Buchdruckerei, 1940.

Koller, Polykarp. *Die Belagerung von Brünn durch die Schweden im Jahre 1645: Das denkwürdigste Jahr aus Brünns Vorzeit: Ein historischer Versuch*. Brünn: R. Rohrer, 1845.

Komareck, Johann Nepomuk. *Albrecht Waldstein, Herzog von Friedland: Ein Trauerspiel in fünf Akten*. Leipzig: K. F. Kohler, 1793.

Köthe, Friedrich August. "Das Jahr 1616 oder die Lage Europa's vor dem Beginn des dreißigjährigen Krieges." *Köthe's Historisches Taschenbuch auf das Jahr 1817* (Leipzig, 1817): 10–15.

Krabbe, Otto. *Zur Geschichte Wallensteins und des dreißigjährigen Krieges: Aus dem kirchlichen und wissenschaftlichen Leben Rostocks*. Berlin: G. Schlawitz, 1863.

Krebs, Julius. *Christian von Anhalt und die Kurpfälzische Politik am Beginn des Dreißigjährigen Krieges (23. Mai–3. October 1618)*. Leipzig: Bär & Hermann, 1872.

———. *Hans Ulrich Freiherr von Schaffgotsch*. Breslau: W. G. Korn, 1890.

Krombholz, Anton. *Die Stiftung des Böhmisch-Leipper Gymnasiums durch Albrecht von Waldstein, Herzog von Friedland*. Leitmeritz: n.p., 1834.

Krönlein, J. H. *Wallenstein und seine neuesten historischen Ankläger und Vertheidiger*. Leipzig: O. Wigand, 1845.

Kugler, Bernhard. *Wallenstein*. Berlin: Lüderitz, 1873.

Kuhn, Adalbert. *Schiller's Geistiger Entwicklung*. 3d ed. Berlin: E. Schweigger, 1867.

Kutscheit, Johann Valerius. *Herr Albert Heising für Tilly und gegen Gustav Adolph, oder wie die ehrlichen Deutschen mit Ruthen gestrichen werden wegen bisher geübter lügnerischer Geschichtschreibung*. Magdeburg: Creutz, 1847.

Kutschmann, Theodor. *Rothenburg ob der Tauber und sein Historisches Festspiel*. Rothenburg ob der Tauber: F. W. Klein, 1881.

Landau, Georg. "Dietrich von Falkenburg, Schwedischer Commandant von Magdeburg." *Allgemeines Archiv für die Geschichtskunde des Preußischen Staates* 15 (1834): 177–80.

La-Roche, Carl du Jarrys. *Der dreißigjährigen Krieg, vom militärischen Standpunkte beleuchtet*. Schaffhausen: Fr. Hurter'sche Buchhandlung, 1848–52.

L.C. "Wallensteins Revolte und Tod; nach der Handschrift eines seiner Zeitgenossen. Bruchstück aus dem Tagebuch eines Reisenden." *Minerva* 4 (October–December 1811): 100–125.

Lempens, Carl. *Pragmatische Geschichte des Dreißigjährigen Krieges, beleuchtung der großartigen Geschichtsfälschung, verlangung der Nationallehre und Verherrlichung des Vaterlandverrats, welche bezüglich dieses Krieges nach heute in Schule und Literatur gefunden wird*. Zurich: Frick-Vogel, 1881.

Lentz, Carl Georg. *Geschichte des dreißigjährigen Glaubenskrieges in Deutschland: Erzählt zum Verstandnisse der Gegenwart.* Quedlinburg and Leipzig: Gottfried Basse, 1853.

Lenz, Max. "Zur Kritik Sezyma Rascins." *Historische Zeitschrift* 59, no. 1 (1888): 1–68; 59, no. 3 (1888): 385–480.

Letzte Belagerung und jämmerliche Erober- und Zerstörung der alten Stadt Magdeburg. Magdeburg: n.p., 1719.

Lichtenstein, G. *Die Schlacht bei Lutter am Barenberge.* Braunschweig: Oehme & Müller, 1850.

Lisch, G. C. F. "Plau während des dreißigjährigen Krieges." *Jahrbücher des Vereins für meklenburgische Geschichte und Altherthumskunde* 17 (Schwerin, 1852): 196–226.

———. "Wallensteins Abzug aus Meklenburg im Jahre 1629." *Jahrbücher des Vereins für meklenburgische Geschichte und Altherthumskunde* 25 (1870): 45–59.

———. "Wallensteins Armenversorgungs-Ordnung für Meklenburg." *Jahrbücher des Vereins für meklenburgische Geschichte und Altherthumskunde* 25 (1870): 80–92.

———. "Ueber Wallensteins Regierungsform in Meklenburg." *Jahrbücher des Vereins für meklenburgische Geschichte und Altherthumskunde* 27 (1871): 3–31.

Lorenz, Ottokar. *Oesterreich's Stellung in Deutschland während der ersten Hälfte des dreißigjährigen Krieges.* Vienna: C. G. Gerold's Sohn, 1858.

———. "Zur Wallenstein-Literatur." *Historische Zeitschrift* n.s., 3 (1878): 22–45.

———. *Leopold von Ranke: Die Generationlehre und der Geschichtsunterricht.* Berlin: W. Hertz, 1891.

"Die Lösung der Wallensteinfrage." *Die Grenzboten* 40, no. 35 (August 25, 1881): 357–72.

Mailath, Johann Grafen. *Geschichte des österreichischen Kaiserstaates.* Vol. 3. Hamburg: F. Perthes, 1842.

Mann, Karl Kristian von. *Kaiser Ludwig IV., genannt der Baier, und Maximilian I. Kurfurst von Baiern, eine historische Parallele.* Munich: J. Lindauer, 1806.

Marcour, Eduard. "Wer hat Magdeburg zerstört?" *Frankfurter zeitgemäße Broschüren* n.s., 10, no. 1 (Frankfurt, 1884–85): 249–82.

Mauritius, Franz. *Gustav Adolf, König von Schweden: Ein Lebensbild.* Unterhaltende Belehrungen zur Förderung allgemeiner Bildung, no. 26. Leipzig: F. A. Brockhaus, 1856.

Mayer, Friedrich Anton. "Ein kleiner Beitrag zur Geschichte des dreißigjährigen Krieges aus einem Manuscripte des Klosters Plankstetten." *Jahresbericht des historischen Vereins in Mittelfranken* 18 (Ansbach, 1849): 97–99.

Mebold, Carl August. *Der dreißigjährigen Krieg, und die Helden desselben: Gustav Adolf, König von Schweden, und Wallenstein, Herzog von Friedland.* Vol. 2. Stuttgart: Comptoir, 1840.

Meinecke, Friedrich. "Kultur, Machtpolitik, und Militarismus." In *Deutschland and der Weltkrieg*, 2d ed., ed. Otto Hintze et al., 750–76. Leipzig and Berlin: B. G. Teubner, 1916.

Menzel, Karl Adolf. *Neuere Geschichte der Deutschen von der Reformation bis zu Bundes-Acte.* Vols. 5–7. Breslau: Grass, Barth, 1833, 1837.

———. *Geschichte des dreißigjährigen Krieges in Deutschland.* 3 vols. Breslau: Grass, Barth, 1835–39.

Menzel, Wolfgang. *Deutschlands auswärtige Politik.* Stuttgart and Tübingen: J. G. Cotta, 1848.

———. *Die Aufgabe Preußens.* Stuttgart: J. B. Metzler, 1854.

———. *Was hat Preußen für Deutschland geleistet?* Stuttgart: A. Kröner, 1870.

———. *Wolfgang Menzel's Denkwürdigkeiten.* Edited by Konrad Menzel. Bielefeld and Leipzig: Velhagen & Klasing, 1877.

Mohnike, Gottlieb. "Gustav Adolph, gezeichnet von Erich Gustav Geijer." *Zeitschrift für die historische Theologie* 3 (1844): 59–61.

Moser, Friedrich Salamo. *Gustav Adolph und die dankbare Nachwelt.* Zwickau: n.p., 1844.

Mühlbach, Luise. *Die Opfer des religiösen Fanatismus: Historischer Roman aus dem dreißigjährigen Krieg.* 3 vols. Prague: Sigmund Bensinger, 1871–72.

Müller, Karl August. *Fünf Bücher vom Böhmischen Krieg in den Jahren 1618 bis 1621.* Vol. 3 of *Forschungen auf dem Gebiete der neueren Geschichte.* Dresden and Leipzig: G. Fleischer, 1841.

Munch, Ernst. "Die Schlacht bei Wimpen, 1622." In *Erinnerungen an die Schlacht bei Wimpfen und den Tod der vierhundert Pforzheimer*, ed. C. B. Sommerlatt, 1–16. Freiburg im Breisgau: F. X. Wangler, 1824.

———. *Pantheon der Geschichte des Teutschen Volkes.* 2 vols. Freiburg am Breisgau: F. X. Wangler, 1825–33.

Murr, Christoph Gottlieb. *Die Ermordung Albrechts, Herzogs von Friedland.* Halle: Hendel, 1806.

Mussinan, Joseph von. *Ueber das Schicksal Straubings und des baierischen Waldes während des dreyßigjährigen Krieges vom Oktober 1633 bis April 1634.* Straubing: F. S. Lerno, 1813.

———. *Befestigung und Belagerung der baierischen Haupt-Stadt Straubing in den Jahren 1633, 1704, und 1742.* Straubing: F. S. Lerno, 1816.

———. *Geschichte der französischen Kriege in Deutschland, besonderes auf baierischen Boden.* 4 vols. Sulzbach: J. E. Seidel, 1822–29.

Nemethy, Franz. *Das Schloß Friedland in Böhmen und die Monumente in der Friedländer Stadtkirchen.* Prague: n.p., 1818.

Neubur, Georg Philipp Anton. *Beytrag zu der Geschichte des dreißigjährigen Krieges.* Leipzig and Stralsund: n.p., 1772.

Opel, Julius Otto. *Onno Klopp und die Geschichte des dreißigjährigen Krieges*. Halle: Verlag der Buchhandlung des Waisenhauses, 1862.

———. "Einige Notizen Eroberung Magdeburgs durch Tilly." *Neue Mittheilungen aus dem Gebiet historisch-antiquarischer Forschungen* 11 (Halle and Nordhausen, 1867): 175–81.

———. *Der niedersächsisch-dänische Kriege*. Halle: Verlag der Buchhandlung des Waisenhauses, 1872–94.

———. *Eine Flugschrift über die Zerstörung Magdeburgs*. Halle: n.p., 1874.

———. *Zur Erinnerungen an Gustav Adolf*. Flugschriften des Evangelischen Bundes, 98/99, series 9, 2/3. Leipzig: T. O. Weigel, 1894.

Ortlepp, Ernst. *Gustav Adolph: Eine lyrische Phantasie zu dem zweihundertjährigen Jubiläum der Breitenfelder-Leipziger Schlacht am 7ten 1631*. Leipzig: Wilhelm Zirges, 1831.

Palacky, Franz. "Jugendgeschichte Albrechts von Waldstein, Herzog von Friedland." *Jahrbücher des böhmischen Museums für Natur- und Ländeskunde, Geschichte, Kunst, und Literatur* 1, no. 2 (Prague, 1831): 78–89.

Palleske, Emil. *Schiller's Life and Works*. Translated by Grace Wallace. London: Longman, Green, Longman and Roberts, 1860.

Pfister, J. C. *Geschichte der Teutschen*. Vol. 4. Hamburg: F. Perthes, 1829–33.

Philippson, Martin. *Wallenstein*. Neue Volks-Bibliothek, series 2, nos. 11–12. Stuttgart: Levy & Müller, 1876.

Pichler, Caroline. *Ferdinand der Zweyte, König von Ungarn und Böhmen: Ein historisches Schauspiel in fünf Aufzügen*. Leipzig: Gerhard Fleischer, 1817.

———. *Die Schweden in Prag*. Vienna: August Liebstind, 1827.

Pierson, William. *Preußische Geschichte*. Vol. 1. 7th ed. Berlin: Gebrüder Paetel, 1878.

Posselt, Ludwig. "Dem Vaterlandstod der vierhundert Bürger von Pforzheim: Eine Rede, gehalten den 29. Januar 1788." In *Erinnerungen an die Schlacht bei Wimpfen und den Tod der vierhundert Pforzheimer*, ed. C. B. Sommerlatt, 17–36. Freiburg im Breisgau: F. X. Wangler, 1824.

Preuß, Johann. "Friedrichs des Großen Wohlgefallen an Gustav Adolph." *Zeitschrift für Preußische Geschichte und Landeskunde* 5 (1868): 209–16.

Prökl, Vinzenz. *Waldstein, Herzogs von Friedland letzte Lebensjahre und Tod in Eger*. Falkenau an den Eger: Müller & Weiser, 1879.

Pufendorf, Samuel. *Commentariorum de rebus Suecicis; libri xxvi ab expeditione Gustavi Adolfi regis in Germanium ab abdicationem usque Christinae*. Ultrajecta: Apud Johannem Ribbium, 1686.

Pütter, Johann Stephen. *Geist des Westphälischen Friedens nach dem innern Gehalte und währen Zusammenhänge die darin verhandelten Gegenstände historisch und systematisch dargestellt*. Göttingen: Wittwe Vandenhoeck, 1795.

Rabenalt, Carl Theodor. *Die Schweden vor Villingen im Jahre 1634: Ein romantisches Schauspiel in 4 Aufzügen.* Deutsche Schaubühne; oder dramatische Bibliothek der neuesten Lust-Schau-Sing-und Trauerspeile, no. 16. Augsburg and Leipzig: n.p., 1816.

Rammelt, Johannes. *Die Frage nach dem Urheber der Zerstörung Magdeburgs.* Halle: E. Karras, 1897.

———. *Wer hat Magdeburg Zerstört? (1631).* Wittenberg: Wattrodt, 1910.

Rango, Friedrich Ludwig von. *Denkmal der verhängnißvollen Jahre 1813 und 1814 jedem deutschen Biedermann gewidmet: Ein Taschenbuch, zum besten der im heiligen Freiheitskampf verstummelten Königl. Preuß. Krieger.* Berlin: n.p., 1815.

———. *Gustav Adolph der Große König von Schweden: Ein historisches Gemälde.* Leipzig: C. H. F. Hartmann, 1824.

Ranke, Leopold von. *Geschichte Wallensteins.* Leipzig: Duncker & Humblot, 1869.

Rathmann, Heinrich. *Der zehnte Mai 1631: Ein Fragment aus der Geschichte Magdeburgs.* Magdeburg: Creutz, 1831.

Raumer, Friedrich von. *Geschichte Deutschlands von der Abdankung Karls V bis zum westphälischen Frieden.* 3 vols. Leipzig: F. A. Brockhaus, 1831–32.

———. *Friedrich von Raumer an Rudolf Kopke: Ein historisch-politischer Brief.* Berlin: E. S. Mittler & Sohn, 1866.

Ravensberg, Otto von [Otto Jacobi]. *Gustav Adolph und Wallenstein: Tragödie in fünf Akten.* Berlin: Georg Reimer, 1840.

Rebmann, Andreas Georg Friedrich. *Albrecht der Friedländer, Hochverräther durch Cabale: Halb Geschichte einer mißlungenen Revolution des siebzehnden Jahrhunderts, halb Roman.* Leipzig: Wilhelm Heinsius, 1794.

———. *Werke und Briefe.* Vols. 1 and 3. Edited by Wolfgang Ritschel. Berlin: Rütten & Leoning, 1990.

Rehlen, Karl. *Zur Säkularfeier der Schlacht bie Nördlingen (am 27 August 1834).* Nördlingen: n.p., 1841.

Reichard, Konrad. *Die maritime Politik der Habsburger im siebzehnten Jahrhundert.* Berlin: W. Hertz, 1867.

Reithofer, Franz. *Denkwürdige Geschichte der Stadt Landshut in Baiern im dreyßigjährigen Kriege.* Landshut in Baiern: n.p., 1810.

Rese, Johann Karl August. *Die Zerstörung Magdeburgs durch Tilly: Ein streng historisches Gemählde.* Magdeburg: W. Heinrichshofen, 1809.

Richter, Friedrich. *Magdeburg, die wieder empor-gerichtete Stadt Gottes auf Erben: Denkschrift zur zweiten Säcularfeier der Zerstörung Magdeburgs.* Zerbst: G. A. Kummer, 1831.

Richter, Johann Wilhelm Daniel. *Geschichte des dreißigjährigen Krieges.* 5 vols. Leipzig and Erfurt: A. F. Böhme, 1840–59.

Ritter, Moriz. *Geschichte der deutschen Union von den Vorbereitungen des Bundes bis zum Tode Kaiser Rudolphs II.* Schaffhausen: Fr. Hurter'sche Buchhandlung, 1867.

———. *Deutsche Geschichte im Zeitalter der Gegenreformation und des Dreißigjährigen Krieges.* Stuttgart: J. G. Cotta, 1889–1908.

Rochau, Ludwig August von. *Grundsätze der Realpolitik.* Edited by Hans-Ulrich Wehler. Stuttgart, 1853; reprint, Frankfurt: Ullstein, 1972.

Roder, Christian. *Beiträge zur Geschichte der Stadt Villingen während des dreißigjährigen Krieges.* Tübingen: H. Lang'sche Buchdruckerei, 1880.

Roepell, Richard. *De Alberto Waldsteino, Friedlandiae duce Proditore.* Halle: C. Grunert, 1834.

———. "Der Verrath Wallenstein's an Kaiser Ferdinand II." *Historische Taschenbuch* n.s., 6 (Leipzig, 1845): 239–306.

Rönnefahrt, J. G. *Schillers dramatische Gedicht Wallenstein aus seinem Inhalt erklärt.* 2d. ed. Leipzig: Byk'sche Buchhandlung, 1886.

Rotteck, Karl von, and Karl Welcker, eds. *Der Staats-Lexikon: Encyclopädie der sämtlichen Staatswissenschaften für alle Stände.* 3d ed. Leipzig: F. A. Brockhaus, 1862. S.v. "Gustav II. Adolf," by Karl Biedermann.

Rüdel, Konrad. *Der Westphälische Friede: Eine Festgabe zur zweiten Säkularfeier desselben für das deutsche Volk evangelischen Bekenntnißes.* Nuremberg: J. P. Raw, 1848.

———. *Die würdige Gedächtnißfeier der Reformation und des Westphälischen Friedens.* Nuremberg: J. P. Raw, 1848.

Rudhart, Georg Thomas. *Einige Wort über Wallensteins Schuld.* Munich: J. G. Weiss, 1850.

Rühs, Christoph Friedrich. Vol. 4. *Geschichte Schwedens.* Halle: J. J. Gebauer, 1810.

Rummel, Carl Johannes. *Kaiser, Gott, und Reich.* Berlin: Vier Falken, 1941.

Schaching, Otto von. *Maximilian I., der Große, Kurfürst von Bayern.* Freiburg im Breisgau: Herder'sche, 1876.

Scharold, Carl Gottfried. "Zur Geschichte des 30jährigen Kriegs in Beziehung auf das Hochstift Würzburg." *Archiv des historischen Vereins für den Untermainkreis* 1, no. 2 (Würzburg, 1833): 107–23.

———. *Geschichte der kön. schwedischen und herzogl. sachsen-weimarischen Zwischenregierung in eroberten Fürstbisthume Würzburg i. J. 1631–1645.* Würzburg: Vogt & Mocker, 1844–45.

Schebek, Edmund. *Die Lösung der Wallensteinfrage.* Berlin: T. Hoffmann, 1881.

———. *Kinsky und Feuquières: Nachtrag zur "Lösung der Wallensteinfrage."* Berlin: T. Hoffmann, 1882.

Scheler, Max. *Krieg und Aufbau.* Leipzig: Verlag der Weissen Bücher, 1916.

———. "Der Genius des Krieges und der Deutschen Krieg [1916]." In *Politisch-Pädigogische Schriften*, ed. Manfred S. Frings, 141. Bern and Munich: Francke, 1982.

Scherer, Wilhelm. *A History of German Literature* [1885]. 3d ed. Translated by F. C. Conybeare. New York: C. Scribner's Sons, 1899.

Scherr, Johannes. *Schiller and His Times* [1859]. Translated by Elisabeth McClellan. Philadelphia: I. Kohler, 1880.

Schiller, Friedrich. *Die Räuber*. 2d ed. Frankfurt and Mannheim: Tobias Löffler, 1782.

———. *Don Karlos, Infant von Spanien*. Leipzig: Göschen, 1787.

———. *Geschichte des Abfalls der vereinigten Niederlande von der spanischer Regierung*. Leipzig: Siegfried Lebrecht Crusius, 1788.

———. *Geschichte des Dreißigjährigen Krieges*. Leipzig, 1791–93; reprint, Zurich: Manesse, 1985.

———. *Correspondence of Schiller with Körner*. 3 vols. Edited and translated by Leonard Simpson. London: R. Bentley, 1849.

———. *Sämtliche Werke. Dramen I*, vol. 1, *Wallenstein: Ein dramatisches Gedicht [1798–99]*, ed. Jost Perfahl. Munich: Winkler, 1968.

———. "Was heißt und zu welchem Ende studiert man Universalgeschichte?" In *Sämtliche Werke*, vol. 4, *Historische Schriften*, ed. Jost Perfahl, 703–20. Munich: Winkler, 1968.

Die Schlacht bei Lützen, am 6. November 1632. Naumburg: K. A. Klassenbach, 1832.

Schmid, Georg. "Die Wallenstein Literatur." *Mittheilungen des Vereins für Geschichte der Deutschen in Böhmen* 17, no. 1 (1878): 68–137.

Schmidt, Friedrich Ludwig. *Der Sturm von Magdeburg: Ein väterlandisches Schauspiel in fünf Aufzügen*. Magdeburg: n.p., 1799.

Schmidt, Julian. "Schiller als Historiker." *Die Grenzboten* 18, no. 25 (June 17, 1859): 441–505.

———. *Schiller und seine Zeitgenossen*. Leipzig: F. W. Grunow, 1863.

Schmidt, Karl. *Geschichte des dreißigjährigen Krieges zur zweihundert Jubelfeier des westphälischen Friedens im Jahre 1648*. Jena: F. Fromann, 1848.

Schmidt, Michael Ignaz. *Neuere Geschichte der Deutschen*. Vols. 7 and 9. Frankenthal: L. B. F. Gegel, 1789, 1791.

Schmidt, Otto. *Geschichte des dreißigjährigen Krieges*. Weimar: Rauschke & Schmidt, 1853.

Schmidt, Richard. "Gustav Adolf: Die Bedeutung seiner Erscheinung für die europäische Politik und für den deutschen Volksgeist." *Zeitschrift für Politik* 22, no. 11 (February 1933): 701–19.

Schottky, Julius Max. *Ueber Wallensteins Privatleben*. Munich: G. Franz, 1832.

Schreckenstein, K. H. von. *Ein gleichzeitiger Bericht über das vom wirtembergischen Kriegsvolke am 15. Oktober 1632 in Hüsingen angerichtete Blutbad.* Freiburg im Breisgau: J. C. B. Mohr, 1867.

Schreiber, F. A. Wilhelm. *Maximilian I. der Katholische, Kurfürst von Bayern und der dreißigjährigen Krieg.* Munich: Flieschmann, 1868.

Schuegraf, Joseph R. "Auszüge aus der Geschichte des 30jährigen Krieges in baierischen Wald." *Eos. Zeitschrift aus Baiern* 57–59 (April 1825): 229–30, 233–34, 237–38.

———. *Belagerung, Eroberung, und Zerstörung der Veste Donaustauf durch die Schweden im Jahre 1634.* Regensburg: G. Joseph Manz, 1831.

Schummel, Johann Georg. *Die Eroberung von Magdeburg: Ein Schauspiel in fünf Aufzügen.* Theater der Deutschen, no. 15. Königsberg and Leipzig: Johann H. Rudiger, 1776.

Schwarzrock, Jeremias. *Frage: Hat Hr. Heinrich Zschokke eine Nationalgeschichte für Baiern schreiben können und Wollen.* Kautzopolis: n.p., 1818.

———. *Theses wider Herrn Heinrich Zschokke's baierischen Geschichten.* Aarau: n.p., 1818.

Die Schweden am Bodensee: Bilder aus dem dreißigjährigen Kriege. n.p.: author, n.d.

"Die Schweden in Hessen." *Historische-politische Blätter für das katholische Deutschland* 19 (1847): 513–21.

Skowronnek, Fritz. *Quellenkritische Beiträge zur Wallensteinfrage.* Königsberg: Kommissionsverlag von Th. Nürmberger's Buch-und Verlagshandlung, 1882.

Sobbe, Eugen von. *Die Erstürmung der Stadt Salzkotten am 22. Dezember 1633 durch die Schweden und Hessen.* Salzkotten: n.p., 1856.

Soden, Franz von. *Gustav Adolph und sein Heer in Süddeutschland von 1631 bis 1635: Zur Geschichte des dreißigjährigen Krieges.* Vol. 2, *Von Gustav Adolphs Tode bis zur Eroberung von Ungarn und Böhmen.* Erlangen: Deichert, 1867.

Söltl, Johann Michael von. *Der Religionskrieg in Deutschland.* 3 vols. Hamburg: J. A. Meissner, 1840–42.

———. "Kaiser Ferdinand II und sein Geschichtsschreiber Hurter." *Historische Zeitschrift* 4 (1860): 366–437; 5 (1861): 1–45.

Sommerlatt, C. B., ed. *Erinnerungen an die Schlacht bei Wimpfen und den Tod der vierhundert Pforzheimer.* Freiburg im Breisgau: F. X. Wangler, 1824.

Spanheim, Friedrich. *Le Soldat Suedois, ou Histoire véritable de ce qui s'est passé depuis l' avenue de roy de Suede en Allemagne jusques a sa mort.* Paris: Chez Olivier de Varennes, 1642.

Sporschil, Johann. *Wallenstein: Historischer Versuch.* Leipzig: J. F. Fischer, 1828.

———. *Der Dreißigjährige Krieg.* Braunschweig: G. Westermann, 1843.

Sterly, Andreas. *Drangsale der Stadt Iglau unter der schwedischen Zwingsherrschaft besonders während ihrer Belagerung im Jahre 1647*. Iglau: Babian Beynhauer, 1828.

Stieve, Felix. *Der Kampf um Donauwörth im Zusammenhänge der Reichsgeschichte*. Vol. 1, *Der Ursprung des dreißigjährigen Krieges, 1607–1619*. Munich: M. Rieger, 1875.

———. *Die Politik Baierns, 1591–1607*. Munich: M. Rieger, 1878.

———. *Churfürst Maximilian I. von Bayern*. Munich: Verlage der k. b. Akademie, 1882.

———. *Abhandlungen, Vorträge, und Reden*. Edited by Hans Zwiedineck-Südenhorst. Leipzig: Duncker & Humblot, 1900.

———. *Der oberösterreichische Bauernkrieg*. 2d ed. Linz: E. Maries, 1904.

———, ed. *Die Deutsche Kaisergedanke in Laufe der Jahrhunderte*. Munich: M. Rieger, 1915.

Stöckert, Georg. *Die Admission der deutschen Reichsstände zum westfälischen Friedenscongresse: Beitrag zur Geschichte des westfälischen Friedens*. Kiel: Schwers'sche Buchhandlung, 1869.

[Stülz, Jodok]. "Kaiser Ferdinand II. im Kampfe gegen die protestantischen Stände Oesterreichs." *Historisch-politische Blätter für das katholische Deutschland* 3 (1839): 673–83, 742–55; 4 (1839): 13–21, 168–77, 219–30, 593–605.

Stumpf, Andreas Sebastian. *Diplomatische Geschichte der teutschen Liga im siebzehnten Jahrhunderte*. Erfurt: Hoyer & Rudolphi, 1800.

Sutner, Georg Karl von. *München während des dreyßigjährigen Krieges*. Munich: Joseph Lindauer, 1796.

Teitge, Hans. *Frage nach dem Urheber der Zerstörung Magdeburgs*. Halle: M. Niemeyer, 1904.

Thiersch, Heinrich W. J. *Luther, Gustav Adolf, und Maximilian I. von Bayern: Biographische Skizzen*. Nördlingen: C. H. Beck, 1869.

Thomas, Georg M. *Hans Ulrich Schaff-gotsch*. Hirschberg: C. W. J. Krahn, 1820.

Tomaschek, Karl. *Schiller's Wallenstein: Ein Vortrag gehalten am 31. März 1858*. Vienna: C. G. Gerold's Sohn, 1858.

———. *Schiller in seinem Verhältniße zur Wissenschaft*. Vienna: C. G. Gerold's Sohn, 1862.

Trauttwein, G. *Der dreißigjährige Krieg und der westfälische Friede*. Berlin: Georg Reimer, 1866.

Treitschke, Heinrich von. *Heinrich von Treitschkes Briefe*. 3 vols. Edited by Max Cornicelius. Leipzig: S. Hirzl, 1920.

———. "Gustav Adolf und Deutschlands Freiheit [1894]." In *Historische und Politische Aufsätze*, 2d ed., 123–37. Leipzig: S. Hirzl, 1920.

Treumund, F. [Eduard Sparfeld]. *Gustav Adolf König von Schweden, der helden-müthige Kämpfer für Deutschlands Religionsfreiheit: Ein Volksbuch für alle Stände*. Leipzig: Freise, 1845.

Tritsch, Walther. *Wallenstein: Herr des Schicksal—Knechte der Sterne*. Leipzig: J. Kittl, 1936.

Twesten, Carl. *Schiller in seinem Verhältniß zur Wissenschaft*. Berlin: J. Gutenberg, 1863.

Unold, Jacob Friedrich. *Geschichte der Stadt Memmingen im dreißigjährigen Kriege*. Memmingen: J. Rehm, 1818.

Usinger, Rudolf. "Die Zerstörung Magdeburgs." *Historische Zeitschrift* 13 (1865): 378–405.

Venedey, Jacob. "Tilly und Gustav Adolf nach Onno Klopp." *Historische Zeitschrift* 7 (1862): 381–444.

Vincke, Carl Freiherr von. *Die Schlacht bei Lützen den 6ten November 1632: Historisches Fragment zur Erinnerung an Gustav Adolph am zweihundertjäh-rigen Jahrestage seines Todes*. Berlin: Nauckschen Buchhandlung, 1832.

Vogt, Nicolaus. *Ueber die Europäische Republik*. 2 vols. Frankfurt: Varrentrapp & Werner, 1787.

———. *Gustav Adolph, König in Schweden, als Nachtrag zur europäischen Republik*. Frankfurt: Varrentrapp & Werner, 1790.

———. *Europäische Staats-Relationen*. 3 vols. Frankfurt: n.p., 1805.

———. *Historische Darstellung des europäischen Völkerbundes*. Vol. 1. Frankfurt: Fr. Andreäischen Buchhandlung, 1808.

Volkholz, Robert. *Die Zerstörung Magdeburgs (1631) im Lichte der neuesten Forschung*. Magdeburg: Faber, 1892.

———. *Jürgen Ackermann, Kapitän beim Regiment Alt-Pappenheim, 1631*. Halberstadt: J. Schimmelburg, 1895.

Voß, Julius von. *Krieg und Liebe, oder romantische Erzählungen, von dreißigjäh-rigen Kriege bis auf unsre Zeiten*. Berlin: J. W. Schmidt, 1813.

Wacek, Franz Aloysius. "Beitrag zu Charakteristik des berühmten Albrecht von Waldstein, Herzogs von Friedland." *Hesperus: Ein Nationalblatt für gebil-dete Leser* 59 (October 1814): 385–90; 60 (December 1814): 478–80; 61 (December 1814): 482–84.

"Wallensteins Tod." *Historisch-politische Blätter für das katholische Deutschland* 14 (1844): 703–10.

Walter, Josef. "Über den Einfluß des dreißigjährigen Krieges auf die deutsche Sprache und Literatur." *Programm des k.k. Kleinseitner Gymnasiums zu Prag*, part 1 (1871): 5–26; part 2 (1873): 39.

Wapler, Richard. *Wallensteins letzte Tag: Ein historisch-kritisches Gedenkenblatt zum 25. Februar 1884*. Leipzig: G. Höfler, 1884.

Wassenberg, Eberhard. *Paranesi ad Germanos, pro communi patria, libertate, gloria tuende repraesentans*. Cologne: Apud Jodocum Kalcovium, 1647.

Watterich, F. C. von. *Kriegsgeschichtsphilosophische Ehrengebuhr dem helden-Charakter und Feldherrnstabe Albrecht Waldstein's*. Prague: C. W. Medau, 1843.

Weinrich, L. *Die Aufhebung der Blockade der Stadt Hanau im Jahre 1636 ("und zur Feieren des zweihundertjährigen Jubiläum")*. Hanau: F. König, 1836.

Westenrieder, Lorenz von. *Geschichte des dreyßigjährigen Kriegs*. 3 vols. Munich: J. Lindauer, 1804–6.

———. *Beyträge zur vaterländische Historie, Geographie, Statistik*. Vol. 8. Munich: J. Lindauer, 1806.

"Wie Gustav Adolph die religiöse Freiheit der Katholiken verstand." *Historisch-politische Blätter für das katholische Deutschland* 11 (1844): 580–84.

Wild, Friedrich Karl. *Geschichte des westphälischen Friedens nebst einem kürzen Abriß des dreißigjährigen Krieges: Zur Erinnerung an den vor zweihundert erfolgten Abschluß derselben*. Nordlingen: C. H. Beck, 1848.

———. *Leben Gustav Adolfs des Großen, König von Schweden: Zur Belehrung, Verehrung, und Erbauung für das Volk*. Basel: Dr. Marriott, 1852.

———. *Erhard Daubitz: Aus der Belagerung von Nördlingen 1634*. Stuttgart: n.p., 1866.

Wille, Richard. *Hanau im dreißigjährigen Kriege*. Hanau: G. M. Alberti, 1886.

Winter, F. "Magdeburg, Gustav Adolf, und Tilly." *Geschichtsblätter für Stadt und Land Magdeburg* 10 (1875): 199.

Winter, Georg. *Geschichte des Dreißigjährigen Krieges*. Berlin: G. Grote, 1893.

Wittich, Karl. "Wallenstein und die Spanier." *Preußische Jahrbücher* 22, no. 3 (1868): 329–44; 23, no. 1 (1869): 19–62.

———. "Kritische Erläuterungen über die Zerstörung Magdeburgs." *Zeitschrift für Preußische Geschichte und Landeskunde* 6 (1869): 317–59, 532–84.

———. *Die Zerstörung Magdeburgs in Jahre 1631*. Berlin: J. Sittenfeld, 1870.

———. *Magdeburg, Gustav Adolf, und Tilly*. 2 vols. Berlin: Carl Duncker, 1874.

———. "Zur Katastrophe des 10./20. Mai 1631." *Geschichtsblätter für Stadt und Land Magdeburg* 22 (1887): 393–417; 23 (1888): 1–132.

———. "Magdeburg als katholisches Marienburg: Eine Episode aus dem Dreißigjährigen Krieg." *Historische Zeitschrift* 65, no. 1 (1890): 431–40.

———. *Dietrich von Falkenberg, Oberst und Feldmarschall Gustav Adolfs*. Magdeburg: Verlag der Schäfer'schen Buchhandlung, 1892.

———. *Pappenheim und Falkenberg: Ein Beitrag zu Kennzeichnung der lokalpatriotischen Geschichtsschreibung Magdeburgs*. Berlin: W. Baensch Verlagshandlung, 1894.

———. *Dietrich von Falkenbergs Ende: Entgegnung auf die Schrift "Jürgen Ackermann, Kapitän beim Regiment Alt-Pappenheim, 1631"*. Leipzig: n.p., 1895.

———. "Noch einmal die Zerstörung Magdeburgs." *Geschichtsblätter für Stadt und Land Magdeburg* 30 (1895): 76–117.

Wolf, Peter Philipp. *Geschichte Maximilians I. und seiner Zeit.* 4 vols. Munich: Joseph Lindauer, 1807–11.

Woltmann, Karl Ludwig von. *Leben, Thaten, und Schicksale Wallensteins.* Zofingen: n.p., 1804.

———. *Oesterreichs Politik und Kaiserhaus.* Frankfurt: n.p., 1815.

———. *Friedrich Schiller's Geschichte des dreyßigjährigen Krieges.* Vols. 3–4, *Geschichte des Westphälischen Friedens.* Leipzig: Göschen, 1816.

———. *Politische Blicke und Berichte.* Vol 1. Leipzig and Altenburg: F. A. Brockhaus, 1816.

Würdinger, Joseph. "Johann Tzerklas Graf von Tilly, bayerischer Heerführer." *Bayerischer Militär-Almanach* 4 (1859): 75–275.

Zehme, Karl Adolph. *Die Einnahme und Einascherung der Stadt Sonnewalde durch die Schweden.* Leipzig: B. G. Teubner, 1841.

Ziemssen, Christoph. *Das Wallensteins-Fest: Gebete und Predigten zur Feier des vier und zwanzigsten Julius 1819 und 1820 in der St. Marien-Kirche zu Stralsund.* Stralsund: n.p., 1821.

Zober, Ernst Heinrich. *Geschichte der Belagerung Stralsunds durch Wallenstein, im Jahre 1628.* Stralsund: W. Trinius, 1828.

Zschokke, Heinrich. *Der Baierischen Geschichten.* Vol. 3. Aarau: H. R. Sauerländer, 1816.

———. *Eine Selbstschau.* Aarau: H.R. Sauerländer, 1842.

"Zur Gustav-Adolf Literatur." *Historisch-politische Blätter für das katholische Deutschland* 35 (1855): 129–52.

"Zur Vorgeschichte des dreißigjährigen Krieges." *Historisch-politische Blätter für das katholische Deutschland* 26 (1851): 73–77.

Zwerger, Franz. *Ein Beitrag zur Geschichte der Stadt Landsberg während des dreißigjährigen Krieges.* Landsberg: X. Kraus, 1882.

Zwiedineck-Südenhorst, Hans. *Die neueste Wallenstein-Forschung.* n.p., 1886.

Secondary Literature

Abusch, Alexander. *Schiller: Große und Tragik eines deutschen Genius.* Berlin: Aufbau, 1955.

Acton, John E. "German Schools of History." *Historical Review* 1 (January 1886): 7–42.

Adamson, J. S. A. "Eminent Victorians: S. R. Gardiner and the Liberal as Hero." *Historical Journal* 33, no. 3 (1990): 641–57.

Adel, Kurt, ed. *Joseph Freiherr von Hormayr und die "vaterländische Romantik" in Österreich.* Vienna: Bergland Verlag, 1969.

Agnew, Hugh. *Origins of the Czech National Renascence.* Pittsburgh: University of Pittsburgh Press, 1993.

Albertsen, Leif Ludwig. *Die Eintagsliteratur in der Goethezeit: Proben aus Werken von Julius von Voß.* Bern: H. Lang, 1975.

Alighieri, Dante. *The Divine Comedy*, vol. 1, *Inferno.* Trans. Mark Musa. New York: Penguin Books, 1984.

Allgemeine Deutsche Biographie. 56 vols. 2d ed. Leipzig, 1875; reprint, Berlin: Duncker & Humblot, 1967–71.

Altgeld, Wolfgang. *Katholizimus, Protestantismus, Judentum.* Mainz: M. Grunewald, 1992.

Aly, Götz. *Macht-Geist-Wahn, Kontinuitäten deutschen Denkens.* Berlin: Argon, 1997.

Anderson, Benedict. *Imagined Communities: Reflections on the Origin and Spread of Nationalism.* London: Verso, 1983.

Anderson, Margaret Lavinia. "Piety and Politics: Recent Work on German Catholicism." *Journal of Modern History* 63, no. 4 (December 1991): 681–716.

Anderson, Olive. "The Political Uses of History in Mid-Nineteenth-Century England." *Past and Present* 36 (April 1967): 87–105.

Angermeier, Heinz. *Das alte Reich in der deutschen Geschichte.* Munich: R. Oldenbourg, 1991.

Ankersmit, F. R. *History and Tropology: The Rise and Fall of Metaphor.* Berkeley: University of California Press, 1994.

Ankersmit, Frank, and Hans Kellner, eds. *A New Philosophy of History.* Chicago: University of Chicago Press, 1995.

Antze, Paul, and Michael Lambek, eds. *Tense Past: Cultural Essays in Trauma and Memory.* New York: Routledge, 1996.

Appian's Roman History. 4 vols. Translated by Horace White. New York: Macmillan, 1912.

Applegate, Celia. "A Europe of Regions: Reflections on the Historiography of Sub-National Places in Modern Times." *American Historical Review* 104, no. 4 (October 1999): 1157–82.

Aretin, Karl Otmar Freiherr von. *Heiliges Römisches Reich, 1776–1806: Reichsverfassung und Staatssouveränität.* Wiesbaden: F. Steiner, 1967.

Aron, Raymond. *Introduction to the Philosophy of History: An Essay on the Limits of Historical Objectivity.* Translated by George J. Irwin. Boston: Beacon Press, 1961.

Auerbach, Erich. *Mimesis: The Representation of Reality in Western Literature.* Translated by Willard R. Trask. Princeton: Princeton University Press, 1953.

Augstein, Rudolf, et al. *"Historikerstreit": Die Dokumentation der Kontroverse um die Einzigartigkeit der nationalsozialistischen Judenvernichtung.* Munich:

R. Piper, 1987.

Baldwin, Peter, ed. *Reworking the Past: Hitler, the Holocaust, and the Historians' Debate.* Boston: Beacon Press, 1990.

Bann, Stephen. *Romanticism and the Rise of History.* New York and Toronto: Twayne, 1995.

Baron, Salo Wittmayer. *Modern Nationalism and Religion.* New York: Harper, 1947.

Barraclough, Geoffrey. *History in a Changing World.* Norman: University of Oklahoma Press, 1957.

Barudio, Günter. *Der Teutsche Krieg, 1618–1648.* Frankfurt: S. Fischer, 1985.

Baruma, Ian, and Avishai Margalit. "Occidentalism." *New York Review of Books* 49, no. 1 (January 17, 2002): 4–7.

Bazillion, Richard J. *Modernizing Germany: Karl Biedermann's Career in the Kingdom of Saxony, 1835–1901.* New York: Peter Lang, 1990.

Becher, Johannes R. "Denn er ist Unser: Friedrich Schiller: Der Dichter der Freiheit." In *Gesammelte Werke,* vol. 18, *Publizistik IV. 1952–1958,* ed. Ilse Siebert. Berlin and Weimar: Aufbau, 1981.

Becker, Frank. *Bilder von Krieg und Nation: Die Einigungskriege in der bürgerliche Öffentlichkeit Deutschlands, 1864–1913.* Munich: R. Oldenbourg, 2001.

Becker, Winfried. "Der Kulturkampf als Europäisches und als Deutsches Phänomen," *Historisches Jahrbuch* 101 (1981): 422–46.

Beenken, Hermann. *Das Neunzehnte Jahrhundert in der Deutschen Kunst.* Munich: F. Bruckmann, 1944.

Beifang, Andreas. "National-preußisch oder deutsch-national? Die Deutsche Fortschrittspartei in Preußen, 1861–1867." *Geschichte und Gesellschaft* 23, no. 3 (1997): 360–83.

Beiser, Frederick C. *Enlightenment, Revolution, and Romanticism: The Genesis of Modern German Political Thought, 1790–1800.* Cambridge: Harvard University Press, 1992.

Below, Georg von. *Die deutsche Geschichtschreibung von den Befreiungskriegen bis zu unsern Tagen.* Munich and Berlin: R. Oldenbourg, 1924.

Benecke, Gerhard. *Society and Politics in Germany, 1500–1750.* London: Routledge & Kegan Paul, 1974.

Bentinck-Smith, William. *Building a Great Library: The Coolidge Years at Harvard.* Cambridge: Harvard University Press, 1976.

Ben-Yehuda, Nachman. *The Masada Myth: Collective Memory and Mythmaking in Israel.* Madison: University of Wisconsin Press, 1995.

Benes, Edvard. "The Unreconciled Czechs [1908]." In *The Austrian Empire: Abortive Federation?* ed. Harold J. Gordon and Nancy M. Gordon, 52–57. Lexington MA: D. C. Heath, 1974.

Benjamin, Walter. "Theses on the Philosophy of History." In *Illuminations,* ed.

Hannah Arendt, trans. Harry Zohn. New York: Schocken Books, 1969.

———. *The Origin of German Tragic Drama*. Translated by John Osborne. London: NLB, 1977.

Berding, Helmut, and Hans-Peter Ullmann, eds. *Deutschland zwischen Revolution und Restauration*. Düsseldorf: Athenäum, 1981.

Berg, Ursula. *Niklas Vogt (1756–1836): Weltsicht und Politische Ordnungsvorstellungen zwischen Aufklärung und Romantic*. Beiträge zur Geschichte der Universität Mainz, 16. Stuttgart: F. Steiner, 1992.

Bergel, Leinhard. "Cervantes in Germany." In *Cervantes across the Centuries*, ed. Angel Flores and M. J. Bernadete, 315–52. New York: Gordian Press, 1969.

Berger, Stefan. *The Search for Normality: National Identity and Historical Consciousness in Germany since 1800*. Providence RI: Berghahn Books, 1997.

Berger, Ulrcke, Ursula Bohn, et al. *Jerusalem: Symbol und Wirklichkeit*. Berlin: Institüt für Kirch & Judentum, 1976.

Berney, Arnold. "Reichstradition und Nationalstaatsgedanke (1789–1815)." *Historische Zeitschrift* 140, no. 1 (1929): 57–86.

Berns, Gisela N. *Greek Antiquity in Schiller's Wallenstein*. Chapel Hill: University of North Carolina Press, 1985.

Bertrand, J. A. *Cervantes et le Romantisme Allemand*. Paris: F. Alcan, 1914.

Bessel, Richard. *Germany after the First World War*. New York: Oxford University Press, 1995.

Beyer, Hermann Wolfgang. *Die Geschichte des Gustav-Adolf-Verein in ihren kirchen- und geistesgeschichtlichen Zusammenhängen*. Göttingen: Vandenhoeck & Ruprecht, 1932.

Bialostocki, Jan. "The Image of the Defeated Ruler in Romantic Art." In *Romantic Nationalism in Europe*, ed. J. C. Eade, 64–71. Canberra: Humanities Research Center, Australian National University, 1983.

Bietenholz, Peter G. *Historia and Fabula: Myths and Legends in Historical Thought from Antiquity to the Modern Age*. Leiden: E. J. Brill, 1994.

Bigler, Robert. "The Rise of Political Protestantism in Nineteenth-Century Germany." *Church History* 34, no. 4 (December 1965): 423–40.

Binhammer, Katherine. "The Sex Panic in the 1790s." *Journal of the History of Sexuality* 6, no. 3 (1996): 409–34.

"Biographische Skizze: Karl Ludwig von Woltmann." *Meyer's Groschen Bibliothek der Deutschen Klassiker für alle Stände* 294 (New York: H. I. Meyer, 1870): 5–6.

Birke, Adolf M. "Nation und Konfession: Varianten des politischen Katholizisimus im Europa des 19. Jahrhunderts." *Historisches Jahrbuch* 116, no. 2 (1996): 395–416.

Birke, Ernst, and Kurt Oberdorffer, eds. *Das böhmische Staatsrecht in der deutsch-*

tschechischen Auseinandersetzungen des 19. und 20. Jahrhunderts. Marburg and Lahn: N. G. Elwert, 1960.

Blackbourn, David. "Progress and Piety: Liberalism, Catholicism and the State in Imperial Germany." *History Workshop Journal* 26 (Autumn 1988): 57–78.

————. *Marpingen: Apparitions of the Virgin Mary in Bismarckian Germany.* New York: Oxford University Press, 1993.

————. *The Fontana History of Germany, 1780–1918: The Long Nineteenth Century.* London: Fontana Press, 1997.

Blake, William. *Jerusalem: The Emanation of the Giant Albion* [1820], in *The Complete Poems*, ed. Alicia Ostriker. New York: Penguin Books, 1977.

Blanke, Horst W. *Historiographiegeschichte als Historik.* Stuttgart and Bad Canstatt: Frommann-Holzboog, 1991.

Blanke, Horst W., and Jörn Rüsen, eds. *Von der Aufklärung zum Historismus: Zum Strukturwandel des historischen Denkens.* Paderborn: F. Schöningh, 1984.

Blanning, T. C. W. *The French Revolution in Germany: Occupation and Resistance in the Rhineland, 1792–1802.* Oxford: Clarendon Press, 1983.

Blight, David W. *Race and Reunion: The Civil War in American Memory.* Cambridge: Harvard University Press, 2001.

Bloch, Renée. "Midrash." In *Approaches to Ancient Judaism: Theory and Practice*, ed. William S. Green, 29–50. Missoula MT: Scholars Press 1978.

Böhme, Helmut, ed. *Probleme der Reichsgründungszeit, 1848–1879.* Cologne: Kiepenhauer & Witsch, 1968.

Botzenhart, Manfred. *Reform, Restauration, Krise: Deutschland, 1789–1849.* Frankfurt: Suhrkamp, 1985.

Boyarin, Daniel. "'Language Inscribed by History on the Bodies of Living Beings': Midrash and Martyrdom." *Representations* 25 (Winter 1989): 139–51.

Boyd, Carolyn P. *Historia Patria: Politics, History, and National Identity in Spain, 1875–1975.* Princeton: Princeton University Press, 1997.

Bradley, John F. N. *Czech Nationalism in the Nineteenth Century.* Boulder CO: East European Monographs, 1984.

Brandt, Peter. "Das Studentische Wartburgfest vom 18./19. Oktober 1817." In *Öffentliche Festkultur: Politische Feste in Deutschland von der Aufklärung bis zum Ersten Weltkrieg*, ed. Dieter Düding, Peter Friedemann, and Paul Munch, 89–112. Hamburg: Rowohlt, 1988.

Breisach, Ernst. *Historiography.* Chicago: University of Chicago Press, 1983.

Breuilly, John. "Nation and Nationalism in Modern German History." *Historical Journal* 33, no. 3 (1990): 659–75.

————. "Sovereignty and Boundaries: Modern State Formation and National Identity in Germany." In *National Histories and European History*, ed. Mary Fulbrook, 94–140. London: UCL Press, 1993.

Brokoff, Jürgen. *Die Apokalypse in der Weimarer Republik.* Munich: W. Fink, 2001.

Bromley, J. S., and E. H. Kossmann, eds., *Britain and the Netherlands,* vol. 5, *Some Political Mythologies* (The Hague: Martinus Nijhoff, 1975)

Brown, Peter. *The Rise of Western Christendom: Triumph and Diversity,* AD 200–1000. New York: Oxford University Press, 1996.

Brownley, Martine W. *Clarendon and the Rhetoric of Historical Form.* Philadelphia: University of Pennsylvania Press, 1985.

Brownmiller, Susan. *Against Our Will.* New York: Simon and Schuster, 1975.

Bruendel, Steffen. *Volksgemeinschaft oder Volksstaat: Die "Ideen von 1914" und die Neuordnung Deutschlands im Ersten Weltkrieg.* Berlin: Akademie Verlag, 2003.

Brunschwig, Henri. *Enlightenment and Romanticism in Eighteenth-Century Prussia.* Translated by Frank Jellinek. Chicago: University of Chicago Press, 1974.

Büchler-Hauschild, Gabriele. *Erzählte Arbeit: Gustav Freytag und die soziale Prosa des Vor- und Nachmärz.* Paderborn: F. Schöningh, 1987.

Buchholz, Werner. "Der Eintritt Schwedens in den Dreißigjährigen Krieg in der Schwedischen und Deutschen Historiographie des 19. und 20. Jahrhunderts." *Historische Zeitschrift* 245, no. 2 (1987): 291–314.

Burke, Kenneth. *The Rhetoric of Religion: Studies in Logology.* Berkeley: University of California Press, 1970.

Burke, Peter. "History as Social Memory." In *Memory: History, Culture, and the Mind,* ed. Thomas Butler, 97–113. New York: Oxford University Press, 1989.

Burrow, J. W. *A Liberal Descent: Victorian Historians and the English Past.* Cambridge: Cambridge University Press, 1983.

———. *Whigs and Liberals: Continuity and Change in English Political Thought.* New York: Oxford University Press, 1988.

Büsch, Otto, and James Sheehan, eds. *Die Rolle der Nation in der deutschen Geschichte und Gegenwart.* Berlin: Colloquium, 1985.

Bußmann, Walter. *Treitschke, sein Welt- und Geschichtsbild.* Göttingen: Musterschmidt, 1952.

Butler, Thomas, ed., *Memory: History, Culture, and the Mind.* New York: Oxford University Press, 1989.

Canetti, Elias. *Crowds and Power.* Translated by Carol Stewart. New York: Farrar Straus Giroux, 1984.

Carlton, Eric. *War and Ideology.* London: Routledge, 1990.

Carlyle, Thomas. "State of German Literature [1827]." *Critical and Miscellaneous Essays,* 1:26–86. London, 1899; reprint, New York: AMS Press, 1969.

Carruth, Cathy. "Unclaimed Experience: Trauma and the Possibility of History." *Yale French Studies,* no. 79 (1991): 181–92.

Casey, Edward S. *Remembering: A Phenomenological Study.* Bloomington: Indiana University Press, 1987.

Certeau, Michel de. *The Writing of History.* Translated by Tom Conley. New York: Columbia University Press, 1988.

Cervantes, Miguel de. "The Siege of Numantia." In *The Classic Theater.* Vol. 3, *Six Spanish Plays,* ed. Eric Bentley, trans. Roy Campbell, 97–160. New York: Doubleday, 1959.

Chickering, Roger. "Die Alldeutschen erwarten den Krieg." In *Bereit zum Krieg: Kriegsmentalität in Wilhelminischen Deutschland, 1890–1914,* ed. Jost Düffler and Karl Holl, 20–32. Göttingen: Vandenhoeck & Ruprecht, 1986.

———. *Karl Lamprecht: A German Academic Life (1856–1915).* Atlantic Highlands NJ: Humanities Press, 1993.

Chickering, Roger, ed. *Imperial Germany: A Historiographical Companion.* Westport CT: Greenwood Press, 1996.

Ciaran, Brady, ed. *Ideology and the Historians.* Buglin: Lilliput Press, 1991.

Clark, Christopher. "The Wars of Liberation in Prussian Memory: Reflections on the Memorialization of War in Early Nineteenth-Century Germany." *Journal of Modern History* 68, no. 3 (September 1996): 550–76.

Clark, T. J. *The Absolute Bourgeois: Artists and Politics in France, 1848–1851.* Princeton: Princeton University Press, 1982.

Classe, Kurt. *Gustav Freytag als politischer Dichter.* Hildesheim: A. Lax, 1914.

Clements, R.E. *Isaiah and the Deliverance of Jerusalem: A Study of the Interpretation of Prophecy in the Old Testament.* Supplement series, vol. 13. Sheffield: Journal for the Study of the Old Testament, 1980.

Confino, Alon. *The Nation as Local Metaphor: Württemberg, Imperial Germany, and National Memory, 1871–1918.* Chapel Hill: University of North Carolina Press, 1997.

Connerton, Paul. *How Societies Remember.* Cambridge: Cambridge University Press, 1989.

Conrad, Johannes. *The German Universities for the Last Fifty Years.* Translated by John Hutchison. Glasgow: David Bryce, 1885.

Conze, Werner, ed. *Staat und Gesellschaft im deutschen Vormärz, 1815–1848.* Stuttgart: Klett–Cotta, 1962.

———. "Deutschland und deutsche Nation als historische Begriffe." In *Die Rolle der Nation in der deutschen Geschichte und Gegenwart,* ed. Otto Büsch and James Sheehan, 21–38. Berlin: Colloquium, 1985.

Corbin, Alain. *The Village of Cannibals: Rage and Murder in France, 1870.* Translated by Arthur Goldhammer. Cambridge: Harvard University Press, 1992.

Coter, Christfried. "Zwischen Habsburg und dem Reich: Ein Versuch über Albrecht von Wallenstein." *Zeitschrift für Geschichtswissenschaft* 4, no. 4 (1956): 713–34.

Cox, Jeffrey N. *In the Shadow of Romance: Romantic Tragic Drama in Germany, England, and France.* Athens: Ohio University Press, 1987.

Craig, Gordon. *Germany, 1866–1945.* New York: Oxford University Press, 1978.

Cramer, Kevin. "Religious Conflict as History: The Nation as the One True Church." In *Religion und Nation: Beiträge zu einer unbewältigte Geschichte*, ed. Michael Geyer and Hartmut Lehmann, 23–38. Göttingen: Wallstein, 2004.

Criegern, Hermann von. *Geschichte des Gustav-Adolf-Vereins.* Hamburg: F. A. Perthes, 1903.

Current, Richard Nelson. *Arguing with Historians: Essays on the Historical and Unhistorical.* Middletown CT: Wesleyan University Press, 1987.

Dahl, Mary K. *Political Violence in Drama: Classical Models, Contemporary Variations*, Theater and Dramatic Studies 36. Ann Arbor: UMI Research Press, 1987.

Dahlmann, Friedrich Christoph and Georg Waitz, eds. *Dahlmann-Waitz: Quellenkunde der deutschen Geschichte.* 6th rev ed. Edited by E. Steindorff. Göttingen: Dieterich, 1894.

Dann, Otto. *Nation und Nationalismus in Deutschland, 1770–1990.* Munich: C. H. Beck, 1993.

———. "Schiller, der Historiker und die Quellen." In *Schiller als Historiker*, ed. Otto Dann, Norbert Oellers, and Ernst Osterkampf, 109–26. Stuttgart and Weimar: J. B. Metzlar, 1995.

Dann, Otto, Norbert Oellers, and Ernst Osterkamp, eds. *Schiller als Historiker.* Stuttgart and Weimar: J. B. Metzlar, 1995.

Demm, Eberhard. *Ostpolitik und Propaganda im Ersten Weltkrieg.* Frankfurt: Peter Lang, 2002.

Denkler, Horst. "Zwischen Julirevolution (1830) und Märzrevolution (1848/49)." In *Geschichte der politischen Lyrik in Deutschland*, ed. Walter Hinderer, 179–88. Stuttgart: Reclam, 1978.

Deutsche Arbeit: Monatsschrift für das Geistige Leben der Deutschen in Böhmen (Prague) 7 (October 1907–September 1908): 628–30. S.v. "Hofrat Dr. Hermann Hallwich."

Dickerman, Edmund H., and Anita M. Walker. "The Choice of Hercules: Henry IV as Hero." *Historical Journal* 39, no. 2 (1996): 325–32.

Dilthey, Wilhelm. "Draft for a Critique of Historical Reason." In *The Hermeneutics Reader: Texts of the German Tradition from the Enlightenment to the Present*, ed. Kurt Mueller-Vollmer, 148–64. New York: Continuum, 1989.

Diner, Dan, and Bill Templar. "European Counter-Images: Problems of Periodization and Historical Memory." *New German Critique*, no. 53 (Spring–Summer 1991): 163–74.

Dippel, Horst. *Germany and the American Revolution, 1770–1800: A Sociohistorical Investigation of Late Eighteenth-Century Political Thinking.* Translated by

Bernhard A. Uhlendorf. Chapel Hill: University of North Carolina Press, 1977.

Diwald, Helmut. Foreword to *Geschichte Wallensteins*, by Leopold von Ranke. Leipzig: Duncker & Humblot, 1869; reprint, Kronberg: Athenäum-Verlag, 1978.

Doblhofer, Georg. *Vergewaltigung in der Antike*. Stuttgart and Leipzig: B. G. Teubner, 1994.

Doeberl, M. "Das Kaiserprojekt und die letzten Absichten König Gustav Adolfs von Schweden nach bayerischer Auffassung." *Forschungen zur Geschichte Bayerns. Vierteljahrsschrift* 15, no. 3 (1907): 202–8.

Donagan, Barbara. "Atrocity, War Crime, and Treason in the English Civil War." *American Historical Review* 99, no. 4 (October 1994): 1137–66.

Donaldson, Ian. *The Rapes of Lucretia: A Myth and Its Transformations*. New York: Oxford University Press, 1982.

Dorpalen, Andreas. *Heinrich von Treitschke*. New Haven: Yale University Press, 1957.

Dower, John W. "The Bombed: Hiroshimas and Nagasakis in Japanese Memory." In *Hiroshima in History and Memory*, ed. Michael J. Hogan, 116–42. Cambridge: Cambridge University Press, 1996.

Dreitzel, Horst. *Monarchiebegriffe in der Fürstengesellschaft: Semantik und Theorie der Einherrschaft in Deutschland von der Reformation bis zum Vormärz*, vol. 2, *Theorie der Monarchie*. Cologne, Weimar, and Vienna: Böhlau, 1991.

Drescher, Seymour, David Sabean, and Allan Sharlin, eds. *Political Symbolism in Modern Europe: Essays in Honor of George L. Mosse*. New Brunswick: Rutgers University Press, 1982.

Droz, Jacques. *Europe between Revolutions, 1815–1848*. Translated by Robert Baldick. New York: Harper & Row, 1967.

Duchhardt, Heinz. *Protestantisches Kaisertum und Altes Reich*. Wiesbaden: Steiner, 1977.

Düding, Dieter, Peter Friedemann, and Paul Munch, eds. *Öffentliche Festkultur: Politische Feste in Deutschland von der Aufklärung bis zum Ersten Weltkrieg*. Hamburg: Rowohlt, 1988.

Düffler, Jost, and Karl Holl, eds. *Bereit zum Krieg: Kriegsmentalität in Wilhelmischen Deutschland, 1890–1914*. Göttingen: Vandenhoeck und Ruprecht, 1986.

Dunbabin, J. P. D. "Oliver Cromwell's Popular Image in Nineteenth-Century England." In *Britain and the Netherlands*, vol. 5, *Some Political Mythologies*, ed. J. S. Bromberg and E. H. Kossmann, 141–63. The Hague: Martinus Nijhoff, 1975.

Dunn, John. *Political Obligation in Its Historical Context: Essays in Political Theory*. Cambridge: Cambridge University Press, 1980.

Eade, J. C., ed. *Romantic Nationalism in Europe.*Canberra: Humanities Research Center, Australian National University, 1983.

Ebersberger, Thea, ed. *Erinnerungsblätter aus dem Leben Luise Mühlbach's.* Leipzig: H. Schmidt & C. Günther, 1902.

Eghigian, Greg, and Matthew Paul Berg, eds. *Sacrifice and National Belonging in Twentieth-Century Germany.* College Station: Texas A&M University Press, 2002.

Ekman, Ernst. "Three Decades of Research on Gustavus Adolphus." *Journal of Modern History* 38, no. 3 (September 1966): 243–55.

Eley, Geoff. "Reshaping the Right: Radical Nationalism and the German Navy League, 1898–1908." *Historical Journal* 21, no. 2 (1978): 327–54.

———. "State Formation, Nationalism, and Political Culture in Nineteenth-Century Germany." In *Culture, Ideology, and Politics,* ed. Raphael Samuel and Gareth Stedman Jones, 277–301. London: Routledge and Kegan Paul, 1983.

———. "Nazism, Politics, and Public Memory: Thoughts on the West German *Historikerstreit.*" *Past and Present,* no. 121 (November 1988): 172–80.

Elias, Norbert. *The Germans: Power Struggles and the Development of Habitus in the Nineteenth and Twentieth Centuries.* Translated by Eric Dunning and Stephen Mennell. Edited by Michael Schröter. New York: Columbia University Press, 1996.

Elshtain, Jean B. *Women and War.* New York: Basic Books, 1995.

Engelhardt, Dietrich von. "Romanticism in Germany." In *Romanticism in National Context,* ed. Roy Porter and Mikulas Teich, 109–33. Cambridge: Cambridge University Press, 1988.

Epstein, Klaus. *The Genesis of German Conservatism.* Princeton: Princeton University Press, 1966.

Erdmannsdörffer, Bernhard. "Zur Geschichte und Geschichtschreibung des dreißigjährigen Krieges." *Historische Zeitschrift* 14 (Munich, 1865): 4–5.

———. *Deutsche Geschichte von Westfälischen Frieden bis zum Regierungsantritt Friedrichs des Großen, 1648–1740.* Berlin: Georg Reimer, 1892–93.

Ergang, Robert. *The Myth of the All-Destructive Fury of the Thirty Years' War.* Pocono Pines PA: Craftsmen, 1956.

Esch, Arnold, and Jens Petersen, eds. *Geschichte und Geschichtswissenschaft in der Kultur Italiens und Deutschlands.* Tübingen: Niemeyer, 1989.

Evans, R. J. W. "Culture and Anarchy in the Empire, 1540–1680." *Central European History* 18, no. 1 (March 1985): 14–30.

Evans, Richard J. *In Hitler's Shadow.* New York: Pantheon Books, 1989.

———. *Rereading German History: From Unification to Reunification, 1800–1996.* London: Routledge, 1997.

Evers, Hans-Gerhard. "Denkmalplastik." In *Die Kunst des 19. Jahrhunderts,* ed. Rudolf Zeitler, 157–63. Berlin: Propyläen, 1966.

Falkenstein, Eugenie T. von. *Der Kampf der Tschechen um die historischen Rechte der böhmischen Krone im Spiegel der Presse, 1861–1879.* Wiesbaden: Harrossowitz, 1982.

Farrell, John P. *Revolution as Tragedy: The Drama of the Moderate from Scott to Arnold*. Ithaca: Cornell University Press, 1980.

Faulenbach, Bernd. *Ideologie des deutschen Weges: Die deutsche Geschichte in der Historiographie zwischen Kaiserreich und Nationalsozialismus*. Munich: C. H. Beck, 1980.

Fenske, Hans. "Gelehrtenpolitik im liberalen Südwesten, 1830–1880." In *Gelehrtenpolitik und politische Kultur in Deutschland, 1830–1930*, ed. Gustav Schmidt and Jörn Rüsen, 39–41. Bochum: N. Brockmeyer, 1986.

Fentriss, James, and Chris Wickam. *Social Memory*. New York: Oxford University Press, 1992.

Figes, Orlando, and Boris Kolonitskii. *Interpreting the Russian Revolution: The Language and Symbols of 1917*. New Haven: Yale University Press, 1999.

Fischer, Fritz. "Der deutsche Protestantismus und die Politik im 19. Jahrhundert." *Historische Zeitschrift* 171, no. 3 (1951): 473–518.

Fischer, Hans-Dietrich, ed. *Deutsche Zeitschriften des 17. bis 20. Jahrhunderts*. Munich: Aufbau-Verlag, 1973.

Flores, Angel, and M. J. Bernadete, eds. *Cervantes across the Centuries*. New York: Gordian Press, 1969.

Foerster, Cornelia. "Das Hambacher Fest 1832." In *Öffentliche Festkultur: Politische Feste in Deutschland von der Aufklärung bis zum Ersten Weltkrieg*, ed. Dieter Düding, Peter Friedemann, and Paul Munch, 113–31. Hamburg: Rowohlt, 1988.

Förster, Ernst. *Aus der Jugendzeit*. Berlin: W. Spemann, 1887.

Fort, Bernadotte, ed. *Fictions in the French Revolution*. Evanston, IL: Northwestern University Press, 1991.

Foster, R. F. *Paddy and Mr. Punch: Connections in Irish and English History*. London: A. Lane, 1993.

Foucault, Michel. *The Archaeology of Knowledge*. Translated by A. M. Sheridan Smith. New York: Pantheon Books, 1972.

Françoise, Etienne, Hannes Siegrist, and Jakob Vogel, eds. *Nation und Emotion: Deutschland und Frankreich in Vergleich 19. und 20. Jahrhundert*. Göttingen: Vandenhoeck & Ruprecht, 1995.

Frantzen, Allen J. *Bloody Good: Chivalry, Sacrifice, and the Great War*. Chicago: University of Chicago Press, 2004.

Friedländer, Saul, ed. *Probing the Limits of Representation: Nazism and the "Final Solution"*. Cambridge: Harvard University Press, 1992.

———. *Nazi Germany and the Jews, Volume I: The Years of Persecution, 1933–1939*. New York: HarperCollins, 1997.

Friedman, Edward H. *The Unifying Concept: Approaches to the Structure of Cervantes' Comedias*. York SC: Spanish Literature Publications, 1981.

Friedrich, Werner. *Friedrich von Raumer als Historiker und Politiker.* Leipzig: F. A. Brockhaus, 1930.

Fuentes, Carlos. *The Buried Mirror: Reflections on Spain and the New World.* Boston: Houghton Mifflin, 1992.

Fueter, Eduard. *Geschichte der neueren Historiographie.* Munich and Berlin: R. Oldenbourg, 1911.

Fulbrook, Mary, ed. *National Histories and European History.* Boulder: Westview Press, 1993.

Funkenstein, Amos. "History, Counterhistory, and Narrative." In *Probing the Limits of Representation,* ed. Saul Friedländer, 66–81. Cambridge: Harvard University Press, 1992.

Furet, Françoise. *Interpreting the French Revolution.* Translated by Elborg Forster. Cambridge: Cambridge University Press, 1981.

Gagliardo, John. *Reich and Nation: The Holy Roman Empire as Idea and Reality, 1763–1806.* Bloomington: Indiana University Press, 1980.

Gall, Lothar. *Bismarck: The White Revolutionary.* Translated by J. A. Underwood. 2 vols. Boston: Allen & Unwin, 1986.

Gay, Peter. *Style in History: Gibbon, Ranke, Macaulay, Burckhardt.* New York: Basic Books, 1974.

———. *The Cultivation of Hatred.* New York: W. W. Norton, 1993.

Geary, Patrick J. *The Myth of Nations: The Medieval Origins of Europe.* Princeton: Princeton University Press, 2001.

Geiss, Immanuel. *Studien über Geschichte und Geschichtswissenschaft.* Frankfurt: Suhrkamp, 1972.

Gellner, Ernst. *Nations and Nationalism.* Ithaca: Cornell University Press, 1983.

Gérard, Alice. *La Révolution française, mythes, et interprétations (1789–1970).* Paris: Flammarion, 1970.

Gerth, H. H., and C. Wright Mills, trans. *From Max Weber: Essays in Sociology.* New York: Oxford University Press, 1958.

Geyer, Michael. "The Militarization of Europe, 1914–1945." In *The Militarization of the Western World,* ed. John R. Gillis, 65–104. New Brunswick NJ: Rutgers University Press, 1989.

———. "The Place of the Second World War in German Memory and History." *New German Critique* 71 (Spring/Summer 1997): 5–40.

———. "Insurrectionary Warfare: The German Debate about a *Levée en Masse* in October 1918." *Journal of Modern History* 73, no. 3 (September 2001): 459–537.

———. "'There Is a Land Where Everything Is Pure: Its Name Is Land of Death': Some Observations on Catastrophic Nationalism." In *Sacrifice and National Belonging in Twentieth-Century Germany,* ed. Greg Eghigian and Matthew Paul Berg, 118–47. College Station TX: Texas A&M University Press, 2002.

Geyer, Michael, and Konrad Jarausch, eds. *German Histories: Challenges in Theory, Practice, Technique.* Special Issue of *Central European History* 22, nos. 3–4 (September–December 1989).

Geyer, Michael, and Hartmut Lehmann, eds. *Religion und Nation: Beiträge zu einer unbewältigte Geschichte.* Göttingen: Wallstein, 2004.

Geyl, Pieter. *Napoleon, For and Against.* Translated by Olive Renier. New Haven: Yale University Press, 1949.

Gibt es ein deutsches Geschichtsbild? Frankfurt: Diesterweg, 1955.

Gilbert, Felix. *Machiavelli and Guicciardini: Politics and History in Sixteenth-Century Florence.* New York: W. W. Norton, 1984.

Gillis, John R., ed. *The Militarization of the Western World.* New Brunswick: Rutgers University Press, 1989.

———, ed. *Commemorations: The Politics of National Identity.* Princeton: Princeton University Press, 1994.

Ginzburg, Carlo. *Clues, Myths, and the Historical Method.* Translated by John and Anne C. Tedeschi. Baltimore: Johns Hopkins University Press, 1989.

Girard, René. *Violence and the Sacred.* Translated by Patrick Gregory. Baltimore: Johns Hopkins University Press, 1977.

Gollwitzer, Heinz. *Europabild und Europagedanke.* Munich: C. H. Beck, 1964.

———. "Zur Auffassung der mittelalterlichen Kaiserpolitik im 19. Jahrhundert." In *Dauer und Wandel der Geschichte,* ed. Rudolf Vierhaus and Manfred Botzenhart. Münster: Aschendorff, 1966.

———. "Vom Funktionswandel Politischer Traditionen: Zum Bild Kurfürst Maximilians I. und Tillys in der bayerischer Überlieferung." In *Land und Reich, Stamm und Nation: Probleme und Perspektiven bayerischen Geschichte,* vol. 2, *Frühe Neuzeit,* ed. Andreas Kraus, 51–80. Munich: C. H. Beck, 1984.

Gooch, G. P. *History and Historians in the Nineteenth Century.* London: Longmans, Green, 1913.

Gordon, Harold F., and Nancy M. Gordon, eds. *The Austrian Empire: Abortive Federation?* Lexington MA: D. C. Heath, 1974.

Gossman, Lionel. *Between History and Literature.* Cambridge: Harvard University Press, 1990.

Gräf, Holger T. "Reich, Nation, und Kirche in der groß- und kleindeutschen Historiographie." *Historisches Jahrbuch* 116, no. 2 (Munich, 1996): 367–94.

Grass, Günter. *The Meeting at Telgte.* Translated by Ralph Mannheim. New York: Harcourt, 1981.

Grassl, Anton. *Westenrieder's Briefwechsel mit einer darstellung seiner innern Entwicklung.* Munich: Verlag der Kommission für bayerische Landesgeschichte, 1934.

Green, Abigail. *Fatherlands: State-Building and Nationhood in Nineteenth-Century Germany.* Cambridge: Cambridge University Press, 2001.

Green, Ian. "'Repulsives vs Wromantics': Rival Views of the English Civil War." In *Ideology and the Historians*, ed. Brady Ciaran, 146–67. Dublin: Lilliput Press, 1991.

Green, William S., ed. *Approaches to Ancient Judaism: Theory and Practice.* Missoula MT: Scholars Press, 1978.

Greschat, Martin. "Krieg und Kriegsbereitschaft im deutschen Protestantismus." In *Bereit zum Krieg: Kriegsmentalität in Wilhelminischen Deutschland, 1890–1914*, ed. Jost Düffler and Karl Holl, 35–49. Göttingen: Vandenhoeck & Ruprecht, 1986.

Gross, Hanns. *Empire and Sovereignty: A History of the Public Law Literature in the Holy Roman Empire, 1599–1804.* Chicago: University of Chicago Press, 1973.

Grote, Adolf. *Unangenehme Geschichtstatsachen zur Revision des neueren deutschen Geschichtsbildes.* Nuremberg: Glock & Lutz, 1960.

Grote, Heiner. "Konfessionalistische und unionistische Orientierung am Beispiel des Gustav-Adolf-Vereins und des Evangelischen Bundes." In *Das deutsche Luthertum und die Unionsproblematik im 19. Jahrhundert*, ed. Wolf-Dieter Hauschild, 110–30. Gütersloh: Gütersloher Verlagshaus G. Mohn, 1991.

Halbwachs, Maurice. *On Collective Memory.* Translated and edited by Lewis A. Coser. Chicago: University of Chicago Press, 1992.

Hansen, Wilhelm. *Nationaldenkmaler und Nationalfeste im 19. Jahrhundert.* Luneberg: Niederdeutscher Verband für Volks- & Altertumskunde, 1976.

Hardtwig, Wolfgang. *Geschichtskultur und Wissenschaft.* Munich: DTV, 1990.

———. *Nationalismus und Bürgerkultur in Deutschland, 1500–1914.* Göttingen: Vandenhoeck & Ruprecht, 1994.

Harrington, Joel F., and Helmut Walser Smith. "Confessionalization, Community, and State Building in Germany, 1555–1870." *Journal of Modern History 69*, no. 1 (March 1997): 77–101.

Harris, Ruth. "The 'Child of the Barbarian': Rape, Race, and Nationalism in France during the First World War." *Past and Present 141* (November 1993): 170–206.

Hatton, R. M. *Charles XII of Sweden.* London: Weybright and Talley, 1968.

Hauer, Fritz and Werner Keller, eds. *Schillers Wallenstein.* Darmstadt: Wissenschaftliche Buchgesellschaft, 1977.

Hauschild, Wolf-Dieter, ed. *Das deutsche Luthertum und die Unionsproblematik im 19. Jahrhundert.* Gütersloh: Gütersloher Verlagshaus G. Mohn, 1991.

Hedetoft, Ulf. *War and Death as Touchstones of National Identity.* Aalborg: Department of Languages and Intellectual Studies, University of Aalborg, 1990.

———. "National Identity and Mentalities of War in Three EC Countries." *Journal of Peace Research* 30, no. 3 (August 1993): 281–300.

Heffernan, James A. W., ed. *Representing the French Revolution: Literature, Historiography, and Art.* Hanover NH: University Press of New England, 1992.

Hegel, G. W. F. *The Philosophy of History.* Translated by J. Sibree. New York, 1899; reprint, New York: Dover Books, 1956.

———. *Hegel: The Essential Writings.* Edited by Frederick G. Weiss. New York: Harper & Row, 1974.

Heilbronner, Oded. "From Ghetto to Ghetto: The Place of German Catholic Society in Recent Historiography." *Journal of Modern History* 72, no. 2 (June 2000): 453–95.

Heineman, Elizabeth. "The Hour of the Women: Memories of Germany's 'Crisis Years' and West German National Identity." *American Historical Review* 101, no. 2 (April 1996): 354–95.

Henning, Friedrich-Wilhelm. *Landwirtschaft und ländliche Gesellschaft in Deutschland.* Paderborn: F. Schöningh, 1979.

Herbst, Peter. "Myth as the Expression of Collective Consciousness in Romantic Nationalism." In *Romantic Nationalism in Europe*, ed. J. C. Eade, 17–26. Canberra: Humanities Research Centre, Australian National University, 1983.

Herkless, John L. "Ein Unerklärtes Element in der Historiographie von Max Lenz." *Historische Zeitschrift* 222, no. 1 (1976): 81–104.

Hermand, Jost. "Dashed Hopes: On the Painting of the Wars of Liberation." In *Political Symbolism in Modern Europe: Essays in Honor of George L. Mosse*, ed. Seymour Drescher, David Sabean, and Allan Sharlin, 216–38. New Brunswick NJ: Rutgers University Press, 1982.

———. *Old Dreams of a New Reich.* Bloomington: Indiana University Press, 1991.

Hermann, Magdelene. *Niklas Vogt, eine Historiker der Mainzer Universität aus 2. Hälfte des 18. Jahrhunderts.* Giessen: O. Kindt, 1917.

Hettling, Manfred and Paul Nolte, eds. *Nation und Gesellschaft in Deutschland: Historische Essays.* Munich: C. H. Beck, 1996.

Higgins, Lynn A., and Brenda R. Silver, eds. *Rape and Representation.* New York: Columbia University Press, 1991.

Hill, Christopher. *God's Englishman: Oliver Cromwell and the English Revolution.* New York: Harper & Row, 1972.

Hinderer, Walter, ed. *Geschichte der politischen Lyrik in Deutschland.* Stuttgart: Reclam, 1978.

Hintze, Otto. "Das monarchische Prinzip und die konstitutionelle Verfassung [1911]." In *Staat und Verfassung*, 2d ed., ed. Gerhard Oestreich, 359–89. Göttingen: Vandenhoeck & Ruprecht, 1962.

Hobbes, Thomas. *Leviathan: Parts One and Two* [1651]. Edited by Herbert W. Schneider. New York: Liberal Arts Press, 1958.

Hoehne, Gerhard. "Das religiöse Charakterbild Wallensteins." *Zeitschrift für Kirchengeschichte* 3, no. 3 (1950/51): 268–90.

Hoerning, Erika M. "The Myth of Female Loyalty." *Journal of Psychohistory* 16, no. 1 (Summer 1988): 19–45.

Hofer, Walther. *Geschichtsschreibung und Weltanschauung: Betrachtungen zum Werk Friedrich Meineckes.* Munich: R. Oldenbourg, 1950.

Hoffmann, Stefan-Ludwig. "Mythos und Geschichte: Leipziger Gedenkfeieren der Völkerschlacht in 19. und 20. Jahrhundert." In *Nation und Emotion: Deutschland und Frankreich in Vergleich 19. und 20. Jahrhundert,* ed. Etienne Françoise, Hannes Siegrist, and Jakob Vogel, 114. Göttingen: Vandenhoeck & Ruprecht, 1995.

Hogan, Michael J., ed. *Hiroshima in History and Memory.* Cambridge: Cambridge University Press, 1996.

Hohendahl, Peter. *Building a National Literature: The Case of Germany, 1830–1870.* Translated by Renate B. Franciscono. Ithaca: Cornell University Press, 1989.

Hohennemser, Paul, ed. *Flugschriftensammlung Gustav Freytag.* Frankfurt: Frankfurter Societäts-Druckerie, 1925.

Hoover, Arlie J. *The Gospel of Nationalism.* Stuttgart: F. Steiner, 1986.

Howard, Michael. *War in European History.* New York: Oxford University Press, 1976.

Hughes, H. Stuart. *Consciousness and Society: The Reorientation of European Social Thought, 1890–1930.* New York: Vintage Books, 1977.

Hüppauf, Bernd, ed. *War, Violence, and the Modern Condition.* Berlin: Walter de Gruyter, 1997.

Hutchinson, John, and Anthony D. Smith, eds. *Nationalism.* New York: Oxford University Press, 1994.

Hutchinson, William R., and Hartmut Lehmann, eds. *Many Are Chosen: Divine Election and Western Nationalism.* Harvard Theological Studies, no. 38. Minneapolis: Fortress Press, 1994.

Hutton, Patrick H. *History as an Art of Memory.* Hanover VT: University Press of New England, 1993.

Huxley, Francis. *The Way of the Sacred.* London: Aldus Books, 1974.

Iggers, Georg G. *The German Conception of History: The National Tradition of Historical Thought from Herder to the Present.* Rev. ed. Middletown CT: Wesleyan University Press, 1983.

Iggers, Georg G., and James M. Powell, eds. *Leopold von Ranke and the Shaping of the Historical Discipline.* Syracuse NY: Syracuse University Press, 1990.

Irwin-Zarecka, Iwona. *Frames of Remembrance: The Dynamics of Collective Memory.* New Brunswick NJ: Rutgers University Press, 1994.

Jacobs, Manfred. "Die Entwicklung des deutschen Nationalgedankens von der Reformation bis zum deutschen Idealismus." In *Volk-Nation-Vaterland: Der deutsche Protestantismus und der Nationalismus,* ed. Horst Zillessen, 51–110. Gütersloh: Gütersloher Verlagshaus G. Mohn, 1970.

Jaeger, Friedrich. *Bürgerliche Modernisierungskrise und historische Sinnbildung: Kulturgeschichte bei Droysen, Burckhardt, und Max Weber.* Göttingen: Vandenhoeck & Ruprecht, 1994.

Jarausch, Konrad H. *Students, Society, and Politics in Imperial Germany: The Rise of Academic Illiberalism.* Princeton: Princeton University Press, 1982.

———. and Michael Geyer, eds. *Shattered Past: Reconstructing German Histories.* Princeton: Princeton University Press, 2003.

Jászi, Oscar. *The Dissolution of the Habsburg Monarchy.* Chicago: University of Chicago Press, 1929.

Jeffords, Susan. "Culture and National Identity in U.S. Foreign Policy." *Diplomatic History* 18, no. 1 (Winter 1994): 92–96.

Jenson, Deborah. *Trauma and Its Representations: The Social Life of Mimesis in Post-Revolutionary France.* Baltimore: Johns Hopkins University Press, 2001.

Johnson, Paul. *The Birth of the Modern: World Society, 1815–1830.* New York: HarperCollins, 1991.

Johnston, David. *The Rhetoric of Leviathan: Thomas Hobbes and the Politics of Cultural Transformation.* Princeton: Princeton University Press, 1986.

Joplin, Patricia K. "The Voice of the Shuttle Is Ours." In *Rape and Representation,* ed. Lynn A. Higgins and Brenda R. Silver, 41–49. New York: Columbia University Press, 1991.

Juergensmeyer, Mark. *Terror in the Mind of God: The Global Rise of Religious Violence.* Berkeley: University of California Press, 2001.

Kahn, Coppelia E. "Lucrece: The Sexual Politics of Subjectivity." In *Rape and Representation,* ed. Lynn A. Higgins and Brenda R. Silver, 141–59. New York: Columbia University Press, 1991.

Kaiser, Gerhard. *Pietismus und Patriotismus im literarischen Deutschland: Ein Beitrag zum Problem der Säkularisation.* 2d ed. Frankfurt: Athenäum, 1973.

Kaiser, Nancy A. *Social Integration and Narrative Structure: Patterns of Realism in Auerbach, Freytag, Fontane, and Raabe.* New York: Peter Lang, 1986.

Kampmann, Christoph. *Reichsrebellion und kaiserliche Acht: Politische Strafjustiz im Dreißigjährigen Krieg und das Verfahren gegen Wallenstein 1634.* Münster: Aschendorff, 1992.

Kaplan, Steven L. *Farewell Revolution: Disputed Legacies: France, 1789/1989.* Ithaca: Cornell University Press, 1995.

Kapner, Gerhard. "Skulpturen des 19. Jahrhunderts als Dokumente der Gesell-schaftsgeschichte." In *Denkmaler in 19. Jahrhundert: Deutung und Kritik*, ed. Hans-Ernst Mittig and Volker Plagemann, 9–17. Munich: Prestel, 1972.

Kaps, Johannes. *The Martyrdom of Silesian Priests 1945/46: Scenes from the Passion of Silesia*. Munich: Kirchliche Hilfsstelle, 1950.

———, ed. *The Martyrdom and Heroism of the Women of East Germany: An Excerpt from the Silesian Passion, 1945–1946*. Translated by Gladys H. Hartinger. Munich: Christ Unterwegs, 1955.

Kawa, Rainer. *Georg Friedrich Rebmann (1768–1824): Studien zu Leben und Werk eines deutschen Jakobiners*. Bonn: Bouvier, 1980.

Kellner, Hans. *Language and Historical Representation: Getting the Story Crooked*. Madison: University of Wisconsin Press, 1989.

Kirmayer, Laurence J. "Landscapes of Memory: Trauma, Narrative, and Disassociation." In *Tense Past: Cultural Essays in Trauma and Memory*, ed. Paul Antze and Michael Lambek, 173–98. New York: Routledge, 1996.

Klebel, E. "Reich und Reichsidee." In *Gibt es ein deutsches Geschichtsbild?* 67–86. Frankfurt: M. Diesterweg, 1955.

Kluckhohn, August. *Ueber Lorenz von Westenrieders Leben und Schriften*. Bamberg: Buchner, 1890.

Klug, Matthias. *Rückwendung zum Mittelalter? Geschichtsbilder und historische Argumentation im politischen Katholizisimus des Vormärz*. Paderborn: F. Schöningh, 1995.

[Koch, Matthias]. *Der mährische Landeshistoriograph Dr. Beda Dudik*. Brünn: n.p., 1890.

Kocka, Jürgen. "The European Pattern and the German Case." In *Bourgeois Society in Nineteenth-Century Europe*, ed. Jürgen Kocka and Allan Mitchell, trans. Gus Fagan, 3–39. Oxford: Berg, 1993.

Köhler, Joachim. *Nietzsche and Wagner: A Lesson in Subjugation*. Translated by Ronald Taylor. New Haven: Yale University Press, 1998.

Koselleck, Reinhart. "Staat und Gesellschaft in Preußen, 1815–1848." In *Staat und Gesellschaft im deutschen Vormärz, 1815–1848*, ed. Werner Conze, 94–105. Stuttgart: Klett-Cotta, 1962.

———. *Preußen zwischen Reform und Revolution: Allgemeines Landrecht, Verwaltung, und Soziale Bewegung von 1791 bis 1848*. Munich: Klett-Cotta in Deutscher Taschenbuch Verlag, 1989.

———. *The Practice of Conceptual History: Timing History, Spacing Concepts*. Translated by Todd Samuel Presner. Stanford: Stanford University Press, 2002.

Koshar, Rudy J. "Building Pasts: Historic Preservation and Identity in Twentieth-Century Germany." In *Commemorations: The Politics of National Identity*, ed. John R. Gillis. Princeton: Princeton University Press, 1994.

Kossovo: Heroic Songs of the Serbs. Translated by Helen Rotham. Boston, Houghton Mifflin, 1920.

Kraus, Andreas, ed. *Land und Reich, Stamm und Nation: Probleme und Perspectiven bayerischen Geschichte.* Vol. 2, *Frühe Neuzeit.* Munich: C. H. Beck, 1984.

Krieger, Leonard. *The German Idea of Freedom.* Boston: Beacon Press, 1957.

———. *Kings and Philosophers, 1689–1789.* New York: W. W. Norton, 1970.

———. *An Essay on the Theory of Enlightened Despotism.* Berkeley: University of California Press, 1975.

———. *Time's Reasons: Philosophies of History Old and New.* Chicago: University of Chicago Press, 1989.

Krill, Hans-Heinz. *Die Ranke Renaissance: Max Lenz und Erich Marcks.* Berlin: Walter de Gruyter, 1962.

Kugel, James L. *The Bible as it Was.* Cambridge: Harvard University Press, 1997.

Kunkel, Franz. *Gustav Freytags "Bilder aus der deutschen Vergangenheit" als schriftstellerische, künstlerische, und dichterische Leistung gewürdigt.* Aschaffenburg: Dr. J. Kirsch, 1926.

LaCapra, Dominick. "Representing the Holocaust: Reflections on the Historians' Debate." In *Probing the Limits of Representation,* ed. Saul Friedländer, 108–27. Cambridge: Harvard University Press, 1992.

———. *Representing the Holocaust: History, Theory, Trauma.* Ithaca: Cornell University Press, 1994.

Lacher, Hugo. "Das Jahr 1866." *Neue Politische Literatur* 14 (1969): 83–99, 214–31.

Lahne, Werner. *Magdeburgs Zerstörung in der Zeitgenossischen Publizistik.* Magdeburg: Verlag des Magdeburger Geschichtsvereins, 1931.

Lambek, Michael. "The Past Imperfect: Remembering as Moral Practice." In *Tense Past: Cultural Essays in Trauma and Memory,* ed. Paul Antze and Michael Lambek, 235–54. New York: Routledge, 1996.

Lampert, Friedrich. "Des Thürmers Töchterlein von Rothenburg: Eine Erzählung aus dem Jahre 1631," *Deutsche Volks-u. Jugendschriften,* no. 9 (Nördlingen, 1873): 90–91.

Langewiesche, Dieter. "Kulturelle Nationsbildung im Deutschland des 19. Jahrhunderts." In *Nation und Gesellschaft in Deutschland: Historische Essays,* ed. Manfred Hettling and Paul Nolte, 46–64. Munich: C. H. Beck, 1996.

Laqueur, Walter, and George L. Mosse, eds., *Historians and Politics.* Beverly Hills: Sage, 1974.

Last, R. W., ed. *Affinities: Essays in German and English Literature.* London: Leonard Wolff, 1971.

Lederer, Wolfgang. *The Fear of Women.* New York: Grune & Stratton, 1968.

Le Goff, Jacques. *History and Memory.* Translated by Steven Rendall and Elizabeth Claman. New York: Columbia University Press, 1992.

———, ed. *La nouvelle histoire.* Paris: Retz, 1978.

Lees, Andrew. *Cities Perceived: Urban Society and American Thought, 1820–1940.* Manchester: Manchester University Press, 1985.

Lehmann, Hartmut. "Martin Luther as a National Hero in the Nineteenth Century." In *Romantic Nationalism in Europe,* ed. J. C. Eade, 194–207. Canberra: Humanities Research Center, Australian National University, 1983.

———. "Martin Luther als Deutscher Nationalheld in 19. Jahrhundert." *Luther: Zeitschrift der Luther-Gesellschaft* 55, no. 2 (1984): 53–65.

———. "Pietism and Nationalism: The Relationship between Protestant Revivalism and National Renewal in Nineteenth-Century Germany." *Church History* 51, no. 1 (March 1992): 39–53.

———. "'God Our Old Ally': The Chosen People Theme in Late Nineteenth- and Early Twentieth-Century German Nationalism." In *Many Are Chosen: Divine Election and Western Nationalism,* Harvard Theological Studies no. 38, ed. William R. Hutchinson and Hartmut Lehmann, 85–108. Minneapolis: Fortress Press, 1994.

Lepore, Jill. *The Name of War: King Philip's War and the Origins of American Identity.* New York: Alfred A. Knopf, 1998.

Lepsius, M. Rainer. "The Nation and Nationalism in Germany." *Social Research* 52, no. 1 (Spring 1985): 43–64.

Lerche, Otto. *Gustav Adolf: Deutsche Bilder und Stätten.* Das Bild zum Wort, vol. 1. Hamburg: Agentur des Rauhen Hauses, 1932.

———. *Hundert Jahre Arbeit an der Diaspora.* Vol. 1. Leipzig: Verlag des Centralvorstandes des Evangelischen Vereins der Gustav Adolf-Stiftung, 1932.

Lestringant, Frank. "Catholiques et cannibals: Le thèmè du cannibalisme dans le discours protestant au temps des guerres de religion." In *Pratiques et Discours Alimentaires a la Renaissance,* ed. Jean-Claude Margolin and Robert Souzet, 233–45. Paris: G. P. Maisoneuve et Larose, 1982.

Linn, Rolf. "Wallenstein's Innocence." *Germanic Review* 34, no. 3 (October 1959): 200–207.

Livy. *The War with Hannibal: Books XXI–XXX of the History of Rome from Its Foundation.* Edited by Betty Radice. Translated by Aubrey de Selincourt. Baltimore: Penguin Books, 1965.

Lorenz, Gottfried, ed. *Quellen zur Geschichte Wallensteins.* Darmstadt: Wissenschaftliche Buchgesellschaft, 1987.

Lowenthal, David. *The Past Is a Foreign Country.* New York: Cambridge University Press, 1985.

Lucas, Karl-Hermann. "Joseph Edmund Jörg: Konservative Publizistik zwischen Revolution und Reichsgründung (1852–1871)." PhD diss., Köln Universität, 1969.

Maas, Annette. "Der Kult der toten Krieger: Frankreich und Deutschland nach 1870/71." In *Nation und Emotion: Deutschland und Frankreich in Vergleich 19. und 20. Jahrhundert*, ed. Etienne Francoise, Hannes Siegrist, and Jakob Vogel, 215–31. Göttingen: Vandenhoeck & Ruprecht, 1995.

Hartmut Mai and Kurt Schneider, "Die Stadtkirche St. Viti und die Gustav-Adolf-Gedenkstätte," *Das Christliche Denkmal*, ed. Fritz Loffler, no. 115 (Berlin: Evangelische, 1981), 1–30.

Maier, Charles. *The Unmasterable Past: History, Holocaust, and German National Identity*. Cambridge: Harvard University Press, 1988.

Mainland, W. F. "Schiller and Shakespeare—Some Points of Contact." In *Affinities: Essays in German and English Literature*, ed. R. W. Last, 19–33. London: Leonard Wolff, 1971.

Malkki, Liisa H. *Purity and Exile: Violence, Memory, and National Cosmology among Hutu Refugees in Tanzania*. Chicago: University of Chicago Press, 1995.

Mann, Golo. *Wallenstein: Sein Leben erzählt*. Frankfurt: S. Fischer, 1971.

———. *Wallenstein: His Life Narrated*. Translated by Charles Kessler. New York: Holt, Rinehart and Winston, 1976.

———. "Schiller als Geschichtsschreiber." Afterword to *Geschichte des Dreißigjährigen Krieges*, by Friedrich Schiller. Zurich: Mannesse, 1985.

Mann, Thomas. *Doktor Faustus*. 1947. Munich: S. Fischer, 1967.

———. *Doctor Faustus*. Translated by H. T. Lowe-Porter. New York: Vintage Books, 1948.

———. "Schillers Wallenstein." *Die Neue Rundschau* 66, no. 3 (1955): 281–92.

Mannheim, Karl. *Ideology and Utopia: An Introduction to the Sociology of Knowledge*. Translated by Louis Wirth and Edward Shils. Bonn, 1929; reprint, London: K. Paul, Trench, Trubner, 1936.

Margolin, Jean-Claude, and Robert Souzet, eds. *Pratiques et Discours Alimentaires a la Renaissance*. Paris: G. P. Maisoneuve et Larose, 1982.

Marx, Anthony W. *Faith in Nation: Exclusionary Origins of Nationalism*. New York: Oxford University Press, 2003.

Mason, Tim W. "Nineteenth-Century Cromwell." *Past and Present* 40 (July 1968): 187–91.

Montaigne, Michel de. *The Complete Essays*. Translated by M. A. Screech. London: Penguin Books, 1991.

Matzinger, Lorenz. *Onno Klopp (1822–1903): Leben und Werk*. Aurich: Ostfriesischelandschaft, 1993.

May, Arthur J. *The Habsburg Monarchy, 1867–1914*. Cambridge: Harvard University Press, 1951.

McClelland, Charles. *The German Historians and England: A Study in Nineteenth-Century Views*. Cambridge: Cambridge University Press, 1971.

———. "Berlin Historians and German Politics." In *Historians and Politics*, ed. Walter Laqueur and George L. Mosse, 191–222. London and Beverly Hills: Sage, 1974.

———. *State, Society, and University in Germany, 1700–1914*. Cambridge: Cambridge University Press, 1980.

McInnes, Edward. "Drama as Protest and Prophecy: The Historical Drama of the *Jungdeutschen*." *Maske und Kothurn: Internationale Beiträge zur Theaterwissenschaft* 17, no. 3 (1971): 191–202.

Meinecke, Friedrich. *Cosmopolitanism and the National State*. Translated by Robert B. Kimber. Munich, 1908; reprint, Princeton: Princeton University Press, 1970.

———. *Machiavellianism: The Doctrine of Raison d'État and Its Place in Modern History*. Translated by Douglas Scott. Munich, 1924; reprint, London: Routledge and Kegan Paul, 1957.

———. *Die Deutsche Katastrophe: Betrachtungen und Erinnerungen*. Zurich: Aero, 1946.

———. *The German Catastrophe*. Translated by Sidney Fay. Cambridge: Harvard University Press, 1950.

———. *The Age of German Liberation, 1795–1815*. Translated by Peter Paret. Berkeley: University of California Press, 1977.

Mellon, Stanley. *The Political Uses of History: A Study of Historians in the French Revolution*. Stanford: Stanford University Press, 1958.

Menzel, Wolfgang. *Die nationale Entwicklung in Böhmen, Mähren, und Schlesien*. Nuremberg: H. Preussler, 1985.

Mergel, Thomas. *Zwischen Klasse und Konfession: Katholisches Bürgertum in Rheinland, 1794–1914*. Göttingen: Vandenhoeck & Ruprecht, 1994.

Metz, Karl-Heinz. *Grundformen historiographischen Denkens: Wissenschaft als Methodologie: Dargestellt an Ranke, Treitschke, and Lamprecht*. Munich: W. Fink, 1979.

Meyer, Henry Cord. *Mitteleuropa in German Thought and Action, 1815–1945*. The Hague: Martinus Nijhoff, 1955.

Milch, Werner. *Gustav Adolf in der deutschen und schwedischen Literatur*. Breslau: M. & H. Marcus, 1928.

Mink, Louis O. *Historical Understanding*. Edited by Brian Fay, Eugene O. Golob, and Richard T. Vann. Ithaca: Cornell University Press, 1987.

Mitteldeutsche Lebensbilder. Vol. 3, *Lebensbilder des 18. und 19. Jahrhunderts*. Magdeburg, 1928. S.v. "Gustaf Droysen," by Hans Schulz; and "Friedrich von Raumer," by Hans Herzfeld.

Mittig, Hans-Ernst, und Volker Plagemann, eds. *Denkmaler im 19. Jahrhundert: Deutung und Kritik.* Munich: Prestel, 1972.

Moeller, Robert G. "War Stories: The Search for a Usable Past in the Federal Republic of Germany." *American Historical Review* 101, no. 4 (October 1996): 1008–48.

Momigliano, Arnaldo. *Essays in Ancient and Modern Historiography.* Middletown CT: Wesleyan University Press, 1977.

Mommsen, Hans. "Reappraisal and Repression: The Third Reich in West German Historical Consciousness." In *Reworking the Past: Hitler, the Holocaust, and the Historians' Debate,* ed. Peter Baldwin, 173–83. Boston: Basic Books, 1990.

Mommsen, Wilhelm. "Zur Bedeutung des Reichsgedankens." *Historische Zeitschrift* 174, no. 2 (1952): 386–94.

Mommsen, Wolfgang J. "Ranke and the Neo-Rankean School in Imperial Germany." In *Leopold von Ranke and the Shaping of the Historical Discipline,* ed. Georg G. Iggers and James M. Powell, 124–40. Syracuse NY: Syracuse University Press, 1990.

———. *Bürgerliche Kultur und politische Ordnung: Künstler, Schriftsteller und Intellektuelle in der deutsche Geschichte 1830–1933.* Frankfurt: Fischer Taschenbuch Verlag, 2000.

Montaigne, Michel de. "On the Cannibals." In *The Complete Essays,* trans. M. A. Screech, 228–41. London: Penguin Books, 1991.

Montgomery, David. *The American Civil War and the Meanings of Freedom.* New York: Oxford University Press, 1987.

Morse, Jonathan. *Word by Word: The Language of Memory.* Ithaca: Cornell University Press, 1990.

Moses, John A. *The Politics of Illusion: The Fischer Controversy in German Historiography.* London: Barnes and Noble Books, 1975.

Mosse, George L. *The Nationalization of the Masses: Political Symbolism and Mass Movements in Germany from the Napoleonic Wars through the Third Reich.* New York: Howard Fertig, 1975.

———. *Nationalism and Sexuality: Middle-Class Morality and Sexual Norms in Modern Europe.* Madison: University of Wisconsin Press, 1988.

———. *Fallen Soldiers: Reshaping the Memory of the World Wars.* New York: Oxford University Press, 1990.

Mueller-Vollmer, Kurt, ed. *The Hermeneutics Reader: Texts of the German Tradition from the Enlightenment to the Present.* New York: Continuum, 1989.

Muhlack, Ulrich. "Schillers Konzept der Universalgeschichte zwischen Aufklärung und Historismus." In *Schiller als Historiker,* ed. Otto Dann, Norbert Oellers, and Ernst Osterkamp, 5–28. Stuttgart and Weimar: J. B. Metzlar, 1995.

Müller, Harro. "War and Novel: Alfred Döblin's 'Wallenstein' and 'November 1918.'" In *War, Violence, and the Modern Condition,* ed. Bernd Hüppauf, 240–99. Berlin: Walter de Gruyter, 1997.

Müller-Salget, Klaus. *Erzählungen für das Volk: Evangelische Pfarrer als Volksschriftsteller in Deutschland des 19. Jahrhunderts.* Berlin: E. Schmidt, 1984.

Murdoch, Brian. *The Germanic Hero: Politics and Pragmatism in Early Medieval Poetry.* Rio Grande OH: Hambledon Press, 1996.

Neubauer, John. "The Idea of History in Schiller's *Wallenstein.*" *Neophilologus* 56, no. 4 (October 1972): 451–63.

Neubuhr, Elfriede, ed. *Geschichtsdrama.* Darmstadt: Wissenschaftliche Buchgesellschaft, 1980.

Neue Deutsche Biographie. Berlin: Duncker & Humblot, 1963.

Neusner, Jacob. *History and Torah: Essays on Jewish Learning.* London: Schocken Books, 1965.

———, ed. *The Christian and Judaic Invention of History.* Atlanta: Scholars Press, 1990.

Nipperdey, Thomas. "Nationalidee und Nationaldenkmal in Deutschland in 19. Jahrhundert." *Historische Zeitschrift* 206, no. 3 (June 1968): 529–85.

———. *Nachdenken über die deutsche Geschichte.* Munich: C. H. Beck, 1986.

———. *Deutsche Geschichte, 1800–1866: Bürgerwelt und starker Staat.* Munich: C. H. Beck, 1987.

Nolte, Ernst. "The Past That Will Not Pass." In James Knowlton and Truett Cates, trans., *Forever in the Shadow of Hitler?* 18–23. Atlantic Highlands NJ: Humanities Press, 1993.

Noltenius, Rainer. "Schiller als Führer und Heiland: Das Schillerfest 1859 als nationaler Traum von der Geburt des zweiten deutschen Kaiserreichs." In *Öffentliche Festkultur: Politische Fest in Deutschland von der Aufklärung bis zum Ersten Weltkrieg,* ed. Dieter Düding, Peter Friedemann, and Paul Munch, 237–58. Hamburg: Rowohlt, 1988.

Nora, Pierre. *La nouvelle histoire.* Edited by Jacques Le Goff. Paris: Retz, 1978.

Nordalm, Jens. *Historismus und Moderne Welt: Erich Marcks (1861–1938) in der deutschen Geschichtswissenschaft.* Berlin: Duncker & Humblot, 2003.

Oberkrome, Willi. *Volksgeschichte: Methodische Innovation und völkische Ideologisierung in der deutschen Geschichtswissenschaft 1918–1945.* Göttingen: Vandenhoeck & Ruprecht, 1993.

Obermann, Karl, and Josef Polisensky, eds. *Aus 500 Jahren deutsch-tschechoslowakischer Geschichte.* Berlin: Rütten & Loening, 1958.

Oexele, Otto Gerhard, and Jörn Rüsen, eds. *Historismus in den Kulturwissenschaften.* Cologne: Böhlau, 1996.

Ohles, Frederick. *Germany's Rude Awakening: Censorship in the Land of the Brothers Grimm.* Kent OH: Kent State University Press, 1992.

Oredsson, Sverker. *Geschichtsschreibung und Kult: Gustav Adolf, Schweden, und der Dreißigjährigen Krieg.* Translated by Klaus Böhme. Berlin: Duncker & Humblot, 1994.

Orr, Linda. *Headless History: Nineteenth-Century French Historiography of the Revolution.* Ithaca: Cornell University Press, 1990.

Ozouf, Mona. *Festivals and the French Revolution.* Translated by Alan Sheridan. Cambridge: Harvard University Press, 1988.

Pape, Walter, ed. *1870/71–1989/90: German Unifications and the Change of Literary Discourse.* Berlin: Walter de Gruyter, 1993.

Paret, Peter. *Art as History: Episodes in the Culture and Politics of Nineteenth-Century Germany.* Princeton: Princeton University Press, 1988.

———. *Imagined Battles.* Chapel Hill: University of North Carolina Press, 1997.

Parker, Geoffrey, ed. *The Thirty Years' War.* London: Routledge & Kegan Paul, 1987.

Paul, Johannes. *Gustav Adolf,* vol. 1, *Schwedens Aufsteig zur Großmachtstellung.* Leipzig: Quelle & Meyer, 1927.

———. "Gustav Adolf in der deutschen Geschichtsschreibung." *Historische Viertaljahrsschrift* 25, no. 3 (September 1930): 415–29.

———. *Gustav Adolf,* vol. 3, *Von Breitenfeld bis Lützen.* Leipzig: Quelle & Meyer, 1932.

Paxton, Nancy L. "Mobilizing Chivalry: Rape in British Novels about the Indian Uprising of 1857." *Victorian Studies* 36, no. 1 (Fall 1992): 5–30.

Pekar, Josef. *Wallenstein, 1630–1634: Tragödie einer Verschwörung.* Berlin: A. Metzner, 1937.

Pennebaker, James W., Dario Puez and Bernard Rimé, eds. *Collective Memory of Political Events: Social Psychological Perspectives.* Mahwah NJ: Lawrence Erlbaum Associates, 1997.

Pestalozzi, Karl. "Ferdinand II. in Schillers *Geschichte des Dreißigjährigen Kriegs*: Eine Rechtfertigung eines Übel." In *Schiller als Historiker,* ed. Otto Dann, Norbert Oellers, and Ernst Osterkamp, 179–90. Stuttgart and Weimar: J. B. Metzlar, 1995.

Peterson, Merrill D. *The Jefferson Image in the American Mind.* New York: Oxford University Press, 1960.

Plaschka, Richard Georg. *Von Palacky bis Pekar: Geschichtswissenschaft und Nationalbewußtsein bei dem Tschechen.* Graz and Cologne: H. Böhlaus, 1955.

Platt, Michael. "*The Rape of Lucrece* and the Republic for Which It Stands." *Centennial Review* 19, no. 2 (Spring 1975): 59–79.

Pocock, J. G. A. "The History of Political Thought: A Methodological Inquiry." In *Philosophy, Politics, and Society,* ed. Peter Laslett and W. G. Runciman, 183–202. Oxford: Blackwell, 1962.

———. *Politics, Language, and Time: Essays on Political Thought and History.* New York: Atheneum, 1971.

———. *The Machiavellian Moment: Florentine Political Thought and the Atlantic Republican Tradition.* Princeton: Princeton University Press, 1975.

Polisensky, Josef. "Zur Problematik des Dreißigjährigen Krieges und der Wallensteinfrage." In *Aus 500 Jahren deutsch-tschechoslowakischer Geschichte,* ed. Karl Obermann and Josef Polisensky, 99–136. Berlin: Rütten & Leoning, 1958.

Porter, Roy, and Mikulas Teich, eds. *Romanticism in National Context.* New York: Cambridge University Press, 1988.

Portmann-Tinguely, Albert, ed. *Kirche, Staat, und katholische Wissenschaft in der Neuzeit.* Paderborn: F. Schöningh, 1988.

Pressel, Wilhelm. *Der Kriegspredigt 1914–1918 in der evangelischen Kirche.* Göttingen: Vandenhoeck & Ruprecht, 1967.

Pressly, Thomas. *Americans Interpret Their Civil War.* Princeton: Princeton University Press, 1954.

Prignitz, Christoph. *Vaterländsliebe und Freiheit: Deutscher Patriotismus von 1750 bis 1850.* Wiesbaden: Steiner, 1981.

Prinz, Friedrich. "Wallenstein, Das Reich und Europa." In *Land und Reich, Stamm und Nation: Probleme und Perspektiven bayerischen Geschichte,* vol. 2, *Frühe Neuzeit,* ed. Andreas Kraus, 81–90. Munich: C. H. Beck, 1984.

Pursell, Brennan. *The Winter King: Frederick V of the Palatinate and the Coming of the Thirty Years' War.* Aldershot: Ashgate, 2003.

Pütz, Peter. "Aufklärung." In *Geschichte der politischen Lyrik in Deutschland,* ed. Walter Hinderer, 114–40. Stuttgart: Reclam, 1978.

Rabb, Theodore K. "The Effects of the Thirty Years' War on the German Economy." *Journal of Modern History* 34 (March 1962): 40–51.

———. *The Struggle for Stability in Early Modern Europe.* New York: Oxford University Press, 1975.

Rad, Gerhard. *Old Testament Theology,* vol. 1, *The Theology of Israel's Historical Traditions.* Translated by D. M. G. Stalker. New York: Harper, 1962.

Rak, Christian. *Krieg, Nation, und Konfession: Die Erfahrung des deutsch-französischen Krieges von 1870/71.* Paderborn: Ferdinand Schöningh, 2004.

Raulff, Ulrich. "Herz der Finsternis. Daniel Jonah Goldhagens Ästhetik des Grauens." *Frankfurter Allgemeine Zeitung,* August 19, 1996.

Raupach, Hans. *Der tschechische Frühnationalismus.* Essen, 1939; reprint, Darmstadt: Darmstadt Wissenschaftliche Buchgesellschaft, 1969.

Redlich, Fritz. "The 'Bibliotheca Reussiana ad Bellum Tricenne' at Harvard." *Harvard Library Bulletin* 14, no. 2 (Spring 1960): 191–200.

Regney, Anne. *The Rhetoric of Historical Representation: Three Narrative Histories of the French Revolution.* Cambridge: Cambridge University Press, 1990.

Reill, Peter Hanns. *The German Enlightenment and the Rise of Historicism.* Berkeley: University of California Press, 1975.

Reinalter, Helmut. "Heinrich Ritter von Srbik." In *Deutsche Historiker,* vol. 8, ed. Hans-Ulrich Wehler, 86–87. Göttingen: Vandenhoeck & Ruprecht, 1982.

Renan, Ernest. "Qu'est-ce qu'une nation?" Translated by Ida Mae Snyder. In *Nationalism*, ed. John Hutchinson and Anthony D. Smith, 17–18. New York: Oxford University Press, 1994.

Reuss, Rodolphe. *Soixante années d' activité scientifique et littéraire, 1864–1924.* Paris: Societé d' édition: Les Belles Lettres, 1926.

Reventlow, Henning Graf, Yair Hoffmann, and Benjamin Uffenheimer, eds. *Politics and Theopolitics in the Bible and Postbiblical Literature.* Supplement series, vol. 171. Sheffield: Journal for the Study of the Old Testament, 1994.

Rhein, Franz. *Zehn Jahre "Historisch-politische Blätter": Ein Beitrag zur Vorgeschichte des Zentrums, 1838–1848.* Obercassel: E. Heeg, 1916.

Richardson, R. C. *The Debate on the English Revolution.* London: Methuen, 1977.

——, ed. *Images of Oliver Cromwell: Essays for and by Roger Howell Jr.* Manchester: Manchester University Press, 1993.

Rigney, Ann. *The Rhetoric of Historical Representation: Three Narrative Histories of the French Revolution.* Cambridge: Cambridge University Press, 1990.

Ringer, Fritz K. *The Decline of the German Mandarins: The German Academic Community, 1890–1933.* Hanover NH: University Press of New England, 1990.

Rippl, Eugen. "Wallenstein in der tschechischen Literatur." *Germanoslavica* 2, no. 4 (1932–33): 521–44.

Ritter, Gerhard. *Vom sittlichen Problem der Macht: Fünf Essays.* Bern: A. Francke, 1948.

——. *Die Weltwirkung der Reformation.* 2d ed. Munich and Berlin: R. Oldenbourg, 1959.

Ritter, Moriz. "Der Untergang Wallensteins." *Historische Zeitschrift* 97, no. 2 (1906): 237–88.

——. *Die Entwicklung der Geschichtswissenschaft an den führenden Werken betrachtet.* Munich: R. Oldenbourg, 1919.

Robert, André. *L'Idée Nationale Autrichienne et les Guerres de Napoleon: L'Apostolat du Baron de Hormayr et Le Salon de Caroline Pichler.* Paris: F. Alcan, 1933.

Rosenberg, Hans. *Bureaucracy, Aristocracy, and Autocracy: The Prussian Experience, 1660–1815.* Boston: Beacon Press, 1966.

Roth, Michael S. *The Ironist's Cage: Memory, Trauma, and the Construction of History.* New York: Columbia University Press, 1995.

Rothfels, Hans. "Zur Krise des Nationalstaats." In *Probleme der Reichsgründungszeit, 1848–1879,* ed. Helmut Böhme, 369–83. Cologne and Berlin: Kiepenhauer & Witsch, 1968.

Rousso, Henry. *The Vichy Syndrome: History and Memory in France since 1944.* Translated by Arthur Goldhammer. Cambridge: Harvard University Press, 1991.

Rublack, Ulinka. "Wench and Maiden: Women, War, and the Pictorial Function of the Feminine in German Cities in the Early Modern Period." *History Workshop Journal* 44 (Autumn 1997): 1–21.

Rudolf, Hans-Ulrich, ed. *Der Dreißigjährige Krieg: Perspektiven und Strukturen.* Darmstadt: Wissenschaftliche Buchgesellschaft, 1977.

Ruof, Friedrich. *Johann Wilhelm von Archenholtz: Ein deutscher Schriftsteller zur Zeit der Französischen Revolution und Napoleons (1741–1812).* Berlin: E. Ebering, 1915.

Rüsen, Jörn. *Begriffene Geschichte: Genesis und Begründung der Geschichtstheorie J. G. Droysens.* Paderborn: F. Schöningh, 1969.

Saint-Pierre, Charles Irenee Castel de. *A Project for Settling an Everlasting Peace in Europe.* London: Ferdinand Burleigh, 1714.

Salditt, Barbara. *Das Werden des Grimmelshausensbildes im 19. und 20. Jahrhundert.* Chicago: University of Chicago Libraries, 1933.

Samuel, Raphael, and Gareth Stedman Jones, eds. *Culture, Ideology, and Politics.* London: Routledge & Kegan Paul, 1982.

Sauer, Wolfgang. "Das Problem des deutschen Nationalstaats." In *Probleme der Reichsgründungszeit, 1848–1879,* ed. Helmut Böhme, 448–80. Cologne: Kiepenhauer & Witsch, 1968.

Scarry, Elaine. *The Body in Pain: The Making and Unmaking of the World.* New York: Oxford University Press, 1985.

Schama, Simon. *Landscape and Memory.* New York: Alfred A. Knopf, 1995.

Schieder, Theodor. *Begegnungen mit der Geschichte.* Göttingen: Vandenhoeck & Ruprecht, 1962.

Schivelbusch, Wolfgang. *The Culture of Defeat.* New York: Metropolitan Books, 2003.

Schleier, Hans. "Ranke in the Manuals on Historical Methods of Droysen, Lorenz, and Bernheim." In *Leopold von Ranke and the Shaping of the Historical Discipline,* ed. Georg G. Iggers and James M. Powell, 111–23. Syracuse NY: Syracuse University Press, 1990.

Schlesische Lebensbilder. Vol. 1. Breslau: W. G. Korn, 1922.

Schmidt, Gustav, and Jörn Rüsen, eds. *Gelehrtenpolitik und politische Kultur in Deutschland, 1830–1930.* Bochum: N. Brockmeyer, 1986.

Schmidt, Hans. "Onno Klopp und die 'kleindeutschen Geschichtsbaumeister.'" In *Kirche, Staat, und katholische Wissenschaft in der Neuzeit,* ed. Albert Portmann-Tinguely, 381–95. Paderborn: F. Schöningh, 1988.

Schmidt, Richard. "Gustav Adolf: Die Bedeutung seiner Erscheinung für die europäische Politik und für den deutschen Volksgeist." *Zeitschrift für Politik* 22, no. 11 (February 1933): 701–19.

Schnabel, Franz. *Deutsche Geschichte in neunzehnten Jahrhundert.* 4 vols. Freiburg im Breisgau, 1929–37; reprint, Munich: Deutscher Taschenbuch, 1987.

Schneider, Falko. *Aufklärung und Politik: Studien zur Politisierung der deutschen Spätaufklärung am Beispiel A. G. F. Rebmanns.* Wiesbaden: Akademische Verlagsgesellschaft, 1978.

Schneider, Friedrich, ed. *Universalstaat oder Nationalstaat: Macht und Ende des Ersten deutschen Reiches: Die Streitschriften von Heinrich v. Sybel und Julius Ficker zur deutschen Kaiserpolitik des Mittelalters.* 2d ed. Innsbruck: Universitäts-Verlag Wagner, 1943.

Schrade, Hubert. *Das Deutsche Nationaldenkmal.* Munich: Albert Langen, 1934.

Schroeder, Paul W. *The Transformation of European Politics, 1763–1848.* New York: Oxford University Press, 1994.

Schubert, Friedrich Hermann. "Volkssouveränität und Heiliges Römisches Reich." *Historische Zeitschrift* 213, no. 1 (August 1971): 91–122.

——. "Wallenstein und der Staat des 17. Jahrhunderts [1965]." In *Der Dreißigjährigen Krieg: Perspektiven und Strukturen,* ed. Hans-Ulrich Rudolf, 185–207. Darmstadt: Wissenschaftliche Buchgesellschaft, 1977.

Schulin, Ernst. "Universal History and National History, Mainly in the Lectures of Leopold von Ranke." In *Leopold von Ranke and the Shaping of the Historical Discipline,* ed. Georg G. Iggers and James M. Powell, 70–81. Syracuse NY: Syracuse University Press, 1990.

——. "Schillers Interesse an Aufstandgeschichte." In *Schiller als Historiker,* ed. Otto Dann, Norbert Oellers, and Ernst Osterkamp, 137–48. Stuttgart and Weimar: J. B. Metzlar, 1995.

Schulten, Adolf. *Geschichte von Numancia.* Munich: Piloty & Loehle, 1933.

Schulz, Hermann. *Vorschläge zur Reichsreform in der Publizistik von 1800–1806.* Giessen: Buchdruckerei Nitschkowski, 1926.

Schulze, Hans K. *Hegemoniales Kaisertum: Ottonian und Salier.* Berlin: Siedler, 1991.

Schwartz, Barry. "The Social Context of Commemoration" *Social Forces* 61, no. 2 (December 1982): 374–97.

——. *George Washington: The Making of an American Symbol.* New York: Free Press, 1987.

Schwartz, Regina M. "Monotheism and the Violence of Identities." *Raritan* 14, no. 3 (Winter 1995): 119–41.

Schweizer, Paul. *Die Wallenstein-Frage in der Geschichte und Drama.* Zurich: Fäsi & Beer, 1899.

Seeba, Hinrich. "'Germany—A Literary Concept': The Myth of a National Literature." *German Studies Review* 17, no. 2 (May 1994): 353–70.

Segev, Tom. *The Seventh Million: The Israelis and the Holocaust.* Translated by Haim Watzman. New York: Hill and Wang, 1993.

Seidlin, Oskar. "Schiller: Poet of Politics." In *A Schiller Symposium: In Observance of the Bicentennary of Schiller's Birth*, ed. A. L. Wilson, 31–50. Austin: Department of Germanic Languages, University of Texas, 1960.

Seier, Hellmut. *Die Staatsidee Heinrich von Sybel's in den Wandlungen der Reichsgründungszeit 1862/1871*. Lübeck: Matthiesen, 1961.

Seifert, Ruth. "The Second Front: The Logic of Sexual Violence in Wars." *Women's Studies International Forum* 19, nos. 1–2 (1996): 35–43.

Semmel, Stuart. "Napoleon in British Political Culture: Early Nineteenth-Century Conceptions of National Character, Legitimacy, and History." PhD diss., Harvard University, 1997.

Shakespeare, William. *King Henry V*. Cambridge text edition. Edited by William Aldis Wright. New York: Garden City, 1940.

Shapiro, Michael J. *Violent Cartographies: Mapping Cultures of War*. Minneapolis: University of Minnesota Press, 1997.

Sheehan, James. "Liberalism and the City in Nineteenth-Century Germany." *Past and Present* 51 (May 1971): 116–37.

———. "The Problem of the Nation in German History." In *Die Rolle der Nation in der Deutschen Geschichte und Gegenwart*, ed. Otto Büsch and James Sheehan, 3–20. Berlin: Colloquium, 1985.

———. *German History, 1770–1866*. New York: Oxford University Press, 1989.

———. "Nation und Staat: Deutschland als 'imaginierte Gemeinschaft.'" In *Nation und Gesellschaft in Deutschland*, ed. Manfred Hettling and Paul Nolte, 33–45. Munich: C. H. Beck, 1996.

Siblewski, Klaus. *Rittlicher Patriotismus und romantischer Nationalismus in der deutschen Literatur 1770–1830*. Munich: Fink, 1981.

Silver, Daniel J. *A History of Judaism*, vol. 1, *From Abraham to Maimonides*. New York: Basic Books, 1974.

Skinner, Quentin. *Meaning and Context: Quentin Skinner and His Critics*. New York: Oxford University Press, 1988.

Smith, Alan. "The Image of Cromwell in Folklore and Tradition." *Folklore* 79 (Spring 1968): 17–39.

Smith, Anthony D. *National Identity*. Reno: University of Nevada Press, 1991.

Smith, Helmut Walser. *German Nationalism and Religious Conflict: Culture, Ideology, and Politics, 1870–1914*. Princeton: Princeton University Press, 1995.

———, ed. *Protestants, Jews, and Catholics in Germany, 1800–1914*. New York: Berg, 2001.

Smith, Woodruff D. *Politics and the Sciences of Culture in Germany, 1840–1920*. New York: Oxford University Press, 1991.

Sondhaus, Lawrence. "Mitteleuropa zur See? Austria and the German Navy Question, 1848–1852." *Central European History* 20, no. 2 (June 1987): 125–44.

Sossenheimer, Maria Anna. *Georg Friedrich Rebmann und das Problem der Revolution.* Frankfurt: Peter Lang, 1988.

Srbik, Heinrich Ritter von. *Das Österreichische Kaisertum und das Ende des Heiligen Römischen Reiches, 1804–1806.* Berlin: Deutsche Verlagsgesellschaft für Politik und Geschichte, 1927.

———. *Deutsche Einheit: Idee und Wirklichkeit vom Heiligen Reich bis Königgrätz.* 4 vols. Munich: F. Bruckmann, 1935–42.

———. *Geist und Geschichte vom deutschen Humanismus bis zur Gegenwart.* 2 vols. Munich: F. Bruckmann, 1950–51.

———. *Wallensteins Ende: Ursachen, Verlauf, und Folgen der Katastrophe.* 2d ed. Salzburg: O. Müller, 1952.

Stannard, David. *American Holocaust: The Conquest of the New World.* New York: Oxford University Press, 1992.

Stargardter, Steven A. *Niklas Vogt, 1756–1836: A Personality of the Late German Enlightenment and Early Romantic Movement.* New York: Garland, 1991.

Starobinski, Jean. *Jean-Jacques Rousseau: Transparency and Obstruction.* Translated by Arthur Goldhammer. Chicago: University of Chicago Press, 1988.

Stein, Leon. "Religion and Patriotism in German Peace Dramas during the Thirty Years' War." *Central European History* 4, no. 2 (June 1971): 131–48.

Steinberg, S. H. *The "Thirty Years' War" and the Conflict for European Hegemony, 1600–1660.* London: E. Arnold, 1966.

Stephens, Anthony. "Kleist's Mythicisation of the Napoleonic Era." In *Romantic Nationalism in Europe,* ed. J. C. Eade, 165–80. Canberra: Humanities Research Center, Australian National University, 1983.

Sternberg, Meir. *The Poetics of Biblical Narrative: Ideological Literature and the Drama of Reading.* Bloomington: Indiana University Press, 1985.

Stowell, Daniel W. *Rebuilding Zion: The Religious Reconstruction of the South.* New York: Oxford University Press, 1998.

Strachan, Hew. *The First World War,* vol. 1, *To Arms.* New York: Oxford University Press, 2001.

Suda, Zdenek. *The Origins and Development of the Czech National Consciousness and Germany.* Prague: Central European University Press, 1995.

Tacke, Charlotte. *Denkmal im sozialen Raum: Nationale Symbole in Deutschland und Frankreich im 19. Jahrhundert.* Göttingen: Vandenhoeck & Ruprecht, 1995.

Tal, Kali. *Worlds of Hurt: Reading the Literatures of Trauma.* Cambridge: Cambridge University Press, 1996.

Taylor, A. J. P. *The Habsburg Monarchy, 1809–1918.* London, 1941; reprint, Chicago: University of Chicago Press, 1976.

Taylor, Charles. *Hegel.* Cambridge: Cambridge University Press, 1975.

Tennenhouse, Leonard. *Power on Display: The Politics of Shakespeare's Genres.* New York: Methuen, 1986.

Theibault, John. "The Rhetoric of Death and Destruction in the Thirty Years' War." *Journal of Social History* 27, no. 2 (Winter 1983): 271–90.

Thom, Martin. *Republics, Nations, and Tribes.* London: Verso, 1995.

Thurston, Anne F. "Victims of China's Cultural Revolution: The Invisible Wounds; Part I." *Pacific Affairs* 57, no. 4 (Winter 1984–85): 599–620.

Tiedemann, Helmut. *Der deutsche Kaisergedanke vor und nach dem Wiener Kongress.* Breslau: M. & H. Marcus, 1932.

Tiefenbach, A. *Wallenstein: Ein deutscher Staatsmann.* Oldenburg: G. Stalling, 1932.

Tilly, Charles, Louise Tilly, and Richard Tilly, eds. *The Rebellious Century, 1830–1930.* Cambridge: Harvard University Press, 1975.

Timm, Hermann. *Die heilige Revolution: Das religiöse Totalitätskonzept der Frühromantik.* Frankfurt: Syndikat, 1978.

Timmermann, Heiner, ed. *Geschichtsschreibung zwischen Wissenschaft und Politk: Deutschland-Frankreich-Polen im 19. und 20. Jahrhundert.* Saarbrücken-Scheidt: R. Dadder, 1987.

Toews, John Edward. *Hegelianism: The Path toward Dialectical Humanism, 1805–1841.* Cambridge: Cambridge University Press, 1980.

Trautmann, René. *Die Stadt in der deutschen Erzählungskunst des 19. Jahrhunderts (1830–1880).* Winterthur: P. G. Keller, 1957.

Tribe, Keith. *Governing Economy: The Reformation of German Economic Discourse, 1750–1840.* Cambridge: Cambridge University Press, 1988.

Ullenberger, Ben C. *Zion, the City of the Great King: A Theological Symbol of the Jerusalem Cult.* Supplement series, vol. 41. Sheffield: Journal for the Study of the Old Testament, 1987.

Updike, John. "New Worlds: German and Austrian Art, 1840–1940." *New York Review of Books* 49 (February 14, 2002): 25–28.

Urban, Otto. *Die tschechische Gesellschaft 1848 bis 1918.* Translated by Henning Schlegel. Vienna and Cologne: Böhlau, 1994.

Veit, Friedrich. *Gustav-Adolfs Vermächtnis: Vortrag bei der Schlußfeier des Gustav-Adolf Jahres 1932.* Nuremberg: Agentur des Rauhen Hauses, 1932.

Venuti, Lawrence. "*The Destruction of Troy*: Translation and Royalist Cultural Politics in the Interregnum." *Journal of Medieval and Renaissance Studies* 23, no. 2 (Spring 1993): 197–213.

Vierhaus, Rudolf. *Germany in the Age of Absolutism.* Translated by Jonathan B. Knudsen. Cambridge: Cambridge University Press, 1988.

———. "Historiography between Science and Art." In *Leopold von Ranke and the Shaping of the Historical Discipline,* ed. Georg G. Iggers and James M. Powell, 61–69. Syracuse NY: Syracuse University Press, 1990.

Vierhaus, Rudolf, and Manfred Botzenhart, eds. *Dauer und Wandel der Geschichte: Aspekte Europäischer Vergangenheit: Festgabe für Kurt von Raumer.* Münster: Aschendorff, 1966.

Vitz, Evelyn B. "Rereading Rape in Medieval Literature." *Partisan Review* 63, no. 2 (1996): 280–91.

Wacker, Annekatrin. "Historisch-Politische Blätter für das katholische Deutschland." In *Deutsche Zeitschriften des 17. bis 20. Jahrhunderts*, ed. Heinz-Dietrich Fischer, 141–54. Munich: Aufbau, 1973.

Walker, Mack. *Johann Jakob Moser and the Holy Roman Empire of the German Nation.* Chapel Hill: University of North Carolina Press, 1981.

Walzer, Michael. *The Revolution of the Saints: A Study in the Origins of Radical Politics.* New York: Atheneum, 1973.

———. *Exodus and Revolution.* New York: Basic Books, 1985.

———. *Just and Unjust Wars: A Moral Argument with Historical Illustrations.* 2d ed. New York: Basic Books, 1992.

Wandruszka, Adam. *Reichspatriotismus und Reichspolitik zur Zeit des Prager Friedens von 1635: eine Studie zur Geschichte des deutschen Nationalbewusstseins.* Graz and Cologne: H. Böhlaus, 1955.

Ward, A. W. "Anton Gindely." *English Historical Review* 8, no. 31 (July 1893): 500–514.

Warner, Marina. *Alone of All Her Sex: The Myth and Cult of the Virgin Mary.* New York: Alfred A. Knopf, 1976.

Weber, Bernhard. *Die "Historisch-politische Blätter" als Forum für Kirchen- und Konfessionsfragen.* Munich: Ludwig-Maximilian-Universität, 1983.

Weber, Max. "Politics as a Vocation [1918]." In *From Max Weber: Essays in Sociology*, ed. and trans. H. H. Gerth and C. Wright Mills, 77–128. New York: Oxford University Press, 1958.

Weber, Wolfgang. *Priester der Klio: Historisch-sozialwissenschaftliche Studien zur Herkunft und Karriere deutscher Historiker und zur Geschichte der Geschichtswissenschaft, 1800–1970.* 2d ed. Frankfurt: Peter Lang, 1987.

Wedgwood, C. V. *The Thirty Years' War.* New Haven: Yale University Press, 1939.

Wegele, Franz X. von. *Geschichte der deutschen Historiographie seit dem Auftreten des Humanismus.* Munich and Leipzig: R. Oldenbourg, 1885.

Wehler, Hans-Ulrich, ed. *Deutsche Historiker.* Vol. 8. Göttingen: Vandenhoeck & Ruprecht, 1982.

———. *Deutsche Gesellschaftsgeschichte.* 4 vols. Munich: C. H. Beck, 1987–2003.

Wertheimer, Jürgen, ed. *Ästhetik der Gewalt: Ihre Darstellung in Literatur und Kunst.* Frankfurt: Athenäum, 1986.

West, Rebecca. *Black Lamb and Grey Falcon: A Journey through Yugoslavia.* New York: Viking Press, 1943.

White, Hayden. *Metahistory: The Historical Imagination in Nineteenth-Century Europe.* Baltimore: Johns Hopkins University Press, 1973.

———. *The Content of the Form*. Baltimore: Johns Hopkins University Press, 1990.

Wilke, Jürgen. "Vom Sturm und Drang bis zur Romantik." In *Geschichte der politischen Lyrik in Deutschland*, ed. Walter Hinderer, 141–78. Stuttgart: Reclam, 1978.

Willems, Emilio. *A Way of Life and Death: Three Centuries of Prussian-German Militarism: An Anthropological Approach*. Nashville: Vanderbilt University Press, 1986.

Willig, Eduard. *Gustav II: Adolf, König von Schweden im deutschen Drama: Ein literär-historischer Versuch*. Parchim: H. Freise, 1908.

Willms, Bernard. *Idealismus und Nation: Zur Rekonstruktion des politischen Selbstbewußtseins der Deutschen*. Paderborn: F. Schöningh, 1986.

Willms, Johannes. *Nationalismus ohne Nation: Deutsche Geschichte von 1789 bis 1914*. Düsseldorf: Classen, 1983.

Wilson, A. L., ed. *A Schiller Symposium: In Observance of the Bicentennary of Schiller's Birth*. Austin: Department of Germanic Languages, University of Texas, 1960.

Wilson, Edmund. *Patriotic Gore: Studies in the Literature of the American Civil War*. New York: Oxford University Press, 1962.

Windell, George G. *The Catholics and German Unity, 1866–1871*. Minneapolis: University of Minnesota Press, 1954.

Winter, J. M. "The Great War and the Persistence of Tradition: Language of Grief, Bereavement, and Mourning." In *War, Violence, and the Modern Condition*, ed. Bernd Hüppauf, 33–45. Berlin: Walter de Gruyter, 1997.

———. *Sites of Memory, Sites of Mourning: The Great War in European Cultural History*. Cambridge: Cambridge University Press, 1998.

Wistrich, Robert, and David Ohana, eds. *The Shaping of Israeli Identity: Myth, Memory, and Trauma*. London: F. Cass, 1995.

Wittram, Reinhard, ed. "Kirche und Nationalismus in der Geschichte des Deutschen Protestantismus im 19. Jahrhundert." In *Das Nationale als europäisches Problem: Beiträge zur Geschichte des Nationalitätsprinzips vornehmlich im 19. Jahrhundert*, ed. Reinhard Wittram, 109–48. Göttingen: Vandenhoeck & Ruprecht, 1954.

Wolf, Maria. *Wallenstein als Dramenheld*. PhD diss., Heidelberg Universität, 1992.

Wolff, Larry. *Inventing Eastern Europe: The Map of Civilization on the Mind of the Enlightenment*. Stanford: Stanford University Press, 1994.

Wolpert, Andrew. *Remembering Defeat: Civil War and Civic Memory in Ancient Athens*. Baltimore: Johns Hopkins University Press, 2002.

Woltmann, Karoline von. *Karl Ludwig und Karoline von Woltmann*. New York: n.p., 1870.

Bibliography

Worden, Blair. *Roundhead Reputations: The English Civil Wars and the Passions of Posterity*. London: Allen Lane, 2002.

Wright, Beth S. "An Image for Imagining the Past: Delacroix, Cromwell, and Romantic Historical Painting." *Clio* 21, no. 3 (1992): 243–63.

Wright, Stephen K. *The Vengeance of Our Lord: Medieval Dramatizations of the Destruction of Jerusalem*. Toronto: Pontifical Institute of Medieval Studies, 1989.

Wünnenberg, Rolf. *Lorenz von Westenrieder: Sein Leben, sein Werk, und seine Zeit*. Tutzing: H. Schneider, 1982.

Yerushalmi, Yosef. *Zakhor: Jewish History and Jewish Memory*. New York: Schocken Books, 1989.

Young, James. *The Texture of Memory: Holocaust Memorials and Meaning*. New Haven: Yale University Press, 1993.

Zantop, Susanne. "Re-presenting the Present: History and Literature in Restoration Germany." *MLN* 102, no. 3 (April 1987): 570–86.

Zeitlis, Rudolf, ed. *Die Kunst des 19. Jahrhunderts*. Berlin: Propyläen, 1966.

Zerubavel, Yael. "The Multivocality of a National Myth: Memory and Counter-Memories of Masada." In *The Shaping of Israeli Identity: Myth, Memory, and Trauma*, ed. Robert Wistrich and David Ohana, 110–28. London: F. Cass, 1995.

Ziegler, Edda. *Literarische Zenzur in Deutschland, 1818–1848*. Munich: C. Hanser, 1983.

Zillessen, Horst, ed. *Volk-Nation-Vaterland: Der deutsche Protestantismus und der Nationalismus*. Gütersloh: Gütersloher Verlagshaus G. Mohn, 1970.

———. *Protestantismus und politische Form: Eine Untersuchung zum protestantischen Verfassungsverständnis*. Gütersloh: Gütersloher Verlagshaus G. Mohn, 1971.

Index

Abraham, and Isaac, 11

absolutism, 12, 38, 63, 68, 101, 111–12, 196;
as anti-national, 46, 79–80, 84, 162; enlightened, 2, 60, 62, 104, 125; and modern
administration, 101, 111

Ackermann Report, 175

The Adventures of Simplicissimus
(Grimmelshausen), 2, 178–79, 197, 226

Alaric, 160

Alexander the Great, 229

Alighieri, Dante, *The Inferno*, 155

Allgemeine Deutsche Biographie, 13

Alte Vest, battle of, 68, 200

Altgeld, Wolfgang, 56

Anderson, Olive, 97

Ankersmit, Frank, 10, 189, 191

Anton, Dietrich, 199

Apocalypse, 295n1

Appian, 144, 285n12

archives, 158; regional, 12

Aretin, Karl Maria von, 28, 83; on Bavarian
foreign policy, 28, 45; on Henry IV (king), 44,
45, 46; on Wallenstein, 119, 121

—Works: *Bayerns auswärtige Verhaltnisse seit
dem Anfang des sechzehnten Jahrhunderts*,
119, 121

Arndt, Ernst Moritz, 152, 170

Arnim, Hans Georg von, 119

art, historical themes in, 179–80

Association for the History of Germans in
Bohemia, 136, 279n97

atrocity narratives, 16, 17, 161, 179–82, 188,
197, 205, 223

Attila, 122, 160, 206

Auerbach, Erich, 143

Augsburg Confession, 68

Austerlitz, battle of, 170

Austria, 6, 26–29, 35, 36, 40, 86, 87, 111, 113,
116, 122–23, 126, 128, 151, 197, 200, 201

Austro-Hungarian Empire, 134;
Ausgleichskommission, 129; federalism in,
128–29

balance of power, European, 45, 59, 60, 90, 106,
126

Balkans, 87, 123

Baltic project, 22, 46–47, 50, 101, 117, 221

Bandhauer, Zacharias, diary of, 158, 163, 167,
291–92n67

Baron, Salo W., 55

Barthold, Friedrich Wilhelm, 85; anti-Prussian
views of, 79–80, 82, 84, 117; on Ferdinand II,
79; on France and Gustavus Adolphus, 79

—Works: *Geschichte des großen deutschen
Krieges vom Tode Gustav Adolfs ab mit
besonderer Rücksicht auf Frankreich*, 78

Barudio, Günther, 199–200

Bauer, Franz August, 214

Bautzen, 200

Bavaria, 102, 133, 178, 190, 200, 205, 211; as
defender of Holy Roman Empire, 210, 211,
213, 215; foreign policy of, 28, 210; histories
of, 27, 210; leadership role in Germany of, 23,
26, 27, 28, 44, 45, 210

Bavarian Academy of Sciences, 27, 36, 306n92

Bavarian Forest, 213–14

Becker, Gottfried Wilhelm, 153–54

Belgium, 44

Below, Georg von, 166

Benes, Edvard, 299n95

Benjamin, Walter, 224

Bensen, Heinrich W., 162

Bensinger, Sigmund, 1

Berlichingen, Götz von, 98

Berlin, 210; archives in, 169; Royal Library in,
168

The Bible: apocalyptic narratives in, 141–42,
197; chosen people narratives in, 7, 8, 54, 55,
75; covenants in, 54, 56, 143, 155, 186–87,
189, 217, 218, 219; divine judgment in, 143–
44, 177, 181, 202, 209, 218, 223, 225; influence on modern history writing of, 10, 54, 55,
143, 154, 176, 186–87, 216, 218–19, 223,
227; prophetic narratives in, 56, 141, 152,
155, 223